For-Giving

A Feminist Criticism of Exchange

Genevieve Vaughan

Foreword by Robin Morgan

In sisterhood for peace, Genevieve

Plain View Press
P O 33311
Austin, TX 78764

Phone, Fax: 512-441-2452
e-mail: sbpvp@eden.com
Website: http://www.eden.com/~sbpvp

ISBN: 0-911051-94-5
Library of Congress Number: 97-065354
Copyright Genevieve Vaughan, 1997. All rights reserved.

Produced by Plain View Press in collaboration with the
Foundation for a Compassionate Society.

Quote from Karl Marx on page 21 is from *The German
Ideology*, Karl Marx and Friedrich Engels, Moscow Progress
Publishers, 1964, p. 41. The quote from "La Folie Perceval" is
from *The Search for the Grail*, Dr. Graham Phillips, Arrow,
London, 1996.

Cover art "The Visible Hand" and line drawing illustrations
for the book are by Liliana Wilson. Computer graphics by
Genevieve Vaughan with the assistance of Liliana Wilson.

Printed in the United States of America

*I dedicate the book to the Earth,
who is Mother, Daughter, Friend
and Beloved, so that all humans
may find a way to love her (and
each other) more.*

*I dedicate it also to the ancient
image of women's power, the
Egyptian goddess Sekhmet, that we
may clearly and fiercely protect
mothering ways and, free from
addictions and misconceptions, give
birth to a better society.*

Table of Contents

Foreword

by Robin Morgan

The book you hold in your hands is a gift—from author to reader, from an individual woman to the Women's Movement (and to men of conscience) everywhere.

In a sense, every work of authentic feminist theory might be said to fit that category. But what Genevieve Vaughan has given us is something unique—a work as impassioned in feeling as it is thoughtful in analysis, one in which scrupulous research and scholarship resonate in synchrony with, not opposition to, the finest impulses of the human heart.

Such a Both/And insistence—to challenge the mind and simultaneously warm the spirit—is not easy in an Either/Or world. It requires a healthy audacity even to *attempt* both at once. Gen Vaughan correctly notes how feminists are already daring to consider "every academic system suspect," and she goes further, urging us to risk regaining our "naiveté," to dare question *everything*. But make no mistake. By naiveté, she doesn't mean sentimentality or blurry-minded romanticism, although she does refreshingly let altruism out of the closet and into the streets. I find her "naive" theories highly sophisticated in the best sense: intelligently worked through, ethical, pragmatic, feasible cross-culturally, and as applicable in intimate relationships as in global politics. In other words, *effectively transformative*.

Different readers will discover different gifts here. Semioticians, linguists, economists, and political scientists will encounter a radical feminist intellectual challenge rare in their rarefied fields. But one needn't know anything about semiotics or other academic disciplines to appreciate this book.

Activists will find an accessible political analysis as applicable to money as to masculation, to anorexia, armaments, or architecture—a theory with implications for closed systems *and* cosmic ones.

Male readers will find a theory that doesn't blame men simplistically yet doesn't flinch to dissect patriarchy and insist on individual moral responsibility as well as on systemic change.

In general, thoughtful readers as weary of pedantic fads as of popu-babble clichés will find in these pages an approach that cheerfully unsettles many such concepts, including deconstructionism, postmodernism, charity, and codependence (to name only a few).

For me, a language-loving poet, there's real pleasure in Gen Vaughan's wit and wordplay (which should delight Mary Daly aficionados). There are constructs here— "constrained reciprocity" for instance—that will, I predict, become verbal-watershed phrases comparable to "reproductive rights," "acquaintance rape," or Adrienne Rich's memorable "compulsory heterosexuality." As a feminist, I revel in the "consciousness clicks" throughout this book—so many that some gems are blithely tossed off in footnotes. As an internationalist, I'm deeply grateful for Vaughan's cross-cultural sensitivity that draws examples from all over the world. As a fiction writer, I enjoy her creative appraisal of fairy tales, myths, archetypes, and stereotypes. As a political theorist, I admire her courage in reclaiming "values" from the right wing. As someone interested in metaphysics, I'm fascinated by the implications of the Gift Paradigm—from the latest left-and-right-brain research to alternative views of existence itself. And as a political activist, I appreciate and admire the way in which Gen Vaughan's life is an example of her theory in *practice*; in fact, she has been so busy for so many years supporting and participating in global feminist energy that it's been difficult to get her to sit down long enough to finish this book.

Her work can now find its audience, and I wish for it a large one. Because this book will not only make you think, but will coax you toward hope, offering a reminder of the human capacity for transformation. And that will make you oddly happy—even surrounded, as you are, by the intensely ungenerous, lethally exploitative spirit of patriarchy. This will offer a third way, in defiance of status quo thinking that posits bifurcated untenable alternatives—selfishness and selflessness, for instance. That possibility, in turn, will give you a sense of your own power—not power *over*, but power *to*. If you've ever been a mother, you'll recognize that power: of giving—whether birth, or nurturance, or time, care, *attention*. If you've ever been in love, you'll recognize that power: of exhilaration, of abundance, of joyous outpouring (Juliet's "the more I give to thee, the more I have, for both are infinite"), the celebration of miraculous dailiness.

However you open yourself to this book, you'll encounter a wiser possible self—and society. The transformation of both is up to all of us. These pages are part of a map-in-progress for the journey; this book is one tool for the task.

A gift indeed.

Robin Morgan

Thanks

I thank Susan Bright for her understanding and illuminated editing which have made the reader's burden lighter and mine as well.

I thank Liliana Wilson for her beautiful artwork and her spirit, her readiness to give her time and creativity.

My greatest gratitude goes to Robin Morgan who over many years has given me encouragement from her disinterested feminist revolutionary heart and has read and commented on various versions of the manuscript numerous times.

I especially thank my daughters, Amelia, Beatrice, and Emma Rossi-Landi who have continued to listen to me, and have encouraged and supported me over the many years I have been working on this book.

I thank my brother Ben Vaughan who has given me much material support and, without at all knowing my ideas on the subject, provides a wonderful example of a nurturing father for his and my sister-in-law's sons.

I thank my parents and grandparents who provided me with the resources of exchange that I could use for giving.

I thank all the women of the Foundation for a Compassionate Society and Feminists for a Compassionate Society who have had to tolerate me while I worked on the book, for their sisterhood and support. I am grateful also for their commitment to peace for all through women's values, and their inspired feminist leadership. I am grateful to San Juanita Alcala, Yana Bland, Rose Corrales, Patricia Cuney, Barbara Franco, Sally Jacques, Suze Kemper. Maria Limon, Sue MacNichol, Aina Olomo, Erin Rogers, Angeles Romero, Susan Lee Solar, Frieda Werden, Debbie Winegarten, and Ruthe Winegarten for proof reading and for their suggestions and reviews of the manuscript. Several people read and commented on earlier versions of the book, including Letitia Blalock, Florence Howe, Kam Magor and

Doll Mathis, for which I thank them. I thank Margaret Nunley for giving me plenty of free time to write. I am especially grateful to Plain View Press for their feminist commitment and innovative organization. Margo La Gattuta valiantly managed the huge job of technical editing, for which I thank her. I also thank Terry Sherrell of Morgan Printing for her expert corrections. I appreciate all people who are trying to bring about a better world through the gifts of time, money, ideas, imagination, good will, and hard work, which make a paradigm shift possible. I especially appreciate and thank the reader for opening your mind to this book and using its contents. Without your attention, the gift would remain ungiven.

I have been very fortunate in the things my life has brought me to do. For example, in 1963 I married an Italian philosophy professor and moved to Italy where I was able to participate in a number of intellectual currents. In 1964 a group of professors in Bologna who wanted to start a new philosophical journal asked my husband to help them apply Marx's analysis of the commodity and money to language. The problem and the way they stated it were fascinating to me. I began to think about it then, and in fact have never stopped. Although the journal did not happen after all, my ex-husband did write about the relations between language and exchange. I did not agree with him but it took many years before I was able to understand why. Finally in 1975-76 I stayed for a couple of years in the United States, and was able to devote myself to thinking the problem through. In 1977-78 I wrote a couple of academic essays which were published in the early 80s. They are cited in the bibliography, and I invite readers who are academically inclined to read them. I was able to go into some issues more thoroughly than I have in this book. For instance, in "Saussure and Vigotsky via Marx" I discuss Saussure's concept of linguistic value regarding the analogy he makes with exchange, correcting for the differences Marx would see in his idea of exchange value. In "Communication and Exchange" I introduce the idea of communicative need, identify exchange as aberrant communication, and analyze money as a 'one word language.' In 1978 I got a divorce and began going to a feminist consciousness raising group. Many of the women in the group worked at the Food and Agriculture Organization of the U. N., which was located near my house in Rome. Women came from many places to talk to us about issues ranging from the protests at Greenham Commons to 'jelly babies' caused by radioactivity from nuclear testing in the Pacific Islands. Issues of women and development were also at the forefront in the group. Many of the women in our group went to the U.N. Decade for Women Conference in Copenhagen and told the rest of us all about it when they came back.

There was a lot of interesting philosophical discussion going on in the Italian feminist movement at the time. I participated in some courses at the Virginia Woolf Cultural Center, an independent women's university in Rome started by feminist philosopher Alessandra Bochetti. It was during that time that I began to realize that women's free labor in the home was the great unseen element that could be the basis of a new philosophy. I had been doing a lot of giftgiving in my own life, both bringing up my daughters and as a wife. I began to see that my values and those of most women differed from the values and priorities of most of the men I had met whether academics or bureaucrats, laborers or activists. It occurred to me that women's free labor could be understood as the economic base for an alternative superstructure, a system of ideas and values different from prevailing patriarchal ideas and values.

In 1983 I came back to the U.S. to try to put giftgiving values into practice in contexts outside the home. The last chapter of this book discusses that attempt, which is still ongoing. This practice, which was somewhat specific to my personal situation, did not leave much time for theoretical work (giftgiving can be very time consuming, which is what happens also in mothering). I was involved in many women's organizations and discussed the idea of the 'gift economy' with everyone, trying to normalize it. One of the people I discussed it with was Sonia Johnson, who used it (citing me) in her book *Wildfire*. I think her treatment was caught in the contradictions between ego and other and could not lead to the kind of social change for all that I think is necessary. I finally began working on the present book in about 1988, though certainly not full time, and without the advantages and disadvantages of academia. It became very long and then short again. The file in my computer under which this version is kept is 'short book.' I have tried to integrate most of the ideas into the text and footnotes, but many had to be left aside.

During the time in which I was living in Italy, we felt the wind blowing from France where many thinkers were dealing with issues of communication, economics, semiotics and psychoanalysis. The school of Jacques Lacan had broken new ground, and anthropologists like Claude Levi-Strauss and Maurice Godelier had broadened the investigations started by Marcel Mauss and Emile Durkheim. Georges Bataille, Michel Foucault and Jacques Derrida investigated language, culture, and the unconscious. For me the most interesting of all of these thinkers was Jean Joseph Goux, whose application of Marx's analysis of the commodity and money to various social structures led in directions which were different from mine (among other reasons, because my reading of Marx was different). The feminist thinkers Luce Irigaray and Julia Kristeva had a difficult patriarchal context in which to operate and sometimes came to Italy to find support among the Italian women philosophers. The Semiotics Summer Institute in Urbino was a place of fine intellectual ferment where many of the French and Italian semioticians and (at the time) ante-postmodernists as well as a few from the U.S. and Eastern Europe gathered to present their theories to the faithful. I heard Jean Baudrillard and Jean-Francois Lyotard there as well as Umberto Eco, Massimo Bonfantini, Augusto Ponzio, Luis Prieto, my ex-husband Ferruccio Rossi-Landi and many others. I wrote a paper on nurturing and communication for the last Summer Institute I attended, but since I neglected to go through the bureaucratic channels to get on the list I presented it only to a small group

15

who got together for the purpose. I also belonged to the Centro Romano di Semiotica and attended many presentations by local and international speakers.

When I moved back to the U.S. in 1983 I encountered Lewis Hyde's book *The Gift, Imagination and the Erotic Life of Property*. While it was heartening to see giftgiving described with honor I thought that the lack of a theory of language as giftgiving limited the scope of the book to literary criticism (which anyway lingered too long on Ezra Pound's anti-Semitic ravings). I had already read Malinowsky's *Argonauts of the Western Pacific* in college and later Marcel Mauss's *Essay on the Gift*. I read in these books about the *potlatch* practiced by the Native American tribes of the Pacific Northwest, and since then I have discussed these 'give aways' not only with anthropologists but with the people for whom they are a living traditional economic way. Then books like Jean Baker Miller's *Toward a New Psychology of Women*, Nancy Chodorow's *The Reproduction of Mothering*, Carol Gilligan's *In a Different Voice* and later Sara Ruddick's *Maternal Thinking* showed me how women in the U.S. were dealing with their difference from patriarchy. Already in Italy there had been a wide movement among feminists dealing with sexual difference in a positive way.

The postmodern criticism of 'phallogocentrism' brings up many important issues. However, I believe that the recognition of the fundamental importance of giftgiving can be the antidote to phallogocentrism on the reality plane (with important repercussions on the psychological and verbal planes). I hope also that my use of the model of Vigotsky's experiment in concept formation can clarify how patriarchy comes to be, how men are 'logofied' and women are 'reified.' The advantage of Vigotsky's model is that it presents concept formation as a dynamic process with stages and is not a static picture of similarities and differences. It transfers to the plane of cognitive psychology an issue that has been important for philosophy from Aristotle's one-many problem to Derrida's questions about exemplarity. I look at this problem as a symptom of centuries of patriarchal mis-conceptions.

16

Vigotsky believed that children were able only to form concepts at puberty. If the concept structure riddles society, as I propose, it alters the context into which children of both genders are born, making it hard for children to understand their own cognitive processes, at least until they are acting them out at another level at puberty. This consideration brings me to a theory of knowledge that I will just mention, which I call 'Nel blu dipinto di blu' ('In the blue, painted blue') from the song 'Volare' by Domenico Modugno. I believe that when we are doing something in our own lives we are more likely to see similar things in the world around us. For example, it was during the rise of 'survival of the fittest' capitalism that 'survival of the fittest' evolutionary theory developed. By this I do not mean to imply that what is seen is not 'true' but only that it might not have been seen at all if people had not been acting in a similar way at a different level. Perhaps it is because men have been embodying the one-many relation in their lives and projecting it into society that it has been important in philosophy. Vigotsky would have been no more exempt from this than anyone else. Moreover, for various reasons connected with the practice of exchange, which I discuss in this book, we are also not recognizing the giftgiving many of us are already doing. I hope that this book will allow women and men not only to practice more giftgiving but to see that they are already doing a great deal of it, to recognize that they are already 'painted blue' and to see the blue of the sky that surrounds them.

I believe that much of the anti-authoritarianism of both women and men can be understood as an appropriate anti-patriarchal attitude. The desire to place heart over head or emotion above reason is a kind of translation of the need to put the gift paradigm above the exchange paradigm. We should do this not just for sentimental reasons (which also have to do with giftgiving) but for practical reasons having to do with the survival of life on the planet. I have written For-Giving in order to understand patriarchy so that we—women and men—can make the deep and far reaching changes that are necessary.

As I was writing the book at a certain point I was wondering whether I would be accused of penis envy and a castrating attitude. As the Goddess would have it, however, just at that moment I received a call from a friend in Germany about the women in former Yugoslavia, and a call from a friend here who is the child of a rape and who was working on that issue. Eighteen thousand babies from the rapes in Bosnia, they said, many of them abandoned. What horror stories. After I hung up and began to write again, I wept and screamed in sorrow, frustration and rage. They said that the men had sometimes been forced to rape to continue in the army. Mothers were raped and killed in front of their daughters, who were also raped. Babies were cut out of their mothers' wombs and dog fetuses put in their place. We could say this is only former Yugoslavia and put it in a context that doesn't belong to the U.S. But I have heard many similar stories from around the world. And in 1991 when the U.S. began the war against Iraq we recieved information that men in U.S. marine bootcamps sang the refrain: "rape the women, kill the children, it's the only thing to do...." I am sorry, my brothers. Those of you who would desert and risk death to avoid this—perhaps it does not apply to you. I hope for all our sakes it does not. But do you realize how much pain and unspeakable horror this 'high' of yours or of theirs is causing? Let the men who read this learn to give by giving me the leeway to go ahead and try to tell it like it is. If you discount me you are enabling that behavior. And the same to you mothers who want to protect your sons from a blow to their self-esteem. Protect your sons not from me, from the truth, but from the society which turns them into ghouls and vampires, their instrument of love into an instrument of hate. Protect them from the phallic images and resonators that radiate validation to them from the society at large, that cause you to think that I am being 'unrealistic,' and that let you allow them to go ahead and join the army or become arms manufacturers or exploitative capitalists. All rapists and torturers had mothers. What can I say? That I am sorry that I see this clearly? I am sorry for us all. But if we see it we *can stop* it. Anything we can do to change the situation is worth consideration. Please read this book knowing *that* is its intention.

Apology

I ask for-giveness for the long time it has taken me to bring these ideas to light. I tried to do it sooner but did not succeed.

I ask for-giveness also for the many inadequacies and inaccuracies that may be found in this book. In my defense I can only offer the consideration that once you stop taking the purveyors of the dominant paradigm seriously, it is hard to remember exactly what they say.

I ask for-giveness of friends who may be surprised at my ideas. A paradigm hangs together and needs to be explained all at once. Though I have expressed my opinions I have often found a lack of comprehension because the wider context of the opinions was invisible. For that reason I did not always try to expose my point of view (though I did try to practice it).

If my anti-patriarchal analysis makes you uncomfortable, dear reader, I want to make it clear that I believe all life is sacred and miraculous—and that means your life too. The problem is a logic and a system, a self-confirming paradigm of dominance, and a dominant paradigm; it is not the individual male or female person. Listen to William Blake's explanation from the poem 'London' in *Songs of Experience*:

> In every cry of every Man,
> In every Infants cry of fear,
> In every voice: in every ban,
> The mind forg'd manacles I hear.

I believe the manacles to be forged not just in the mind but, through a feedback loop, on the material plane also. Perhaps we cannot break the manacles—because that would require the violence that confirms patriarchal domination. However, we can unlock them. In this book I try to find a key so small it fits into the mind. Please use it.

"Language is as old as consciousness, language is practical consciousness that exists also for other men [sic] and for that reason alone it really exists personally for me as well. . . ."

Karl Marx

"Whom does the Grail serve?"

La Folie Perceval, 1330 A.D.

Chapter 1
Where to Start

Capitalism and communism are both patriarchal. The philosophy of social change which is wider and deeper than either of them is feminism. I believe that feminism is a collective philosophy, a body of thought and action based on the values of women worldwide, which is presently revealing itself to the consciousness of all. Patriarchy has infected women *and* men for centuries, distorting our view of the world and warping our socio-economic practices. The agenda of feminism is to liberate everyone—women, children and men—from patriarchy without destroying the human beings who are its carriers and the planet where they live.

Trying to think outside of patriarchy puts women in a situation similar to that of the ancient pre-Socratic philosophers who were thinking at the beginning of Western patriarchal culture. If we reject the patterns of thought that have riddled and plagued European culture, there is a great deal of untrodden ground before us. We need to reconnect with our innocence, with the hearts that have not made war, that have moved us to take care of children and old people in spite of great difficulties rather than abuse them. We need to reject the patriarchal world view and start over—naively looking through our own eyes.

When we stop believing what we have been told, we find that the truth is there but our ability to recognize it has been numbed and buried deep within by the strata of the history of individuals, of cultures and of the species. It is the re-awakened, collectively-formulated women's perspective that proves the human species was not Mother Nature's mistake. By adopting it, women, and the men who follow them, can reverse the destruction of human beings and the planet.

In order to reject patriarchal thinking, we must be able to distinguish between it and something else, an alternative. The disciplines of academia have a tendency to mushroom into worlds to which thousands of international researchers and thinkers contribute. In spite of many 'advances,' they validate a view of the world and a reality in which the perpetration of abuse and domination is endemic at many levels. I believe that there is a relatively simple fatal flaw which undermines all so-called 'First World' thinking, including the thinking of the academic worlds. We usually begin our investigations into different subjects downstream from this flaw and, therefore, we are already under its influence. The naive point of view allows us to begin at the beginning. Usually academics build upon the past and begin at a place so far down the course of the river that the flaw can no longer be identified. Indeed, it seems to constitute reality. It is at the beginning that we can hope to find the alternative.

Because of the circumstances of my life, I have been able to turn my own naive attention towards one area of academic concern which has been particularly important in the Twentieth Century: the study of language and other sign systems. Whatever their other achievements, the disciplines of linguistics and semiotics and the philosophy of language have brought forward the fundamental importance of language for the human character and condition. If language is important, it follows that the study of language—in the disciplines of linguistics and semiotics—is a good place to begin an investigation of patriarchal thinking.

Communication by means of language is now considered by academics to be a separate and independent rule-governed activity. Some linguists believe that the fact that all human communities use language is evidence that language is transmitted, for the most part, not culturally but genetically. Syntactic rules and sometimes even elements of vocabulary appear to be part of the hardware handed down from generation to generation. It seems to me that such genetic endowments would predetermine our linguistic behavior in a "Biology is destiny" sort of way. In this, language would appear similar to gender, the characteristics of which were for centuries culturally considered to be biologically transmitted and, therefore, unchangeable and unchallengeable, especially by the 'genetically inferior' gender.

Making language a gift given by our DNA, not a cultural inheritance, locates it in an area which is beyond human intervention. If we believe instead that language is a social endowment which must be learned by flexible young mind-body complexes in the making, our idea of the human character varies accordingly. What is learned can be subjected to collective revision; its mechanisms can be investigated by the learners, its consequences altered.

Strange as they seem to me, considerations such as the genetic transmission of language are taken seriously and have far-reaching ripple-effects for other disciplines. An environment is created in which some ideas fit together and thrive because they are validated as permissible and respectable, while their alternatives are discredited. The so-called 'free market' of ideas, like the economic free market, often promotes the benefit of a (genetically superior?) few while appearing to be good for everyone.

Whenever we are talking about the human condition, we should subject our own discourse to at least two tests: "What's in it for me materially?" and secondly, "What's in it for me psychologically?" Criticism of ideology has shown that whole systems of thought have served the dominance of some groups over others. Every academic discipline should be suspect. Systems of ideas which we have been taught as the truth back up the political and economic systems of which they are a part.

Fortunately, I have been outside the academic world and not dependent upon it for my material well-being. Thus, I have been able to remain naive. I desire radical social change; as a mother, I want my children and the children of all mothers to receive a healthy and sane future, free from the collective psychosis of patriarchy. Contributing effectively to this future is my psychological reward.

I hope to show that there is a feminist explanation for language, and that much of our thinking can be re-framed as deriving from a woman-based practice. There is an entirely different paradigm which exists and is accessible beneath the abstractions of linguistics and semiotics. Feminists who have been rightly distressed by the male dominance of language have sometimes chosen to speak and write poetically as an alternative. They have even sometimes chosen to remain silent in order to subtract themselves from patriarchal discourse. I suggest that, by finding and consciously embracing the hidden paradigm, we can begin to liberate both language and social practice from patriarchal control.

In spite of endless discussions, philosophers have not been able to answer the question, "How are words 'hooked on' to the world?" This question is the end of a thread which is bound up in the tangle of patriarchal philosophy—a good place to begin a naive investigation. All the answers that have been given to this question have been influenced by the patriarchal stances of the mostly male philosophers who were doing the thinking. Their points of view grew up in denial of a women's model and have served to support patriarchal hierarchies throughout the centuries.[1] I do not want to try to refute current or past theories of language one by one, which would make this book an endless academic undertaking, conducted on the territory of those I want to challenge. I will simply propose an alternative theory.

Let me identify some questions that need to be answered. We need to know how words, phrases, discourses 'mean.' How are they related to each other and to the world? What is the significance of language for the nature of human beings as individuals and as a species? Why is it important for us to know this? Since language has been considered to play an important role in making us human, answering these questions in terms of an abstract system causes us to attribute our humanity to our

---

[1] In looking at the surface of language I question the psychological significance of terms used by philosophers and linguists, especially those having to do with giftgiving and need such as genetic 'endowment' or popular economic terms like 'haves' and 'have-nots.' They are clues to patriarchal psycho-social hidden agendas.

capacity for abstract thought, with the consequence that those of us who are best at abstract thinking appear to be somehow more human than the others.

Women have been stereotypically assigned the province of 'emotion' while men have appropriated the area of 'reason.' If we see language as an abstract system having the capacity to make us human, men's 'superiority' would seem to be justified by their presumed capacity for abstraction. Theories of language back up theories, or at least popular conceptions, of gender.

At another level of complication, considering syntax as a collection of rules imputes the rule-governed character to the human being as well. Thus it validates our systems of laws, making them seem natural because they are also collections of rules and require rule-governed activity. What happens in academia regarding language can have far reaching effects on the rest of the world. Academic economic theories also have important effects on the way goods are produced and distributed everywhere. Even when the effects are not direct, the assumptions underlying these disciplines influence individual and group behavior in many areas of life.

Changing the basic assumptions would have a far-reaching ripple effect. They form the motivation and backup rationale for policies and behaviors in much the same way that the existence of the military industrial complex forms the motivation and backup for US foreign policy.

Co-creation of Patriarchy

It has become commonplace in the US New Age movement to talk about the co-creation of 'reality.' It is said that, by our thoughts, we cause certain things to occur and others not to occur. I hope to be able to show how we are collectively creating a patriarchal reality, which is actually bio-pathic (harmful to life), and I propose that we dismantle that reality. Our values, and the self-fulfilling interpretations of life that we make because of them, are creating a harmful illusion which leads us to act and to organize society in harmful ways. This is one sense in which our thoughts do make things happen. If we understand what we are doing, however, patriarchal reality can be changed. First, we must have the courage to change the basic assumptions which serve as fail-safes to keep deep systemic changes from occurring.

Although male domination exists in many (or perhaps most) cultures, it is towards the domination of the white male that I want to direct my attention. In fact, I believe that many patterns of domination and submission have come together to create a pattern of domination for that group at all levels.[2] By this, I do not mean that every white male dominates, or that only white males dominate, but that the patterns of sex, race, and class fit together effectively to allow and encourage white males to dominate in many different areas of life. The patterns of domination propagate themselves and the values upon which they are based.

In the history of Europe, the rise of capitalism and technology, the slaughter of the witches, the invasion of the Americas and genocide of indigenous peoples, the slavery of Africans, and the Nazi holocaust are all extreme moments of a culture in which sex, race, and class work together like a giant mechanism to over-privilege some and under-privilege many others. Unfortunately, this mechanism often sets the standard and validates similar behavior in other cultures. Dictators throughout the world climb the stairs erected before them by their European brothers, perpetrating horrors.

At present, white males are still the most successful purveyors of patriarchy. Through mechanisms such as the free market, they continue to dominate the global economy. It is therefore the responsibility of their caregivers, especially white women, together with white women's allies among women and men of color *and* white men, to turn against patriarchy and dismantle it from within. We must all cease rewarding bio-pathic behaviors

[2] I do not pretend to cover all the different kinds of patriarchy that occur in different cultures: instead I am using Euro-American patriarchy as an example with which other patriarchies can be compared, their common qualities found and their differences identified. See chapter 5 for this type of reasoning.

and systems. Women and men with caring values must stop nurturing patriarchy.

Capitalism has had advantages for many women, especially white women, in that it has allowed us to take on the structural position which had formerly been reserved for men. Becoming part of the work force and becoming educated for positions of authority have allowed many women to acquire the voice—the ability to speak out and to define situations—which is very difficult for women who only have access to traditional family roles where males have all the authority.

Many women are using their freedom to speak against the system which 'liberated' them regarding its many defects, which weigh upon them personally through low wages, lack of child care, and the continued privileging of males. They also condemn the system's exploitation of their sisters and their sisters' children in the so-called 'Third World' here and abroad, its enormous waste of resources through the arms business and war, and its endemic devastation of the environment.

I think that women in capitalism are in a particularly good position to see through its apparent advantages, because we are still being educated to bring up children at the same time that we are being encouraged to climb the economic ladder. The contradictions involved in the values which accompany these two mandates draw our attention to the deep contradictions in the system itself.

Therapies and drugs of various kinds tend to try to make us 'adjust' by concentrating on ourselves as the cause of our discomfort. However, many feminists are turning outwards, against the bio-pathic system. We are not using the violent methods of the system but are looking for other ways to change it from within.

I believe we have not yet succeeded because we do not realize that we have a common perspective with women everywhere and that the problems we are facing are systemic. By showing the links among different aspects of patriarchy, and by uncovering

29

and asserting our common alternative values, women can begin to dismantle patriarchy, to re-create reality and to lead everyone back from the brink of disaster to peace for all.

The Gift Paradigm

There is a fundamental paradigm, with widespread and far reaching effects, which is not being noticed. It may seem strange, in the time of space travel, computers and genetic engineering, that anything really important could be ignored. However, we may remember the idea of the "elephant in the living room" talked about by Alcoholics Anonymous. People who are in denial of someone's alcoholism do not mention it. In order to maintain the *status quo*, they turn their attention to other things.

I believe there is a large part of life that is being denied and ignored. Unlike alcoholism, it is the healthy normal way of being, but we are indeed turning our attention away from it in order to maintain a false reality, the patriarchal *status quo*. I call this unseen part of life 'the gift paradigm.' It is a way of constructing and interpreting reality that derives from the practice of mothering and is therefore woman-based (at least as long as women are the ones who are doing most of the mothering).

The gift paradigm emphasizes the importance of giving to satisfy needs. It is need-oriented rather than profit-oriented. Free giftgiving to needs—what in mothering we would call nurturing or caring work—is often not counted and may remain invisible in our society or seem uninformative because it is qualitatively rather than quantitatively based. However, giving to needs creates bonds between givers and receivers. Recognizing someone's need, and acting to satisfy it, convinces the giver of the existence of the other, while receiving something from someone else that satisfies a need proves the existence of the other to the receiver.

Needs change and are modified by the ways they are satisfied, tastes develop, new needs arise. As they grow, children need to become independent, and mothers can also satisfy that need by refraining from satisfying some of the children's other needs.

Opposed to giftgiving is exchange, which is giving in order to receive. Here calculation and measurement are necessary, and an equation must be established between the products. In exchange there is a logical movement which is ego-oriented rather than other-oriented. The giver uses the satisfaction of the other's need as a means to the satisfaction of her own need. Ironically, what we call 'economics' is based on exchange, while giftgiving is relegated to the home—though the word 'economics' itself originally meant 'care of the household.' In capitalism, the exchange paradigm reigns unquestioned and is the mainstay of patriarchal reality.

Even many of those who wish to challenge capitalism envision only an economy without money—a barter economy— which is of course still based on exchange. I believe they misplace the dividing line between the paradigms, making money the responsible factor rather than exchange, so they cannot clearly see the alternative that giftgiving presents. Aiding the maintenance of the *status quo* and the exchange economy is a view of 'human nature' as egotistical and competitive—qualities which are required and enhanced by capitalism. The qualities required and enhanced by mothering are other-orientation, kindness and creativity. Though they are necessary for bringing up young children, these qualities are made difficult, even self-sacrificial, by the scarcity for the many which is often the consequence of the exchange economy. They are considered not 'human nature,' not part of reality.

I believe that the gift paradigm is present everywhere in our lives, though we have become used to not seeing it. Exchange, with its requirement for measurement, is much more visible. However, even our greeting "How are you?" is a way of asking "What are your needs?" 'Co-*muni*-cation' is giving gifts (from the Latin *munus*—gift) together. It is how we form the 'co-*muni*-ty.'

By satisfying the needs of the infants who are dependent upon them, mothers actually form the bodies of the people who are, and live together in, the community. They also care for and maintain the implements, houses and locations where the community interactions take place. We communicate with each other through our gifts of goods, through co-munication. Each gift carries with it something of the thought process and values of the giver and affirms the value of the receiver. In fact, goods and services that are given freely to satisfy needs give value to the receiver by implication.[3]

Exchange

Exchange, on the other hand, is self-reflecting. It requires attention to be concentrated on equivalence between the products, and the value that might have been given to the other person instead returns to the giver in the satisfaction of her own need. In exchange, the satisfaction of the need of the other is only a means to the satisfaction of one's own need. When everyone is doing this, the co-munication that occurs is altered and only succeeds in creating a group of isolated, unbonded, independent egos, not a co-munity.

In their isolation, these egos tend to develop new artificial needs for nurturing and bonding and use domination to procure for themselves the sense of community and identity they lack, forcing others to nurture them. They use everything from personal violence to manipulation of abstract systems to achieve the satisfaction of their needs, satisfaction which they are no longer receiving from participating directly in gift interactions.

In fact, we might look at our society as starving for free gifts and the bonds that are created by them. Our compassion is blocked, and it appears that only by denying giving-and-receiving can we survive. Yet not giving is killing those who could give just as surely as not receiving is killing those who have the material needs. In order to maintain this aberrant

---

[3] It would be interesting to look at anorexia as a refusal not only of food but of the value that would have been transmitted to the receiver through the reception of nurturing. Perhaps the anorexic takes on the exchange paradigm too profoundly or too soon.

situation, laws have been established, and armed forces are paid to back them up.

Huge amounts of money are spent nurturing the justice system, the government, the police and the military, thereby creating the scarcity which makes giftgiving difficult, and exchange a necessary survival mechanism.[4] Abstract systems of laws and hierarchical organizations like the government and the military are delivery systems for gifts, taking them away from the needs of the many in the community and directing them towards the needs of special groups of exchangers who have been socialized with an ego hungry to have 'more.'

While we may be grateful to the exchangers (entrepreneurs) for creating jobs, we should realize that the jobs are ways of getting for the entrepreneur what Karl Marx called 'surplus value'—what we could call a free gift of labor time given by the worker. In order to survive, the worker also has to receive many free gifts from his or her nurturers. Gifts are distributed from the bottom up in the hierarchy, from the poor to the rich, from giftgivers to exchangers, while it looks as if the flow is going in the other direction.

The interaction of exchange itself has seemed so natural that it would not require investigation. However, exchange is actually artificial, deriving from a misuse of co-munication. If we no longer consider exchange natural or one of the mainstays of reality, we can stop considering our participation in it as the criterion of our worth. In fact, many women have believed that the purpose of our liberation has been to allow us to participate more fully in society. In the US, this society is capitalist patriarchy. Women have also felt discomfort in it because our values are different, and at times this keeps us from being successful. The answer to our problem is not to change ourselves to adapt to the bigger patriarchal picture, but to change the bigger picture to adapt to women's values. This change requires

---

[4] World-wide, 19 billion dollars is spent on armaments every week. This would be enough to feed all the hungry on earth. Since the expenditure on armaments does not create any life-sustaining products, it acts as a drain on the nurturing economy. For a clear view of military expenditures see graphic on page 421-422.

33

asserting those values as more viable than the values of patriarchy. We must understand and deeply criticize patriarchy, so that we can realize we already have the alternative in our hands.

Rather than attempting to achieve the respect of those who have succeeded in the system, we need to stand our ground outside the system. Even 're-spect' has to do with looking again, evaluating and being equal to, which are criteria deriving from exchange, and are important only when caring is not already considered the norm.

As we shift our focus towards validating the gift paradigm and seeing the defects of the exchange paradigm, many things acquire a different appearance: Patriarchal capitalism, which seemed to be the source of our good, is revealed as a parasitic system, where those above are nurtured by the free gifts of their 'hosts' below. Profit is a free gift given to the exchanger by the other participants in the market and those who nurture them. Scarcity is necessary for the functioning of the system of exchange and is not just an unfortunate result of human inadequacy and natural calamity.

Chapter 2
Language and Giving

Since we use language throughout our daily lives, and much of our thought takes place in language, it seems obvious that it would have a strong effect on us—not only as a process or instrument, but as a model. Language also has the power of having come from others, from the many. It is a deep connection that we have with other people in our society. It is an important part of our socialization as children.

The fact that all human societies have languages does not have to imply that language is genetically based. There is something else that all societies have in common: the caregiving done by mothers. This social constant does not depend so much upon the biological nature of mothers as upon that of children, who are born completely dependent. If someone does not take care of their needs, they will suffer and die. The satisfaction of their needs must also take place without exchange, because infants cannot give back an equivalent of what they receive.

The caregivers of infants are thus forced into what we might call a kind of functional altruism. Society usually interprets the biological abilities of women—such as pregnancy, birthing, and lactation—to assign the role of mother and caregiver to women. Girls are brought up with the values that allow them to act in the other-oriented ways necessary for that role.

If we look at co-munication as the material nurturing or free giftgiving that forms the co-munity, we can see the nurturing that women do as the basis of the co-munity of the family unit. The nuclear family, especially the relation between mother and children, is just a vestige of what a community based on widespread giftgiving may have been at some time in the past, or could become in the future. The isolation of pockets of community from each other keeps the gift model weak, while the scarcity in which most of us are forced to live makes giftgiving difficult, even self-sacrificial and, therefore, 'unrealistic.'

While material nurturing is made difficult by scarcity, there is one thing of which we have an unlimited abundance, for which almost all of us possess the 'means of production.' That unlimited supply is language, with which we are able to produce ever-new sentences. Our vocabularies are finite, though almost infinitely re-combinable. We receive words and sentences free from other people and give them to others without payment. Language functions as a sort of free gift economy.[1] We do not recognize it as such, because we do not validate giftgiving in our economic lives and, in fact, we usually recognize the existence of nurturing specifically only in the mother-child relation. It, therefore, does not occur to us to use giftgiving as a term of comparison for language. With language, we create the human bonds that we have stopped creating through material co-munication. Language gives us an experience of nurturing each other in abundance, which we no longer have—or do not yet have—on the material plane.

This idea has led me to think that, if language is what made humans evolve, perhaps it is the giftgiving-in-abundance aspect, not the abstract system, that made the difference. If we were able to reinstate a material giftgiving co-munity, perhaps we would evolve again, as New Agers and many others hope. In fact, I believe it is the exchange economy itself that is impeding our evolution.

The logic of mothering requires that the nurturer give attention to the needs of the other person. The reward for this behavior is the well-being of the other. There are many different kinds of needs, and it is sometimes a challenge to understand and provide for them. Giving and receiving in an on-going way create expectations and rewards, a knowledge of the other and of the good that satisfies the need, a commitment to further caring, and

[1]Many of the words we use to talk about language are gift words: 'attribute' a property, 'convey' a meaning, a message, 'transmit' information. Language, the collective means of expression, has been talking about itself, but we have not been paying attention because we have been listening to patriarchy. Language was not saying what we expected it to say. Instead we have looked at it according to a postal metaphor—the packaging or encoding of information, sending and then unpacking or decoding it. I think the postal metaphor is just a way of keeping the gift under wraps.

36

an expectation that it will occur—an on-going relationship. Each participant is somewhat altered by the experience.

Even when material goods are not available or not being used, a need for bonding with the other person may still arise. I would call this a communicative need, a need to bond, a need for the relationship. Words are the social verbal items that have been devised to satisfy communicative needs. Since we use words to satisfy communicative needs regarding something, we can consider words as gifts. The mother first nurtures her child with goods and services, but she also nurtures her with words. The child is actually able to participate in turn-taking with the mother, verbally giving her communicative gifts before she is able to give her material gifts.[2]

Words as Gifts

A question arises here about the materiality of the verbal gift. Although we can identify a word as a repeatable sound unit, and it shares this character with other words, it can only be used for satisfying communicative needs, not for satisfying material needs directly. The word 'bread' does not satisfy the need to eat. However, communicative needs can sometimes be indirectly functional to the satisfaction of material needs. For example, 'There is bread in the cupboard' can be seen as a service that helps someone to satisfy her material need for bread. Saying the word 'bread!' as a request satisfies the listener's need to know what we want. We could consider the lexicon as a collection of gifts satisfying different communicative needs. Each word is a sequence of phonemes, a program of vocal behaviors which may be identified by the communicative need, or needs, it satisfies.

Boiling an egg is a sequence of behaviors having to do with various material objects, which satisfies the need to eat a cooked egg. Saying the word 'egg' is a series of vocal behaviors which satisfies a communicative need, establishing a relation with others

[2]We look at the world through the glasses of exchange so we may tend to see turn-taking as exchange. The motivation in turn-taking is not constrained reciprocity, but sharing, alternating giving and receiving, and communication.

regarding an egg or eggs. The ability to give information derives from the specification of experience through the use of these word-gifts, because the relation established is not only to the words themselves, but to things on other levels of reality, as well. The ability to receive information based on the use of words gives those words a value in the satisfaction of material needs, as well as in the satisfaction of communicative needs.

Whether we should consider word-gifts as goods or as services is something like the question whether light is made up of particles or waves. The kinds of communicative needs the word-gifts satisfy have proliferated to make use of them, much as the eye and the visual cortex have developed on our planet to make use of the light. It is useful also to consider the materiality of words as somewhere between goods and services, because the gifts on the nonverbal plane which they re-present, may also be of varying degrees of materiality.

From loving to the color green, from the moon to capitalism, all kinds of nonverbal things are re-presented by verbal things, creating verbal co-munication, and the formation of linguistic, and sometimes of material co-munities.[3] Just as material giftgiving-and-receiving of goods forms the physical bodies of the people in the community, verbal giftgiving-and-receiving contributes to their formation as social subjects, with psychological identities.

Relationship

Giving and receiving word-gifts organized in sentences and discourses creates a human relation among people with regard to things in the world. Communicative need is the need for the relation to others with regard to something. We cannot ourselves make the other person relate herself to something. However, we can interpret her lack of a relation as a need for a means to that

[3]The O.E.D. says that the word 'thing' derives from the old Norwegian word for 'court' which to me implies a collective judgment about the value of cultural items. I feel justified in thinking of both words and nonverbal things of varying degrees and kinds of materiality, in terms of a collective judgment about their value.

38

relation, and we can satisfy that need—with a word-gift. The need arises from the circumstances in which people find themselves, to talk about something. One person gives to the other word-gifts which re-present (give again) the pertinent parts of the world. We are social beings, and language allows us to include others in experiencing the world with us.

If I say, 'Look at the sunset,' I satisfy the need of the listener to know the sunset is happening, and to know that I think it is something worth looking at. By providing her with these words (which she already knows) in the present, I satisfy her need for a momentary relation to me and to the sunset, which is the same as my need for a relation to her and the sunset. Presumably, I would already be perceiving the sunset, so the motivation of my speech would be to include the other person in that experience, satisfying what I understand as her need to be put in that relation. The word 'sunset' has been supplied by the society in general to everyone, as a word-gift which can be used to satisfy communicative needs about sunsets.

The listener's creative reception of that word-gift places her in an inclusive human relation with me and, at the same time, draws her attention to the sunset, so that we can include each other, not only with regard to the words, but by relating ourselves in similar ways through our attention to a shared nonverbal experience. The relation to the nonverbal experience is also to some extent a gift, which we usually call 'information.' While looking at a sunset together can be a positive experience for both participants and, therefore, a need-satisfying aesthetic experience, there are many pieces of information which seem decidedly negative.

For example, 'I hate you' creates a common relation between us to my negative emotion towards you. This emotion is certainly not itself a gift to you, but it is useful to you to know that I have it and, thus, my phrase could be considered a gift or service in spite of its negativity. I believe there are many levels of gifts in life, as in language, but they have been hidden from us, because we have not been looking at them. We can say positive things to each other and nurture each other in that way, but even when we say things that are negative or neutral, the listener has many ways of receiving what has been given to her, transforming them into gifts by her creative use of them.

The phrase by Karl Marx that I have used on the frontispiece of this book, "language is practical consciousness that exists also for other men [sic] and for that reason alone it really exists personally for me as well," identifies a logic of other-orientation as the logic of communication. It also brings up the second grail question, "Whom does the Grail serve?" or in simpler terms, "Who is it for?" This question, always pertinent to giftgiving, often remains unasked and unanswered in our profit-based society.

General and Particular Processes

One aspect of communication through language is that it narrows down the range of possible experience at the moment to a shared present which, of course, may include mention of other times and places, as well. It often provides a theme or story line around which we can organize our behavior, revisit and interpret our experience together. The story line, and the topics of our conversations, are also gifts of common ground from which our diverse subjectivities grow.

I believe the way language works is by combining constant and general items in particular and contingent ways. We can identify the constant and general items by taking them out of the flow of speech in naming and definition. Their generality is in evidence when they stand 'alone' in this way. 'Dogs are four-legged tail waggers that bark' lets us consider dogs in general and the word 'dogs' in its generality. However, it is the use of words by the many in innumerable combinations in particular sentences that gives them their generality. Words are the common products of the collective, but so are general communicative needs.

When any 'thing' becomes pertinent or valuable enough to the many, so that people often need to form inclusive relations

40

with each other in its regard, a word arises socially to fill that need. If the need to form the inclusive relations is only contingent and fleeting, we satisfy it by creating a sentence— combining words that satisfy needs regarding the constant aspects of the thing or topic. A contingent and fleeting communicative need can arise regarding any part of on-going experience.

In 'After the storm, the sun made the water drops sparkle,' a contingent communicative need for a relation with others regarding a particular transitory situation is satisfied by combining words, which are also used elsewhere in other sentences regarding other contingent situations. The elements of those situations are relevant to the society of verbal communicators repeatedly, so that a common need arises for a verbal gift that can be given for them, and a constant word arises to satisfy the need.[4] A single word can also be used to satisfy needs regarding different kinds of things in homonymy. One kind of 'thing' can become related to different words in synonymy.

Needs build upon each other, and communicative needs can arise with regard to verbal as well as to nonverbal contexts. If the situation giving rise to a contingent communicative need is complex, we can put together a discourse by combining sentences, which we use to satisfy a variety of contingent communicative needs regarding that situation. Sentences work together in discourses to bring forward a common topic and to satisfy a variety of communicative needs arising in its regard.

Giftgiving is the Ur-logic

Linguists and philosophers have sometimes thought of explaining language in terms of underlying logical structures— either a simpler language, which would still not explain how language itself works, or some other elementary structure or process. One such process was that of cause and effect. It was

[4]The needs that give rise to idiomatic expressions can be seen as somewhere between the constancy of the word and the contingency of the sentence.

thought that it might be possible to reduce subject-verb-object structures to an underlying cause-and-effect structure. One example that was often used was 'John killed Mary,' which was given a 'translation' in cause-and-effect terms: 'John caused Mary to die.' I am often horrified at the (probably unconscious) hostility to women that can be found in linguists' examples. Perhaps it is evidence of the guilt they feel in denying the mothering paradigm (Mary?) as an explanation for language. Cause-and-effect was found by most linguists not to be an appropriate process to which to reduce language, perhaps because it is not informative enough. It certainly does not carry with it the human relational consequences that giftgiving does.

I am proposing giftgiving as the logical process to which to reduce language. Not only can words be seen as need-satisfying gifts, but the syntactic structure of subject, predicate, object can be seen as deriving from giver, gift (or service), receiver. For example, in 'The girl hit the ball,' 'girl' is the giver, 'hit' is the gift, 'ball' is the receiver. The 'translation' would be, 'The girl gave a hit to the ball.'

The intentionality of giftgiving can be found in many human actions and in the intentionality of speaking. A sense of motion and completeness which comes to us from a simple transitive sentence is similar to the motion and completeness that take place in giftgiving. In fact, giftgiving is transitive, a motion of something from one place or person to another. In the passive sentence 'The ball was hit by the girl,' emphasis is placed on the receiver rather than the giver of the gift.

Mothering is the necessary social process in the beginning of life, and this is also the time in which language learning takes place. Mothering is a cultural universal, required by the biology— not of adults, but of infants. To each different culture, mothering may appear as simply part of the nature of things but, for the mothers, the need to nurture is social and its accomplishment is intentional. Women's ability to give milk is a biological advantage that makes caretaking more convenient, but women must do the caretaking in a cultural context within social

42

parameters. In mothering, there is an intentional transfer of goods and services from adult to child, from giver to receiver.

This experience is fundamental for children, because their lives depend upon it, and it is important and formative for the caretakers as well—if nothing else, because it is enormously time-consuming. It is not surprising that half of humanity is socialized from birth to do caretaking, because it requires a great deal of attention and commitment. A recent book, *The Language Instinct*, by Steven Pinker,[5] attributes our linguistic capacity to a biological endowment. Similarly, mothering was considered instinctual until recently. In both cases, the logic of the gift is what is being covered by denial.

The caretaking situation is more fundamental than the condition of objectivity. The experience of free gifts given by the mother and received by the child is more basic to the human being than is the knowledge of cause and effect. The mother is the giver—her care is the gift or service—and the child is the receiver. This process is laid down when the child is learning language in alignment with a syntactic structure of subject (giver), predicate (gift), object (receiver).[6]

If words are verbal gifts that satisfy constant social communicative needs, in the structure of an interpersonal speech situation, the speaker would be the giver, the words and sentences the gifts, and the listener the receiver. Sentences are combinations of words, satisfying contingent communicative needs. It would not be far-fetched to think that the word combination process might also take place according to the logic of the gift.

The hypothesis that language is based on giftgiving and receiving allows us to look at many different levels at which they may occur, so that aspects of language which seem to be mysterious can be explained as elements of a gift process at some

[5]Steven Pinker, *The Language Instinct*, Penguin Books, London, 1994.
[6]The fact that there is variation in the ways these functions are expressed in different languages in word order and syntax does not undermine the hypothesis that giving and receiving could constitute universal behavioral structures from which they are derived.

level. First, there is the level of material co-munication—the mother gives gifts or services to the child. Second, there is verbal communication—the mother talks to the child.[7] Third, words are social gifts, each satisfying a constant communicative need. Fourth, words are combined into sentences, which satisfy contingent communicative needs. Fifth, the message and the topic may also be considered gifts, as when we satisfy someone's need to know something or to talk about something. Sixth, at the level of syntax (within the sentence), the relation between subject, predicate and object re-traces the relation between giver, gift, and receiver.

It is important to look at this as a syntactic relation taking place at the level of words themselves, because at the level of things the words re-present, the 'gift' may be negative, as in 'The boy hit the girl,' or even 'John killed Mary' (translation: 'John gave death to Mary'). At the level of material communication, such violence is contradictory and harmful, causing more grievous needs rather than satisfying needs. Nonetheless, at the level of sentence structure, the gift process can function independently from the level of experience. Thus, 'The girl hit the ball,' 'Mother made a cake' and 'John killed Mary' all have the same giver, gift, receiver sentence structure though on the level of reality, they are very different events.

At the syntactic level, we can also look at the relations between adjectives and nouns, adverbs and verbs, as relations between gifts and receivers. In 'The brown dog ran fast to the gate,' 'brown' is *given* to 'dog' and 'fast' to 'ran.' Philosophers used to say brown was a 'property' of the dog, and fast would be a 'property' of its running. Brown can be called a 'property' because . . . it is given to the dog by allowing the word 'brown' to modify the word 'dog,' joining them as transposed gift and receiver in order to satisfy a contingent communicative need, arising from a dog of that color.

[7]There is a great deal of nonverbal communication as well which occupies a spectrum between material nurturing and language. However it is the more abstract end of the spectrum—language, that needs to be understood first in order to see nonverbal communication in its light.

Linguists are used to following a mathematical, algebraic or scientific model, not a life model—but they still talk about words 'filling the slots' of other words in a phrase. We could look at the 'slots' as needs and the words as gifts satisfying them. If a word can only be related to a specific kind of other words (for instance, a determiner like 'the' can only be related to nouns), it is a kind of gift that can be given only to a certain kind of receiver. Only that kind of receiver has a need ('slot') for it. Some words or groups of words have to attach themselves to others; they cannot give their gifts alone, but serve or are served by another group.

For example, 'to the gate' has to serve; it cannot stand alone. It is not itself a gift transaction, or even a giver, but a gift to a gift. If bonds are formed between the receiver and the gift, perhaps we attribute the same process to our words. 'Brown' is given to 'dog' by the speaker for the moment, satisfying the communicative need arising from a brown dog. 'Dog' receives the gift of 'brown' and bonds with it for the present.

Transparency and Giving-Way

Gifts are given at the verbal level, which interpret 'reality' by re-presenting it in terms of giftgiving, but they are actually transparent to experience. In our example, they are transparent to the dog's being brown (it had that color), bringing it forward as part of an experience or topic the interlocutors can share.[8] The transparency of the gift structure recalls another characteristic of giftgiving—the giver gives-way, self-effacing in order to give value to the receiver. We may, therefore, notice only that what we say is a gift—as when some information that we transmit is understood and used by the listener. We do not notice that the way we say it is a gift process at many levels.

At the 'reality' level, things which could have been gifts in co-munication give way to the word-gifts which take their place. They graciously stand aside and let words take over. In fact, their

---

[8]Similarly 'the sick woman' attributes sickness to a woman according to a gift structure, creating a shareable topic though sickness is not a gift to be shared.

lack of competitiveness makes us forget that many of them never could have been actually transferred from one person to another anyway. Abstract ideas, huge material objects, creatures of fantasy, subjective states, etc. all stand aside with equal equanimity, allowing their places to be taken and giving value to the words that take their places.

At another level, the emotions that accompany our speech, or sometimes the very act of speaking to others, may also be said to nurture them, creating bonds. However, we do not usually notice gift structures in language because, in fact, they also stand aside; they give way in order to give value to what is being said and to the listener, the receiver of the verbal gifts. Another reason we do not usually see gift structures is that they are different from definition-exchange structures, and their levels are usually not formed the same way. Definition structures overtake gift structures like military facilities built on women's sacred springs.

The interpretative capacity of giftgiving has been denied and overtaken by viewing interpretation as a kind of 'penetration' by the mind. Phrases such as 'the way words are hooked on to the world' and even 'filling the slots' suggest metaphors of male sexuality. Instead, from a mother-based feminist point of view, we can see the relation between words and the world as the relation among gifts at different levels, where reality itself is a gift, all the way from sense 'data' to experiential givens.[9] The world is made accessible to humans by the gifts of language at many different levels—resulting in the sending of messages, the transmission of ideas and information, and the handing-down of culture. In fact, from this point of view, we could call our species, not *homo sapiens*, but *homo donans*. Giftgiving and receiving are prior to and necessary for our human way of knowing. They are the basis of a universal 'grammar,' not only of language, but of life.

[9]Gifts, whether verbal or nonverbal, are not arbitrary, in that they are given to satisfy needs and to create relations. However, the substitute gifts do not have to look or sound like the originals.

Transitivity

Still another level at which we can see giftgiving is that of logical transitivity. The syllogism upon which the discipline of logic was founded "If 'A' then 'B,' and if 'B' then 'C,' if 'A' then 'C' could be seen as the transposition of the transitivity of the gift: "If 'A' gives to 'B,' and 'B' gives to 'C,' then 'A' gives to 'C.'" Logic, like language, could thus be seen as deriving from mothering, not from the capacity for abstraction. Logical connectors (articles, prepositions, parts of speech, prefixes, suffixes) alter the kinds of gifts that words are, by the fact that they are given to them and become attached to them from time to time in various ways. The answers to questions about 'how,' 'where,' 'when,' etc. satisfy communicative needs that grow up around the capacity to give and receive itself.

When an experience being described is not a complete gift transaction, we may nevertheless use the gift structure to give our message to the listener: 'The brown dog ran fast to the gate' is 'intransitive.' The dog is only given ostensively; it 'presents (gives) that behavior' to us to perceive. The additional information given by 'to the gate' increases the useful character of the sentence by saying where the running behavior was directed. 'To the gate' serves 'ran' by giving it a location, making it more specific.

Patriarchy has assigned 'activity and creativity' to men and 'passivity and receptivity' to women, because it has been blind to the creativity of giftgiving and of receiving. Both giftgiving and receiving are creative. The use of what has been given to us is necessary to make what has been given into a gift. If we do not use it, it is wasted, lifeless. The fact that the capacity to receive is as important as the capacity to give is manifested in our ability to transform sentences from active to passive and from passive to active. Moreover, the receiver in one moment can become the giver in the next, passing the gift along: 'The girl hit the ball, which hit the window.'

The speaker herself could be considered the receiver of an experience, which she is transmitting again to the listener. Perhaps the speaker might be considered as the middle term in a gift transaction, 'A gives to B, and B gives to C.' The speaker (B), by describing an event, passes on to another (C) the gift that has been given to her by life, by 'the way things are,' reality (A). She gives a gift which also involves her own creative receptivity: she has already necessarily selected some of the features of her experience as more important than others. Her re-presentation gives value to the elements she has selected.

The listener too will emphasize some of the elements in what she has been given. She actively collaborates in the creation of the product she receives. The stereotyping of gender and the emphasis on exchange in our society make it seem as if there is a great deal of (male) human activity which is not a gift, not need-directed. Reinstating the gift paradigm to its central place in the group of interpretative registers through which we address the world, lets us see that most human 'activity' is oriented towards the satisfaction of a need at some level. Language consequently appears, not as a mechanical concatenation of (verbal) activities, but as a collection of gifts and of ways of giving and receiving, in alignment with communicative needs, which arise from experience and proliferate at many levels, given that there are abundant means available for their satisfaction.

Chapter 3
Reciprocity

The logics of giving and of exchange contradict each other, but the one is also built upon the other. Exchange is a constrained double gift in that the receiver must give back to the giver an equivalent of what she has received. The product of one person takes the place of the product of the other. I believe that this requirement of equivalence and place-taking is a derivative of naming, where the verbal gift takes the place of the nonverbal gift, and of definition, where some verbal gifts take the place of other verbal gifts. In exchange, which operates on the material plane, a return 'gift' takes the place of one's own, and may seem to serve, as the verbal substitute gift would, to create a bond between the exchangers.

The road to hell is paved with good intentions however, and acquiring the equivalent return 'gift' becomes the whole motivation of the first 'gift.' Transforming the gift process into an equal exchange, erases the other-orientation of both exchangers— making their equality only the equality of their self interests. Exchange becomes a kind of magnetic template around which our society organizes itself. Our thinking gravitates towards it, giving it a great deal of credit, perhaps because of its similarity with naming and definition (the linguistic processes from which it derives and which we continue to use). Giftgiving continues unabated, but remains invisible and does not become generalized as a model which is validated by having conscious followers. In fact, the gift paradigm gives-way: it does not compete with the exchange paradigm. It is thus in the situation of giving value and giving many gifts to exchange.

Exchange is self-reflecting and therefore self-validating. It has a symmetrical form and the requirement of equivalence between the products subverts the focus on the need of the other. Because exchange is based upon and promotes the self-interest of both exchangers, there is an equality not only in the products but also in the motivation of the persons involved.

As instances of equality, the two are then again equal to each other and a hall-of-mirrors effect begins, which is again equal to that effect in all the other exchanges taking place—for instance, in the market. The processes of substitution and equivalence in language also resonate with and confirm the derivative processes in the market, giving the hall-of-mirrors many abstract reflections.

The abstract need for equations, which is set up by the process of exchange in function of the self-interest of each of the exchangers, acquires an independence, a sort of life of its own. Anything that can be substituted by an equivalent appears to be a value (an exchange value), whether or not it is directed towards someone's need. I believe that the over-emphasis on the equation, while ignoring giftgiving, is the source of the idea that there is much human activity which is not need directed. The abstract needs of the process of exchange are not considered needs but part of 'the way things are.' However, satisfying them becomes more important than satisfying human needs, and the exchange process takes over from giftgiving, seeming to be the source of 'human' values. Thus we have the inhuman and inhumane market-driving category of 'effective demand.'

Because exchange requires an equation, which is equal to other equations on the market and elsewhere, it brings with it a sort of built-in meta level[1], which allows it to self-propagate and to

[1] A 'meta-language' is a language which talks about language. Terms such as 'noun,' or 'sentence' are part of the meta-language of grammar. The 'hall-of-mirrors' effect spawned by exchange makes all the other equations and reflecting structures in the society validate exchange. By their similarity to it they appear to say 'This is norm-al.' The self-reflecting focus warps our view by overemphasizing the exchange process and decontextualizing it—taking it away from its context—its other—in giftgiving. In *Principia Mathematica*, Bertrand Russell discussed his theory of logical types where 'higher' logical levels are of a different type than the levels beneath them. For example, the class of all classes is a meta-class at a higher logical level than its members. Meta-messages are messages about messages and tell us how to interpret them. I believe that the hall-of-mirrors effect creates many meta-messages which keep our focus locked onto the exchange process. See also Gregory Bateson, *Steps to an Ecology of Mind*, Ballantine Books, New York, 1972. Bateson discussed the potential for resolving schizophrenogenic double binds by changing meta-messages. I believe the double binds are caused by concealed exchange motivations and processes at the meta level. Recognizing giftgiving as the context in which exchange and classification are embedded could cause us to re-focus our economics and our logic, validating giftgiving and achieving sanity.

remain in evidence in the foreground. At the same time, giftgiving (which only requires an imitator in order to serve as a model) is pushed into the background and made invisible, even though it continues to be practiced in many ways. In fact, exchange is parasitically embedded in a wider process of giftgiving, which actually gives to the process of exchange, allowing it to continue to prevail. Exchange itself becomes the 'other' of giftgiving.

The generality of giftgiving is captured by its being practiced on exchange; then it is redefined as an inferior or failed exchange. Giftgiving thus appears to be a special case of incomplete one-sided exchange which cannot exist on its own. Actually the logic and practice of exchange are parasitic upon the logic and practice of giftgiving. The gifts they receive help them dominate the lives and the world views both of those who practice exchange and of those who practice giftgiving.

There is an upward flow of gifts, against gravity, towards the superior positions in patriarchal hierarchies and away from needs. The presence together of many of these gift-exchange hierarchies, which bolster each other by their similarity and sometimes by service is called 'social reproduction.' The hall-of-mirrors creates abundant images of the same structures—and thus once again looks similar to language—but we are led by the reflecting equation to take the cue for understanding the world from the aspect of the propagation of similar one-many images instead of from the gift aspect of language.

Perhaps it is because of similar structures at different levels that the parasitic exchange paradigm is elevated to the level of a self-perpetuating system with a 'mind' of its own. If these processes are functional in the formation of our individual minds—conscious vs. subconscious for example—perhaps they are also forming the same patterns on a very large social scale.

The self-perpetuation is facilitated by the confirmation of finding or creating self-similar images at different levels. I look at such similarities between patriarchal structures at different levels not as analogies, historical isomorphisms or homologies, but as self-similar social patterns created by the reciprocal feedback of

51

the form of the definition into the definition of gender (and vice versa, the definition of gender into the form of the definition) at many different levels.

The idea of self-similarity was developed by Benoit Mandelbrot in the study of fractal geometry, where he found that the same patterns were repeated at widely different levels or 'scales.' The cauliflower is the common example: each flower and piece of each flower looks like the whole head.[2]

I think the same thing happens in society in what we call 'social structures.' In fractals, the patterns are created by feeding the result of an equation back into the equation millions of times. Socially, we are doing the same thing—feeding back the definition of gender and its resulting 'masculine' characteristics into the structure of other definitions endlessly and thus we are actually creating the same patterns at different levels.

Figure 1. A fractal image is generated by feeding back the results of an equation into the equation millions of times.

Copyright © Clifford Pickover; reprint of graphic with permission. From *Fractal Horizons: The Future of Fractals* by Clifford Pickover and J. C. Sprott, 1996. This book is a clear recent discussion of fractals.

[2]For another useful explanation of fractal geometry and self-similarity see James Gleick, *Chaos, Making a New Science*, Penguin Books, New York, 1987.

Is Reciprocity Exchange
or Turn-Taking?

Homo economicus, the protagonist of neo-classical economics, is made in the image of exchange. Even the word *homo*, meaning 'the same,' brings with it the idea of an equation. We educate our boys to be similar units of masculinity and then to vie with one another for economic and symbolic superiority. We educate our girls to nurture this process and to bring up their children in its image. This has the effect that in the 'free market' (an oxymoron) society more males can be found in the practice of exchange, while more females can still be found practicing giftgiving.

Our economic systems are based on exchange and our study of them, economics, is based on exchange as well. Capitalism itself practices the values of masculinity and masculinity the values of capitalism. Since these are social roles, they can also be practiced by persons of the other biological sex. However, this may be rendered more difficult because the social interpretation of genders creates many impediments against the success of one gender in areas usually occupied by the other. One of these areas is economics, the academic discipline that studies capitalism.

Because the study of the production and distribution of goods in our society is based upon and directed towards self-validating exchange, it does not consider giftgiving as 'economic.' Yet giftgiving is indeed the production and distribution of goods. The micro-economics of a different (gift-based) macroeconomic system takes place in every household. Women's un-monetized gift labor has been invisible to economists until recently because those who were practicing the values of exchange were the only ones studying it.

Now some women economists, who like other women have been socialized towards mothering and the practices of giftgiving, are applying gift values to the study of exchange and to their profession and are experiencing a great deal of healthy cognitive dissonance. However, they have not yet begun to question the validity of the exchange paradigm itself as a world view, perhaps because they are still more or less successfully operating within it.[3]

It is easier for those who are at least partly outside the exchange logic to identify and promote giftgiving as a socially relevant paradigm—indeed as the solution to the problems being caused by exchange. This 'revolutionary vanguard' would include not only women, housewives and mothers (whether or not they do monetized labor), but all those who do not make profit from exchange and instead are unconsciously giving to it—the male and female 'hosts' of the parasite.

Most of us are still blinded to giftgiving by the internalization of the self-reflecting logic of exchange. Even while we are practicing it, we do not 're-cognize' giftgiving, think about it at a meta level or have a meta language with which to talk about it. We continue to think in exchange terms about our own culture, as well as about examples of institutionalized giftgiving in other cultures.

A recent school of thought in France, based upon the work of the anthropologist Marcel Mauss, devotes a great deal of attention to giftgiving, which it sees as composed of three moments: giving, receiving and giving back.[4] The insistence upon reciprocity hides the communicative character of simple giving and receiving without reciprocity and does not allow this group to make a clear distinction between giftgiving and exchange as two opposing paradigms.

It seems to them that giftgiving is just a variation on exchange, with a longer pay back time and less emphasis upon equality. The bonds still seem to be caused by constrained reciprocity, rather than by the direct satisfaction of needs. Like

[3]The International Association for Feminist Economics (IAFFE).
[4]See, for example, the work of Jacques Godbout, Serge Latouche and the review MAUSS, which is an acronym for *Mouvement Anti-utilitariste des Sciences Sociales*.

most men, these investigators are limited in their thinking because they have not been socialized towards the adult experience of creating bonds directly through mothering. Giftgiving appears to be a curiosity, not the mother-based (mammalian) life logic or a program for social change.[5]

Years ago, French anthropologist Levi-Strauss's description of the symbolic 'exchange of women' among family groups[6] inspired much further speculation in the exchange mode by anthropologists, psychoanalysts, linguists and semioticians. From the gift paradigm point of view, women are themselves the source of nurturing, so that the 'giving' of women is a gift of givers—a meta gift. The exchange (if it is constrained and seen through our capitalistic eyes) or turn-taking (if it is not) has a content which, in the case discussed by Levi-Strauss, is women, who are the source of giving.

Giving and receiving, rather than the constraint of reciprocity, is what causes bonding. The interaction of nurturing and receiving nurture (or nurturers) is the mutually creative factor, not the imposition and following of the law, not the equivalence of exchange, nor the constraint of reciprocity. In societies which are less deeply etched by exchange than our own, gift practices (gift cycles) serve definitional purposes, defining relationships among the members of the group. We might consider them descendants of language, of another lineage than exchange, but using the giving and receiving of gifts—co-munication—for the purposes of status. (See Figure 2.)

[5]In an influential foreword to a re-edition of Marcel Mauss' *The Gift*, W. W. Norton, New York, 1990, Mary Douglass discusses exchange—or reciprocity—as the bond-creating aspect of the gift. She refers to her experience in a foundation where she learned that "the recipient does not like the giver, however cheerful he be." She believes that free gifts should not be given because "refusing requital puts the act of giving outside any mutual ties." p. vii. Women too can be mesmerized by the exchange paradigm into believing that reciprocity, not the satisfaction of needs, is the source of human relations. I would just like to mention that there is great psychological distress around free giving and that charities often give paternalistically, demeaning the receivers—another reason why the recipients may not have liked Douglass's "cheerful giver."
[6]Claude Levi-Strauss, *Anthropologie Structurale*, Paris, Plon, 1958.

55

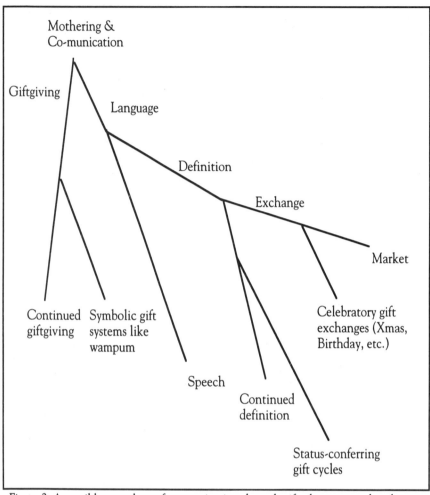

Figure 2. A possible genealogy of co-munication through gifts, language and exchange.

Women are the Vanguard

Lewis Hyde, Jerry Martien and other writers on gift 'exchange' have done work[7] which re-interprets historical and anthropological literature, at least partially liberating the idea of the gift from the constraints of capitalism. Perhaps because they have not had the experience of mothering, they tend to see the gift way as a poetic thing of the past, which has been forgotten,

[7]Lewis Hyde. *The Gift, Imagination and the Erotic Life of Property*. Random House, 1979, New York, and Jerry Martien, *Shell Game, a True Account of Beads in North America*, Mercury House, San Francisco, 1996.

marginalized and covered over—much as their own experience of the gift way (with their mothers when they were children) has been covered over but still remains in the unconscious and in myths and stories. Continuing to see giftgiving in terms of reciprocity (that is, exchange) maintains the discourse within the parameters of the patriarchal *status quo*.

Women can more easily recognize the presence of giftgiving everywhere because we have an actual example of it in our adult practice of our social role (however socially disqualified and devalued that may be). That is why women are the vanguard, the carriers of giftgiving as a social program, a way of organizing society now and for the future.

The lack of a theory of language as giftgiving makes the understanding of giftgiving as a living principle more difficult. However, the discussion of money as a 'gift' and wampum as 'words' and 'speech acts' proposed by Martien is a bridge between language and material giftgiving (as was wampum itself). Martien lets us see that wampum was a means of material co-munication (interpreted by European settlers only as a 'primitive' kind of money). The strings of shell beads were sent from place to place to define situations and satisfy special needs for bonding, attention and care. For example, special beads were sent to those in mourning, to satisfy the need for consolation. Beads were given to create pacts and maintain promises among social groups. Wampum would appear to be a many-word material language, which went beyond definition to create solidarity and mutual inclusion, while money remains at that stage which names everything quantitatively in order to facilitate a more 'primitive' human relation of mutual exclusion—of having and not-having private property.

In our own lives, as well as in the investigation of other cultures, the question arises as to whether it is possible to follow and assert a clear model of giftgiving or whether, by focusing on giving back, any transaction becomes assimilated to the model of exchange. This is really a problem of the intersection of two logics; but it is often read as a moral question(we ask, "Is she really being altruistic, or is this just a hidden manipulation?"), which only clouds the picture and sometimes makes us pay for our acts of love with shame. We wryly comment, "No good deed ever goes unpunished." Self-interest appears to be the basic motivation of all humans, with scarcity as its natural complement. The good of the whole seems to be, after Adam Smith, the compendium of the self-interests of all, while orientation towards the other is unrealistic and self-sacrificial. Reciprocity is a way of maintaining the self-interest of both of the parties involved in the interaction.

The custom of giving back a bit extra, more than one has received, is a way of affirming the gift model—even when, through reciprocity, one is running the risk of being perceived as exchanging. However, this process has also been assimilated into exchange as interest on loans. In fact, lenders give their money in expectation of the extra gift of interest they will receive. (This kind of exchange has become so much the norm that an interest-less loan is now considered a gift).

Anthropologists, like the rest of us in patriarchy, have difficulty taking off the mirror glasses of the exchange paradigm. Thus they talk about 'gift exchange,' confusing the two modes from the beginning. Again giftgiving appears to be an under-developed version of exchange rather than a different and more viable method of organizing society. In so-called 'primitive' societies, giftgiving often has a symbolic function. I believe that is because, in imitation of language, as we just saw with wampum, special material substitute gifts (like verbal substitute gifts) are given in organized ways for the purpose of creating specific bonds among givers and receivers.

In other words, both the exchange of commodities for money and 'symbolic gift exchange' are variations on the theme of co-munication. They are two alternative uses of the intertwined patterns. In fact, both language and the production and distribution of material goods are found in all societies and have co-existed for millennia. Societies have learned to use their own processes in a variety of ways to create new processes of communication.

Language is a second (verbal) gift economy, while definition and naming are special de-contextualized processes of language. These de-contextualized processes evolve into exchange when they are transposed onto the material plane, as people substitute one product for another and equate them quantitatively.

The introduction of money provides a 'general equivalent,' a single substitute gift (like a word) in which the values of all the products on the market can be expressed and evaluated. While money provides an additional abstract element in the exchange process, it does not alter its basic logic. Thus barter is not a solution to the problems caused by exchange. Rather it is only an example of the same logic without money. By taking the distinction between giftgiving and exchange as the watershed between two basic paradigms of human interaction, we can clarify a number of different and seemingly unrelated problems.

Many Gifts

We can understand many of the irrational and harmful aspects of patriarchal capitalism as a point of contact between the two paradigms. Surplus labor—that portion of the workers' labor time that is unpaid and goes towards the profit of the capitalist—can be considered as a gift under constraint, from the worker to the capitalist. The tendency to pay women less than men for comparable labor, can be interpreted as an attempt to maintain women in a giftgiving position, reinforcing our practice of the invisible gift model by making us give even more unpaid (gift) labor than our male co-workers do. Because of the equality of exchange and the value we attribute (give) to it, we are apt to give credit to the market as 'just' even when it is penalizing us (Father knows best).

Women's unpaid labor in the home has been calculated as adding some 40% or more to the Gross National Product. It is one of the most glaring examples of unrecognized gift labor that exists. Consider also the gifts that come to the rich from the poor, to the North from the South, to exchange-based economies from economies that are still to some extent gift-based. Differences in exchange rates, levels of life and self-sufficiency in the 'developing' countries permit a flow of gifts from them to the so-called 'developed' countries.

Not only is this flow not recognized as such, but it is actually read in the opposite direction so that the North appears to be giving loans, material aid, information, technology, markets, protection, even a 'civilizing influence' to the South, which becomes depleted and crippled trying to pay back the 'more,' the interest on what it has been 'given,' but which has actually served to stimulate more hidden gifts which drain away its capital.

For example, the lowering of the level of life in Third World countries serves the First World by lowering the price of labor—transforming the differential of low-cost labor and raw materials into collective gifts from the many in the South through the few in the South to the few in the North. The manipulative use of giftgiving for the purpose of profit making (leveraging more gifts) is itself an exchange. However, misinterpreting giftgiving as an exchange and profit as 'deserved' confuses the two paradigms and is not just a bias of academicians. It is a very widespread view that is part of and supports the practice of exploitation.

The many examples of actual slavery that have poisoned human history are evidence of the tendency to place groups of people in constrained giftgiving positions through 'owning' them. Women of all races and cultures have also often been in these positions with regard to their husbands, whether or not they were actually 'owned.' In order to accumulate capital, surplus gifts must come from somewhere. Slavery provided that surplus 'free' to the slave 'owners' in the South of the US, for example, though it cost immense human suffering to the slaves.

But exchange also provides an efficient mechanism for accumulation, by hiding the gifts it receives behind the screen of an equation which appears to be 'fair,' and a transaction which appears to come from a 'free choice' (no matter that the absence of alternatives often reduces poor people to a situation similar to slavery). Capital can be seen as the combined gifts of the many captured by exchange and understood within exchange's self-reflecting parameters as coming from fair profit on an investment. Equal exchange does not produce a profit. Gift labor is necessary for that purpose.[8]

Gift labor is easy to hide because, as we said regarding language, giving is transitive. If 'A' gives to 'B' and 'B' gives to 'C,' then 'A' gives to 'C.' Thus, if a wife gives her free labor to her husband and he gives his surplus labor to the capitalist, the wife's labor passes transitively through her husband to the capitalist. The gift is also unseen because we avert our gaze from the original source. At most we look at 'B' giving to 'C.' What is in full evidence, however, is the so-called 'equal' exchange between 'B' and 'C,' where the capitalist pays the worker a salary which is determined by the price of that kind of labor on the market.

Focusing on the salary as the 'just' price of labor draws our attention away from the quantifiable *and* unquantifiable giftgiving which is also taking place. Exchange validates itself and fits with the other exchanges which are occurring in the market. It floats like a cluster of bubbles on a sea of hidden gifts—given by women, workers, the unpaid, the underpaid, the poor, the unemployed (who with their demand for jobs keep the 'just' price of labor low), and all those in classes and countries which are in a giftgiving stance towards privileged classes and countries.

Then there are the many gifts of consumers who consistently overpay for products like gasoline, which have a relatively low production cost but a high utility to people whose needs have been determined by transportation industries. There are the gifts of the past, of the surplus value contained in 'fixed capital,' but also in (mostly women's) free gifts of maintenance of the buildings, goods, use values and people of previous generations— their children, their language, their art, their culture, and the by-products of their lives. There is a great unrecognized flow-through of gifts from the past to the present, as well as from

[8] Jack Weatherford, *Indian Givers*, Fawcett Columbine, New York, 1988, discusses the impact the gold and silver of the Americas had on European capitalism, along with the numberless other (unrecognized) gifts the native people gave to the rest of the world.

people in groups and in countries in the giving stance to the people and countries in the taking stance.

There are the gifts of nature ready for our use, air and water and sunlight, which we are adapted by evolution to creatively receive—but which are becoming polluted and scarcified by being covertly expended, wasted, to cut costs (give gifts) in the service of the exchange paradigm. This pollution forces unborn generations to hand over to us their potential use of nature's gifts so that we can make a quick profit. We are blocking the flow of gifts towards the future. New types of commerce invade previously giftgiving areas, from fast food restaurants to laundromats. The inheritance of all is becoming commercialized by the industry of bio-genetics, turning even the (biological) free gifts of the many to the profit of the few.

Chapter 4
Definitions and Exchange

Naming and its more complicated form, definition, constitute special moments of language where words themselves are given to satisfy the meta linguistic needs (needs regarding language itself) of the listeners. By telling others the names of things, or giving definitions of words, we are giving them the means of production of linguistic co-munication. This situation is different from speech proper, because naming and definition are at least somewhat de-contextualized, and their internal processes are of a special kind. We step outside the flow of speech to a meta level, to provide the listener with something she does not already have, a 'new' term which satisfies some constant general communicative need.[1]

The need satisfied by the flow of speech, instead, is a need for a present and contingent relation to something(s), satisfied when the speaker gives the listener a verbal product, combining words (each of which, taken alone, would provide a constant relation) into sentences. In speech, the listener could, in principle, make the speaker's sentences herself, but has not (in that instance) recognized the need to make them. In the case of naming or definition, the listener needs, because she does not yet have and cannot yet use, the appropriate words. Her need is like a material need for the means of production—in this case it is a need for the means of production of verbal gifts.

In the processes of naming and definition, the speaker performs a service for the listener, understanding what she needs

[1]Ferdinand de Saussure, in *Course in General Linguistics*, Mc Graw Hill, New York. 1959, distinguished between what he called '*langue*,' the lexicon, the collection of words taken out of context and related to one another purely differentially, and '*parole*' or speech. Naming and definition may appear to be pre-requisites for the rest of speech (though we also learn words from simply hearing them in others' speech). My point is that the processes by which we acquire words and consider them on their own out of context, in their generality, are different from the processes in which we use them by putting them together. I believe that the definition's internal gift processes are different enough from speech that they are the hidden model for exchange. They are what Roman Jakobson called 'equational statements.' 'The Speech Event and the Function of Language' in *On Language*, edited by Linda Waugh and Monique Monville-Burston, Harvard University Press, Cambridge, Mass, 1990.

to know and providing her with a word in a way that is fashioned so that she can learn it. If she is talking to a child or to someone who speaks a foreign language, she may say the word at the same time that the 'thing' is present as an experiential given. She may also point at it, pick it up, hold it out towards the other person, etc. However, if she thinks the listener already has some knowledge of the vocabulary of that language, the speaker can fashion a defining phrase[2] using terms she imagines the listener already knows.

In order to do this, she has to put herself in the place of the other person, thinking of her knowledge, 'mind reading' about the other person's vocabulary and life experience. The definition requires other-orientation on the part of the speaker. Her guess is informed by her having heard the words others used when they were speaking and she was listening. Even when she is defining something for the general public, the speaker or writer has to use terms she thinks the others already know. If a written definition is not clear, the reader has to supply the further linguistic knowledge from some other source—for instance a dictionary. However, even those seemingly impersonal dictionary definitions require that their definers use terms that others will understand. Definitions do not stand on their own, as philosophers (influenced by equations and exchange) seem to think. They are gifts of words from one person to another or to many others.

The *definiens* is a phrase which is the part of the definition which functions as a provisional substitute gift for the thing defined, allowing the thing's general social relation to its name to be brought forward. The name is the constant social gift-word, which satisfies the general communicative need regarding that kind of thing in the society at large. The speaker provides an individual provisional gift, substitutes it for the given thing and for the social gift-word and makes it available to the listener. 'Furry friendly animal like Aunt Mary's pet' and 'domestic feline'

[2]I will use the term '*definiens*' as the name for the phrase which allows the listener to identify what the 'new' word represents, and '*definiendum*' for the word under definition, the 'new' word itself, or the name. In 'A cat is a domestic animal with a long tail and pointed ears,' 'Cat' is the '*definiendum*,' and 'a domestic animal with a long tail and pointed ears' is the '*definiens*.'

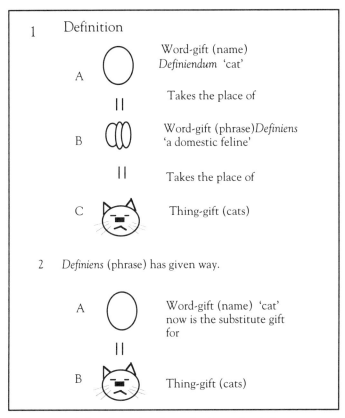

Figure 3. Gifts taking the place of gifts in the definition.

are both provisional gifts that might be given to listeners to define the word 'cat.' Their selection, or the selection of other variations, depends upon the listener's vocabulary and experience (and her communicative need), as interpreted by the speaker. The *definiendum* is provided as the constant social communicative substitute gift (the name) for that kind of thing and for any number of other *definiens* regarding that kind of thing. (See Figure 3.)

The implication is: What the *definiens* has done regarding the thing, the *definiendum* can do—and more. In our examples, 'furry friendly animal like Aunt Mary's pet' picks out a 'sample' cat, while 'domestic feline' locates the animal in a taxonomy, which requires a complex interrelated system of *definiens* and *definienda* to distinguish among similar categories. 'Cat,' the *definiendum*, is more general than any *definiens* (any defining phrase), and it takes the place of all possible defining phrases as the name of that kind of thing for the speakers of that language.

By providing a name through the process of substituting the *definiendum* for the *definiens*, the speaker is also passing on the gift, a word she has received from others. This free process of giftgiving, receiving, and passing it on creates human subjectivities in relation to language, to each other and to an immense variety of qualitatively different things, events and ideas. In this linguistically mediated relation, we humans find ourselves to be a self-constituting species, able to bond with one another in almost as many ways as there are experiences. And we use gift processes and verbal gifts to bond with each other, also at a newly-created level of organization of experiences—the level of shareable topics which are linguistically given.

The definition can be seen as a 'package' containing several gifts at different levels. By creating a *definiens*, arranging terms the listener already has, the speaker performs a service for the listener. She relates something in the world and the *definiens* to the *definiendum*, providing the listener with the use of a new word. The 'things,' for example cats, are made to give way for the moment as co-municative gifts, because now indeed there is a substitute gift phrase which is being given in their stead—the *definiens*, for example, 'domestic felines.' Then the combination of words, the phrase which constitutes the *definiens*, 'domestic felines,' is also made to give up its equivalent position in favor of the *definiendum*, 'cat,' which takes over. Both the experiential givens, 'cat,' and the *definiens*, 'domestic felines,' give way to the *definiendum*, 'cat,' as the verbal gift by means of which co-munication usually happens with regard to that kind of thing, for people in that co-munity.

The word 'cat' is used by people more often to talk about cats, and is therefore more general than the *definiens*, 'domestic feline,' or 'an animal like Aunt Mary's pet,' or 'a furry friendly animal with a long tail.' It is used by more people, more often, than are any of these *definiens*. However, they could be used if a contingent communicative need arose for talking about those animals in that way, at that level of specificity. 'Cat' is more constant and more general than 'a furry friendly animal with a long tail.' We give the name 'name' to 'cat,' not to phrases such as 'a furry friendly animal,' etc.

All these gifts are tied together by the meta linguistic communicative need of the listener and the need-satisfying service of the speaker. She does not keep her knowledge of the lexicon to herself (though some elites and in-groups do this), but gives it freely to the listener, taking it upon herself to create and provide a *definiens* the listener can understand.

In spite of its being a package of gifts, the definition does not function internally according to the giver-gift-receiver process the way we have been saying a transitive sentence does. Instead, it functions by an internal and an external substitution. Both a nonverbal given and a phrase give way to a general word, the name which takes their place as the constant co-municative need-satisfying substitute gift.

Let me just mention that contained in the definition, the verb 'to be'[3] is the substitute for the acts of substitution which are the *definiens* and the *definiendum*, which also both give way to it, implying that these acts are the same because, as acts, they are substituted by the same word, thus bringing the whole operation neatly into the present. (See Figure 4.)

The relation of words to words and things to words in 'the girl hit the ball' is different from the relation of words to words and things to words in 'a ball is a round object used for games.' In the former, the whole sentence is a gift, and within it there is a gift of a predicate given by subject to object. In the definition, someone is providing the gift of a word to someone who doesn't know it, through substitutions of something the listener does know—for example, 'a round object used for games' by something she doesn't know, the new word 'ball.' The speaker is the giftgiving subject who gives the *definiens* and the *definiendum* to the listener, who is the receiver of the *definiendum* as a

[3]See Chapter 9 for a more complete discussion of the verb 'to be.'

67

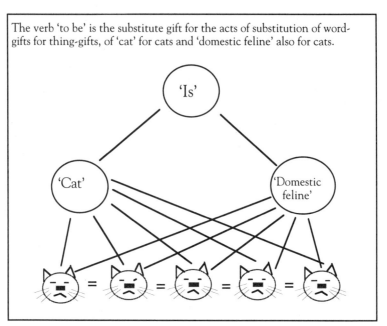

Figure 4. 'Is' substitutes for acts of substitution in the sentence.

permanent acquisition. The *definiens* gives-way to the *definiendum*, which takes its place, much as the kind of thing 'gives-way' first to the *definiens* and then (in a permanent way) to the *definiendum* as its name.

The listener has an immediate meta linguistic need for a word she does not 'have.' The memory and understanding of that phonetic pattern constitute 'the means of production' of a word-gift speakers can give to satisfy others' communicative needs, and listeners can receive, creating bonds with them regarding that kind of thing. The speaker gives the new word to the listener, satisfying the listener's meta linguistic need.

Origin of Exchange

I believe that the processes of substitution and giving way in the definition and in naming are the original processes from which exchange derived. In exchange these processes have been transferred back into nonverbal patterns of interaction and distorted to mediate the kind of co-municative need that arises from the mutually exclusive human relationship of private property. Statistics show that very little private property—perhaps 1% world wide—is owned by women (who nevertheless are well able to perform the processes of naming and definition). Moreover, private property is an institution of so-called 'developed' societies, not of so-called 'primitive' ones, which nevertheless must have naming and definition processes. Thus, mutually inclusive gift-based language precedes exchange and the mutually exclusive property relations which are mediated by it. The processes of naming and the definition, where substitution and giving-way are predominant, have been stretched and altered as they have been transferred onto the material plane. This is particularly visible in monetized exchange where because of its function as a substitute gift, money creates a self-similar image of the word on a different scale. Moreover, in the absence of giftgiving and without a process of exchange, the institution of mutually exclusive private property would become sclerotic and unmanageable, since each owner would have no peaceful access to the satisfaction of her needs by others.

The use of these linguistic processes to avoid giftgiving and maintain the isolation of each economic operator contradicts the fundamental giftgiving-and-receiving principle of life and language, and creates a misogynist and hostile environment to which human groups have had to adapt. In fact, we have adapted to it so well that it appears to be natural, while the kinds of aggressive and competitive behaviors that are made necessary for survival in it appear to be 'human nature' (which expresses itself 'his-torically').

The existence of the same processes on the verbal and the nonverbal planes creates many re-verberations. In our present capitalistic society, for example, there is a feedback loop between verbal definition and nonverbal exchange, whereby the one validates the other and takes on the function of the other. A person or a product is defined by the amount of money s/he or it is 'worth.' Names, categorizations, titles from 'policewoman' to 'doctor' have a monetary value.

Controlling people through salary, which is definition by money, backs up naming, labeling, and defining others as a way of controlling them. Product names and brand names justify higher prices. We look at definitional processes as giving 'meaning' to our lives. If we have a title, a university degree, a married name, we 'are somebody.' However, all this naming is taking place in a society that does not recognize giftgiving as the underlying principle of meaning for language and life.

Restoring Gifts to the Definition

Exchange reflects back on the idea we have of the definition, making it seem aseptic—an intellectual equation instead of a package made up of many gifts. Among the gifts we have already enumerated, we must also include the wider consideration that the definition sometimes serves to transmit words socially between generations, linguistic groups, etc. Moreover by finding a 'common language,' using the words which many others already have, both in speech and in performing the service of the definition, the speaker or writer is able to co-municate with people who are elsewhere in time and space. She must succeed in identifying, using and/or building upon the terms others already have—though of course the others may themselves have made the effort to acquire these terms through education, developing a body of knowledge about some discipline or area of life (sometimes with its own specialized language).

Because the need for the definition of terms is common, since none of us was born knowing them, definitions abound in books, dictionaries, and treatises. The nature of things is explored as well, in discussions which seek to define kinds of things. If it is well-fashioned, using words others commonly have, the gift package of the definition can continue to function independently of its maker. Its gifts leap to the satisfaction of the reader's need, as soon as she opens the dictionary.

This ability to continue to satisfy (meta) communicative needs independently makes it appear that the definition's human source and the relation between giver and receiver are unimportant. In one sense, we might say that it is society itself, the collective, that gives us these verbal 'means of production,' establishing a bond with us. On the other hand, the definer's unconditionally generous service is easily forgotten when we use the words we have been given to establish relations with others.

Equivalence

When the service or gift aspect of language is ignored, we tend to look at the way words take the place of other words in the definition as the basic process of language, rather than need satisfaction. A kind of fetishization occurs in which 'meaning' seems to come from the relation of words to each other, rather than from the relation of people to each other using things or using words regarding things. Then since philosophers have concentrated on definitions to tell us about everything from mankind to God to Being itself, we investigate definitions to find out the relation of words to the world—and we only see words taking the place of other words in closed systems. We do not look at nurturing as co-munication, nor do we look at linguistic communicative need as a socially relevant need, already necessarily arising from the world and from others, the satisfaction of which is an end motivating verbal and nonverbal interaction among individuals.[4]

Because of the magnetic template of the exchange logic, we see the need of the other only as functional to our own need. Her 'demand' must be 'effective;' she must have the proper amount of money to substitute for our product to satisfy our co-municative need for money.[5] We do not see the 'service' side of the definition but only its so-called 'truth function,' whether its 'intension' (or

---

[4] Without altruism and other-orientation, we cannot justify society or culture. There is no group which can survive as a compendium of isolated egotists. Social cohesion is provided by the hidden giftgiving and other orientation of all, and especially of women.
[5] Typically, we do not consider the listener's understanding as the satisfaction of her need, but have to see it expressed in other words, just as the need of the buyer has to be expressed in money as effective demand. Otherwise it does not 'exist' for the seller.

meaning) corresponds to its 'extension' (the instances of that kind of thing in the world).

For example, 'A bachelor is an unmarried man' is an example which is often used because the *'definiens'* and the *'definiendum'* appear to completely correspond. Any man who is a bachelor is also an unmarried man. Definitions of this sort are gifts which only satisfy the meta linguistic need for philosophical examples of definitions. The aspect of the meta linguistic gift of the word has become secondary. The other-orientation of the definer also seems to be irrelevant to the equivalence of 'extension' and 'intension.' The other-orientation is therefore ignored while the definition appears independent and aseptic, untouched by human relations. The aseptic appearance might disappear if the listener were an unmarried woman. Some questions could arise about a bachelor being an unmarried man. Why is she, the listener, not also called 'bachelor?' Are her material and communicative needs being considered? Why presuppose an insensitive male definer?

In our thinking about language, we are being influenced by the priorities of exchange, the necessity for identification of goods, their measurement, and the aseptic and objective assessment of their equivalence to the satisfaction of both parties (or of society as a whole). The correspondences involved in selling and buying become the model for the correspondence between language (price) and reality (commodities). The motivation towards the need of the other as an end is ignored both in exchange and in the study of language.

Since definitions are made with words substituting for other words, the relation of words to the world seems to come from the form of the definition, the form of substitution as an end in itself—and without seeing the creative activity of giving, receiving and giving-way. The relation of words to the world appears to come from the form of the equation (x = y), or from the words themselves, or from the will of the people who are saying them. By concentrating on substitution without the idea of giftgiving, it is difficult to get back to the world from language, and it appears only that "the sense of a sign is another sign,"[6] and so on in infinite (albeit systemic) regress as if words were not 'hooked on' to the world at all.

Giftgiving at Both Levels

It seems that 're-present-ation' is the process without there being any prior 'present-ation' to back it up. Instead, 're-presentation' (taking-the-place-of) is only one moment in a giftgiving process which is both linguistic and non-linguistic. We can indeed substitute one gift for another, but the whole process from the identification of the need to the fashioning of the particular gift—words or sentences—which will satisfy it, involves much more than taking-the-place-of or substitution. It involves other-orientation, the ability to recognize others' needs in relation to the world, and things in the world as relevant to those needs. It involves recognizing oneself as a potential satisfier of other people's needs, using appropriate kinds of things, and the motivation to satisfy at least their communicative needs if not their material needs. It also involves recognizing others as the satisfiers of one's own needs. A patriarchal point of view would see the world as made up only of things for which we should compete, not things as having value as relevant to the satisfaction of others' needs.

Other-orientation is also necessary in order to be able to use words others will understand, put ourselves in their places and consider what they do not know as a need we can satisfy. Each need is a theme with many variations. The general need to communicate about cats—to form human relations regarding cats—comprehends all of the ways cats can be present or relevant to humans. We individually recognize those ways as needs, arising from the extra linguistic or linguistic contexts, which others may have for a relation with us in regard to cats. The word 'cat' has

[6]The approach of unlimited semiosis begun by Charles Sanders Peirce, *Collected Papers*, Harvard University Press, Cambridge, 1931-35, (1931, 2.230) has captured his (and Saussure's) deconstructionist descendants in an infinite regress, inside the definitional stance, far from the plane of material giftgiving co-munication. Chains of substitutes deny the importance of the 'present,' the need satisfying gift.

73

been given to us socially as a means for satisfying any of those communicative needs, at least in part.

We have to have been able to receive from others materially and linguistically in the past, in order to be able to give to others in the present. That is, we must have been receivers of others' co-municative other-orientation. We must also be able to fashion new sentences according to transposed gift patterns—like matchmakers putting words in the position of giving to other words. Moreover, we have to seek and use the bonds that we create with others linguistically and with regard to the gifts of the world to develop our own, and their, social subjectivities. Giftgiving is the content of the form of substitution, which is the very reason for the existence of the form. It is what matters about the form; it is the (mothering) matrix.

Giving and giving-way have not been understood as fully human behavior. In patriarchy winning, power-over, and over-taking have been over-valued. However, giving-way is a necessary complement of taking-the-place-of. *Being* substituted is an active and necessary relational complement of substitution. Similarly receiving is the active creative complement of giving. In the definition the process of substitution and giving-way of gifts are the functional elements. In most sentences of speech in context, the substitution process is not in focus and gift processes at other levels create transparency.

Substitution and being substituted are the processes at issue in the definition and naming because what is being given is a general word, a social gift for a kind of thing, given through a series of substitutions. The need which is being satisfied in this case is not primarily a contingent need for a mutually inclusive relation to the world, but a meta need of the other for the means of production of gifts regarding kinds of things. Perhaps because of the strength of the pattern of exchange (which is, as we said, the definition's descendent), the process of substitution and being substituted has been unilateralized, leaving aside the so-called 'passive' side of the relation. With one side lacking, the relation of substitution (and being substituted) or over-taking (and giving-

74

way) has seemed to be no relation at all.[7] Language no longer appears to have anything to do with what has been substituted. Instead it appears to be a unilateral, purely verbal activity unrelated to the world, a self-sufficient system which uses arbitrary sounds in a rule governed way to 'convey' (give) a 'meaning' (which is not understood either).

To some philosophers who ignore giftgiving, the relation of 'cat' to cats seems abstract, a *sui generis* act on the part of the speaker (or the community), who somehow equates 'cat' with cats, or imposes 'cat' upon cats, keeping them separate from dogs and monkeys, perhaps through a genetically 'transmitted' (given) ability. It seems that, by naming something, we put it in a category, which appears to be the purpose of communication.

The question then arises, what does categorization have to do with understanding? We slip into a kind of reasoning akin to private property—asking what things belong to what categories. Then the most knowledgeable person is the one who 'has' the most categories. We arrange the categories in hierarchies of inclusiveness and function, 'transforming' particular phrases by substituting more general for more specific names, all the way up sentence trees, seeing their interaction as governed by laws or rules according to what is appropriate for their identities or kinds. Then we equate these hierarchies with 'understanding.'

The Sentence Tree (or Root) Diagram

A kind is only a collection of things that is important enough to have a name because communicative needs arise regarding it. At a meta linguistic level, in fact, such names as Noun Phrase (NP) or Verb Phrase (VP) name kinds of phrases because linguistics professors need to talk about them. The rules of syntax show how words and phrases can 'give' to one another, while sentence tree diagrams visually express the gift relation as

[7]Gandhi's movement for non-violence demonstrated the political importance of 'giving-way,' allowing us to see what women had already been practicing personally. Using 'giving-way' as a response to 'over-taking' made the over-takers realize, among other things, that their action was relational. Gift giving and giving-way are the presents which underlie the relation of re-present-ation.

branches of dependency. The tree diagrams always looked upside down to me—until I realized they are not trees at all but root systems, with the flow of gifts going upwards (from the particular to the general) not downwards (from the general to the particular).

Linguistic creativity, the ability to generate ever-new sentences using a limited number of words, is accompanied and elicited by the ability to recognize the needs which those words and sentences satisfy. Collective human need-satisfying practice with things of a kind gives a value to those things which in turn is partially transferred or given by implication to the word-gifts that substitute for them. It is not a top-down categorizing relation that makes language work, but a creative dynamic of need satisfaction that moves both language and life.

I believe that the gift relations within the sentence itself, not an interplay of categorizations, are the motors of its meaning. We have mistakenly taken the naming side of language as the key to the dynamic. It is not the 'application' of words to things that promotes the change of levels, causing the move 'up' from the level of nonverbal experience to the level of verbal practice; there is a different process going on that we are not seeing.

We give a group of things something that they can be related to as their substitute. Then we transfer to it something of their value, in the sense of their importance for humans, because needs become associated with them. The substitute gift receives a destination in the satisfaction of a communicative need, which may make it also be useful from a distance in the satisfaction of material needs, for example: 'the bread is in the cupboard' or 'the train is leaving from track 12.' There is an upward flow of meaning or value from the world of which we are a part, not just a top-down application or cutting-out of categories. A meta language is only a hierarchical collection of categorizing terms, a parasite upon the object language because it lacks its own gift dynamic.

The branching of a sentence tree should be seen instead as the coming together of elements which can give to each other, a cooperative assembly of terms. We can give 'the,' or 'the' can give itself to 'girl,' and we name this gift act 'noun phrase.' Then as a unit they can 'give' the verb 'hit' to the unit which is made when 'the' gives itself to 'ball.' We can diagram these units, giving them names such as 'determiner,' 'noun phrase,' 'verb,' 'sentence.' They tell us which are givers, gifts, receivers. We give some of the parts of the sentence, 'the girl hit the ball,' to such words as 'noun phrase,' to be substituted by them. We believe we know more when we can show the hierarchy. We know who controls who and can get along ourselves better in it. But we do not notice the gifts of value percolating up from below.

The sentence tree is the one in the garden that grew from Adam's doing too much naming. It is not because they are categorized together or because they follow the rules that words stick together (bond) in sentences. Rather it is because they give to each other, combine, and then together give to another word or part of the phrase. They can do this because they have been 'given to' by things (and people). If we deny the flow upwards it appears that the only thing there is the top-down naming mechanism, and we are at a loss to see how it is attached to the world.

The question should not be, "Where does the (fractal) tree divide into branches?" but "Where does the root system come together carrying the gifts of value upward to the plant?" The question is, "Who is feeding whom?" and "Who is doing the nurturing?"—the naming mechanism or the giftgiving, value-conferring mechanism?"

Masculation

Words themselves, ruled by syntax, may appear to contain the secret of their own relation to the world. I believe this is an illusion coming from the gender definition, which exacerbates the aspect of substitution.

What happens when a boy child learns he belongs to a different gender from his giftgiving mother? As with other instances of naming or definition, the name or *definiendum* 'boy' causes him (as a material thing) to 'give way' as the nonverbal gift. Before he understands what adults are saying, he considers himself to be like his mother. But when he begins to understand the implication of his gender term, he must realize he is not *supposed* to be like her. His being named or defined as a boy (with the social definition of 'male') contradictorily makes him give up the gift-giving character, in order to be different from his mother. (See Figure 5.) His gender name is thus much more harmful for him than we imagine.

Since his very life depends upon his mother's care, a change of category, to be like his father, would seem to be a very frightening thing. The boy becomes 'like' someone he usually does not know very well, who may appear to be (like the word which is 'taking over') just an abstract dominator. An aspect of language becomes grafted on to the gender behavior of the child. Substitution, part of the definition process, self-reflectingly takes the place of the process of the gift, which gives-way. Categorization becomes more powerful than co-munication. Words are no longer benign co-municative gifts, but magic wands that can change a child's identity.

The question "What is man?" really derives from this question: "What is man if he is not like his mother?" The answer is—this is a false question. He *is* like his mother, a nurturing being, but he is altered by the naming of gender, which becomes a self-fulfilling prophecy. Since it is only a word that spirits the boy away, words must appear to be very powerful. And since his fathers before him have had the same experience, males find commonality in that respect. It does not seem to the child—or perhaps to anyone else in the society—that an arbitrary and false distinction is being made. Rather, the community bases the boy's difference from his mother upon his genitals—upon the biological fact that he has a penis like his father while she doesn't. But if nurturing is the basis of communication and community, there is really nothing, no content available for his oppositional category. In order to fill this void, substitution, definition, and

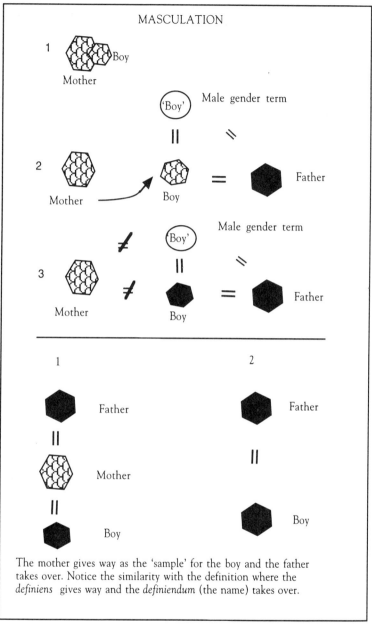

MASCULATION

The mother gives way as the 'sample' for the boy and the father takes over. Notice the similarity with the definition where the *definiens* gives way and the *definiendum* (the name) takes over.

Figure 5. Masculation: forming the boy's gender.

categorization themselves become the content of the (masculine) identity of those who are told that they are not nurturers.

Words are cast socially in this case, not as gifts, but as powerful abstract categorizers which overtake and control a person's identity. According to the survival mechanism of imitating the oppressor, the children then become like the word—as did their fathers before them. Male gender identity imitates the naming or 'definitional' side of language and the process of taking-the-place-of—giving importance to equivalence with the other, the father who is taking the place of the mother (who gives-way) and of other males as well. The penis plays an important part in this because it is that physical characteristic which places the boy in the category with his father.

Phallic symbols are everywhere, though we have learned to ignore them and to deny their importance. The equation itself, as a moment of similarity and of exchange, receives gifts of attention and value from the many. The equal marks (=) are perhaps originally two little phallic symbols. It is this characteristic (or property), which the boy has and the mother does not have, which takes him away from her nurturing category. The psycho-social effects of 'having' or 'not having' this physical characteristic have become immensely important, as we shall see.

The boy receives many privileges. In fact, he is often given more nurturing because he is a male than he would have been given if he had been a female, like his mother. Often he is validated as superior, even to her. Like the word, he has the ability to take-the-place-of, which, in the absence of other-orientation and giftgiving, becomes over-taking and domination. He is 'compensated' with that ability and those privileges because he has given up the nurturing identity.

I have coined the word 'masculation' for this process in which the boy is socialized into a false, non-nurturing identity, incarnating the word which alienates him. It seems to me that this is an essential moment in male development that is not recognized and that, therefore, spawns self-similar images in many different areas of life. By acting out this process on different social scales, the collective unconsciously hopes to rid itself of this self-created fatal flaw. At the same time, there are many fail-safes which keep it in place and keep us from clearly seeing what is happening.

Chapter 5
The Concept of Man

Like language, the capacity to form concepts can be allocated to biological hardware or to socialization. Much investigation is taking place of both possibilities. Some say our ability to recognize similar things must be a genetic endowment. Others believe that we form concepts by a process of comparison and generalization. For some, this process uses a prototype, possibly the image of the first thing of a kind a child has seen, or something of a kind, present in her immediate environment. Through repeated comparisons of things of a kind some common qualities are abstracted. An experiment which was conducted by Soviet psychologist Lev Vigotsky[1] in the 1920s originated the prototype theory and Vigotsky is identified with that current of psychology.

One-Many

Vigotsky described a number of stages of concept development, leading up to a final 'one-many' stage, where the prototype or 'sample' object acquired a stable 'one-many' relation with a number of objects which were compared to it, excluding objects which were different. The many objects also acquired a common relation to each other by being compared to the sample and found similar to it in the same ways. This generalized the sample, and the common quality of the similar objects was a reflection of that generality. The sample was given a name, and the objects that had the common quality also had that name.

The description usually given of Vigotsky's experiment was provided by E. Hanfmann and J. Kasanin in their book *Conceptual Thinking and Schizophrenia*, 1942, pp. 9-10:

"The material used in the concept formation tests consists of 22 wooden blocks varying in color, shape, height and size. There

[1]See L. S. Vigotsky, *Thought and Language*, Edited and translated by Eugenia Hanfmann and Gertrude Vakar, The M.I.T. Press, Cambridge, Mass, 1962.

are 5 different colors, 6 different shapes, 2 heights (the tall blocks and the flat blocks), and 2 sizes of the horizontal surface (large and small). On the underside of each figure, which is not seen by the subject, is written one of the four nonsense words: 'lag,' 'bik,' 'mur,' 'cev.' Regardless of color or shape, 'lag' is written on all tall large figures, 'bik' on all flat large figures, 'mur' on all tall small ones, and 'cev' on the flat small ones.

"At the beginning of the experiment, all blocks (well-mixed as to color, size and shape) are scattered on a table in front of the subject. The examiner turns up one of the blocks (the 'sample'), shows and reads its name to the subject, and asks him (sic) to pick out all the blocks which he thinks might belong to the same kind. After the subject has done so, the examiner turns up one of the 'wrongly' selected blocks, shows that this is a block of a different kind, and encourages the subject to continue trying. After each new attempt, another of the wrongly placed blocks is turned up. As the number of turned blocks increases, the subject by degrees obtains a basis for discovering to which characteristic of the blocks the nonsense words refer.

"As soon as he makes this discovery, the 'words' come to stand for definite kinds of objects (e.g., 'lag' for large tall blocks, 'bik' for large flat ones), and new concepts for which the language provides no names are thus built up. The subject is then able to complete the task of separating the four kinds of blocks indicated by the nonsense words. Thus the use of concepts has a definite functional value for the performance required by the test.

"Whether the subject actually uses conceptual thinking in trying to solve the problem can be inferred from the nature of the groups he builds and from his procedure in building them. Nearly every step in his reasoning is reflected in his manipulation of the blocks. The first attack on the problem, the handling of the sample, the response to correction, the finding of the solution—all these stages of the experiment provide data that can serve as indicators of the subject's level of thinking." (See Figures 6 and 7.)

Figure 6. Visualizing Vigotsky's experiment.

The 'one-many' concept structure itself is important in cognitive psychology, while Vigotsky's experimental demonstration of possibilities of different ('wrong') kinds of uses of the sample lets us see what is not being done in one-many conceptual reasoning. Two of the possibilities of 'wrong' reasoning show this clearly: the 'family name' complex, in which the sample is held firm and the qualities by which the other objects are found similar to it vary; and the 'chain' complex, in which the one-many character is lost because an object is found similar to the sample by one characteristic, and the next is found similar to the second object by a different characteristic, and so on. The 'wrong' strategies show the importance of keeping the sample firm and trying to develop generality by repeatedly comparing objects to it with regard to the *same* similarities. At the end of the experiment, the sample itself is no longer necessary because a type of thing has been recognized as having one of the names that were given to the different kinds of things in the experiment.

I thought about this for a long time, and it occurred to me that the word actually takes the place of the sample and takes over its generality. This gave me a second characterization of words, which I could add to that of words as co-municative need-satisfying gifts. In fact, it was fitting that a word-gift could take the place of the sample, which could not itself always be given as such, and which could probably usually not remain stable for very long except as an image. The word, on the other hand, with its infinite repeatability, has the character of being 'the same thing,' even when every instance of it is actually a different event from every other instance. By taking over the one-many function of the sample, the word helps in the organization of the concept so that the concept's members were considered similar to each other because of their common relation to their name, as well as because of their common relation to the sample.

Once the relation of things to each other as similar according to the same qualities is established, the sample is no longer necessary and the word can bring them to mind as a kind by itself. The reason for this is that, in the 'one-to-many' relation, a

Imaginary illustration of Vigotsky's experiment, 2

Chain Complex

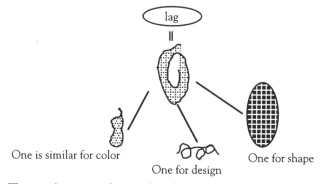

mur

= Added because color similar to previous   = shape similar to previous   = size similar to previous

The characteristics do not remain constant but change in each step.

Family name Complex

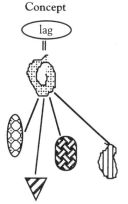

lag

=

One is similar for color   One for design   One for shape

The sample remains the same but characteristics vary.

Concept

lag

=

The sample is constant and the objects are related to it and to each other by the same similarities.

Figure 7. Visualizing Vigotsky's experiment.

polarity is established whereby the one is maintained as a point of reference and the many are compared to it one-by-one. The word, taking the place of the 'one,' maintains the polarity, bringing forward the relation of the 'many' to each other, as well as to itself. (See Figures 8 and 9.)

The sample or prototype must be kept firm with its qualities. If not, a consistent kind or category cannot be constructed, and our thoughts may wander from one association to the next. However, *any* thing of a kind may be chosen as the 'one' which will be held firm as the sample and, once the category has been constructed, the sample can be demoted from its 'one-many' position and become again just a member of that kind. I make a point of saying this because I think the one (or sample) position has been misunderstood as constituting part of the gender definition and, therefore, over-emphasized, invested with special privilege and projected into the structures of the society as self-similar patterns at many different levels.

The father and his family, the king and his subjects, the general and his army, the CEO and his business, etc., embody the one-to-many polar relation established in concept development. The relation between money and products[2] is also an embodiment of the concept, and we can use this polarized relation among objects to elucidate the one-many relation among persons. Even the relation between a person and her/his property can be seen as a one-many relation deriving from the (gender-invested) concept structure. (Though perhaps it is more like the 'family name' complex).

The Privileged One

Privileging the sample position is particularly dangerous because the polarity and the concepts formed with its help are themselves originally innocent, useful ways of organizing our thoughts and perceptions. It is a very intimate and basic level of

[2]See Marx's discussion of money as the 'general equivalent' in the first book of *Capital*, (1890), translated by Eden and Cedar Paul, J. M. Dent and Sons Ltd. London, 1962, Chapter 2.

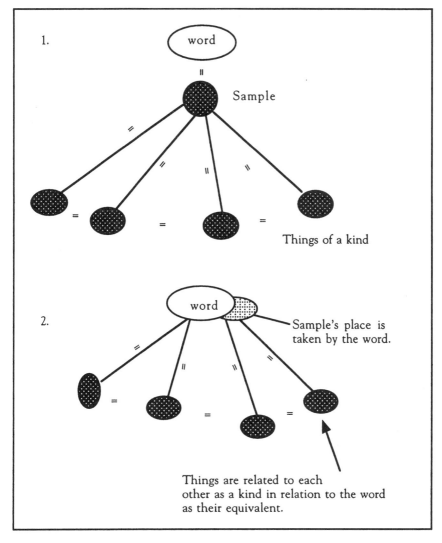

1.

word

Sample

Things of a kind

2.

word

Sample's place is
taken by the word.

Things are related to each
other as a kind in relation to the word
as their equivalent.

Figure 8. Schematized images of the stages of concept
formation. (Continued on next page.)

thinking that becomes invested with the pernicious privileging of
the one position. Because it is so basic, this 'investment' is hard to
investigate, and we project it outside ourselves so that we can
deal with it. Since we never think of tracing the origin of our
strange one-many behavior back to concept development, we
continue to act out the process at many different levels of society,
creating structures which then interact with each other, compete,
support each other, arrange themselves in one-many hierarchies

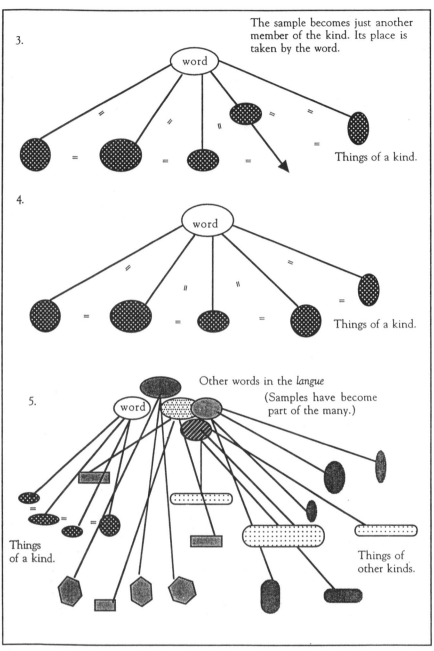

3. The sample becomes just another member of the kind. Its place is taken by the word.

word

Things of a kind.

4.

word

Things of a kind.

5.

word

Other words in the *langue*

(Samples have become part of the many.)

Things of a kind.

Things of other kinds.

Figure 9. More schematized images of the stages of concept formation.

again. Together these structures form the self-propagating social systems which we call 'patriarchies.'[3]

At the root of these systems lies, once again, the question of the male gender identity and masculation. Males have been taken as the samples for the category 'human.' Boys' categorical gender difference from their nurturing mothers has made males seem to have to be 'samples' (in the 'one' position) if they were to be included in 'humanity' at all. Women have nurtured them in this, giving way, not appearing as the ones to whom the many would be compared to find their human identity. Therefore, women have appeared to be lacking, deficient in the supposed human characteristics which men have. Abstract thinking, aggressiveness, individualism, leadership, independence (qualities having to do with competitively achieving the 'one' position) appeared to be 'human,' and women seemed to be 'inferior humans' because that was not their focus.

In fact, the women continued practicing the gift paradigm whenever that was not made impossible by scarcity, war, and individual violence of various kinds. The concept 'human' was interrogated for centuries for its meaning, while philosophers considered women as not appropriate samples for that concept. Meanwhile, the gift paradigm (which the women were practicing) was and continues to be the source of meaning, community, and even of life itself.

What we have considered to be the defining characteristics of the male gender are actually characteristics of the 'one' position patched together with the patterns of taking-the-place-of deriving from the role of the word in the definition and naming. They are taken up by boys in order to carry out the self-fulfilling prophecy

[3]Vigotsky's experiment showed children being able to consciously identify concepts and use conceptual thinking strategies at puberty. More recent developmental psychology work has shown that children appear to be using the prototype relation from infancy. I believe that Vigotsky's experimental situation tested a certain conscious level of the concept's use. Interestingly, Carol Gilligan *et al* have written about the choice girls make at puberty between two modes, which appear to me much like the gift and the exchange modes. See *Making Connections: The Relational World of Adolescent Girls at Emma Willard School*, edited by Carol Gilligan, Nona P. Lyons and Trudy Hanmer, Harvard University Press, Cambridge, MA, 1990. Perhaps both 'one-many' thinking and the privileging of the male arrive at a new level of emphasis at puberty.

of their gender concept, as different from their mothers. The 'one' position held by the father towards the family as many, appears to be what the boy must achieve if he is to be called a 'man.' The Oedipal injunction is thus not so much to kill the father as to overtake his position as the 'one.'

The simple logical consideration that not everyone can be the 'one' in a polar way, and that this is a relational not a permanent characteristic, may not be clear to children at an early age. The mandates of the male gender appear to say, "Be different from women and grow to be equal to or larger than the father, so as to be able to overtake his position and deserve the name *man*."

The boy appears to be related to the nurturing sample himself before he understands the implications of his gender name. Then the word 'boy' takes the boy out of the category of the mother. Thus the father's role of overtaking and dominance may seem to come from the word's ability to take the boy away from his identity with the mother. The ability to put things into categories appears to be a capacity of the father and an aspect of the role of the 'one.' The father is the standard (like money), and this standard has the capacity to speak and (because he takes the place of the mother sample) to *be* the word, which categorizes and divides. Every judgment resonates with the power he (or his gender name) seems to have had—to divide male from female.

The relation of a boy to his father becomes one of inferiority, of many to one, of property to owner, of things to a word or sample (a sample which is not giftgiving). Masculation is a kind of original de-humanization because the father model is objectified, like a non-human thing. Then women are defined as not (even) that, while the relation among male concept members is over-valued.

The Bible story of Joseph and his brothers deals with a situation in which the many brothers vie with each other for the 'one' position to be inherited from the patriarch. Joseph's dreams about the many sheaves of corn and the sun, moon and stars bowing down to him express this relation symbolically. When a boy takes on the father as the sample for his own concept, he is part of the real or potential many with regard to the 'one.' His gender identity may appear to be that of striving competitively with others of the same gender for the 'one' position. His father may be doing this himself in his work life. 'Taking-the-place-of' may also seem to be a mandate of his gender role as males take-the-place of females, and the male sample (and word) takes-the-place of the female sample and its giftgiving way.

Thus, what little boys perceive as their gender role at an early age is the incarnation of the sample position itself and a partial incarnation of the word. Being equal to or like the sample and taking-the-place of others become important in the male identity, while other-orientation and giftgiving remain principles of the female identity. Making the male the sample for the concept of 'human' cancels the perceived importance of giftgiving. Females (and other males) nevertheless continue to give to the males whose identities are constructed in this way, over-privileging them and especially rewarding those who do achieve the 'one' position. Thus giftgiving supports this identity-construction, even while being is canceled by it and judged by it as 'inferior' (even less than human) 'instinctive' behavior. Giftgiving permeates human activities and is still the way we transmit goods and messages, co-municate and form our co-munity. We have altered and distorted giftgiving, however, using it for the 'ones' and against the many. We are all taught from our earliest days to mis-recognize the giftgiving way, and we give it other names ('activity,' 'housework,' 'leisure,' 'surplus value,' 'profit'). As we begin to recognize the dynamics of the two paradigms, we can finally give the appropriate value and the appropriate names to giftgiving.

The Incarnate Word

In masculation, males incarnate themselves as the substitute gift, taking-the-place-of the mother, taking the father as sample, and giving-up giving.[4] This is the moment of the Fall—when the

[4]This transition itself looks a lot like exchange as we shall see in the chapter on "Market and Gender."

boy child realizes he cannot participate in the material giftgiving co-municative way because of the definition of his gender.

Perhaps the greatest (and smallest) mistake humanity has made is to give our babies opposite gender names—such an innocent but terrible mistake, heavy as a snippet off the feather on the scale of Maat. Do we sometimes wonder why the Spirit of Good has not destroyed us, given all the horrors we commit— genocide, rape, genocidal rape, child rape and battery, the rape and pollution of land and sea, murder of species and of individuals, physical and mental torture? Perhaps it is because the origin of all this horror is such an innocent misinterpretation, so easy to make.

We have incarnated the word, the process of naming itself, and the word we have incarnated is 'male.' It was only a word, but we have let it dominate our psychology and our social structures. We have used it to alienate half of humanity from the giftgiving norm.

After alienating our sons into the non-giving category, we (mothers and fathers) over-privilege and reward them, give more to them than to our daughters. Later, we try to teach them altruism through authoritarian morality or religious precepts coming from the Law. We wonder why this is so difficult to achieve and explain the difficulty by thinking that 'human nature' is cruel.

A communicative need has arisen now for all of humanity— the need for a new term to mediate our human relations with regard to our babies. We need a new word-gift for all of those small creatures who are our greatest gifts to each other, to the future and to themselves. Using this new word-gift, one term for both genders, we could stop recreating the problems that are destroying our species, our mothers and our Mother Earth.

Chapter 6
'Marksist' Categories

Co-munication creates the mutual inclusion of co-municators, regarding all the different parts of their world. The naming of gender divides the co-municators into two mutually exclusive, oppositional categories from the beginning, contradicting the mutual inclusion of co-munication. Like the opposed modes of giftgiving and exchange, the genders enter into a kind of complementarity, though they are not a perfect fit. The over-valuing of domination makes mutual inclusion and bonding according to creative giving and receiving difficult. Bizarre developments, like viewing dominance and submission *as* mutual inclusion, sometimes appear to be the resolution of this contradiction. Giving to the dominator can become a stable pattern—as occurs with so-called 'family values.'

What happens in the distinction of gender is that the aspects of language which involve giving and giving-way are identified as the behavior of biological females, while the aspects of substitution and categorization are assigned to males. These two roles eventually develop into dis-empowered nurturing on the one hand and domination/exchange on the other. The mutually exclusive aspect of gender comes from language itself,[1] where 'female' and 'male' are connected by direct opposition. In order to carry out behavior which is supposedly appropriate for a bearer of one's own gender term, one could conceivably look at the behavior of the other gender, and simply do the opposite.

In a founding text on the universals of language, Joseph Greenberg[2] discussed 'marked' and 'unmarked' linguistic categories, which are found at the phonological, grammatical, and lexical levels regarding terms in opposition. For example, terms

[1]For Saussure, ibid, Chapter IV, *langue* is a system of purely differential oppositional units. Each word is related to all the others by mutual exclusion. Each is identified as itself by not being the others. When signifier and signified are considered together, other associations and oppositions also apply, such as binary oppositions and regular paradigmatic variations.
[2]Joseph Greenberg, *Language Universals*, The Hague, Mouton, 1966.

like 'short' and 'tall,' or 'wide' and 'narrow,' 'up' and 'down' imply opposite ends of a continuum. One of these opposites is usually the linguistic norm.[3] We ask, 'How old is the girl?' not 'How young?' 'Old' is the norm, what linguists call the 'unmarked' term. According to Greenberg, 'man' is the 'unmarked' term, while 'woman' is 'marked.'

To me, the meta-linguistic expressions 'marked' and 'unmarked' seem to be backwards. It would seem that the more general, more inclusive term should be 'marked' (calling our attention to it) and the less inclusive, 'unmarked.' Instead, the term which is less important has an extra 'mark,' a prefix or suffix, while the more important term, which is called a 'zero sign,' is without additions. For example, in English we add an 's' to the singular to form the plural. The plural is the 'marked' category, the singular 'unmarked.' Even the two terms themselves have their meanings strangely crossed. 'Marked' is un-marked, while 'unmarked' is marked.

Greenberg cites Jakobson's article that defines the distinction: "The general meaning of a 'marked' category asserts the presence of a certain property 'A;' the general meaning of the corresponding 'unmarked' category does not assert anything regarding the presence of 'A' and is used principally but not exclusively to indicate the absence of 'A.'" Then Greenberg goes on to say, "Thus in Jakobson's terms 'woman' asserts the presence of the 'marked' category 'feminine,' while 'man' is used principally but not exclusively to indicate the absence of 'feminine.'"

This analysis is counter-intuitive for women who have been taught by 'the school of hard knocks' that it is being a male that is the important property, the lack of which defines us as women. Greenberg continues, "'Man' therefore has two meanings, to indicate the explicit absence of 'feminine' in the meaning 'male human being,' but also to indicate 'human being in general.'" Thus, according to Greenberg, the term which indicates the absence of the feminine also includes the feminine

[3]Op. cit., On Language, Roman Jakobson, "The Concept of 'Mark,'" Chapter 8.

94

when it is used in general. Women are included while the feminine is explicitly indicated as absent.

It occurs to me to fantasize that if men and women were words, men would be the 'marked' term, with the prefix of the phallus—so according to this theory, less important, different—while the women would be 'zero' signs, without a prefix, more important, the norm. If it is true that 'man' is defined according to the absence of the feminine property, what is this property? Women's property is just the absence of the distinctive property, the 'mark,' and (added to this) the absence of property in the sense of private property. Women are indeed the norm, as the lacking and unaccepted 'samples' of the human species.

It is on the basis of the absence of the female sample that men define themselves and define humanity. The phallus would be the double negative, the absence of the absence. (Jacques Lacan talks about the 'lack of the lack.') It is not surprising that both children and linguists are confused. And the word 'wo-man' itself is 'man' marked with a prefix which perhaps hides the fact that the mother doesn't physically have one. The difference, her not having a 'mark,' is seen as *her* difference, a lack with regard to the norm to which the male child instead is similar. The word 'mankind' demonstrates the problem. By taking the phallus as the 'mark' of men, and men as 'samples' of the species, women appear to be 'defective,' members (sic) of an inferior kind.

Being the norm has itself become a male gender characteristic, and the phallus has become, paradoxically, a 'mark' of the norm. The word 'male' and all other words which are used for domination through definition become phallically invested, because of the similarity of the male gender mandate and the definition (from which it derived). The word 'male' over-takes males, those who have a 'mark,' who become themselves over-takers, and who use their 'mark' to dominate or take over. Placed in positions of 'author-ity' by their 'marks,' they use their words to define and conquer.

Verbal communication among males and females thus must attempt to create mutual inclusion among those who are culturally defined as polar opposites, one pole being defined as 'superior' to the other, the marked norm and the sample for the species. The logical contradictions involved in this situation create damaging double binds which society has not yet resolved. In fact, many meta messages about gender are ego-oriented, constructed upon the exchange logic, and confirm the superiority of the male gender. This book is an attempt at an alternative giftgiving meta message about gender categories which would serve the need for abolishing them.

Over-Valuing Substitution

Since more value is socially given to masculated males, more attention is socially given to the substitution side of language, which therefore holds sway over the gift-giving side, in our understanding. A number of self-reflecting patterns develop, which both express the contradictory character of language-based gender and perpetuate it. Substitution or taking-the-place-of becomes domination and repeats itself, taking the place of giftgiving, which nurtures it. The male takes the place of the female as model of the human, and women continue to give to males and to give value to the male model. Male behaviors of domination and competition take the place of noncompetition, of giftgiving and giving-way. These behaviors replay aspects of the service and substitution mechanisms which we saw in the definition. Giving value is an aspect of giving that continues to support substitution-domination in our society.

At the level of language, we give value to the substitute gifts which are words, while at the level of genders we give value to the substitute, the male who takes the place of women (and other men). Our attention becomes focused on the place-taker, and we no longer look at Mother Earth or the mother, or any gift-giver— the one whose place is being taken. Giftgiving itself appears to be inferior (value is not given to it) when compared to substitution, which has usually been stripped of its gift aspects so as to appear more completely the opposite of giving. Then in economics, exchange—which is a mechanism of substitution and giving-way—self-similarly substitutes the whole giftgiving mode, which gives-way. (See Figure 10.)

Another expression of masculation is the use of the definition and naming to control the behavior of others through command and obedience (the giving-way of the will). After the members of one half of humanity have been given the mandate to be non-nurturing, it is difficult to convince them they should do it at appropriate moments and to a limited degree. Thus children may paradoxically be beaten (a physical over-taking) for not giving and giving-way, for being disobedient or disrespectful. Morality and the law are also structured according to command and obedience, domination by the word. Revenge and reprisal are the consequence of disobedience. 'Just' punishment is given in exchange for breaking the law. Giftgiving is made to seem unrealistic, while what is actually needed is not justice—based on the definition, masculation and exchange—but kindness, the restoration of the gift paradigm and the mothering model.

A Divided Community

Virtually everyone in the co-munity takes turns in the roles of speaker and listener (linguistic giver and receiver). Co-munication takes place also among people of the same gender, of course, so that speakers and listeners (givers and receivers) can also be of the same sex. Each gender develops its own kind of co-munity of mutual inclusion with those of the same sex while attempting to bridge the mutual exclusion, by forming a co-munity with those of the opposite sex.

There are thus two different processes for each gender. If forming the co-munity also produces our individual identities at the same time, there will be two kinds of identities for each gender—an identity constructed by co-municating with the same sex and one constructed by co-municating with the opposite sex. (The givers give to givers. They also give and give-in to those who are engaged in taking-the-place-of; the place-takers form a community of similars who also compete to take each other's place.) The basic functioning principles of co-munication—giftgiving and substitution are acted out in the two opposed gender roles.

The misuses of definition and naming—which would otherwise have been relatively neutral and collectively beneficial linguistic processes and mechanisms—are made possible by the invisibility of giftgiving in language and in life. These are both causes and results of masculation and the cancellation of the mothering model. Restoring giftgiving to our view of language and life (and restoring the idea of service and co-municative need-satisfaction to the definition and naming) can debilitate the patriarchal possession of a reified and de-humanized definition process, while taking away the phallic investment of the word.

Family Values

In practice, the mothering model has been kept in the family and dis-empowered, not extended to the rest of society. It has been interpreted by the ideological Right as subservient to the dominant father model. Families built upon such oppressive 'family values' are the cornerstone of patriarchy. In them, the caretaker and giftgiver is captured in the (permanent) service of one who dominates her and usurps her position of model for her sons—a fact which at the same time makes her a model of weakness and subservience for her daughters. Instead, mothering could provide the reasonable, workable basis for our social institutions, and giftgiving could be liberated as the principle of a better social order.

I do not mean by this that the patriarchal state should co-opt nurturing, as has already been tried in many kinds of exchange dressed up as gift and welfare programs. In the US, aid to the 'Third World' at home and abroad is almost always a hidden exchange to the benefit of the 'givers' and to the detriment and humiliation of the 'receivers.' Nurturing from the male model, even the collective male model, has not worked, as many costly examples of communism (state capitalism) and bureaucracy have shown.[4]

Rather, governments should be re-organized to rid them of competition for dominance, so that individuals and relatively small groups could take part in nurturing one another. A transformation of this sort would also require the creation of abundance through the cessation of waste. Presently scarcity is being artificially created through waste-spending on products which do not nurture life—armaments, drugs, symbolic luxuries. These expenditures deplete the economy of the many in order to allow the continuation of patriarchal socio-economic systems of exploitation and the over-privileging and power of the few.

It is important to look at language for clues about how to organize society, because language has the characteristic of being both individual and social, both in our own minds and in those of our groups. As a major creative factor in the formation of our individual and collective identities, it helps to bridge the gap between the single person and the multitude.

Exchange, constituted by a mechanism of substitution and giving-way as a derivative of the definition, is a very strong self-reflexive template which pulls us towards interpreting everything in its image, while at the same time hiding giftgiving. If we can point out, understand and de-mystify its mechanisms and restore the principle of giftgiving in abundance to our idea of language, we can then use language as a guide towards

[4]Though communism may be seen as an attempt to satisfy needs, it has been undermined, like capitalism, by patriarchal structures. Marx, and other male economists up to the present day, did not understand women's free labor as value-producing work. If women's work were counted (See Marilyn Waring, *If Women Counted, A New Feminist Economics*, Harper and Row, San Francisco, 1988), we would have to add on at least 40% to the GNP of most Western countries, more to Third World countries. Economists who leave aside such macroscopic elements must be skewing their analyses, as if a student of the solar system were to leave aside 40% of the planets. S/he would have to find other explanations for their effects—irregularities in orbits, for example, and would not be able to map an itinerary for successful space travel. Feminism is a more complete analysis, deeper and farther reaching, and a better basis for social planning than communism or capitalism, because unlike them it gives value to free labor.

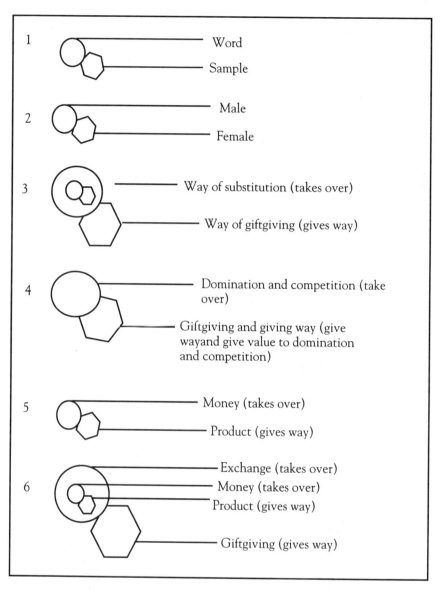

Figure 10. Taking-over and giving-way at different scales.

creating a Mothering Society at home here on Mother Earth. Giftgiving and its values are already available. We must only alter our perspective and take off our patriarchal glasses to see them.

Genderless Categories

Even when we talk about the 'Good' or 'Justice,' which seem like 'unmarked' and gender-neutral terms, we still have males as the unacknowledged models. The 'Good' is loaded with images of male God figures, while 'Justice' usually depends upon male judges and male law. The value given to equality, which is an important factor in the one-many concept form and a main principle of masculation and exchange, also perpetuates the male model. (Mothers nurture babies who are different from them, not equal.) The male images and actors bring with them the values they have been given socially, including the privilege of their 'mark.'

Moreover, the seemingly neutral categories are given a nobility as categories to which we should try to belong. They are a sort of artificial, 'unmarked' state of being, a broader norm to which little boys who had to leave the category of their mothers can as adults strive to return—without going through the terrors of the illusory need for castration. By behaving according to the laws, commandments, rules and regulations of the fathers, they can become similar to their father and brothers, who are not really different from their mothers in this, since the rules are valid for all, even though the males have more authority.

By this, boys as they become adults can partly divest themselves of the invented difference that ruined their primordial integrity, the wholeness and identification with their mothers— the original true experience they had to deny when they found out they belonged to the other category. Their mothers and other females are 'raised' to a level of equality with them, following the same rules and supposedly having the same privileges.

The neutral, objective ('unbiased') categories promise a sort of utopia to which children can aspire if they behave correctly, or if all people behave correctly. By acting in such a way that we can belong to the category of 'good' (or even 'Democrat' or 'American'), we seem to have a chance to overcome the original estrangement due to the 'mark' or lack of the 'mark,' the gender difference. I want to insist here that this sad journey is unnecessary, because the original estrangement is unnecessary. It is the social interpretation of gender that estranges the little boy from his mother because of his 'mark.' And we can change a social interpretation. The little boy really is still a member of the category of the human with the giftgiving mother as model, as is the little girl, and the 'mark' really is irrelevant to the category of the human from the beginning.

'Hum'

Adults socialize children into these roles both by their own behavior and by actively telling the child he is a boy, pushing him towards his father's identity, away from the interactive giftgiving identity he experiences every day with his mother. (The problem is even worse if the father is not available at all, but the child only sees other men on the street or perhaps on television.) We adults divide his conceptual identity from his experience. He is just trying to use language with regard to himself as he uses it with regard to other things to understand what they are.

Similarly, a little girl learns from society that the category to which she and her mother belong is 'inferior,' that it is often not even visible as a category, and that her mother, who is still her model, probably values the male with his 'mark' more than she does her daughter, herself or her gender.

Another effect of masculation is that privilege of one kind or another appears connected to a 'mark.' Money, cars, possessions function as 'marks' of class; skin color, height, and other physical differences function as 'marks' of racial or cultural categories, but all of these dynamics originate from the phallic 'mark,' and from defining the boy's difference from the mother as a physical difference. They promote the idea of a privileged 'deviant.' Then it may appear that we should behave in a masculated obsessive way because we are connected to (or own) a 'mark.'

Money for instance, like the phallus, is the 'mark' which appears to identify the norm. It disqualifies the (giftgiving) norm

102

whose place it has taken, making those who do not have it 'inferior.' Other kinds of biological characteristics like white skin, can function as the culturally imposed 'mark' of the norm, interpreting other skin colors as 'lacking' or 'less normal' categories. We all act according to our definitions just as boys and girls do. We blindly follow the self-fulfilling prophecies of the names of our categories, which bring with them the erroneous social readings of our physical and non-physical differences. Or we have to grapple with the prophecies and contradict them. It would be much easier to change the definitions than it is to change the lives and social patterns that have already been distorted in their image.

Both women and men can learn (and many are already doing so) to speak to children from a meta level about gender, telling them something like "The words we use to talk about ourselves are not quite right; we are a little different from the way it sounds. Even though we say 'male' and 'female,' 'boy' and 'girl,' 'mommy' and 'daddy,' we are all human. We are really all part of the same category." In fact, when children are small, they have to also overlook some other major physical differences (such as size) in order to be able to grasp the category 'human' and themselves as part of it. Surely they are open-minded enough to overlook the difference in genitals for their definition if we don't impose it upon them.

Listen to how people with young children talk about gender. With clothes on, boy and girl babies look very much alike, and the gender is the first thing people ask about. "Is the baby a boy or a girl?" Even the practice of distinguishing babies according to the colors they are dressed in, pink and blue, is misleading.[5] We should not impose stereotypes upon our children, but rather allow them to grow up through giftgiving interactions, and to become conscious of what they are as they grow. Perhaps we should allow children to choose their gender at puberty according to sexual preference, enhancing their choices with rituals and celebrations.

[5]Distinguishing sexes according to the color of their clothes is like distinguishing (and privileging) races according to the color of their skin.

103

We should not burden them with a self-fulfilling prophecy which alienates them from us and from themselves.

We may think children are not smart enough or logical enough to catch these distinctions. But if that is the case, it is probably because we have confused them from the beginning by loading the terms of their identities with such difficult and false differences. We are not doing this only individually; it is part and product of the whole misogynist social drift. Categorization itself has become a tool of oppression linked with the economic evaluation of everything according to its price. But giftgiving and need-satisfaction are more important than categorization for the well-being of humanity. Categorization has just been distorted and over-emphasized as a consequence of masculation.

We could also avoid masculation by abolishing gender terms altogether for children. We could call children 'hums,' for instance, short for 'humans.' We could say, "How's my little hum?" To the question, "Is your baby a boy or a girl?" we could reply, "E's a hum." Or perhaps we could just hum. Maybe adults could finally begin to refer to ourselves that way as well. This would solve the problem of separation-based masculated identity, of the definition of females as inferior and of the over-evaluation of the neuter or objective, by not imposing false distinctions in the first place. The penis is not a special gift or a 'mark' of a superior category. It is only a body part.

I do not mean by this to take the positive and life-enhancing character from sexual differences, but to liberate them from the stereotypes and especially from the obsession of masculation that is murdering us and our Mother Earth. Is it perhaps because we cannot hear Earth saying, "You are like me! You are in my giftgiving category," that we have done this? Or is it that we cannot hear her because we have the obsession? As a species, we have defined ourselves as something ('Man') that is 'other' than the Mother and have to act according to our self-fulfilling prophecy.

In other words, we have done the same thing regarding Mother Earth that we have done as little boys regarding our human mothers. We have denied our similarity and identified ourselves as 'something else,' but we don't quite know what it is (so we end up identifying with the word itself). Our sample seems to be a male god a lot like us, up in the sky and bigger and more important than the Mother. We try to act according to what he tells us to do, invent a hierarchical great chain of being, of over-taking and giving-way, and forget about the giftgiving impulses of our hearts.

Trusted and allowed to play according to their own lights, however, children become enormously intelligent and creative as Maria Montessori discovered. We need to let our definitions of ourselves grow up from our experiences of our free activities— play, creativity, interactions of giftgiving—filling our sensitive learning periods with living reality. We should not make our children have to try to become adequate to pre-existing oppositional adult gender categories. All this is easier where there is abundance and the experience of the child is not blighted by abuse or scarcity.

Maybe 'hum' could also stand for 'humus,' part of earth, the ground which we and our whole cultures are for one another, the foundation from which we grow and to which we return. Maybe we can finally act according to giftgiving, in a continuation of the original mother-child situation which we can finally allow to flower sanely and untwisted in the whole society.

A Personal Experiment

It is really not difficult to change the language we teach to children. I tried it myself in the 1960s with my oldest child, Amelia. I avoided using the possessive pronoun with her, not teaching her 'my' or 'mine,' 'his,' 'hers.' Since the mother really is the original sample, a child learns from what she says better than from others. I did ask the other people who were with us to avoid these possessives also. Of course, Amelia heard them when we were with people we did not know well, on the radio, and so forth. I got around the difficulties in ideas by saying, "Daddy uses that," for example, instead of "that's Daddy's." It was interesting that she did not learn possessives until she was around three, though she was talking well by then.

I know how she learned. She wanted to play with some dishes and another person there told her, "Don't touch those; they're your mother's." I always felt that the illogical reason (actually she was not supposed to play with them because they would break—not because they were mine) coupled with the fact that the person who possessed the dishes was me, the mother, finally made my daughter start to use that category. It would be hard to say whether not learning the possessives made my daughter any more generous than she otherwise would have been, or whether it had any effect at all. In fact, the experiment ended too soon, there were too many variables, and doing it alone was not terribly effective.

On the other hand, it didn't hurt her either. Possession is not as basic as gender, and anyway, the fabric of life absorbed any negativity that might have been involved. Avoiding gender terms at an early age, however, could really have a far-reaching effect in children's self-concepts, at least if it was done in their most sensitive language-learning periods.

We could also use androgynous terms in nursery schools. We could talk to children about gender terms from a meta level on *Sesame Street* and *Mr. Roger's Neighborhood*. We could give TV examples of mothers and children (boys and girls) using genderless terms to define their categories as part of a common humanity. I believe that here, too, the fabric of life would correct any unknown negatives that might be involved in the experiment.

Women have made such a difference in language in the last decades, eliminating sexist terminology. Surely we could devise new ways of talking to and about our children which would let them continue to identify with us in an ongoing way outside of stereotypical gender concepts. Then perhaps all of us could recognize and acknowledge our kinship to each other, to our mothers and to Mother Earth, returning to the giftgiving norm.

Chapter 7
The Collective Source

Through language, every individual weaves an answer to the deepest philosophical question of our time: "What is the relation of the one to the very many?" The relation of the individual to her culture and from thence to the five-and-a-half-billion other humans now living is very different from her relation to her village or social group in centuries past. The media brings us images and information about billions of people we will never see or meet, who are just as human as we are. Similarly, astronomy has brought us a view of our one planet Earth in the midst of millions of galaxies and billions of other stars and all their possible planets. As our knowledge of humanity and the universe has increased, our dimensions as individuals relative to the whole have shrunk incredibly. Yet each of us remains in the foreground for herself and thus appears very large, because she occupies her own view.

The answer to this question from the point of view of the gift paradigm goes something like this: Each human is a part of the collective because her/his identity is formed by using the collective's material, cultural and linguistic gifts, which are given to each of us by others, and are given by each of us to others. Our physical and psychological subjectivities are made of that matter, that matrix (or mother) which we ourselves re-form and become again for others. Each of us is a point or locus, a stitch in the fabric made by the transmission of innumerable gifts. In this fabric, the collective process relates things to words, words to words, things to things and us to each other—to and through the gifts at all the different levels.

The reiteration of masculation at different scales has altered the configuration of this collective process, directing the flow towards a category of self-motivating dominant ones, who attempt to expand their individual importance by establishing relations of control over the collective and its gifts. These ones are often served by other ones who access a relation to the many indirectly through their relation to the one who dominates the many. While it is conceivable that the expanded ones could give their gifts back to the many, this is not in accord with the gender mandate towards over-taking. Unfortunately, the relation of dominance by the one over the many appears to have a possible outcome in the destruction of the many by the one. Recently, the ability to cause nuclear devastation has made that power available and some 'ones' have played with it. We must reveal the illusory character of the motivation to dominate and expand and re-create ourselves through the giving and receiving process, finding a way to relate as nurturers, ones among many and many among many.

Environmental Niches

An environmental niche is a gift for which receivers evolve; creatures develop with needs that can receive that kind of nurturing. Language is a product and a by-product of the life of past generations, which present generations and individuals can receive and use. It is a collectively created cultural environmental niche.

We need to interact with each other in regard to things because they are valuable to us collectively and individually in various ways. And we have to be able to use things collectively and individually in various ways to bring their value to fruition. Others in the society have contributed a lot to the value of things, but the same is true of the value of words. Usually, the 'how to use it' side of our immediate environment at least, has been given to us free—just left there for us to pick up or handed down to us by our mothers. This, as well as the knowledge of what it would be appropriate for us to use, is transmitted to us by others in the society. But all of that, all of our material culture, happens to be there because others have been interacting with it through the centuries and mediating their interactions with language. Not only have women and things been left out of consideration, but the life processes of the multitudes of the past (and present) have often been ignored by philosophers who value words above things because they are viewing the world from a decontextualized, masculated point of view. The attitude of sexism is much broader than the issue of gender. It initiates denials and distortions of points of view which influence many other issues. It enters into the interactive dialectic between words and things, definer and defined, deeply altering the collective perspective and the world picture that is presented to its view.

Exchange has mis-taken some of the processes of language and, by transferring them onto the material plane, created a situation in which the gift is actually canceled by the requirement of an equivalent counter gift. This artificial situation is created by re-using the part of the pattern where the word takes the place of a thing, making the gift of the thing unnecessary for the creation of the human relation at the moment: I do not need to give you this flower to create a human relation of co-munication with you at the moment. I can simply say the word 'flower.' The word also serves as a sample-equivalent. In the description of the concept process, we discussed how the sample 'thing' is no longer necessary when the word takes its place as the equivalent for things in that category. On the material plane in exchange, when the counter gift is given, it also cancels the gift character of the first gift and expresses its value, re-presenting it. This is particularly clear when money is the counter gift.

Money takes the place of the product as the equivalent of other products (thus replacing and canceling that product as an equivalent). It measures and re-presents the value of the product in exchange as the substitute 'gift.' (Curiously, money, the arbiter of exchange, functions only by being given away.) Money also cancels both the qualitative value and the gift value (the inference that the other person is valuable), replacing them with quantitative value and exchange value so they are seen within the category of all the other products on the market.

The nurturing human transaction of giftgiving is altered, and part of the concept process is put in its place to mediate the mutually exclusive relation of private property. This material use of the concept (and transposed linguistic) process allows each exchanger in turn to act out the definition, to give and receive the substitute gift-word, money. The exchangers can thus give without depriving themselves. They give value to things and their substitute, money, rather than to one another. Money is the means of communication by which the product is defined, and the buyer gives it to the seller much as the definer gives the *definiendum* to a listener. The seller in turn has to give up the product—what for the definition process would be the thing defined. As it passes through the incarnated concept process, the product's gift value is canceled and transferred on to the money, which is exchanged for it and which we therefore call the exchange value of the product. As the product becomes the property of the buyer, it exits from the market process and becomes a use-value.

When it cancels the attribution of value to the receiver, the process of exchange cancels the gift value of the product in a way which has not usually been recognized. The use value is, as it were, wiped clean of previous experiences. Having bought it and paid its price, we no longer think of where it came from. We usually pay no attention to whether the source of the product we are using is underpaid 'Third World' workers, child labor, or US union members. The product is ready for our use, but gratitude and recognition are not given to its makers—nor is the product received from its makers as a nurturing gift, transmitting value to its receivers by implication. Instead, recognition and gratitude are given to the one who 'made' the money, or perhaps to the buyer, the seller, or the market process itself. For this reason, I believe there is an invisible, logical difference between use values which have passed through the process of exchange and use values which are made by people directly for others and which transmit gift value. The person who uses the use values, preparing and adapting them for the satisfaction of the needs of people in her family, does add gift value to them, but the gift value given to them by their makers has been canceled (or diverted into others' profit) by the exchange process.

Starting with the World

In his analysis of money and commodities (products in exchange), Marx took commodities as his starting point. He believed that previous thinkers had been wrong to begin with money. A similar consideration can be made about the relation between words and the world. In formulating our questions about that relation, we usually take words as our starting point, which sets us off on the wrong path to begin with. We need to start with the world, not with words—with material co-munication, not verbal communication. The answer, in either case, passes through the gift activity of human beings. However, by starting with words themselves, we cannot see the gift character of words *or* things. The gift character is also hidden because of the word's transparency, because the word position is burdened by masculation and because there is a motivation towards 'taking-the-place-of' in the definition, etc.

Placed in an 'inferior' giftgiving stance towards masculated men, the position of women is similar to the position of things in relation to words. Thus, it is easier for women to understand language starting from the point of view of things, while men usually take the point of view of words. Of course, all humans are also 'things related to words' when we are being talked about: 'that person over there,' 'the next one in line,' 'Janie's friend.' However, because the word has been incarnated in the male gender, women analogously take on the role of things in relation to that 'word.' We have known what it is to be spoken about rather than to speak, to give way to the one who takes our place, stands for us, re-presents us in public, while we continue our giftgiving at home.

But women actively put ourselves in relation, do the work of maintenance, caregiving and child rearing—all the myriad tasks that women have had—continually giving gift value to others in many ways. Things do not do this in first person as we do. They do not put themselves into a relationship with people. What accounts for their active side? It is the activity and creative receptivity of the collective—beyond the focus of the individual, the background of the many, in which women have also been anonymously standing for centuries. Our unacknowledged giving, providing for others directly and indirectly, is the process and result of an ongoing collective interactive dialectic with things. Not only do humans practice giving but, in the process, we leave a considerable amount of by-products available for the taking. Sometimes, it has seemed that women (and other excluded people) were only a few men's by-products, and like things, had only the value given by the collective, not value coming from themselves as givers in interaction. Things are also like women in that they give-way to words, letting them take their place.

The treatment of women as 'things' which nurture and give way in a 'many-to-one' relation to those men who take over and own or control them, repeats the relation between things and words that has always been so hard for philosophers to understand. The male philosophers were starting from their own point of view, the point of view of the over-takers, the owners, and controllers, the 'ones' as opposed to the 'manies.' Women, treated as things, can take the point of view of things, the many, those that give and give-way.

Someone might ask, "Do things really give and give way to words, like women give way to men?" In the fabric of innumerable gifts that make up the process of life of the collective, are things enlivened by our magic hands to become Pinocchios obedient to their Fathers' words at last? Or is it all a projection? Leaving aside Geppetto's words, witches (and the Blue Fairy) feel the life of inanimate things, perhaps because, as women, we know we are like them, under a spell of objectification. Anyway, our words are different, less empty than masculated men's, because we also speak things.

Starting with Words

Starting with words, relating words to things causes the investigator to concentrate on words but divides the idea of words into at least two parts: the 'vehicle' (sound, signifier, sign, writing, gesture of sign-language) and the 'meaning' ('idea,' 'signified,' 'referent,' *designatum*,' etc.). I believe we are actually packing some of the value of the characteristics of things into what we see as the 'meaning' of the word. Things are then split off from the word, rendered bereft of their value for communication because neither things' nor words' for-others aspects are recognized—or given value. We should look at words, not so much as having their own value, but as substitute gifts that carry the value of things in and for communication. This value contributes to forming the community in all its variety by letting each of us bond with other people in specific ways regarding all the parts of the world. It is the general existence of things for others.

In the community distorted by masculation, the genders act out the relation between things and words (which they do not understand.) We have gotten ourselves into this problem because, of course, humans are better able to respond to definitions as self-fulfilling prophecies than things are, however animated things may seem. Men act out the role of the word, women of things. Men, taking the place of women, are women's (for-others) substitute gifts, bearing women's value in communication for the kind of community that we call patriarchy. Women help to create the specific kinds of bonds that form and maintain this community. Men are the communitary substitute gifts of these individual hidden gifts who are gift-givers. Things, too, have a hidden gift side that is attributed to the words that take their places. Words and men are self-referential, while things and women seem not to be. All this confusion comes from dividing the community of self-and-other-creating mutually inclusive speakers and listeners (and givers and receivers) into two original inescapable and opposite categories of gender.

'Meaning'

If we start with things instead of words, we can locate 'meaning' in things in all their varieties of appearances and uses,

113

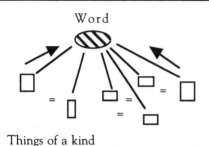

Things of a kind are related to one another as equals also nominalistically because they are related to the same word-gift as their substitute and name. This inclusive relation is the opposite of the mutually exclusive relation of words to each other in the *langue*. Homonymy and synonymy are variations of the pattern.

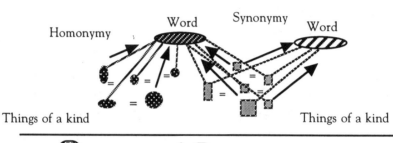

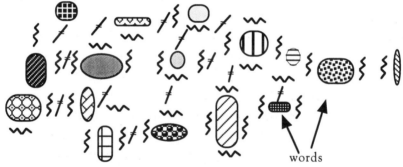

words

Words in the *langue* are related to each other in a purely differential, mutually exclusive way. Each word is what it is because it is not the others. Most words in the *langue* are equivalents and substitute word-gifts to which things of kinds are related. Some words such as logical connectives are not equivalents and substitutes but are still related to other words by mutual exclusion in the *langue*. They could be considered instructions for the use of words and sometimes for the use of things.

Figure 11. Things related to words, words related to each other.

with their relation to words as their relation to their substitute gifts for human beings. Different kinds of things that are related to a word (what we usually call the different 'meanings' of the word) can also be similar to each other. For example, the word 'sweet' can convey a taste of honey, or cakes having that taste, or a person with a pleasing attitude. The honey, or the cakes, or the attitude themselves have relevance for human beings. If they were not related to the same word, they would be related to different words. If they were not related to any words as their names, they could nevertheless be related to sentences composed of words to which some of their aspects are related. The fact that things are related to a word implies that they (or things like them) have been used to satisfy the needs of the many. They have a certain amount of generality. It is not just the words themselves that are general, but the things that are related to them through human use. In the formation of the concept, the capacity of things to be repeatedly for others as things of the same kind is brought forward by the generalization of the sample with regard to the many and the final assumption of the polarity by a general word. The fact that there is a word for that kind of thing expresses the generality of those things—not just of the word. In fact, the word by itself is nothing; it is dependent on the relation of things to it.

'Meaning'[1] is the top-down word-based term for the relation between things and words. This relation is established by human beings in an on-going way for each other collectively and individually. We usually believe only in a word-to-thing relation, but it is the thing-to-thing and thing-to-word relation that gives value to words for human beings. Without it, words would not have any utility for us. The thing-to-word relation is also functional in the making of our identities for several other

---

[1]We should ask, "Which others is it for?" We attribute qualities of things to words and of words to things. In the linguists' example: 'man' = + adult + male, 'man' does not have the quality of adulthood, or maleness, because 'man' is a word, while a man is not. We cover up the relation of things to words with the idea of a word-based concept, to which qualities can be attributed (given). We transcribe the qualities of men in a notation based on addition and subtraction, which are the quantificatory translation of giving and taking, creating un-kind 'mean-ing'—activity without giving. Whom does this attribution serve? If we restored the gift paradigm, perhaps we could call mean-ing 'kind-ing.'

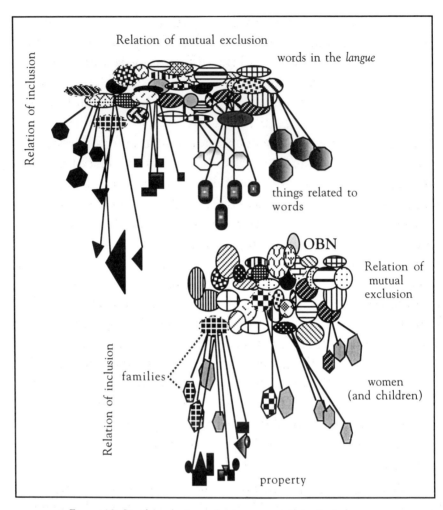

Figure 12. Similar relations of things to words in the *langue*, traditional wives and children to husbands and property to property owners.

reasons: humans are also 'things related to words' for each other (we talk about each other); we nurture one another at many levels materially and linguistically; and as we have been saying, many of us are modeling ourselves on some linguistic processes.

We have projected these linguistic processes into the organization of the collective, economically, politically and in the structure of the family. The projections confirm and reward some types of behavior and discount others, 'training' us, influencing our identities. They make up the contexts in which we live, imposing the parameters of the 'reality' in which our self-made artificial identities operate (which we call 'patriarchy'). (See Figures 11 and 12.)

Not only do women in the US take the names of our husbands but, in traditional roles here and elsewhere, men take our place in the public sphere, speak for us and often make decisions for us. We are known by who it is we are in relation to. In order to know about the relation between things and words, we need to start with things—just as, in order to know about the relation between women and men, we have learned in feminism that we need to start with women. Men have reasoned from words to things for centuries, just as they have reasoned starting with themselves when trying to understand women (and children and 'things'). It seems to me that those who are looking for the meaning of life are, like those who are looking for the meaning of words, starting from a top-down, word-based approach. Instead, we all need to start with material giftgiving rather than linguistic, substitute, re-presentational giftgiving. We need to be giving things, not words, satisfying material needs of others, to create abundance for all, co-municating to form the physical subjectivities (the bodies) not just the linguistic or psychological subjectivities of the co-munity. We need to create the systemic changes that will make generalized material co-munication possible for everyone at all levels.

Parasitic Relations

Altruism may sometimes seem fake, but that is because the artificial masculated exchange ego has learned how to do altruism, but not in a mothering way. Paternalistic charities give small amounts, just enough to take the pressure off a few individuals without changing the big picture. They maintain control of their gifts and of the receivers through 'due diligence' with the idea that the receivers have to earn their trust. Then women (even mothers), overvaluing these 'charitable' procedures, take them as the norm of how to be altruistic. If women continue to discredit the model (concept sample) of mothering, to look at it only from the self-reflecting and self-validating point of view of masculation and exchange—whether this is due to our own success in the system or to our taking the point of view of the over-valued male 'other' who degrades us—we will lose the revolutionary (the re-evolutionary) potential that now inflames the heart of the worldwide women's movement.

Having for centuries accepted the male bill of goods that we were inferior ('things'), and now accepting the bill of goods that we are or should be 'equal' to their model, we risk relinquishing our alignment with Mother Earth, our possibility of saving her, our mothers, ourselves, our daughters and our sons from the hungry mirror of the exchange paradigm. This is a species that is eating itself alive, because it cannot value the concept sample of the abundantly giving mother, or even see her.[2] We have made giftgiving, which is the source of life and joy, a slave to the artificial masculated ego and its expressions at the economic, political, and ideological levels. This drains the gifts of humanity into the coffers of the few, whose priapic excesses are kept from the needs and transformed into phallic armaments, deadly 'marks,' by which one group can demonstrate its 'superiority' (occupation of the privileged concept sample position) over another, which is forced to give way.

In this way, the constrained gifts of the many are wasted on non-nurturing expenditures of destruction, not to mention the immolation of millions of giftgiving hearts, minds and bodies. By un-making the bodies of the community, co-munication turns against itself, in the image of the concept sample. Meanwhile, this same process, supplying the needs of war (nurturing a phallic exchange), conveniently destroys (through spending wealth on armaments) the abundance which would have facilitated giftgiving in parts of the world not directly affected by the war. We have created a many-tiered relation in which a relatively small number of people act as a parasite on the rest, recreating a

[2] I find it fascinating that breasts have been both degraded and sexually objectified in our society. Until recently, our baby bottles were phallic—another symptom of our malady, of replacing the mother with the father model.

situation of privilege which is originally created by transferring half of all our babies into a linguistically mediated non-nurturing 'superior' category. This category is over-valued and given *to* by the nurturers, because of its mandate to achieve the concept sample position. (The sample position is only a conceptual mechanism functional for organizing our perceptions, not a way of 'deserving' love or abundance). The host must re-educate and convince the parasite (which is anyway part of itself). We must not allow the parasite to continue to convince the host.

The parasite is made of mirrors—exchanges, definitions, judgments—and it has to receive energy, money, food, time, nurturing from somewhere else in order to grow big enough to become a privileged 'one' by overcoming many others. But this aberrant state of affairs is not anybody's fault. In fact, blame and guilt are part of the exchange paradigm, ways of making the other 'pay back.' We cannot fix the exchange paradigm by re-applying it again and again to itself. Our prisons and electric chairs are overflowing with people 'paying' for their mistakes. We do not need justice; we need kindness. Justice is really an attempt to define the crime so that it will not happen again. We try to perform this definition through a kind of exchange because exchange derives from the definition. The 'payment' involves a forced material co-munication whereby the criminal is required to give up something, and give way. Perhaps we believe that, by returning to the material level requiring goods, time, or even life in an 'equal' exchange, we will have more effect upon the wrongdoer. An attempt is made to evaluate the gravity of the crime with respect to other crimes (a kind of quantification). The criminal is masculated again, physically distanced (de-contextualized) and put into a category of 'other' with a 'term' or a 'sentence.'

Many 'One-Manies'

Thinking about all this, I saw I had three areas of similar relations to work with: 1. commodities were to money as; 2.

things were to words as; 3. women were to men. I could use each to clarify the others.

For example, all of these areas have many to one relations as part of their make-up. All commodities are many, related to money as their equivalent. They are also many in relation to a particular price as one. Things are related to words in various ways as many to one: as many with regard to language as one kind of thing; as many with regard to a single word (for example, the word 'things'); and as many as kinds of things with regard to the word which 'means' that kind or re-presents it. As the 'inferior' gender, all women are related to every man as many to one. Each of these relations also involves potential one-to-one relations. The human couple is a one-to-one relation like the more fleeting relation of the exchange of a product for money, and like Saussure's idea of the sign as union between signifier and signified. Variations and changes in the one-to-one relation take place in the on-going relation of women to men with the family's relation to the father. The mother herself figures as one with regard to whom her children are potentially many, but she is replaced by the father as the 'head' of the family. Such examples of the double standard as the Don Juan syndrome or polygamy also involve many-to-one relations. Another many-to-one relation is that of property to its owner, which has often combined with the relation of family as chattel to the father.[3] Then, of course, there are subjects to a king, constituencies to their elected representatives, nations to their presidents, employees to their bosses. There are successive many to one stages, for example: Catholics to their priests, priests to their bishops, bishops to their cardinals, cardinals to their popes. Armies are related in the same stairsteps to their officers and finally to their generals, etc. The overlapping of one-many structures creates a giant mechanism.

[3]Children may participate in many of these relations at different levels. The property relation looks something like Vigotsky's complexes. It is 'one-many' but does not depend upon similarity. The child may also be an owner, of toys, for example, at an early age—while s/he is 'owned' by the father in the family relation. Associative complexes or their incarnations in property or the family may be held together also by a 'feeling tone' as Carl Jung said about word association and about psychological complexes. The feeling tone of concepts would be influenced by masculation. Carl Jung, 1973 [1906] "A psychological diagnosis of evidence" *Experimental Researches, Collected Works of C.G. Jung 2*, Leopold Stein and Diana Riviere eds. London, Routledge and Keegan Paul, pp. 318-332.

Perhaps, when some of its pieces are missing, it can be more benign, but the re-enforcement which occurs among the structures in First World patriarchy has made it more deadly and priapic than ever before—with the nation's nuclear weapons ready to obliterate the many, its phallic mushroom cloud evidence that it has achieved the one (1) position.

We have been reasoning and acting from the point of view of words in relation to things, money to commodities, men to women. It seems to me that the explanation for this is that the exchange economy provides a focus on the individual ego and gives value and importance mainly to the 'one,' the abstract isolated consciousness. The importance (and the ways of using) the collective consciousness, group consciousness and other-tending gift experience have been ignored, because we have only known how to start from ourselves as isolated individuals—and only those who have succeeded as isolated individuals have been given credence and the authority to speak. This self-focus is due to masculation, to the self-reflecting logic of exchange and to the top-down hierarchical model. It is consistent with capitalism, especially with the 'independent producer' or entrepreneur cultural hero. Academics are no more free from this syndrome than others, though perhaps they would like to be. The competition, in terms of a certain type of creativity and acumen (the reward of which is ego validation, authority and prestige), influences the world views of academics just as much as if the rewards were only economic ones. Language has become an instrument of power, and those who study it are usually not free from the ego-validating patterns which make this power possible.

Light and Shadow

Women can also develop a self-focused ego, but we often remain to some extent other-oriented because we continue to be required to be the nurturers of our children. Inside or outside academia, our world views are likely to be broader than men's, especially when we are not intellectually subservient to the patriarchal way. With one foot in each camp, it is easier to see the contradictions. In fact, what we see is that we are standing half in the shadow, half in the light. Even while we compete and succeed in the exchange economy, as individuals we often view ourselves as belonging to the masses of women who are unseen and unrecognized.

Our place in the shadow also lets us look at the others who are in the dark, the masses of people, cultures, women, children, and men, who are placed in the background by the masculated ego. Along with these are all the things, animals, creatures, plants, inventions, art and household effects which have been the objects of our care, use and maintenance throughout the centuries. Here in the dark lie all the tables we have polished, corn we have ground, fields we have planted, horses, cows and chickens we have fed, snow we have shoveled, roofs we have thatched, assembly lines we have worked in, sinks we have unstopped, dances we have danced, children we have raised. In all this variety of activity, we have conferred value upon things and imbued them with the stuff of life freely, which others may freely use. Even when our activity has cost us a lot, humanly or economically, the results of our acting according to nurturing principles still remain as a free legacy for others. The legacy consists of material reality—the house that was lived in and taken care of has survived to this day, the one that was abandoned has decayed and gone—caring ways and unmasculated value-giving hearts and minds.

The male ego notoriously fears death and loves what it fears, because by shifting its vision away from others, it denies what it has received from them—and their existence and importance for it, as well. Thus, it is likely to see itself as the lonely source of what instead has been given to it by others, from the masses of humanity that preceded it, to the workers in its factories and fields, to its mother, wife, sister, child, and (even at times) brother. This is a bit rarer, because the Old Boys Network and male bonding serve to increase the sense of power and autonomy of the isolated male ego as such. Men learn to recognize the self-reflecting image and validate each other. The 'one' position works particularly well within the denial of the fact that it has received from others. The ego sees everything in the framework of taking—or at least of deserving what it gets. (Deserving is another transposition of exchange, requiring an equivalence between past actions and present rewards.) The emphasis that we have put on the monetization of labor in capitalism has concentrated attention only on that area of our activity and on the kind of human relation which is 'making money.' Since the ego thinks of its perceptions, its world, and its abilities as all coming from itself, its own social artificial character is concealed from it, and it runs the risk of solipsism.

Looking at language from the point of view of the gift paradigm is a good cure for solipsism. If we consider each word as a by-product of the linguistically-mediated life processes of the multitudes of people before us, by which they satisfied each others' communicative needs and which is also freely given to us, we find ourselves in contact with millions of other giftgiving and communicating people, because we have received our words (and our culture and our material goods) from them. Actually, solipsism is not so much a philosophical position in our society as a psychological and a political one. It allows cruelty without responsibility, blissing out in our own well-being in the face of others' pain. Our compassion withers and dries up and our souls become prisoners of our egos. We allow our governments to make innumerable decisions which kill other people or let them die, perpetrating economic and military genocide while we stay safely at home wondering whether those other people really existed in the first place.

People who talk about creating our own reality are perhaps unknowingly inspired by the limitless creativity and magical quality of the gift of language, without however acknowledging the source of the gift as others-in-general. Some religious attitudes, both New Age and Fundamentalist, are prone to weaseling out of the human race, so as not to feel powerless among the multitude, and instead to belong only to the privileged 'one' position. When we begin to relate only to God (who is often also seen as a masculated 'one,' and therefore similar to each of us as an isolated individual) and not to the human race and the planet, our attitude tends to become megalomaniacal and paranoid. Then we act in singularly discompassionate ways, ignoring those people outside our immediate focus—whose spirituality, after all, is just as great or as small as our own. If we can re-conceptualize ourselves as having received from the people of the past and present, beginning with our own mothers, we are no longer separate and disempowered. In fact, seeing oneself as a masculated ego (as not receiving from others except through 'deserving') does really make us powerless. Then we overcompensate.

At any rate, solipsism is disproved by the fact that we think in language, which we have gotten from others. There used to be a creationist theory that God had buried those dinosaur bones out there to 'test our faith' in the Bible story of Genesis. Similarly, for solipsists, s/he would have to have implanted language in our minds to test our faith by making us suspect there were other people out there. Actually, our earth is so vast and varied we could never begin to live on it as individuals. We need the common perceptions of the many to give any kind of real context to our individual lives. Society is a sort of enormous fly's eye which, by putting together its many facets into a collective vision, is able to see the big picture. This picture is facilitated by and transcribed into language in order to mediate our social relations with each other. And the transcription, in turn, provides a sort of enormous collective eardrum, which reverberates in response to everything that is important at a certain threshold of intensity beyond the individual level. Through collective elaboration, the cultural values of the things the co-munity responds to are stored in words, kept alive as gifts available for all, constantly in use.[4]

Still, the patriarchal ego looks only at the things which are within its own focus, shining its own light upon them. It is because people, in first place in the so-called 'First World,' are in this mode that we are able to ignore the flow of goods, money and

[4]Though most of us arrive at an effective linguistic competence, the lack of access to experiences of cultural variety, and to the positive aspects of education, sometimes deprives economically disadvantaged people of many of these gifts.

value from the so-called 'Third World' at home and abroad to US. When the CIA is not directly destabilizing Third World governments or the US funding fascist tyrants against the interests of the many poor, 'First World' patriarchy takes over economically. While our media and our therapy focus on the here and now, our government uses our money, their influence and their armaments to devastate the people in the dark. Big businesses relocate in the Third World, causing economic and environmental disaster, while some of us at home reap the profits and others lose their jobs. When the businesses are unable to hide, they cover up with lies, re-defining what they do as 'development.' Under the appearance of helping people, they bring the gift mode into focus, though falsely, to cover the bitter exchange-mode, exploitative things that they are really doing. This has the effect of portraying the gift-mode as something other than it is, and of identifying it with the men, especially in the government and big business, who are farthest away from the truth. Often, as individuals these men have never nurtured anybody, having themselves always functioned within the exchange mechanism.

Our 'First World' needs are actually being satisfied free or at very low cost to us by 'Third World' people. An equivalent of their work does not go back to them. The difference in the economies allows the business people to pocket most of the price we pay them, put it in our banks, transferring that value one more time from the have-nots to the haves, from the dark to the light, the invisible to the visible. Like a lock in a river, the flow of value is blocked and maintained at a 'higher' level. The 'First World' economies, as a whole, have received an enormous amount from the 'Third World' economies. Individually, it may be hard to see this, or we may not feel the benefit directly. But the much larger amount of value circulating here than there is due to the unequal exchange, an exchange which in practice ends up as a free gift from 'Third World' people to US.

Our short-term profit motive, which fits so well with the privileged ego mode, lets the people in the dark (those of the past, those of the present in the 'Third World' at home or abroad, and those of the future, all our children) be damaged or destroyed by poverty, pollution and war to pay for what is in the 'light,' our own continued well-being. The problem is not moral depravity and a psychological penchant towards greed but a 'normal' world view, an ego structure, and an economic way which fit and function together to the detriment of all. Individually, I do not think we know we are doing this, or we would stop, make each other stop. Collectively, our consciousness is in denial—which makes it hard to come to individual consciousness. That is why we so desperately need a paradigm shift.

The mandate towards over-taking and being 'one' by having and domination is broadcast at every level in our society. The scarcity that is artificially created by the powers that be, in order to maintain the system of exchange, intensifies the penalties for not succeeding in the mandate. We do not realize that it is logically impossible for everyone to be a 'one' related to the many and that no other life agenda is available to most males beyond masculation per se. Meaningful work, education and entertainment are offered almost exclusively to economic 'haves,' and all of those areas are anyway part of the exchange economy. Gangs and criminal behavior are the only chance many people have to carry out the masculated life agenda, though violence against women continues to be an option for males needing to act as dominant 'ones.' While all of these activities need to be defined as 'wrong,' it is only through a re-vision and re-definition of society itself that the problem can be solved.

We have to shift paradigms and educate everyone into the nurturing way, not masculate our boy babies into an ego structure that requires dominance and privilege to feel it is carrying out its gender identity mandate. We have to restore the mothering model for all, educate our boys to be giftgivers too, from the beginning. After they have had to give up the mother and learn how not to nurture, how can they at a later date learn to be 'good' by following the rules, the behavioral syntax deriving from the naming of gender, the overtaking Law of the Father?

126

Chapter 8
Castration Envy

A war between the haves and the have-nots is being waged. I think its root causes are in what I have decided to call 'castration envy.' The relation of private property is a product of the mutual opposition of gender categories combined with the privileged concept sample position. The boy finds he is in the category opposite to giftgiving, because of what he has (the penis), while the mother is defined as female because she gives (nurturing) and because she does not have (a penis). A 'having' category is opposed to a 'giving' category. Giftgiving and not-having are identified with each other—and with being female. Since he is in the same category as the father (who is a privileged concept sample, a 'one'), the boy has to take part in the role of the 'many,' things, those who give way, the weak, before this relation can be overturned and, as an adult, he can become the sample or 'one.' The boy's role is also similar to the commodity, compared again and again to a general quantitative standard of value. While 'having' puts the boy in a competitive situation, which might be considered difficult and negative, he is consoled by the fact that he belongs to the privileged gender to which more is given.

Property and Money

Money is the substitute (material) gift for the commodity, and the sample for the category of value. It takes the place of all other concept models as sample for the value of products in exchange—in their transition out of the gift way. The owner is to property as money is to commodities, as father is to child, as father's penis is to child's, as sample is to the many that are compared to it.[1]

---

[1] Money takes the place of the owner as the concept 'sample' to which commodities are related as values, until it is given up and the commodities become related as property to new owners as 'samples.' A 'one-many' property relation is taken over by a 'one-many' value concept relation, and then a new 'one-many' property relation occurs.

The male is one who has the 'mark,' which points him out both as potential sample man and as potential owner, in a one-many relation to his property. The penis is perhaps the sample piece of property. But it is inalienable—he cannot and will not give it up.[2] The patriarchal father stands in a similar one-many relation to his family, of ownership. In a way the father's control of the family seems to be required by the consideration that, in scarcity, those who give will lack if they do not receive from others, and those who keep and do not give will not lack. (There is surely an anal-retentive aspect of all this as well.) Mothers and children under the control of the father can be made not to practice giftgiving outside the family, not to satisfy others' needs sexually or materially. Those who have will therefore presumably continue to survive in scarcity. By owning large quantities of money, the sample of value, the one who *has* assures more nurturing for himself and those related to him, under his one-many control in the concept-structured family.

Exchange, by requiring equivalence, brings a relative item to comparison with a standard, so into the concept process. The same process happens in many different areas of life: in the masculation of the baby boy, in measurements and tests of all kinds, grades in schools, sports records, beauty contests, role-modeling. The relation of presidents to citizens, movie and music stars to fans, first prize hogs to piglets are variations on the theme.

Similar to exchange is the Western marriage ceremony, where the woman is an item being transferred out of the family group, which is relative to her father as sample 'one,' to a new relation to her husband as sample 'one.' This pattern is changing to some extent in the US, but we are still influenced by it, and it continues in many variants in other parts of the world. Though her wedding day is supposed to be the happiest day of her life, a sample day, and the woman herself is seen then as sample of Woman, she is only playing the role of a sample thing in the

[2]See Annette Weiner's book on the cross-cultural economic logic of not-giving: *Inalienable Possessions, The Paradox of Keeping-While-Giving*, The University of California Press, Berkeley and Los Angeles, 1992.

process of being over-taken by its (new) substitute, the husband, who is functioning very much like a word. It is fitting then that the woman should take her husband's name.

A new self-replicating concept-family unit is formed, where the boys will continue to learn to become 'male' by renouncing the gift process (and sometimes by punishing and degrading it), and the girls will learn to give their gifts and allegiance to the male sample. Property, like marriage, is based upon the mutual exclusion of the 'ones'.[3] Each owner is in a one-many relation with his/her properties and in a mutually exclusive relation with every other owner. Money steps in as the sample for the concept of value, to which products are related and by which they are replaced, much as the priest steps in between father and husband to regulate the transfer of the woman (still a giver) from one family 'concept' to another. Altering the relation of those who belong to a category, relative to a sample, so that they can be transferred to a different (mutually opposed) category and a different sample requires a definitive word pronounced by the priest or presented as an actual portion of the material word and value sample (money) by a buyer. Deeds, licenses, and contracts are enduring re-presentations of the definitive words.

Labor and Money

The sale of labor time takes place in much the same way, although labor is often given freely to family and acquaintances

---

[3] I believe the OBN (Old Boys' Network), like the group of property owners, incarnates the differential values of words opposed to one another in the *langue*. Women and children have historically been to their husband and fathers as properties are to their owners and as things are to the words which stand for them. Each of the members of the category of husbands/fathers is in a differential, mutually exclusive relation with every other while in a one-many relation with his own family. The husband/father has to keep the other 'ones' from taking his place and property owners face the same challenge. In the *langue*, each word is in a differential relation with all the others, while it is in a 'one-many' inclusive relation with the things which are related to it as their name. We said that when the sample is no longer necessary for forming the concept, it becomes just another thing of that kind. However, its removal might also be attributed to its being incorporated or subsumed into the word, a kind of logofication. Males (especially those in 'superior' categories) appear to become words, while females (and others in 'inferior' categories) appear to become things, 'reified.' (Look back at Figure 12.)

129

and gifts and services actually permeate much of life, so labor is somewhat more flexible than private property. Because of scarcity, jobs (monetized exchange labor) seem to be gifts. Many women and men do not receive this gift of being defined by money, which allows survival. Monetization, or the lack of it, is an instrument of power, because it defines one group as relevant to the concept of economic value, the other as irrelevant (they do not have the 'common quality' of exchange value). This categorization implies that those outside could become part of the privileged group if only they were good, efficient, or educated enough. Their success or failure seems to depend upon qualities which they have or have-not.[4] The importance of exchange value is that it gives access to the category that has a chance to survive. However, the scarcity (not having) that is necessary for exchange to prevail as a process is artificially created so that the monetized (having) category will be privileged.

Masculated men traditionally need women who have been abandoned and left bereft of the gift of belonging to a privileged category, having a degree or title (another verbal masculation), or even having a monetized job (monetary masculation), who take care of them in order to make them better able to succeed in the fierce competition to be in the highly monetized categories. Here is the leverage point where capitalism and patriarchy are locked together with those they define as 'different.' The total system needs and uses the individual needs of those who are outside the category of the employed. For example, the job market needs the unemployed who want to become employed, in order to keep the price of labor down. Those who do monetized work need the free labor of those who do not, which passes through them and permits them to add more gift labor to their jobs. The system rewards the employed by contrasting their relative well-being with the suffering caused by the unsatisfied needs of the

[4] The idea of buying and selling labor time seems clear enough, but there are many differences between the ownership of our lives and the ownership of property. Our relation to our lives is really not 'one-many,' as our relation to property is, even though we can divide it into time periods, and we may or may not have many marketable qualities or abilities.

unemployed.[5] Thus, those who 'have' are encouraged to attribute more relative value to what they do have, through fear of the abandonment and suffering experienced by the have-nots. Similarly, the mistreatment of women and girls, even (in some cultures) the abandonment of girl babies to die, makes those who have the 'mark' attribute more importance to it and to being in the masculated category because of fear that they would undergo similar mistreatment if they were female have-nots.

The Primordial Error

It is as if there were an unconscious reasoning of this sort: if a boy has been put into the non-nurturing category because of the penis, he might remedy this estrangement through castration and, therefore, wish for castration in order to be like his nurturing mother. (Freud revealed that we often fear what we desire.) But through misogyny, society shows him that girls, who are born 'castrated,' are even more grievously punished than he is, so he should value what he has. He might be seen as having *castration envy* but being healed of it as an adult through the mistreatment of the have-nots. And the more goods he gets *from* them, the larger his 'having' is and the less he presumably wants to be like them or envies their lack.

Perhaps the boy wants to give the penis to the mother, because she doesn't have one, and satisfy her 'need' to be in the superior category. However, he decides to keep it (treats it as an inalienable possession and, therefore, as more valuable than what he would give away). He gives up giving it and gives up the gift paradigm at the same time. Thus, he demonstrates that the gift way is alienable, or less important to him than keeping the penis (not being castrated) and remaining in the category 'male.' In ex-change, he takes on genital sexuality in the place of nurturing, much as the whole society takes on

[5]The institution of welfare defines the excluded category as 'poor' and allows some minimal giftgiving to be done by the patriarchal state. This is a paradoxical masculation of people as 'have-nots' with consequent humiliation, allowing the subsistence of an underclass who believe their poverty is due to their personal defects ('lacks').

economic exchange in the place of giftgiving. As an adult, by amassing possessions and money (which can be both kept and given), he has a chance to engage again in selective nurturing towards others.[6] In fact, if he arrives at a state of wealth, he can give abundantly if he wishes and finally appear even more nurturing than the mother, who was only useful to him anyway in infancy. By giving to a few, he can repeat the pattern, privileging them over others who lack, repeating his own entrance into the privileged category, making them 'haves' as opposed to their 'lacking' (economically female) counterparts.

Another defect of the mother's giving-way or standing aside as the boy's model is that the child is not validated as precious by seeming inalienable. She may also seem to have given up her penis, even given it to the boy. The father, however, does not have this defect, because he kept his, and he keeps the boy in his gender category. He seems to have known how not to give away too much. If the father had only been the mother, the boy may reason, s/he would have the penis, and the boy would still be like him/her and still be able to be a nurturer. These speculative trains of thought are moot, of course, because it is not the penis that takes the boy away from the category of the mother, but the social interpretation of the penis and the construction of gender around the opposition of the gender terms. Socially, we *name* him 'male' because he has a penis. If he wants to remain nurturing, and well he should as a little *homo donans*, he would not have to change his body, giving up his penis, but only change the name and the concept of gender in his society (an arduous job but definitely less threatening than losing a body part). This healing of language would keep the boy from wanting what he also must fear, and must not achieve—his castration. The society would be able to stop over-privileging 'having' and penalizing 'not having' both as regards to male genitals and as regards money and other kinds of properties.

[6]Perhaps the monetary support he gives his wife is a way of making her 'have' what he could not give his mother.

Puerarchy

Rich people often fear not having, even though they might want to participate in a gift economy with those who do not have. The same kinds of privileges that reward boys over girls are given to the rich over the poor. The fear of symbolic castration besets the rich and they perceive the need of others as a desire to take what they have, and castrate them of their goods, relegating them to the unprivileged category. Wealthy women are in a contradictory position, because they only have money or property, not the male 'mark' of privilege. This may be the reason they buy expensive portable objects, like jewelry, that demonstrate they are members of the superior category.

Guns and knives are marks that restore the phallic equation and sometimes do make it possible for poor people to force giftgiving from the rich through robbery. The rich often force giftgiving from the poor through the leverage of low salaries and other means of exploitation. However, they do not define it as robbery but as profit. The system of profit taking is defended by hierarchies of police or military armed with guns and knives. The poor are punished for 'not having' while the rich are rewarded for 'having.'

The intensification of the needs of poor people demonstrates the necessity for the practice of the gift economy on a large scale. However, giving up money resonates with giving up the penis (castration), giving up the privileged category and thus the possibility of living in abundance. Abundance itself is a good thing, but it is being used to reward 'having,' not-giving and the kind of categorization, definition, and de-serving that come from masculation. By creating widespread scarcity, capitalism provides the conditions for the exchange economy to prevail and makes what is the birthright of all into the reward of the lucky few, just as masculation does with the mother's abundance. The relation between the 'haves' and the 'have-nots' acts out the combination of *fear* and *desire for* castration that arises from the false categorizations of masculation. The anxiety of our boy children has cast its spell upon society as a whole, causing incredible harm. It may be hard for us to acknowledge this situation, because we unconsciously feel we should pay back for the harm that has been done. However, in that case we are needlessly reasoning according to the exchange paradigm.

There is no payment that could equal the harm that has been done, but the fact is that if we want to enter the gift paradigm, we must anyway be for-giving. We can begin by re-defining the system as something that needs to be changed, not just 'the way things are,' and we can begin by addressing that need. We can re-interpret patriarchy in the light of the gift paradigm as a bad dream and start all over again. Perhaps we should re-name the system that is based upon this childhood castration nightmare, calling it not patriarchy but '*puer*archy,' the rule of the boy. Or even '*puer*' archy—the rule of the word 'boy.'

Misogyny

The mistreatment of females in general can also be seen as a reprisal against the mother for giving up the boy into the other gender. Such an exchange (or evening of the score) is perhaps not just a mercenary attack, but a renewed attempt to form a concept by creating repeated instances of the problem of inclusion/exclusion according to physical properties. This attempt has not succeeded, though the abandonment of the 'have-nots' by the 'haves' has taken place on ever larger scales. Now the 'haves' are some 250 million people, while the 'have-nots' are 5.5 billion. One reason for this is that the translation of the problem of having and lacking the penis into the economic terms of having and lacking the means of livelihood has created numberless new problems and disguised their common origin in the infantile misperception. Here, differently from the childhood nightmare (where it may be feared that mothers give away their penises to their male children), the 'have-nots' do actually give to the 'haves'—though this is concealed by an over-emphasis on the presumed value and deserving of the 'haves,' whose 'one' positions are held in place by hierarchies and gained by competition and domination.

The misunderstanding that is creating this terrible distortion in values (and in reality itself) is very profound but so innocent and obvious as to be invisible. It is just masculation and the consequent turning away from the mothering model that is making us value death and destruction over life and well-being for all. The 'haves' should be giving to the 'have-nots,' giving to satisfy needs, not abandoning or killing them to punish them for not having—or so that the 'haves' will value their possessions, jobs, money, and phalluses more. I am trying to explain patterns that I believe underlie our problems. I do not deny that many men love their children, and that boys often retain the capacity for nurturing (perhaps for some of them masculation just doesn't 'take'), but I believe these patterns cut deep channels in our culture, profoundly bias our institutions, and influence the behavior of all in needlessly negative ways.

Nurturing Exchange

The abstraction, boy = father, is made more important than the concrete creative nurturing relation in the internal ('marginal')[7] priority list of the parents. The visible physical similarity is more important than the behavioral or the ongoing *ad hoc* construction of the self, based on love. Yet, that has to happen, too, though it may be travestied through servitude by the mother and deserving by the child. Equivalence between the child and father is self-confirming by such mirroring effects as the child reflecting the father reflecting himself in him (the father fulfilling himself as sample 'one' through being the equivalent to which the boy is relative) and through other examples of the concept relations in the wider context. Giftgiving is other-confirming. Presently, it is wrongly nurturing exchange as its 'other' and confirming

[7]Marginalism in economics is based upon the consideration of the relative alienability and inalienability of possessions. Economic operators presumably have to ask themselves what they are least willing to give up.

equivalence, the principle of substitution. It nurtures the contradiction of itself, the substitution *of* giftgiving, and its replacement by the phallic equation. Giftgivers give to the process of exchange as our 'other,' and we also make the boy our 'other' by letting the father sample substitute *us*—creating the male image (of equivalence and substitution) for the boy to follow. A simple other-oriented process gives to a complex and artificial self-reflecting one.

The mother upholds and nurtures the boy's similarity to the father; she affirms the importance of their similarity, while it is both obvious and unseen that she does not require the boy's similarity to herself, because she is in fact nurturing him—who is someone different from herself (different first because he is a child, and then because he is being made male). The privileging and the father's attention seem to be conditional upon the boy's similarity to the father, and perhaps on the size of the child, and therefore also upon the size of the penis, which is not really like the father's anyway. (Their equation is therefore only counter-factual and programmatic in the beginning.)

To this can be added the need or desire to assert paternity and, therefore, also a privileging of other individual physical similarities, such as facial features, hair and skin color, height. Even behavioral traits can be identified as similar. Then, also, obedience to the father's word makes the boy act according to his father's plan, thereby showing who the child 'belongs' to. The character of 'belonging to' is important also for girls. They need to belong to the father and, therefore, should be obedient to his Law, even if they have to be like the mother, eventually. This requirement comes about because property and the concept coincide as one-many patterns. Since the father cannot be the gender model for the girl (the other one-many pattern), the property relation emerges more strongly. Girls follow the model of their mothers in belonging to the father, and in giving importance to the one-many concept relation among males.

To keep the gift and exchange paradigms in place, it is often necessary for exchangers to avoid even the *appearance of giftgiving*.

However, a lot of giftgiving in exchange does happen, through surplus labor, gift labor, and just as the result of cheating. Even things like inflation, printing new money, and exchange rate differentials provide free gifts for some. All this is all hidden by an *appearance of equal exchange*. That is why we have to keep our gaze fixed on the appearance of equality, and that is one gift of equality—that it hides the gifts of giftgiving and the bridging of diversity. It does the same in the boy's change of categories. The equality with his father hides what he has lost to gain his privilege—the giftgiving way he seems to have been dispossessed of, cheated out of—where the good actually comes from. Once giftgiving is given up, it is as if society decides to cut its losses in the compromise. Equal exchange seems to be the best that can be had, so we focus on its gifts which are the values of patriarchy: safety under the rule of the honored and (occasionally) benign patriarch, equality, and justice. They are accompanied by the domination and blotting out of the values of giftgiving and abundance: other orientation, kindness, tolerance, diversity, and the leap of love across the synapse.

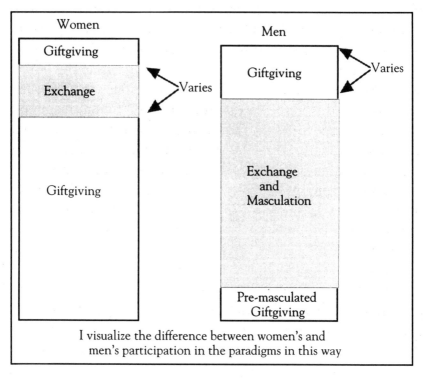

Figure 13.

Chapter 9
Is = $

The need which a word-gift satisfies is not a need directly for the object, or a need to consume it. That is why we do not have to carry the things we are talking about around with us, like the philosophers in Jonathan Swift's *Gulliver's Travels*. As our experience goes on, ever-new communicative needs arise to establish human relations of inclusion with one another, in regard to all the parts of the world. We satisfy those communicative needs by giving verbal gifts to establish the relations, instead of giving and receiving material gifts. By doing this, we transform what might have seemed an objective world into an intensely giftgiving world, in which humans interact with each other on the gift basis, at least in this one area of their lives, all the time. Linguistic giftgiving continues to happen, whatever else we do, even when we are acting in very inhumane ways towards each other. Indeed, if we could bring our actions in the material world into alignment with the gift aspects of language, we would have the basis for the flowering of humanity.

Word-gifts, however, have several advantages over most material gifts. First, words are easy for humans to make and store. Second, the different instances of a word are used by us as one word. This collapsing of the different sound events into one allows the possibility of the word's being for each of us the 'same thing' that it is for others. It also makes the word something which can easily be in two, or many, places at the same time. Third, these peculiarities give rise to the generality of the word, in that it can be used over and over by many, as something to which things can be related and with regard to which human relations can be established. A word can be made by virtually anyone and also received by virtually anyone.

The act of substitution of verbal gifts for material gifts, as well as for 'immaterial' things, events, situations, ideas which are seen as for-others, is a specifically human act. The word is a special

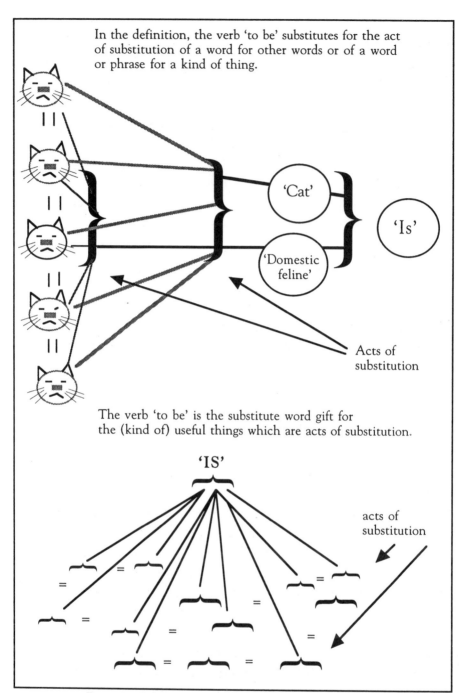

In the definition, the verb 'to be' substitutes for the act of substitution of a word for other words or of a word or phrase for a kind of thing.

'Cat'

'Domestic feline'

'Is'

Acts of substitution

The verb 'to be' is the substitute word gift for the (kind of) useful things which are acts of substitution.

'IS'

acts of substitution

Figure 14. Substituting the acts of substitution inserts a meta moment into the sentence. As the single substitute for acts of substitution, 'is' becomes very general.

kind of substitute gift and the communicative needs which it satisfies are specifically human needs, which have also adapted to the means of their satisfaction. Multiply the needs by the number of things there are to talk about that are relevant enough to people to occasion a single word-gift (a name) to arise in their regard, and we have a linguistic gift *plenum* of an immense variety and combinability, in which each word participates as one among many and which everyone in the community can potentially use.

To Be Meta

There is one abstract word, the verb 'to be,' which has given philosophers a great deal to think about. Although it is not used in all languages, where it does exist its presence is intriguing. Its quantitative and logical transcription as '=' seems to be as widespread as the market economy. I believe that in the definition, the verb 'to be' is a word-gift which satisfies a communicative need arising from the very sentence in which it is embedded. It substitutes for the acts of gift-substitution just performed or about to be performed by the other words in the sentence. In 'a cat is a domestic feline,' 'is' is the substitute gift for the act of gift-substitution, which is performed by means of 'cat.' At the same time, it substitutes for the next gift-substitution, 'domestic feline,' which can thus be seen as an act of the same kind as 'cat.' Taking the verb 'to be' as a word-gift substitute for other gift acts, which are happening within the sentence of which it is a part, allows us to consider it a 'meta' part of the sentence. (See Figure 14.) This accounts for the present-time character of the verb 'to be,' since its referents (the 'things' related to it) are immediately there, happening in the same sentence. This act of word-gift substitution is itself a service, done for the other person. It satisfies a meta sentential communicative need, the need for a re-presentation of the acts happening in the present sentence, establishing a relation between persons to them in the here and now. This insertion of a shift into a meta moment inside the sentence mediates its function as a definition, allowing the *definiendum* to substitute for the *definiens*.

141

If language does indeed function according to the principle of substitute giftgiving, it should be clear that a very large number of acts of substitution must be occurring all the time as we speak. The act is itself a very general one. The word which functions as substitute gift for the act of substitution is therefore the most general of words. There are no other words at the same level of generality. This does not prevent it from remaining humble and being used abundantly. It is because of its unique position that the verb 'to be' is itself difficult to define, but we do try to define it, since it seems to be just a word like any other. Our minds boggle and seem to expand to the whole world and contract to the immediate present, when we say such things as 'being is.' Perhaps this is because 'being'—the verb 'to be'—is a meta word-gift (not a simple substitute, but the gift-substitute for the act of word gift-substitution itself). It is both very general and does not have a group of terms at its own level of generality to which it could be opposed as a value.[1]

In order for words and the communicative needs which they satisfy to develop, there has to be a verbal plane that is maintained as a common-place alongside the rest of life. When things become important enough on the nonverbal plane, they acquire a permanent collective communicative gift on the verbal plane in the form of a word. We use that word as we shift our communicative giftgiving from the nonverbal to the verbal plane. That shift may be seen as a substitution: we can access the verbal gift and use it in place of the nonverbal gift (or in the definition, in place of other verbal gifts) to create bonds with another. It is this shift or act of substitution itself that we name when we say 'is.' That is why we can use 'is' both when we speak of something that is nonverbal, pointing it out (*deixis*), as in 'That is a cat,' and when we use a verbal *definiens*, 'A cat is a furry friendly animal with a long tail.' In both cases, 'is' re-presents the shift from a nonverbal to a verbal gift. One shift moves from the reality plane to the

[1]Perhaps 'to exist' is almost as general.

verbal (passing through the relatively empty place-taker 'that') and the other from the reality plane to the verbal plane, and then again to a more constant element of the verbal plane.

Sentences combine general collective word-gifts to satisfy contingent and particular communicative needs. Each of the aspects of a situation or event, taken singly, can be seen as related to a word-gift, its name. When the words are taken together in sequence (what linguists call the axis of 'metonymy'), they combine and collaborate with each other (by transposed processes of giving to and receiving from each other), particularizing each other to satisfy a true communicative need arising from the situation which the speaker and listener are addressing. Together, they are a provisional and fleeting way of bringing forward some elements of the world as relevant, distinguishing them from elements that are not relevant. They provide a combination of words to which the relevant elements are related, at least for the moment.[2]

The relation between words and things, as well as the concept relation we have been discussing, take place on what linguists have called the axis of 'metaphor.' Here terms at different levels are related to one another on the basis of an equivalence and the ability of an element on one plane to take the place of others on another. The axis of metaphor often involves the one-many polarity.[3] Metonymy and metaphor work together in discourse, as well as in definitions. Strings of words (metonymy), many of which are individually in one-many relations with the things for which they are substitute gifts (metaphor), are put together according to transposed gift relations. Providing a word as a substitute gift is

[2]In the definition, a continuing tension or polarity between what is said and what is not said, what is present as an equivalent and what is excluded, aids in the foregrounding of relevant elements or items, as opposed to those which are not relevant or valuable at the moment. If I say 'a cat is a four legged animal,' for instance, I do not need to say 'a cat is not a two-legged animal' or 'two-legged is not four-legged, because the assertion of 'four-legged' already excludes 'two-legged.' The foregrounding of elements that takes place gradually in the concept formation process (and more or less deliberately in the definition) is simply implied in the use of words for communicative need satisfaction in the flow of adult speech.
[3]Metaphor and metonymy (substitution and combination) are two poles of language function which are also found in aphasia (speech loss) in a 'similarity disorder' or a 'contiguity disorder.' See Roman Jakobson, *op. cit.*, Ch.7.

itself a particular kind of service.

The verb 'to be' constitutes an intersection and a passage between the two axes of metonymy (contiguity) and metaphor (substitution). As a substitute gift for the act of substitution, it is metaphor, but as a substitute placed alongside the things for which it stands (the other acts of gift-substitution in the sentence), it is contiguous and forms a metonymical succession. As we saw above, on the axis of contiguity, a sentence replays gift relations which could take place on the nonverbal level. However, the definition differs from other types of sentences, because it is constructed according to layers of substitution, in which the *definiens* serves as provisional word-gift phrase for the kind of thing being defined, and the *definiendum* then takes the place of the *definiens* as the constant and general name of that kind of thing for the listener. The definition is a service the speaker performs for the listener, creating an inclusive relation and giving, in the moment, something (a word gift) that may last the listener's lifetime.

Such logical connectives as 'both/and,' 'either/or,' and 'not' modify (are given to) the verb 'to be,' so as to make it the substitute gift for the act of substitution of two or more items 'a cat is both a feline and a domestic animal,' one of two items 'a cat is either feline or canine,' or for something other than the item mentioned. 'A cat is not a canine' says that the first term does not satisfy the same general communicative need as the second term and, therefore, cannot be substituted for it. Syllogistic 'if/then' ("if all a's are b's and all b's are c's, then all a's are c's") says that 'a,' 'b,' 'c' are gift substitutes for the same 'thing.' The principle of gift-substitution, shifting planes, functions between language and the world, as well as within language itself in the definition and at a meta level with the verb 'to be' in the definition.

On the other hand, when we use the verb 'to be' to describe something in the world, 'the dog is brown,' we use 'is' to 'give' or attribute 'brown' to 'dog.' The dog has the 'property' or gift of being brown (given by the universe or the dog painter, the source

144

is not at issue). A thorough discussion of all of the possibilities of the interpretation of language using the gift paradigm, though fascinating, would make this book too long and academic. I want only to suggest some of the possibilities in order to go on to the discussion of exchange for money in their light.

The definition is different from the sentences of ongoing discourse, because it has more to do with the process of gift-substitution itself and serves a meta linguistic gift function, satisfying the need of the listener for a word she does not have. However, in a sense, the definition has been drained of its giftgiving aspects for centuries by patriarchal philosophers and linguists, for whom it seemed to be expressing 'objective'[4] aseptic relations among words, instead of relations among persons. These objective relations among words are regulated by abstract laws of syntax similar to the abstract laws which regulate our masculated society.

We can restore the gift principle to language, recognizing that the patterns of gift relations among persons continue in language and are also trans-lated or shifted from the human level to the verbal. Since misogyny has blinded us and kept us from recognizing those gift relations among persons, we have never thought of looking for them in language. Instead, we have recognized abstract and arbitrary laws similar to those we create for the regulation of masculated behavior in patriarchy. We might ask if our laws are a syntax used to regulate the self-supremacy of each of our isolated incarnated (male) words, or if our idea of syntax is extrapolated from our rules of domination, command and obedience. It might also seem that the verb 'to be' drains the sentence of giftgiving just as masculation drains the society.

---

[4]We should suspect 'objectivity' as a reification or fetishization having to do with phallic property and its analogs, from toy cars and trains to guns and missiles. The boy's male identity concept and private property are two transposed concept relations among things as opposed to an ad hoc giving-and-receiving identity. Thus a concept relation among things constitutes the masculated identity, not a configuration of subjectivities constructed through giving and receiving. When things which have been deprived of their gift character are proposed as 'presents' to be re-'presented' the gift connection between the levels becomes invisible. The 'present' appears to have only to do with time not with the gift. However, perhaps the temporal aspect of 'present' derives from the fact that the satisfaction of needs focusses us on the here and now.

Actually, I believe that this appearance comes from the fact that the verb 'to be' is associated with the definition (which is itself originally a benign process) where the mechanism of substitution is used internally in a way which is different from the flow of speech. The giftgiving in the definition takes place between persons at a meta linguistic level through a substitution of words for other words. Since the process is different from the rest of speech, its gifts may not be apparent, and the 'over-taking' function of the *definiendum* may appear to be the 'fault' of the verb 'to be.' However, it is really the primordial use of the definition in masculation (the different levels of substitution contribute to the hall-of-mirrors effect) that rubs off on the verb 'to be,' giving it a bad name. Some people involved with General Semantics have felt that they should avoid the verb 'to be' altogether, and they have eliminated it from their speech.[5] It is not the verb 'to be' which is parasitic upon humanity, however, but *puer*-patri-archy. Returning to the gift paradigm in economics (as in language) will allow, among many other things, the restoration of the verb 'to be' to its rightful place as part of the mother tongue.

Being and Money

The same thing happens in the definition with 'to be' that happens now in exchange for money—which is a substitute for the act of substitution of another's product for one's own, and one's own product for that of another. The substitution happens even though the products themselves are particular—not standing as general, but only as particular equivalents and substitutes for the products of the person with whom the exchange takes place. Moreover, the act of substitution is not yet complete when money has been substituted for it. Like 'to be,' money forms a metonymic succession with that for which it stands, but it does so by actually interrupting that act and placing itself in the middle of it, pushing the first product away. The buyer's money often begins the process in the same space with the

[5] *To Be or Not: An E-Prime Anthology*, ISGS, San Francisco, 1992.

product it is being exchanged for (contiguous with it), but then, acting on the axis of metaphor, it physically supplants the seller's product, changing hands.

The substitution of money for a product anticipates the substitution of the money for another product, and a reversal of the roles of seller and buyer. Since money takes the place of all products as their general equivalent, it has the character of generality, which they do not. Every time it takes their place, it provides this character of generality and connection with others in the society, for that particular transaction. Every time it is given away for other products, this character of generality and connection is given away by the buyer. The substitution of the act of exchange for money for the direct act of substitution of one product for another does almost the same thing in the economic realm that the verb 'to be' does in the definition. It creates a metonymic moment with what it has substituted (the products)—but this requires human beings to take part in the 'phrase' as actors. The actors take turns in their roles of seller and buyer, and this symmetry alters the metonymic succession, keeping it from developing into other kinds of 'sentences' beyond the 'definition.'[6]

The exchangers can, however, operate upon the plane of substitution and buy in order to sell, so as to increase the quantity of general equivalent that they hold. The linguistic axis of metonymy is recreated in another way in the addition of quantitatively and qualitatively similar units to one another (one plus one plus one) in the numerical system by which value is assessed in price. This also permits the addition of sums of money to one another, which provides the possibility of hoarding and the

[6]In barter, exchange remains a particular dyad, not in relation to a general equivalent. A barter system provides many moments of dyadic exchange requiring calculations of equivalence according to time or some other standard. It is important not to confuse barter with giftgiving. Barter is still giving-in-order-to-receive, while giftgiving is directed towards the need of the other. The logics are different. The barter systems and alternative monies that are presently being developed in green and bio-regionalist groups might be considered a step towards a gift economy. However, they continue to be based on exchange and contain the defects of exchange, one of which is taking-the-place-of giftgiving. I want to be very clear that giftgiving and barter are not the same thing. Abolishing money is like abolishing the verb 'to be.' It doesn't solve the problems caused by masculation and exchange.

development of capital.

Since it has retained the character of material gift and concept sample in a situation of private property, money actually does have to be physically substituted for products and received or given away in their place (axis of metaphor). When it is present in one's hands, they are not; when they are present, it is not. And we do actually have to carry it around with us in order to give it to others, as a substitute for their products. The process of linguistic substitution has come full circle; the word has been re-incarnated. Swift's scenario has also proved true. (Little do we know, we have the verb 'to be' jingling in our pockets.) I believe that subconscious reasons often influence the symbols, as well as the words that 'stick' in our culture. Thus, the striking similarity of the dollar sign '$' to 'is' seems to me to support the identification of 'to be' with money.[7]

Money substitutes the seller's product, and exchange for money substitutes the act of substitution for her own product, which will take place when she, the seller, becomes a buyer. If the situation had been one of barter, each person's product would have been substituted by the product of the other. Rather than receiving the buyer's product directly, the seller receives its substitute in the artificial product, money. At the same time, this substitution anticipates the next substitution by the next seller. The whole process takes the place of the process of barter, which takes the place of giftgiving. Exchange for money creates a temporal lapse in the metonymic succession of the moments of barter. Money can be exchanged for one product and then held for days or years before it is exchanged for another. It pulls the interaction together in its different moments, creating its own social space, the market. Exchange takes the products and the material 'word,' which defines them out of context (physically decontextualizes them) in a way which emphasizes the decontextualized aspect of the definition.

---

[7]Money is actually an icon of words in that every instance of a coin or bill of one denomination is considered the 'same thing,' making it possible for 'one thing' to be many places at once, which is what allows money to become general like the word.

Since money has the character of measure of value, it functions also as a word in that respect, on the axis of 'metaphor' (substitution). In its defining mode, it answers the question 'what is it?' with a price.[8] The market may be seen as the social area in which products and their general equivalent are taken out of context in order to define, evaluate and exchange them. This co-existence and shifting of planes, and the use of verbal mechanisms in nonverbal areas, allows for the introduction of variables which would not exist with either giftgiving or barter.

In the situation of barter, one person's product equals the other's. However, both are individual products, and they belong to a dyad. They only substitute each other and, though this gives them a common quality reciprocally as substitutes, no general concept can be formed with regard to them because a one-many relation is necessary for that to happen. Then the whole process of exchange for money takes the place of barter, so that a concept-formation type of process is put into effect regarding those two or any individual products, expressing their common quality as substitutes for each other but related to all other products and, therefore, having general value.

Because of the situation of scarcity and the mutual exclusion of private property, the exchangers only want to exchange quantitatively equal items, so they must be able to evaluate them, to know 'what they are' in terms of price. The linguistic dialectic comes into play again: What they are 'for others' in general in the society determines what they are, what price they will have, for the individuals, as well. A social need for this evaluation (and for the substitute equivalent in which it is made) begins to exist as a communicative need, an element which is necessary for the communication and interaction of the persons regarding the transmission (giving) to one another of their private property.

---

[8]Both the market and language are ways of determining whether something is the 'same thing,' having the same value for the people involved, whether this is cultural-linguistic or economic value. The determination of a price is a collective process similar to the collective attribution of value which gives rise to a name.

Then we seem to need the substitute equivalent, money, for itself, not for the products it substitutes. What was a linguistic communicative need has become a material need on the economic plane. This has happened because private property alters the giftgiving co-munity, isolating us from each other as owners of goods. Our lack of material co-munication creates a situation similar to that of isolated consciousnesses without language. We therefore have a common need for the means of co-munication, of establishing and altering our relations to each other with regard to things—in this case our private property. This means of co-munication is the material gift concept-sample substitute, money. Exchange value is the product's value (relevance) to distorted material co-munication (exchange) in a situation of private property. It is quantitatively assessable through the material sample equivalent and substitute gift ($).

From a third person, outsider point of view, the 'phrase' in which money is the verb 'to be' becomes complete by repetition (for example, one shirt equals twenty dollars equals ten pounds of beans). And from that point of view, the interactors are indeed satisfying each other's needs, each giving to the other what she does not have and receiving from the other what she needs. Money is simply a substitute gift, given from one to the other, satisfying the communicative need that arises every time she has to decide what to receive from others. But of course, these are rose-colored 'objective' glasses. In fact, if a person's product or work cannot be sold, it is outside the market (as if it were beyond the confines of the concept) and does not 'exist' as far as exchange is concerned. It is not substitutable by another product, and there will be no act of substitution by the money-verb $ in regard to it. If her work is valueless for others, her decision as to what to receive to satisfy her need is completely powerless. Her demand is not 'effective.' Her need does not 'exist,' because giftgiving to needs has itself been substituted.

Being and the Aberrant Norm

The similar functions of the verb 'to be,' the Phallus and money suggest a connection among the different realms of language, sexuality, and economics. This is a connection which is 'genetic' in the sense that masculation provides the genesis of the Phallus and of money, as well as the phallic investment of 'to be.'[9] If the father did not take the place of the mother as sample, there would be no possibility of substituting that act of substitution. (There would be no act of substitution there to substitute.) Masculation would no longer exist to project exchange onto society as its economic way, so there would be no communicative need for money, and it would not have the function of the word. The verb 'to be' itself would not become hypostatized, because it would not be invested psychologically by equivalence with the Phallus. Thus, while the connections may indeed be there, they are artificial—because masculation itself is an artificial, unnecessary and damaging aspect of the boy's socialization. Together, the Phallus, money, and 'to be' confirm a false picture, or to say it in another way, they are all the 'marks' of the aberrant norm.

Perhaps the real problem is precocious Phallic genitalization taking the place of the oral stage for children. The penis or Phallus would take the place of the breast as invested object of interest. The boy's 'mark' 'gives' him privilege, because it puts him in the 'superior' category—in a manipulative, if 'x' then 'y' way—while the mother's breasts gave to him directly. Its erotization coincides with the estrangement of the boy into the privileged, non-nurturing category. Thus, it may appear not only that he gave up the breast and got the penis, but the gift process

[9]For the present argument, the Phallus re-presents or takes the place of the act of substitution of the father for the mother, making its function similar to that of the verb 'to be,' with the general social symbolic character that Lacan believed was norm-al. Jean Joseph Goux has much to say on the Phallus and money as the general equivalent in *Symbolic Economies: After Marx and Freud* translated from the French by Jennifer Curtiss Gage, Cornell University Press, Ithaca, 1990 [1973]. I highly recommend Goux's book for a more psychoanalytic and historical approach to many of these issues, at least those regarding exchange.

may become identified with the internal sensations of eating and evacuating (having to do with the oral stage), while his change of category has to do with genitalization and the penis (an external part of the body). The gender identity of the boy then depends upon a polar equation with the (bigger) father, who is always in the equivalent position and is the large sample of genitalization. Thus, the boy's identification in relation to a polarized equivalent takes over from the giftgiving, turntaking and sometimes playful construction of identity with the mother. Here quantification begins to be important, because the quantity (size) of the phallus may appear to be the reason the father, not the boy, is in the polarized 'one' position. Phallic quantity appears to be the most important quality.[10]

Quantitative Material Co-munication

It is not a qualitative word or evaluation that is given in exchange but a quantitative word or evaluation. Money does the same thing on the material plane that words do on the verbal. Prices explicitly express material co-municative needs as quantities of money. They are served by quantities of material money taking over the role of words-as-gifts. The co-municative need that prices express is the need for a means of co-munication the sellers of those products do not have. Money is the word, but differently from language, the 'communicators' have to produce (and actually give up) the things it stands for in order to get it. Money, like male identity is an incarnated word. In its transference onto the material plane, it too has become somewhat distorted away from the original word functions. Like a word, its only real use is in being given to others; yet money can be hoarded and accumulated.

[10]Jerry Fodor says that Vigotsky's idea of the concept is too philosophical and criticizes his belief that the concept requires the abstraction of a 'sensory invariant.' Yet we have been describing a widespread situation in which the male 'mark' is the sensory invariant of the privileged category, 'abstracted' by our childrearing practices. Money is the sensory invariant for the privileged category of people who have succeeded in being economic 'ones.' See J. A. Fodor 1972 "Some Reflections on L.S. Vigotsky's *Thought and Language*" in *Cognition 1*, 83-95.

Because money is the general gift substitute for the act of substitution, it influences every particular act of substitution (exchange) by relating it to all the others. Money is the material in which the values of products relative to each other and to us can be quantitatively expressed. As such, it is like language in which words are available to express the qualitative values of all the parts of our world in relation to each other and to us. Money is a one-word (material) language.[11] Those who do not have it cannot 'speak.' They do not belong to the 'species,' the category of those who do have it.[12]

[11]As Jerry Martien shows (*op. cit.*), wampum was a many-word material language. It is not surprising that the Europeans redefined wampum in terms of their one word material language, money.

[12] It is as if there were a moment in pre-history when those who could speak became part of the group and those who could not were left to die, in a cruel 'evolutionary' strategy. We seem to be imitating that pre-historic moment. Those who 'have' the word are privileged and those who 'have not' seem to deserve to die. From the Greeks for whom everyone who did not speak Greek was a 'barbarian' to modern speakers of any language other than standard English, those who do not possess the 'sample' language are excluded from the privileged category.

Chapter 10
Value

"Gracias a la Vida"

If we take giftgiving seriously, we can at last understand more about our human relation to reality as a given. I believe there is a certain 'grain' to our experience that comes from our capacity to give and receive. We have evolved to perceive things at this level. For example, we perceive apples as round, red objects which we can pick from trees and eat or give to others to eat, not as collections of atoms, because we cannot give and receive them as atoms. It is conceivable that we might nurture ourselves with parts of nature as atoms (by osmosis perhaps), but it would be very difficult to nurture each other with them. For instance, transporting atoms to a different location, handling and preparing them, supplying them to the other person, etc. would all be difficult. At the level of perception, physical integrity and dexterity to which we have evolved, we can nurture each other relatively easily with things of certain sizes and kinds. Language expands this giving and receiving 'grain,' giving it added dimensions of collective importance, abstraction, generality, imagination, space and time.

A theory of knowledge could be developed which identifies knowledge with the gratitude experienced by the individual as the recipient of the gifts given by life, nature, culture and other individuals. In gratitude, we respond to our on-going experience and remember both gifts and their sources—the food we eat and the words we learn, the people who give them to us and the cultures they came from. Those who are deprived of the good things of life by poverty, cruelty or disease are being deprived of their human right to knowledge, to experience the givens of life with gratitude. (The song *"Gracias a la Vida"* by Violeta Parra expresses the gratitude all of us, rich or poor, can feel for the most basic gifts of life.) Unfortunately, we have misplaced our gratitude away from the mother onto the father, and we have placed our faith in this change and in ex-change. We are, therefore, more conscious of the father and of exchange; we know more about them than we do about giftgiving, towards which we have learned to be ungrateful. We see ex-change and the ego as necessary for our survival and are grateful for a chance to participate in the market.

Creative Receptivity and the Giving 'Grain'

If we consider receptivity as passive (and passivity as receptive), we will never understand our own interactions with our environment, our language, each other. In fact, things have qualities which are valuable to us because we can respond to or receive them. (It is not that they exist because we can receive them, but that they are useful because we can use them for our needs.) An apple seems red, round and good to us, because we are physically, psychologically and socially adapted to creatively receive and use it. We are also physically, psychologically and socially adapted to creatively receive the word 'apple,' to which we attribute some of the cultural value of apples, because it substitutes for them as a gift in co-munication (even though it is not itself red, round, or good to eat). If we had been able to give and creatively receive apples as collections of atoms, we might have evolved to perceive them in that way. We do not have any way of handling them or giving them to each other at that level. Instead, we have physically and culturally evolved to perceive them as round and red, aided by our language. The kinds of sense perceptions we have are pertinent to the level of complication of our activity. At this level, we can also perceive sounds as such instead of as vibrations of air.

Perceptions having to do with a finer grain, for example, collections of atoms, or the actions of enzymes in our digestive processes, or a grosser grain, such as the migration of human families or groups, are not available to us *per se*, because we do not have ways of giving and creatively receiving them. Instruments

156

and methods, such as microscopes and sociological statistics, have indeed been developed to study events at different levels of complication with the goal of satisfying needs—which are themselves finally perceived at the everyday level. The goal is also usually that of making a profit, for example, in the case of enzymes by devising medicines, or, in the case of the migrant workers, by accessing cheap labor. Without the information provided by specialized disciplines, we must receive the influences of finer or grosser-grained reality passively. Once food enters our stomachs, we no longer perceive it at the level of gifts, but can only passively allow our enzymes' automatic processes.

Our language and the world we perceive are fine-tuned to a level in which we can give to and receive from each other without special instruments, microscopes, telescopes, surveys or statistics. If we consider this level apart from language, it is the level of 'sense data,' the world as a given. We can only consider it this way when we have language, however. If language originally derives from material gift giving co-munication, its grain has become, by now, much finer than that of the material gifts that can actually be given by humans to each other. We can communicate about the color red with each other, its location on the breast of the bluebird singing in the tree, yet we cannot actually give each other the color or the location.

Much scientific and philosophical investigation goes into the nature of our sense data and experiential givens. However, both kinds of investigations take place as such after the giving-and-receiving co-municative mode has been established in childhood nurturing, and language has been learned by the investigators. Sense data and experience become interpretable by people as givens after nurturing has established gross-grained giftgiving and receiving as important and language has given them the fine-grained analysis made by the life process of the collective.

The extension of the number of substitute word-gifts to cover aspects of experience which cannot be directly given provides the collective fine-grain which allows ungiveable gifts to be understood as finer-grained givens. Thus, we can receive the color red, the momentary location of the bluebird, the detailed geological, horticultural, biological and cultural histories of the world as givens, because we can communicate about them and satisfy one anothers' communicative needs, forming our relations with each other linguistically in their regard, even though we cannot actually hand them over to each other.

There are various reasons why some kinds of gifts cannot be given. For example, a mountain is ungiveable because it is too large. The color red is ungiveable as such because it is too firmly attached to the objects of which it is a part: we can give a red ball but we cannot give the color red without the ball—or the ball without some coloration. Alternatively, if the red color we are talking about is a subjective sensation, like an after-image, it cannot be perceived by others as such, much less handed over to them. Some things, such as facts and events, cannot be given directly, because they are too transitory and evanescent.

For example, the fact that the bird is singing in the tree cannot be given, as such, because it is fleeting and its components can be easily changed. The bird can stop singing and fly away, creating a new, or many new events. However, we can grasp (receive) fleeting events as givens and give them again as gifts if we relate their constant and repeatable elements (the bird, the singing, and the tree) to the substitute gifts—the words which people in our society use to give to each other in their place. By combining those words in orderly ways (together with some meta-gift instruction words or 'marks' like 'the' or 'in' or 'ing'), we make them also give to and receive from each other—forming relatively short-lived substitute gifts (sentences) which we give to each other. In this way, we make ungiveable events giveable, forming ourselves as a co-munity in regard to them. Through our gifts to each other, we are able to creatively receive ever-changing experience as a common ground, given to us together.

Once we learn how to co-municate and to use language, we do not need to put either ability into practice all the time. We can leave language aside and simply consider sense data as givens, but the gifts of language are usually already in place when we approach the world as a given without them. Moreover, leaving language aside is itself a procedure which requires language. The world we experience is a gift and a given, because we can creatively receive and give aspects and parts of it, enhanced by our ability to receive and give the verbal (and nonverbal) substitute gifts to which the givens give up their value for comunication. (Most things are probably not actually giving gifts to each other, but because we have the gift framework we can interpret them in that light.) Like receiving, giving-way can be creative and attribute value to the other. Things give way to words as gifts because we make them do it[1]—we give them a substitute—but we make words do what we want them to do also. Giving way attributes value to the other by implication in the same way that giving implies the value of the other. The value given to words by things which allow their place to be taken as gifts is met by the value people give to words as the means of satisfying the communicative needs of others. Words are thus the recipients of value attributions from at least two directions (in addition to their value-as-position in the *langue*). By standing aside together in the present, allowing their place to be taken by words in combination, things appear to be related to each other and more valuable for the moment than their surroundings, and we give our attention to them.

The linguistic mediation of a perception or an experience constitutes a secondary gift that gives us common access to the perception or experience as a value or as a communicative or material need-satisfying good. We can consequently act in a variety of ways towards the good, which we can give to and receive from each other, consume alone, take turns using, combine with other goods, take apart, save for later, etc. We can also simply satisfy communicative needs in regard to something, making ourselves

---

[1]Does it make a difference if this is just a projection upon things as long as it works to let them give value to words for us? In patriarchy we have believed women were passive in giving way to men but they were still giving value to the men by implication. The kinds of giving way that are done by apples, mountains and a bird singing in the tree or a girl hitting the ball are similar enough to give value to the word-gifts which take their place even if they are very different as parts of the world. Abstract ideas (e.g., justice) and fantasy creatures (e.g., unicorns) put up even less resistance to having their places taken.

who we are as its common perceivers—perceivers of apples, for example. When we know a language we can also just think about apples in their substitutability without directly relating them to words. We maintain a direction towards the community in our thinking[2] because the potential for communicative needs and word-gifts which satisfy them is always there.

The value given by things to words and by words to things at the level of the lexicon (*langue*) is somewhat grosser-grained than the value attributed through sentences. In fact, like things, words are general gifts of the culture which are creatively received by the culture, as well as by individuals (the many being more than just a collection of 'ones'). Except for the special cases of naming, definition and language teaching, the uses of words in combination in sentences provide the gifts of individuals to others who creatively receive them, the satisfaction of communicative needs and attributions of value, at a finer grain than that of words taken alone. There are really two different processes going on—the meta-linguistic gift of words through naming and the definition (upon which masculation and exchange are constructed), and language which uses gift processes to facilitate on-going communication, the development of the social subject and object, her community, her world and world view. The existence of different levels allows individual giving and receiving on the basis of social giving and receiving, an interplay of 'grains.'

Things that are important or valuable require our creative-receptive attention. We appreciate the value they already have, while at the same time we attribute value to them. Appreciation and attribution are similar to creative receiving and giving. Gratitude is an aspect of both. We use things to satisfy needs, and we attribute value to others (or to ourselves) by satisfying needs.

[2]In reading about the philosophical standpoint of women's caring labor, I finally recognized what fit for me into Marx's phrase about language as practical consciousness that exists for others and, therefore, really for me. Caring labor is practical consciousness—language is one of its general aspects. For the perspective of care, see Sara Ruddick, *Maternal Thinking*, Ballantine Books, New York, 1990. In a more specifically economic context, Nancy Folbre, *Who Pays for the Kids?*, Routledge, London and New York, 1994.

The many values of the world for the community of humans are registered in language. A similar process causes the exchange value of commodities to be registered in money. When we receive the satisfaction of our needs by others (and the consequent implication of our value for them), we can appreciate what has been given to us, and the others as its source, in gratitude. We can also ignore the source, or see ourselves as the cause of our own good. In linguistic (and other sign-based) communication, we can share a point of view and attribute value or give attention to the same things, selecting them as relevant from our on-going experience and using the social gifts that take the place of those material (or immaterial) gifts or givens.

What we give value to is in our focus; we direct our creative receptivity towards it. What we do not give value to remains outside our focus. Our motivation in giving value to something depends upon our needs and upon a synthesis of previous experiences and previous attributions and appreciations of value. The collective means of attributing value, which is a collective gift (the word), hovers in our minds in easy access for our use in on-going experience whenever the need for it arises. That need is originally interpersonal, though we can also use words to satisfy our own communitary communicative needs when thinking alone, attributing socially mediated value to various parts of our experience, and foregrounding them in the present when we need to.

Value, a Meta Gift

Value can be interpreted as a kind of meta gift, a giving of attention to something so as to cause or alter the giving of further gifts. It is a singling out of something upon which creatively receptive attention is focused. We also often attribute to the object of our attention the quality 'something for others and, therefore, for ourselves.' Since giftgiving has been invisible and unvalued, we have not thought of connecting value with the process of giftgiving, and it has therefore remained mysterious.

161

Exchange value has taken over the concept of value, becoming its 'sample.' In exchange, the other-oriented aspect of giftgiving does not dissolve, but it is hidden and instrumentalized for the purposes of the ego. Giftgiving is embedded in exchange and made to contradict itself. This logical two-step requires us to measure our satisfaction of other's needs against their satisfaction of our own, and both against a standard which is common to all. All needs then become dependent upon this contradictory process for their satisfaction.

Exchange becomes an ever-present fact of life, and we give value to *it* as the prerequisite for the survival of all. By doing this, we hide and discredit giftgiving, thereby denying the other-oriented gift-based aspect of value. When this aspect is made invisible, value cannot be understood correctly, and the connections between exchange value and other cultural values are concealed and denied. Value is divided and conquered. Only by giving value to giftgiving can we begin to solve the puzzle of value, restoring its other-oriented content.[3]

Value is basically a gift (re)distributing device. It is a gift of energy and attention *to* gifts, which helps us select some over others for other people and for ourselves. By overemphasizing exchange value, we distort this collective device for distribution—away from giving and needs and towards the relatively limited number of things that are valuable to the processes of exchange and the market. Egotism and the value (and attention) we give to it can be seen as effects of preparing

[3] 'Use value' is a category of the market, defined in opposition to 'exchange value' and similarly taken away from giftgiving. Gifts are goods with a source and a destination, part of a human relation. It is from the point of view of the exchange paradigm that we see something as a use value, having a generalized and indifferent potential to satisfy a human need—'nameable' with money, objectified as property. Use value is the pre-requisite for exchange value, which at the same time renders the product extraneous to the gift process, outside the giving 'grain.' From the point of view of the gift paradigm, use values would be part of a more complete process involving people. While it is true that, after exchange, people use products to satisfy their needs, the relation to the producer as the original source of the products is usually broken. Moreover, in capitalism, producers do not produce use values as gifts but as objects people will pay to use. Gratitude is given to the market, to the exchange process itself. That the gift logic is still strong is shown by the 'brand name' phenomenon which identifies the source of goods in a particular company as if it were a gift, reinstating an artificial human relation with the 'giver' so the 'receivers' will buy more. Bargains, sales and give-aways have a similar dynamic.

for and practicing those processes. We have been accustomed to looking at this the other way around—as if exchange and the market were natural outcomes of human egotism and greed. This very view and the values (the re-distribution of gifts) it promotes help to maintain the monopoly of the exchange processes.

Value Modes

Value is both attributed and appreciated—freely given to people, things and words, and received from them. It may involve a process of self-stimulation in the sense that we give value to something by singling it out, focusing on it. Then we turn our creative receptivity upon it, appreciating its value. We may then forget our part in the attribution, which was freely given. Selecting something among other things, foregrounding it, adapting it to needs and giving it to others for their needs are processes by which we attribute value to something and appreciate its value. That value is also transferred to others and their needs by implication, as we give things to them satisfying their needs. (We can also attribute-appreciate their value directly, simply by giving them our attention.) Giving something a gift-substitute, mutually including others in its regard, also gives value and appreciates value in that kind of thing and in the mutually included others.

There are four major modes of value attribution-appreciation: nurturing, language, masculation and exchange. I believe two of them are the norm (nurturing and language) and two are distortions (masculation and exchange). As we look at the norm we are better able to understand the distortions. As we look at the distortions and their consequences, we are also better able to understand the norm.

Nurturing Value Attribution

Happiness—not the pursuit of happiness—is not only a right but an epistemological necessity, if gratitude is a basic template for knowledge. 'Grasping' is usually associated with understanding and considered necessary for knowledge, but it is only a small specific part of receiving—made necessary by scarcity. By depriving people of abundance, of the possibility of receiving and giving, we deprive them of their human being. *Homo donans* (and *recipiens*) precedes *homo sapiens*.[4] That is because it is gifts that we know, and our knowledge is our grateful response to them, whether they are milk from our mothers' breasts, experiential givens, words and sentences, topics of conversation, kind actions, babies, rain storms, new cars, works of art or blueberry pies. (We are grateful to know negative things, as well as positive, because that knowledge is useful for our coping.) If someone satisfies our needs, we can appreciate her value to us and attribute value to her. Part of our gratitude is a disposition to care for things which have particularly nurtured us. We do this not as an exchange but, momentarily, taking upon ourselves the giver as model, we nurture in our turns.

Nurturing transfers value to the receiver by implication. The giver often self-effaces as the source making it appear that the value or importance of the receiver is the cause of the gift. For example, a mother believes she nurtures her baby because the baby is important, not because she attributes value to her. Yet, if she did not attribute value to her and nurture her, the baby would die. Value is thus a useful projection, both of the individual and of the culture and community. The fabric of everyday life is made up of enumerable attributions of value and it is perhaps that reason that it has recently (at last) attracted attention of philosophers.

Part of the way we give value to others is by eliciting, honoring, enhancing, specifying, educating their needs. Mothers, for example, can be fascinated when their children

---

[4]Food sharing practices were widespread in prehistory among the early hominids. Masculated archaeologists typically see hunting as more important for the development of man.

begin eating solid food, trying different things to see what they like. Teaching itself can be seen as enhancing others' needs to know about different kinds of things.

The knowledge of the means of nurturing that used to be passed down through the women's line from grandmothers to mothers and daughters attributed value and appreciated it in material culture. These values and the manner of attributing them are being lost as nurturing is being absorbed into exchange. Advertising now educates our desires not the love, intelligence, or other-oriented, need-satisfying imagination of our grandmothers. The value of the receiver is not implied directly or maternally but only through the market—as a 'deserver' or as the responsibility of the care taker state.

We attribute value to things we think may be particularly useful for others or ourselves. Then we appreciate the value of those useful things.[5] Attribution of value is itself a gift of our disposition to behave with care towards something, and it is an element of our gratitude. Conversely, appreciation (of which gratitude is an aspect) is an element of the attribution of value. The two attitudes are intertwined, though attribution is more active and reflects giving, while appreciation is more receptive and reflects receiving.[6]

[5] V. N. Volosinov, *Marxism and the Philosophy of Language*, New York, Seminar Press, 1973 [1930] says, "Every stage in the development of a society has its own special and restricted circle of items, which alone have access to that society's attention, and which can be endowed with evaluative accentuation by that attention. Only items within that circle will achieve sign formation and become objects in semiotic communication." Any such item ". . .must be associated with the vital socio-economic prerequisites of that group's existence." pp. 21-23. I am thinking also of the prehistoric cave paintings, which (it is now believed) were done through mouth painting—spitting the color onto the walls—as is still done by some Australian aboriginal cave painters. The paint is spewed upon the wall (attributed), then it is viewed. The analogy, which seems to me stronger than painting with hands or brushes, comes from the physiological alteration of breath and saliva that must come from spewing the paint. An acceleration of breath or an increase of saliva might serve as a physiological 'anchor' for value accents or attributions, which are always taking place in our on-going experience, and of which we are not even conscious. The attribution, appreciation (and projection) of value through language thus would coincide with emphasis given through alterations of the breath. Breathing also involves receiving (inhaling) and giving (exhaling).
[6] Michel Foucault in his chapter "Exchanging" in *The Order of Things, An Archaeology of the Human Sciences*, Vintage Books, New York, 1994[1966] discusses value from within the exchange paradigm as 'attributive,' 'appreciative' and 'articulative.'

Language Value Attribution

Things become relevant to humans by our use of them in relation to needs. Needs proliferate and diversify according to the ways in which they are satisfied. They are also, to some extent, identified by the things which satisfy them.[7] In language, we attribute some of the co-municative qualitative value of a kind of thing to a word which takes the place of a (usually) nonverbal sample, and functions as a substitute gift for use in forming human relations and interactions. The thing or kind of thing give way as a possible gift for the moment and the word (which also has a value-as-position in the *langue*) becomes the vehicle for its value in communication, i.e., in establishing or modifying human relations regarding that kind of thing. The word becomes the vehicle for the value of things in their use for establishing or modifying human relations. Because each kind of thing (and therefore each word) has a value which is qualitatively different from the others in that it is related to different human needs,[8] the combination of a few words according to gift patterns in any statement or proposition can also serve to convey (give) specific information.

We select parts of our experience as givens to which to give our attention, and we give new gifts by rearranging the old. We satisfy the listener's communicative needs at the moment and, therefore, our own as well. We can remember what was selected and emphasized in our co-munication, storing this information to apply to future material or communicative needs. Not codes

[7]See Karl Marx, *Critique of Political Economy*, trans. N.I. Stone, Charles H. Kerr & Co., Chicago 1904 [1859],(pp. 274-292), for a discussion of the relational character of production and consumption, the specification of needs through the production that satisfies them, as well as the specification of the production by the kinds of needs that are to be satisfied.

[8]I believe this relation to different needs underlies the 'purely differential' values Saussure recognized as the abstract organizing principle of the *langue*. Different kinds of things are used in different gift processes, to satisfy different kinds of needs, and they give way to different words which take their place as communicative gifts. Cases of hononymy and synonymy are not problematic as long as the mutual exclusion is maintained on the phonetic plane and the needs satisfied are clearly different from each other. The mutually exclusive value-as-position which is found in the *langue* is repeated in the structure of institutions deriving from masculation like the OBN or private property. Hierarchies have structures similar to those of terms which are superordinate or subordinate according to generality and inclusiveness. For example, a superordinate such as 'plant' is more general than, and includes subordinates such as 'flower,' 'tree,' 'vine,' while 'flower' is a superordinate which is more general than, and includes 'rose,' 'daisy,' 'mimosa.'

but the logic and practice of giftgiving are the basis of our understanding.

A code is only a collection of abstract marks. In the cryptographers sense, it serves to disguise, rather than express the truth. Language, like life, is need-driven. The ability to satisfy others' needs is the aspect of life that creates society and makes us evolve culturally—and eventually, perhaps, biologically. In other words, we use our gift for another purpose—not to get back an equivalent as in exchange, but to alter the others' relation to the environment, bringing something forward as a value for them in the present. This allows us to share our relation to it. Each of us knows what the other knows or appreciates as a value for the moment. We select that part of our experience as social beings on the basis of what has been selected to satisfy the needs of others before us as evidenced in the lexicon. By giving substitute gifts to each other, we give a social value to the same thing together at the moment, and we can, therefore, co-ordinate our actions and attitudes towards it.[9]

The selections we make in our on-going experience are similar to the selection process we perform in developing concepts. But in discourse (because we are satisfying present and contingent communicative needs, rather than the general process-needs of the concept or the meta linguistic needs of the definition), we are practicing giftgiving at many other levels. Our on-going experiences and interactions with each other bring things into focus verbally and nonverbally (making them 'givens') and consequently push other things into the background all the time (making them 'not-givens' for the present). Even saying something as simple as 'the girl hit the ball,' picks out part of a complex experience. We could have said instead 'the sky was blue above the baseball field' and/or 'a mockingbird was singing.' If we

[9]The postal metaphor: sender (encoder) package (message) and receiver (decoder) is giftgiving seen as 'mail.' A code is a shared collection of 'marks' which one group 'has' and another group 'has not.' Encoding and decoding, sending and receiving a message are metaphors of packaging and opening a gift. In fact, another locus for the gift economy in our society (besides mothering) is the sending and receiving of celebratory gifts on birthdays, Christmas etc. See David Cheal on celebratory gifts, *The Gift Economy*, Routledge, London, 1988.

go on to say 'the ball hit the window' we are building on the givens which are the gifts of 'the girl hit the ball.'

Communicative needs (and desires) arise for relating ourselves to each other (confirming each other as valuable) with regard to a focus on aspects of things which may not be obvious to the other person already. In fact, we might consider our attention as telling us something like, 'There might be a gift there.' Satisfying their communicative needs focuses some aspects of a situation for the interlocutors. It gives them a common valued foreground and a (more or less) common un-valued background. Together, speakers and listeners consider some elements of a situation relevant and others irrelevant. They attend to the same things. Then, what has been backgrounded in one instance can be foregrounded in another. When we satisfy the others' communicative needs regarding something—what we have seen as a gift to them in relation to us—they are brought to participate with us in the present.[10] A relationship is established as shared in regard to the gift which the speaker has given but the listener who 'has' most of the same words could have given (different in this from satisfying material needs where we give something the other person does *not* have). The listener's relation is established by the speaker but, perhaps as unspoken potential, has as much influence on behavior as the overt part of the communication.

A shared interaction is also the matrix of exchange—where others show they give value to our product by giving up an equal amount of money. Then money (with its abstract social quality) becomes the hidden but powerful model for our understanding of language, and of life. That is not only because money is the 'child' of language, but because of the actual similarity of the processes— of giving value by giving something (else).

[10]I think what semioticians call 'natural signs' can also be interpreted as gifts, even though the behaviors in which they are useful for animals maybe less complex than our own. Flowers by their color and odor say to insects, "Here is nectar." The color and odor are secondary gifts, which lead to the material gift of the nectar. The gift depends on the receiver for its existence as a gift. The black cloud is a gift (a natural sign) for anyone who can use it to get home before the rain starts. The tree falling in the forest is a gift to anyone who can use it as such. I recently heard an environmental song about trees falling in the rainforest.

Both speech and experience can occasion further attributions of value and further communicative needs. Moreover, the kinds of things we attend to, the kinds of value we discover (and attribute), depend on an on-going synthesis of our previous life experiences, which may be similar to or very different from other people's experiences. What appears irrelevant in one moment may become relevant in the next, or to another person (and with regard to something else), so that actually everything is always valuable *potentior* (even when presently excluded as irrelevant).

This possibility makes experience like an immanent Garden of Eden, from which we gather and share the fruits only a few at a time whenever we need them, plucking them from its fantastic abundance. The material scarcity in which many people live hides the gift character of life, exiling them beyond the wall of the Garden. Restoring abundance would allow value to be bestowed again according to the collective and individual experience, rather than pitting the individual against the collective (as happens in scarcity-based exchange). Our economics could be in alignment with the humanizing and bonding part of our language, rather than being at cross purposes with it because of the excessive value we (unconsciously) collectively attribute to the definition and masculation.

Masculated Value Attribution

The kind of ego that is useful for exchange is actually the masculated ego. The value system that promotes this ego reinforces it through economic rewards and punishments, having and not-having kinds and quantities of properties. The ego is vulnerable to the advertising which educates its desires. Value may appear to be transferred to a person who receives the satisfaction of such desires or needs through the market. However, it is actually being transferred to the seller of the object, who has caused the consumer to buy the product through a manipulation of the truth. The kind of value-as-position which is acquired by a person through comparative 'havings' can be understood as status and does not really satisfy the gift-based subjective needs of the individual. The consumer always needs to have more, because his/her having does not actually give him/her value, but contributes more economic value to the seller.

While it may sometimes be true that without an instrument of technology (or phallic tool) men may not know the objective world (because they, and it, are outside the 'grain' of giving and receiving), women are more often inside that 'grain' because of our caregiving roles. We are, therefore, more likely to turn our knowledge as gratitude upon the givens of our experience. Without the object, there would be no instrument. Women are objects as well as subjects. For example, the penis and the vagina are the psychological archetypes for the instrument of knowledge and the object of knowledge. If the purpose of sexuality is other than giving and receiving, satisfying one another's needs, instrumental 'knowledge' treats the 'object' as if it were a nonliving, noncreatively receptive thing to be forcefully 'penetrated.' The 'gratitude' experienced in this case by the masculated phallic knower is only for the reinforcement of his ego, in a one-many over-taking earth-dominating position. It is not other-oriented gratitude or knowledge. In fact, it is more like receiving the property transfer of exchange.

Much phallic instrumental knowledge of the objective world has been inspired by the ego profit motive and reflects the limitations of the focus with which it is seen. Backgrounding the human needs of the many has given it the destructive power of acquisition by force or of nonnurturing indifference. Those who continue to view reality through the giftgiving grain oppose the products of scientific knowledge which threaten the possibility of all to give and receive. No amount of purported benign uses of nuclear technology, genetic manipulation or chemical poisons can bring the negative aspects of those technologies into the giftgiving grain, or convince those who care for needs that they are really gifts to humanity.

Women can gratefully know the vagina, the 'object,' internally without the phallic instrument. It is interesting to

170

think that if women are reified 'things,' the vagina would correspond to the philosopher's supposedly unknowable 'thing in itself.' Then in sex it would become for another and therefore really for ourselves as well.

As caretakers of things for others, we know more about them than those who do not satisfy others' needs with them. We can point out the healing plants, the caring ways, as well as the flaws in the arguments for violence. Our life energy has often gone into the care and maintenance of others' bodies and our own directly, without exchange and without an interposing definition or evaluation based on exchange.

Exchange Value

Exchange value is communicative (linguistic) value in the kind of distorted communication that is exchange. Exchange is like definition which locates something with respect to its name and thus with respect to everything else. The fact that something has a name depends on the cultural value of that kind of thing for human beings. The specific name it has depends on the totality of the *langue*. That differential relation has become quantitatively ordered in prices.

The language value-attributing process is used again in exchange, when we each give the same value to the products we are exchanging on the basis of their general social value. We do it every time we say one pound of beans = one dollar. The fact that one person gives up the beans and the other gives up the dollar demonstrates that they give the same value to beans and to a dollar. The beans have that price as a function of all the other exchanges happening on the market at that time, particularly those regarding beans. Similarly the use of words depends upon how they are being used by others speaking that language.

The principle of exchange is *do ut des* (I give so that you will give). The principle of gift-based communication is similar, except for the watershed difference that giftgiving is mutually inclusive while exchange is mutually exclusive. In gift-based

171

communication, one gives so that the other may give—attention and value to the topic, as well as to the speaker and the listener themselves. Both speaker and listener have a need for a means to be able to give value to something together; words serve this purpose and the interlocutors give value by giving them. Agreement upon a price allows exchangers to give equal value. The consequences of the co-munication and the attribution of the same value by speakers and listeners and by sellers and buyers are different because exchange is mutually exclusive where verbal communication is mutually inclusive. In exchange, the material *do ut des* principle requires that the receiver give back an equivalent to the giver. Giftgiving unilaterally satisfies the other's need.

In our altruism we give the same value so as to establish common relations between us as human beings regarding things. But in exchange this altruism is used to serve our egotism. The very similarity of the processes has hidden the giftgiving altruistic side of communication behind exchange, given that exchange has become such an important activity for everyone in our society. We only give under the constraint that the other gives an equivalent, because living in a system based on scarcity and the market, we consider ourselves in terms of a quantity of things (or of exchange values) which are necessary for our survival.

Everything we give or spend, every value we attribute, seems to take away from that totality, assessable as salary—the 'living' that we make. Exchange is like a language in which things are actually 'given up' when words are spoken (and the words are 'given up,' as well). We are always calculating whether we have or are enough, as if we had performance (or competence) anxiety. There is an economic value-assessment of human beings, an economic (masculated) name, a salary, which is 'given' to us. It seems that people don't exist or deserve to exist unless they are masculated, and if they don't exist they don't deserve to eat—though perhaps they can eat anyway, if they correspond to a masculated 'one' like a wife does.

Both individually and socially, we invest our energy in what we consider valuable, even when this is to our own or others' degradation and detriment. For example, we invest energy and money in drugs and violence. Individuals attribute value to these activities, perhaps because of physiological pleasure and short-term ego reinforcement. Even if it does not consciously approve of these individual activities, society gives value to the kind of ego with which they are in alignment. In fact, hedonism fits with masculation—with ego-orientation not with other-orientation. It also seems that, by amassing large amounts of capital, we can have more value than others in an almost unlimited way, a consideration which provides the artificial ego with the kind of validation it needs to continue to amass more. Power over others, which appears to be the prerogative of the sample position, is used to provide the rewards which motivate the masculated ego. Interactions based on giftgiving are more genuinely satisfying, however, and they are often co-opted as the 'spoils' of success.

Exchange value seems to be the most valuable, or even the only kind of value. The society based on it purports to provide an access to the general good by promoting the sum of ego-oriented values as its goal. Of course, this leaves out other-oriented values and people, as well as those who simply don't succeed. The OBN's view of *homo economicus* as bringing about the general good has recently been challenged by feminist economists.[11] I believe that seeing exchange value as the main or only kind of value prevents us from a genuinely radical criticism of *homo economicus*. As an alternative, I am proposing that we consider as primary the cultural value of things for humans as created through giftgiving and expressed in language, which functions according to giftgiving. Exchange value can then be seen as a distortion of the value-giving process.

[11]The Journal of the International Association for Feminist Economics (IAFFE) *Feminist Economics*, Diana Strassman ed., began in 1995 and is published by Routledge, New York.

Re-present-ation

Language continues to maintain our giftgiving way even while we are doing our experiencing in an economy based on exchange and thus are no longer co-municating materially. Technology, motivated by profit, expands perception in another direction, beyond giftgiving to a kind of inhuman objectivity. It sees below the level of possible gifts to sense impressions understood as electro-chemical reactions, and above the level of gifts through telescopes that allow us to see the origins of the universe. It also works against the giftgiving co-munity, using its knowledge to create conventional, biological, chemical and nuclear armaments. While the levels of 'objective reality' discovered by technology beyond giftgiving may sometimes be utilized for human need-satisfying endeavors, they are often also used to great harm. They are patriarchal exchange-driven (not gift-driven) enterprises. By embracing the nongiftgiving grain, which indeed produces a useful income in the exchange economy for researchers, academics can discount those who embrace the giftgiving grain as 'naive realists.' (Because of scarcity, the 'naive realists' anyway do not usually have access to the technology that would allow them to see things differently.) When giftgiving has been drained from the 'present' by exchange the link between life and language is obscured. Then re-present-ation, not patriarchy appears to post modern thinkers as the reason for tyranny.

Linguistic value and economic value both have to do with re-presentation—that is, with communication through systems of substitute gifts. We have to recognize their commonalities in order to understand value itself. It was in looking at these commonalities that I began to see masculation as an off-shoot of representation, a mis-representation of the identity of the boy—making him in its image, overvaluing him because of it, and then broadcasting that mechanism into the society at large. (It is as if a broken piece of the movie projector were being projected onto the screen along with the movie.) Masculation is a distortion of the value-attributing process—on a par with exchange and

174

occurring prior to it. It feeds back through exchange and mysogyny into re-present-ation over emphasizing the 'one-many' and hierarchial over-taking aspects and denying giftgiving.

Exchange value is nurturing (or gift) value filtered through the anti-gift process of exchange, modeled on masculation. Masculation de-values giftgiving and instead gives value to the one-many position, its incarnations in hierarchies, and competition to be first. Many of the gifts and much of the value given by masculation to its priorities actually flow through it transitively from the nurturers, who give preferentially to males and to the masculation process itself. Norm-al, undistorted nurturing gives value directly to needs, to the receivers of its gifts and to the means for the satisfaction of the needs. Language provides co-munity value-based, fine-grained verbal giftgiving, which mediates finely tuned interaction and co-operation, creating the value given by the many working together on common endeavors and contributing to the individuated physical and psychological subjectivities of the co-municators.

We are considering noneconomic value as the concealed norm, rather than a sub-case of economic value. Grounding our idea of noneconomic value in linguistic value, our idea of language in giftgiving and our idea of linguistic value in the varied importance of the gifts of the world to the community, gives us a different perspective from which to look, not only at economic value, but also at what are usually called 'moral' values. By disconnecting the different kinds of values from each other and denying giftgiving (or at most considering it a curiosity due to an irrational propensity towards nurturing), patriarchy has imposed the values of masculation upon the society at large. It practices domination by categorization, repeating everywhere in different terms, the masculation that was done to boys through their gender definition when they were categorized as separate and superior. In this situation, 'moral' values are an attempt to regulate the mutually exclusive interests away from harm, to mitigate their negative effects, and to reintroduce giftgiving after the fact in an auxiliary way. Instead, giftgiving rather than masculation is the basis for creating a society where everyone can care for everyone free from harm.

Other cultural values, such as aesthetic, historical, spiritual, and ethnic values, are originally located within a context created by nurturing and language, but are usually now altered by masculation and exchange. What cultural values might be beyond that alteration will be seen when we are finally able to dismantle patriarchy. However, many of them already contain the hope for a better world. They are gifts of the imagination which heal some of the suffering endured by humanity throughout the centuries.

Shift into Exchange

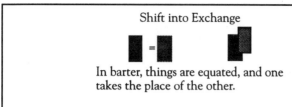

In barter, things are equated, and one takes the place of the other.

In monetized exchange, products and money are equated, and money substitutes for each of the products in turn.

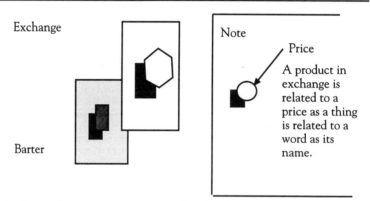

Exchange for money, as a process takes the place of barter.

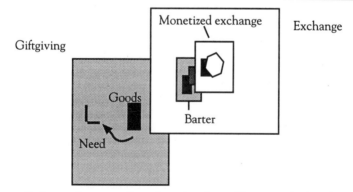

Exchange for money has taken the place of barter, and takes the place of giftgiving, which gives way though it continues to exist.

Figure 15. Exchange over-takes giftgiving and barter.

Chapter 11
Shifting into Exchange

When we use words instead of material gifts to communicate, we shift to another plane that we have created—language, which works according to similar co-municative principles. But when we shift from material giftgiving to economic exchange, we actually shift to the logic of substitution in place of the logic of the gift. The logic of substitution (which has a linguistic function) in a self-similar process, itself takes the place of the logic of giftgiving. Because of the double, two-level substitution of money for a product and of one logic for another, we cover more ground than we realize; there is a wider gap between giftgiving and exchange than there is even between things and words. (This gap is filled on the one hand with 'deserving' and on the other with correspondence between word and thing—perhaps what we sometimes call 'truth.')[1] There is a move from the micro to the macroscopic through the self-similar structures of substitution and exchange. (See figure 15.)

The alignment of self-similar structures creates a sort of mind warp, a hole in the roof, a breach with a strong updraft which draws us up into the 'new' mindset of exchange. Then this new mindset or paradigm attracts the attribution of value to itself. (It is only 'new' as opposed to giftgiving, which preceded it ontogenetically and phylogenetically.)

Because of the similarity and self-referentiality at the different levels, we give at least the amount of credence to the substitution of the whole logic of giftgiving by the logic of substitution that we do to the simple substitution of one thing for another. The new grosser-grained material level is familiar. We

---

[1]Actually telling the truth should be seen as other-oriented communication, satisfying others' communicative needs to know about a situation in order to satisfy their other complex needs. Lying is ego-oriented. Like exchange, it uses the other for the satisfaction of the needs of the ego. False advertising is a lie which promotes an exchange. 'Objective' truth, the correspondence between words and things, might be seen as a reflection of equal exchange, outside the giving and receiving grain.

know unconsciously how the fine-grained micro level works, because we are using that substitution process all the time when we learn language and define things. We did shift to a new level when we gained language, and having language has mediated everything we are. The similarity to masculation of receiving a new 'name' in the price, of being given away by the 'producer' and out of giftgiving into the new logic of substitution, again sets up reciprocal confirmations. Exchange draws us in, and the exchange paradigm takes over, taking the place of other possible models for our concepts of human interactions.[2]

If superior value were not being continually attributed to exchange, it would not continue to exist as such. Nor would the masculated male continue to exist as such if superior value were not attributed to him. Giftgiving, and the extension and valuing of the gift paradigm, would make exchange unnecessary. So actually, at present, giftgiving is sustaining its 'competitor' (competition is of course an aspect of the exchange, not of the gift paradigm). The logic and the practice of exchange need this attribution of value, and everyone satisfies this need, even those practicing the gift paradigm. Having been given superior value, exchange becomes the only way to achieve survival—occupying the field, pervading our lives, and marginalizing or excluding its alternatives.

The social institution of exchange for money lets us shift paradigms every time we buy and sell. The shift itself becomes so common we do not notice it; it permeates our lives. Both the 'new' paradigm and the shift become natural and normal for us. The 'old' paradigm of free goods and services is dis-counted and valueless by contrast, though it continues to function.

Ego-oriented people attribute value to exchange, not only because they need it to survive, but also because by engaging in it they can individually deserve and receive extra value, appearing to be self-made (the source of their own superiority). Moreover,

[2]The new naming also happens in fundamentalist Christianity with baptism and with being re-born, which is similar to acquiring a new (exchange) value by relating oneself to the general equivalent. It is also similar to masculation and almost creates a third gender identity, with its own mandates for behavior.

180

the masculated pattern of exchange repeats their own over-coming. Other-oriented people also attribute value to exchange by logical consequence, because they attribute value not only to themselves but to others who need exchange to survive. Exchange occupies center stage, and it also attracts attention, because it promotes competition to which visibility is useful. The seller must elicit the choice of the buyer through the visibility and attractiveness of the product-in-exchange.

The substitution of giving—precluding it—makes the transaction of exchange adversarial. Since the other person is doing the same thing in a different phase of the process (giving money while we are giving a product, for example), she is our delayed or anticipated reflection and like ourselves, in scarcity is always ready to get our product for less or sell her product to us for more—even to cheat us. In exchange, when we 'put ourselves in the other's place,' we recognize our adversarial interests. A mechanism of our altruism thwarts itself by the realization that the other person needs to cheat us, as we need to cheat her. It would be in each of our mutually exclusive 'interests.'

The shift into exchange cross-validates with masculation, so it attracts some of the value which is given to masculation and vice versa. Like masculation, it cancels and invalidates the giftgiving source, making its practicer appear to stand alone. It sets the standard for the economic field and often even for 'reality' itself. What is similar to exchange appears to be not only more valuable but real and normal, while everything else is unconfirmed and uncertain (another way women and giftgiving are discounted). Exchange deals with evident value overtly, names it, accumulates and stores it as money, foresees its social fluctuations. It seems to be the crux of the matter. In other words, at this level the exchange process attracts the gift of value. We move back and forth from appreciating it to attributing value to it, contradictorily receiving from it—from the process—and giving to it. We breathe the living breath of value into the exchange process, like God breathing the breath of life into Adam. The value given to exchange by those who participate in it, as well as those outside it, is influenced by market forces and finally accumulated in capital, which provides the rewards for having and the punishment for not having that motivate the whole process.

The importance of exchange is overdetermined, as might be expected, but giftgiving too would be receiving value and confirmation from many different areas, if its gifts and its value were not being drained into exchange. Many processes can be interpreted as giftgiving-and-receiving—from sexuality to birth, to breastfeeding, to breathing, to Mother Nature dropping her handkerchief for us to pick up (in windfalls and synchronicities), and to all the many ways of nurturing we have mentioned at all levels. These can be and are symbolized in many different ways, beginning with Mother Earth and Sister Water, the cornucopia and the grail. However, giftgiving is often concealed because exchange (like masculation) is in competition with giftgiving and parasitically depends upon it for the value that is attributed to it. Exchange needs to be in the forefront, to disguise giftgiving or blot it out, and to seem to receive value because it deserves it.

Exchange actually needs its value to appear to be revealed as its own rather than as attributed by others. That is, it needs to seem to have the source of its value in its own double logic, as if it were only getting back an equivalent of what it, exchange, 'gave.' It appears to re-institute giftgiving at its own (partial) meta level, and we may be led to believe that exchange is a very beneficial gift to the community. In fact, so-called 'developing' communities often have this idea when they begin to raise crops for sale instead of for their own consumption. The initial increase in prosperity and 'independence' appear to be almost magical, but they are soon off-set by the defects of dependence on a market economy. This dependence actually privileges only the very few, while making it appear to the others that their own defects—lack of intelligence, ineffective strategies, wrong choices, bad luck, etc.—are the reasons for their failure. Blaming individuals (instead of the system) for their failure allows excessive value to continue to be given to exchange and to the market.

Since exchange appears to be the only source of goods for survival in an economy based on scarcity, it does seem to deserve all our attention. However, the system has to create the scarcity as the prerequisite of exchange—because giftgiving in abundance subverts exchange by making it unnecessary. As the monetized economy expands, it occupies the space that previously was available for gift production and consumption, making it difficult for those not participating in exchange to survive. Natural resources are employed or destroyed (intentionally or unintentionally), so that they cannot be used as a source of livelihood for those who traditionally were nurtured by them. The economic marginalization of Native Americans and the destruction of the huge herds of buffalo on the North American plains, which were the free source of livelihood of many tribes, are one tragic example among many.

By showing how exchange is parasitic on the gifts of the paradigm which it hides and denies, we can finally see that it is not the primary source of economic well-being and that, even on its own criteria, it does not *deserve* the attention and the value we give to it. Giving value to a wider meta view for the good of all, we can shift the paradigm back from exchange to giftgiving.

Chapter 12
Giving Value to Exchange

Giving to the Market

Exchange does not itself give value, though it may appear to give through the process of monetary definition—by including something in the category of things which are exchangeable for money. Whatever is included in that category actually receives value that is given to it, and to the category as a whole from the outside. Not only is value attributed to things in that category because people want to buy them, who then give up their money in order to receive them, but value is given by everyone to the process as a whole (as they do to the process of masculation), to that part of it which is the category 'products on the market,' and to all the intricacies of capitalism that are built upon it.

In giftgiving, value passes transitively from giver to receiver, but in exchange the value of the gift does not pass to the other because the satisfaction of the need passes back to each exchanger. The implication of the exchange is not that the receiver of the product or her needs are important, but instead that the initiator of the exchange and her needs are important. The money which is given to the seller allows a product having that exchange value to return to the buyer—who was a seller previously and thus de-serves the return. If the buyer does not receive 'her money's worth,' more of the value passes to the seller—which may be another part of the motivation for cheating.

Buying in order to sell attempts to increase the amount of value which will be given to the product by others and, consequently, the amount of money which will be given up for it. For instance, by transporting a product to another location, we may expect more value will be attributed to it by others. Its rarity may even make it a prototype or sample product, and as such, highly desirable. Commerce is made possible because products are placed in positions and given aspects of availability, durability, convenience, etc.—by which others will give more value to them from the outside. The threat of unsatisfied needs also causes people to give extra value to products. Scarcity serves this increase in the attribution of value and is often created for that purpose. The creation of scarcity is euphemistically called 'increasing the demand.'

The rarity of the product seems to enhance its owner's value—and the buyer pays for that, repeating the pattern. Many products also are given value as 'marks' of (masculated) status which increases the value the buyer gives to him or herself through the exchange. All these attributions of value influence the buyers' priorities and 'marginal' decisions. Her attributions of value seem to be expressed in her choices, which are all ultimately interpreted by economists in terms of her self-interest. They are, of course, choices taking place within the parameters of exchange, with the market as a 'given.'

Being in the category of exchangeable things makes products available to receive the attribution of value from the outside. Products on the market are given more value than abundant necessities, such as air and water, or things that cannot be sold, because they are broken or defective or overly abundant. Being on the market also reveals the value that products already have, which has been given to them by others in the past—a value which is usually calculated and expressed as costs of production. The market puts things—and people—in a decontextualized position where their value is 'revealed' by substitution, and where value is given to them by contrast with what has no exchange value. Bringing something to the market is thus similar to attending to something about which we will communicate—with regard to which we will alter our human relations—appreciating its value and attributing value to it. It is a slow motion replay of semiotization on a material plane.

In the market, we alter our mutually exclusive relations of property regarding that particular product, transferring the product to a new owner while keeping its value in the form of money. In language, we alter our mutually inclusive relations regarding the things we are attending to, creating a shared experience and a common ground on the basis of shared substitute gifts. Altering our mutual human relations in a consistent and coordinated way with regard to something reveals and utilizes its general relation to the group. And vice versa, we use its general relation to the group to include ourselves, altering our relations to it in the moment, by making them specific.

In the market, we usually bring things physically to a place, for example, a store, where they will be categorized as valuable to the human relational process of (distorted) material communication, exchange, and given up. In speech, we usually alter our relations to things using the words to which they specifically give way and give value showing that those things are already appreciated as valuable to the human relational process of linguistic communication and, thus, to the communicators. In exchange, the product enters the category 'valuable' as it becomes related to money. In language, something first becomes a value in the culture, which leads to semiotization. It is socially related to other things of the same kind (and to a word as its name) and is capable of being explicitly related to the words of present communicators. Its categorization is part of its relation to the many, just as is the categorization of a product on the market as an exchange value. Value is appreciated and attributed by the exchanger or interlocutor, to products or to things related to their names. The first case provides the category of exchange value, the second provides the cultural or semantic value of each different category.

The attribution of value to a category or to the market is similar to the attribution of value to hierarchies with their different levels (for example, we attribute value to the army as a whole from the outside). Hierarchies transfer value and goods upwards. They are vertical strings of masculating definitions. The many give upwards both to the privileged categories and to their privileged sample 'ones.' The structures of exchange and

187

hierarchy often combine (for example, in the military or the church), where those inside the valued category are supported by those outside (for example, through taxes or tithes). A hierarchical structure channels commands downwards and the obedience and services of the many upwards, towards ever higher levels of ones.

The value of particular products is revealed by their position within the totality of things on the market, and value is given to the totality from the outside by free labor and other gift practices.[1] Value is attributed freely to the market because in scarcity the market seems to be the source of all goods; survival depends upon it. Other possibilities for survival are few. Scavenging from the garbage and begging are alternatives which are viewed as socially valueless ways of surviving, and so-called 'self-sustainable communities' are relatively new and isolated developments. Thus, value for the market becomes the sample of the concept of all value.

Value is given to the market from outside by everyone, but it is usually appreciated as coming from exchange, from the market itself, or from the products themselves. The fetishism of commodities comes from the denial and cancellation of gift value-attribution. Any value that is not 'deserved' through the market is considered a rip-off, because giftgiving is not recognized as contributing to the whole. If we get something free or pay less for something than its market price, it seems that there has been no original contribution to the market, through our production, corresponding to our consumption. It may seem unfair for us to receive 'something for nothing.' Yet this question is completely misplaced, because we have usually contributed to others and to the market itself through caregiving, and through the surplus labor which creates profit, as well as through giving credit to the market as a system, and to all the worthless and destructive products, politicians and ideas that validate it. In fact, enormous contributions are given free by everyone to the market, but are unrecognized.

[1] This situation is similar to that in which knowers freely give value to the concept, a value which instead is usually perceived as coming from the concept itself or from the things involved.

188

If I buy a useless toy or breakfast food or face cream that is available on the market and has been advertised, I am giving extra value, not only to the producers and sellers of the product, but also to the market process, without which I would not have bought it. Advertising elicits the free gift of our attention endlessly. Our minds, hearts, and houses are filled with products coming from or destined for the market, as is a large amount of our time. The central recipient of our attention for most of our lives is the market and all the varieties of our participation in it.

Giving Value

Value is also one side of a binary opposition with what is unvalued. It is the doorway for a relation to human beings, because we relate to each other more strongly regarding what is valued than regarding what is unvalued. It is likely that we would begin to create a concept about things that are valued. There is also negative value, to which we may give attention, and we may have to give many gifts to counter its effects. Satisfying another's need gives value transitively to that person.

Because the satisfaction of the other's need is used only to procure the satisfaction of one's own need, exchange cancels the gift and creates an equilibrium, so that neither the gift nor value pass transitively to the other person. The stimulation of more needs to increase production is even less compassionate than equilibrium, because it creates also more unsatisfiable needs.

Supply and demand in equilibrium are a lot like question and answer. Effective demand is the expression of the need (the explicit question or request) through money. Production is the 'right' answer. But their interaction is an imitation and transposition, even a travesty of the giving and receiving, which honors needs directly. A symmetrical closed circuit is created, in which each self-interested, self-valuing person who gives only in order to receive is equal to all the others doing the same thing, and finds the 'human' valuable common quality in that equality. Market equilibrium is a projection of the symmetrical circuit of exchange. But giftgiving and the needs it satisfies, as well as needs which remain 'ineffective' and unsatisfied, lie outside this circuit while at the same time they feed and feed into it.

Hierarchies and Makeshift Communities

The mutually independent and indifferent mode of exchange imposes a characteristic structure, through which we distortedly communicate materially to become a community. It is the hierarchical transposed concept structure of over-taking (power-over) and substitution, which is incarnated as the needs of the people in privileged one positions are satisfied by others—the many—who are kept in positions of giftgiving (so the attribution of value goes upwards). (See Figure 16.) These many de-servers are those who are paid to create capital through surplus labor, or to service their privileged samples in various ways, providing them with the rewards which are at least in part the motivation for their capital accumulation.

In exchange, we do not give value to need or the person who has the need, but to the product that might satisfy the need, as a member and quota part of the category of things in exchange. The assessment of the product in terms of money, and the instrumental assessment of need for that product of those who have the money to pay for it, capture our attention and our production, leaving little energy for the needs of other de-servers much less those of the 'undeserving.' Communitary bonds wither and fall away. Compared to what they might have been, our communities as a whole are pitifully 'lacking.'

This human void is filled in various ways: through more of the same hierarchical behavior in 'law and order,' but also through much unrecognized giftgiving. There are volunteer activities, done for the express purpose of bonding, by which many community bonds among those who would otherwise be indifferent or strangers are created or revived. A good deal of work has recently been done[2] by various authors on the giving of

[2]David Cheal, op.cit.

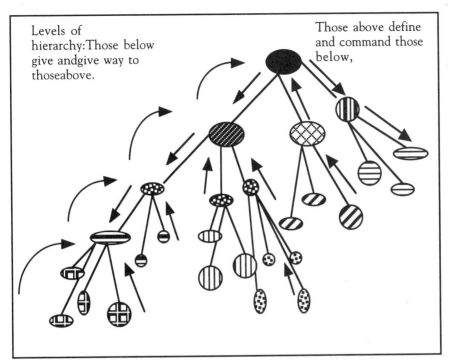

Figure 16. Gifts flow upwards.

Christmas and birthday gifts, an activity done mostly by women. Volunteer work, nonprofit organizations, charities, attempt to heal the wounds and bridge the gaps that are continually being created by closed circuit ego-oriented economics. Religious organizations encourage or require much free giving of money and of time and, therefore, give value to their own need for self-propagation. A sense of community among their members is created, because they are all giving instead of exchanging, and they are giving to the same overarching organizational need. Allegiance and obedience are also explicitly given to the priorities, interpretations and rules of these organizations. Each masculation and exchange-based ego thus finds itself having qualities and beliefs in common with others beyond its own egotism.

By stimulating pheromones and loosening inhibitions, alcohol and other social drugs make bonding more immediate. Drinking alcohol socially perhaps replaces giving each other milk, i.e. mothering each other! or at least being nurtured together—in

191

spite of alcohol's macho mystique. In fact, drinking excessively often stimulates masculated behaviors of overcoming, such as loudness, hyperactivity and physical violence. Alcoholics require special tending by others, which makes them seem to assume a superior hierarchical position with regard to their 'servers.' Such groups as Alcoholics Anonymous create community through serving one another's needs for support to solve a common problem. The community that is created replaces the bonds that were formed by drinking alcohol together which replaced the bonds made difficult by the exchange economy. The letting go attitude and trust in a higher power are healing alternatives to the power-over, masculated attitude.

Sports activities give us the shared (often vicarious) experience of attempting to achieve common goals through relatively short-term masculated competitions. Perhaps it is the sharing of the experience and its priorities as valuable that allows us to communicate about them successfully, forming bonds regarding their exclusion or entrance into the category of winners. These social institutions and habits and many others respond to a need for community that is created by the economic way based on exchange, and on the ego-oriented instrumentalization of the other's need, which creates the isolation of each individual ego. The responses of volunteer, self-help, community organizations are, in their way, gifts at a group level. They do succeed in creating community through giftgiving. Many women may become aligned with them, because they give a social location and a wider range of action to the other-tending they are already doing in the family. (For women who are still being socialized towards giftgiving, a contradiction and an internal tension are created between self and other-orientation, gift and exchange paradigms.)

The community organizations and institutions themselves remain hybrids between giving and exchange and often serve to maintain the status quo of the exchange paradigm by satisfying the needs for community created by it. They do have the positive effect of allowing space for the gift paradigm to be

192

practiced outside the family. However, the giftgiving that does take place is often at the service of patriarchal ideology, or it is re-assimilated into an exchange context. The recent criticism of other-orientation as co-dependent takes the isolated individual as the norm, and the other-tender as aberrant, discrediting the very giftgiving that is the cause of the healing. Of course, we also need to know how not to give care when we or other people need to be independent. That is, in itself, a needed gift. The exchange economy requires isolated individuals, privileged one behavior, and many de-servers serving them. It is this economic way that is the culprit, not other-orientation.

It seems to me that the movement for radical social change, now occurring in the US and worldwide, combines a number of the advantages of these efforts, while approaching the society itself from a wider view and trying to change the system— whether this is understood as capitalist patriarchy, organized racism, or fascist tyranny. Much volunteering and many common activities are done by those in the feminist, ethnic, peace, and environmental movements. An on-going community is created. Although there seems to be a common consciousness among activists in the US that 'all the issues are connected,' exchange has not yet been considered as negative, and much masculated, 'privileged one' behavior still occurs.

The exchange principles of equality and equilibrium are still embraced by the social change movement, although some attempts are being made to celebrate diversity and to honor the Mother. Using exchange principles as the final court of appeal re-infects the movement with some of the values of the very system it is trying to change. This weakens and makes more superficial the alternatives that are proposed, such as using moneyless barter instead of the present system of exchange for money. Such attempts cannot solve the problems. They could perhaps provide moments of transition towards a gift economy, but only if they were clearly not themselves being taken as a final solution. On the other hand, these principles of equality and equilibrium may cause us to repeat the exchange paradigm by calling for reprisal, payment, and punishment for the grievous wrongs that have been committed. These values re-confirm the principles of the system that caused the wrongs. Therefore, however well-intentioned they may be, they only reform the system locally and in the short term, but do not radically change it.

Giving the Givers

Value can also propagate self-similarities at the meta level as the gift of the giving of giving. We mentioned above that when French anthropologist Levi-Strauss argued that an 'exchange of women' between men of different kinship groups created bonds among them, and functioned like an exchange of commodities, what he did not realize was that the 'giving' of women is actually a meta gift—of givers. Needs for givers are present in every society, and the gift of the giver is the gift which, like the cornucopia, can potentially satisfy all needs. Women are the bearers of material co-munication and, as such, create the bonds of the community wherever they are—whether or not they are themselves subjected like commodities to 'exchange' or are given like gifts or decide upon their own destiny. Women often don't recognize their own contribution or attribute to themselves the meta gift of value any more than they or masculated men consciously recognize the mother as the source of giving or the gift paradigm as a viable Way.

From a feminist ('gynophilist') point of view, we can see value as the giving of giving, which in exchange value is made to double back and cancel itself out. Whereas originally there was a binary opposition between valuable and valueless based on other-oriented giving, exchange is a new kind of giving which is not for others, in its final destination. Exchange value creates a new opposite of giving (the giving of not-giving), an opposite of value different from valuelessness. Value-in-exchange constitutes a third opposition, and there is no longer a binary but a tri-polar, three-pronged opposition, consisting of value, valuelessness and exchange value.

194

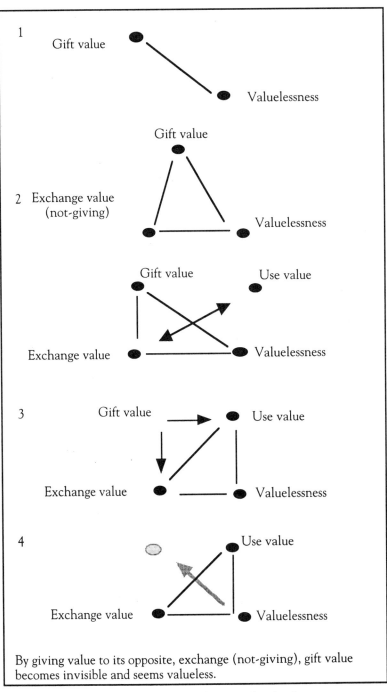

1 Gift value — Valuelessness

2 Exchange value (not-giving) — Gift value / Valuelessness

Gift value — Use value / Exchange value — Valuelessness

3 Gift value — Use value / Exchange value — Valuelessness

4 Use value / Exchange value — Valuelessness

By giving value to its opposite, exchange (not-giving), gift value becomes invisible and seems valueless.

Figure 17. Value is given to exchange; gift value becomes invisible.

195

This three-pronged picture is soon altered by the addition of a fourth prong: use value. Then the gift of value is given to exchange, and to use value, canceling out gift giving. (See Figure 17.) We mistakenly attribute the gift of giving to exchange, to the market, and what is not exchange value or has not been through the exchange process seems to be valueless. Exchange value becomes the sample of the concept of value. Exchange over-takes giftgiving. We collectively and individually *give* it too much importance while denying any importance to giving. We are not conscious of the giving we are actually doing. We do not give it any value.

Giving value to exchange also gives value to the ideal 'sample' of the successful capitalistic masculated male as the opposite of the mother. The gift of value and of the giver (mother) are imprisoned in exchange value by giving value to their opposite and to not giving. (And many mothers and daughters are literally imprisoned by husbands, fathers, sons, brothers, etc.) The giving of giving is not usually visible as such, also because visibility is connected with language and with the characteristic of substitution, which is part of the process of exchange. If exchange subsides (or we start thinking outside the binary opposition), we can appreciate the value of the giving of giving, and the need for it, that depends on a widespread complex social situation and not just on the deserving which seems to come from self-similarity and participation in the exchange process.

For-Giving

Letting money (like a word) take the place of a product (or a thing) says about the product: 'Here is a gift, a satisfier of need.' Since the money-word is actually transferred as property from one person to the other, it enters into the anti-communicative logic of the not-gift: 'For me, therefore not for you—for you (or others), therefore not for me.' Our culture nevertheless identifies this anti-gift process as a gift, a socially useful process, and gives it the name 'exchange,' by which we can satisfy our linguistic communicative need in its regard. In fact, we do engage in the process of exchange a lot; it is valuable. It satisfies our need for a source of goods in a situation where goods have been made artificially inaccessible through keeping property and abolishing giftgiving. By making access to goods conditional upon the production of other goods of equal value and their measurement and exchange, we interrupt the material giftgiving value-conferring process and cancel the bonds and community which it could have produced. We relate to exchange as the source, as if it were the mother—though it is an analog of masculation and thus concomitant to the process that alienated the boy (and the father in his time) from the mother. Perhaps this is why people feel so passionately attached to exchange, the market, capitalism and masculation itself. They bond with these processes, because the processes appear to nurture them.

The 'gift' of exchange contradicts giftgiving. The needs that surround it are the needs of a not-community, of people living within the 'adversarial' relations of buyer and seller. Though we continue to communicate by means of language and other signs, our material co-munication has become drastically altered and contradictory, and our attitudes towards one another have appropriately become fear and resentment.

For-giving becomes a moral issue, whereas it is actually only the psychological manifestation of the gift paradigm. When we forgive we refuse rancor, reprisal, 'measurement' of wrongdoing, and other psychological reflections of exchange. (We refuse to give up giving the gift for the not-gift. We do not change into exchange.) We try to understand others' motivations in terms of their unmet needs. And we try to understand the personal and social reasons for those needs, satisfying them and changing the contexts if possible, solving the problems. Shifting the paradigm back to giftgiving is a way to for-give everyone.

It is almost as if the word 'forgive' were pointing the way towards the paradigm shift. In fact, forgiving is not something we do to another person; it is a change in our values, in our own

197

attitude towards giftgiving and away from guilt, blame, manipulation, and punishment, which are ways of remaining in and promoting the exchange paradigm at the psychological level. By modeling it, we also give the logic of giving a multiplier effect, since others can see it at last unconcealed—and follow our example. If we can shift paradigms and consciously change our behavioral logics, collectively demystifying and diminishing exchange and reprisal, we can have a permanent effect. We should look at the shift as a practical solution for all rather than just as a moral choice. The framework of morality limits the scope of for-giving to the individual, while the need of all the children of the earth is for a collective shift towards the Mother.

Supporting the Alien Noncommunity

We continue to have to give without exchange to very young children, and to form a community with them, socializing them as communitary beings. Yet, our most important and widespread material communication with others at large, as adults, is exchange. We have formed an alien noncommunity in which our children then have to try to adapt and survive.

The noncommunity of exchangers requires many free gifts. It needs gift (surplus) labor in order to supply the reward of profit, by which capitalists are motivated to create and maintain enterprises. It needs women's free labor, which cares for use values, gives to workers and reproduces the workforce, increasing the profit margin. It needs the gift of our credence, our belief that it is viable and even 'just.' But it also needs the giftgiving among humans that continues to take place beyond or in spite of exchange, not only as communication through language, but also through all the acts of kindness, love, generosity, hospitality and camaraderie that 'make life worth living.'

The aesthetic experience is, to a large extent, the creative reception of a gift, though owning the object of art is not free. The nonprofessional thought that goes into any kind of business or work or activity is free. Sometimes bringing products to the market is done free, and the travel of buyers to the market is done at their own expense. The needs of consumers are greatly influenced by their care-giving of each other, especially through the choices of the women (and men) who have to buy the means of nurturing. The development of needs and desire itself is done free through caregiving—though it is now being profoundly altered by advertising.

The gift of value is also given, not only to exchange, but to a systemic adversarial (and instrumental, conditional) ego need to know or appraise how much a person has given, assessing his/her production quantitatively with regard to all the others. Ostensibly, this appraisal is made in order to give back to her/him the same amount, but it is actually made to give power to the one who *judges* who 'deserves' to be given access to the exchange itself, who 'deserves' to be given to, and eventually who 'deserves' to be the privileged one, the sample. (The privilege and generality of the sample, come from the polarization of the concept process in which it is immersed, and are not due to the sample's having given more than others.) In our judgments about 'deserving,' excessive value is given to the equivalence or correspondence between thing and word, or product and money, or work and salary—and very little value is given to needs as such.

Even equations do not have value on their own; they are given 'values,' but they are also given their value from the outside. We have seen that equations take the place of the consideration of things in their relation to needs, and we over-value them in that role. Exchange could not exist if it were not embedded in giftgiving of many kinds and at many levels. The 'gift' of not-giving and the alien community of not-givers are possible because they are immersed in (and nurtured by) a community of givers.

Among the gifts we give to not-giving, which consumes those gifts in its processes, are our attention to exchange and our blindness towards gift processes. We do not form our community regarding giftgiving, our linguistic communicative needs do not arise regarding it, because in fact we are forming our community mostly according to exchange. Thus, we do not communicate much about giftgiving. (This 'functional' reason supports the more misogynistic motivations for our denial of giftgiving and helps us for-give ourselves for it. Guilt, self-reprisal, 'paying ourselves back,' only confirm the logic of exchange more strongly.) Exchange has taken the place of material gift co-munication, as communication with language has taken the place of material co-munication, as men have taken the place of women. In fact, the exchangers are related to each other in a very individualistic way, which is a perfect fit with the ideal of masculation, the individualistic and adversarial lonely hunter.

Of the gifts that are given by the community, which is still acting according to giftgiving at an abstract level, the most important is the meta gift of value, by which other gifts and services are directed. We appreciate value and attribute it to art, music, literature—all of which themselves attribute value in complex, beautiful and surprising ways. We value the gifts of the painter or the story teller, as well as those of the political organizer, and even the salesperson's gift of gab. They direct our attention in new ways, altering our habitual attributions of value. We love the gifts of nature, of culture, of history, of science, which by satisfying our needs attribute value to us, as well. However, by giving value to exchange and to things in the exchange mode, we continue to maintain it, directing most of our goods and services towards it.

Another way in which value is attributed to exchange, to the self-similar shift into the logic of substitution and all the manifestations of masculation, is through confirmation by reflection, by their reciprocal similarity. Unless we consciously understand its causes and negative effects, the repetition of the pattern seems to give value to its different expressions. The pattern itself acquires a certain amount of independence, and we can imagine it floating through the universe validating other masculations whenever they form.

In fact, by acting it out, by giving the pattern of masculation repeated manifestations, humanity can make it into a 'kind of thing'—a thing which could be related to a word, to which we can begin to give value, and towards which we may direct our concept forming attention. We look for a sample and try to find the common qualities of the things related to it as similar. We both appreciate the importance of the pattern and attribute importance to it. We talk about it and give it a name.

For example, we call it 'patriarchy.' By naming it, we relate it to a word; we begin to transform it by making it 'give way' to the word which is our gift to each other. Women form ourselves as a co-munity by talking about patriarchy, as I am doing in this book, and as the progressive and the feminist movements are doing everywhere, pointing out the patterns of oppression and grasping the connections among them. We must also give to each other—time, attention, nurturing goods, forming material co-munities beyond exchange. We are working now to transform 'reality,' so that we can give the gift of a good earth to the future.

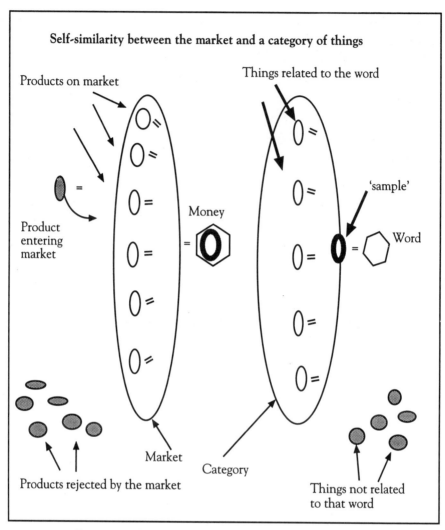

Figure 18. The relationship between products and money and things of a kind and a word are self-similar at widely different scales.

Chapter 13
Market and Gender

An Altered Reality

I am trying to trace the self-similar patterns of patriarchy in different areas of life, so that we can recognize them. Women and other have-nots may feel that if only we 'had,' we would realize our potential, becoming 'equal' to the haves—and finally, fully human. Thus, we aspire to the rewards of patriarchy and unwittingly help to motivate the system. If we can recognize the patterns, we can use the system for survival while we are changing it, without giving it value, without giving it our hearts. (See Figure 18.)

The market is like a language which is evolving from a past into a future state, according to quantitative (rather than qualitative) value and having only one word, money. The constraints upon this language derive from the kinds of human relations it is required to mediate, the mutually exclusive relations of private property. Money 'names' the products again and again as values, but because of the exchange mode, which preserves the ego-orientation of all, no further mutually inclusive material relations can develop.[1] The human exchangers cannot evolve fully as a co-munity.

The market seems normal, 'given' to us by the way things are. Instead, it is actually an altered reality. Why, indeed, should human beings allow the naming process to stand between those who have goods and those who have needs? The market involves naming or defining with the money word, over and over. 'This coat = $20.00. This other coat = $100.00. This bag of potatoes = $4.00.' The equation between products and money, which is a moment of the naming process, becomes an important moment

[1]We have been talking about exchange as definition. Because there is only one material word, money, I am now talking about naming. Several of the functions of the definition are collapsed into each other in monetized exchange.

for the society as a whole. It seems to be the gateway to all value. In fact, it is used to bring some products into the category of 'valuable,' while others appear to be valueless because they are not saleable, or because they are free (gifts of nature: air, water, sunlight, etc.).

Masculation has made everyone expect to be 'elevated' or fear being demoted by being put in one category instead of another. The moment of naming with the gender term: 'John is a boy,' or with money: 'one pound of coffee = $2.00,' puts the person or the product in the category of those having value in relation to that word or that amount of money. Girls and products which are unsaleable or free (giftgivers and nature's gifts) do not belong to the superior category. Thus, the gender term for females already attributes to the person the contradictory value of not being in the superior, valued, category. Being put in a superior category by '... is a boy' seems to deprive the members of the category of their ability to give in the present, while giving them another mode with something else—words, positions, money to strive for (a distraction and a kind of addiction). The naming of gender and the exchange of products for money focus us in the present, but only through the mis-recognition of gifts and overemphasis on the equation and substitution.

We give value to definitions rather than to people or to the nurturing way, which remains concealed, in the shadow. Gifts give value to the receiver, exchange does not—except through the process of 'deserving,' where the exchanger appears to cause the payment herself through her own value, her previous production, etc. As in masculation (where boys learn to 'deserve' the name 'male'), the definition takes over, and the gift model gives-way. The social gift, the name, takes over from individual gifts and, because it is general, appears to be something else, to have an arcane power. The one-many position, when used as a privileged, phallically invested sample with power in the real world, backs up this fetishized power of the name. When we 'earn' a profess-ional qualification, we can call ourselves a 'journalist' or a 'doctor.' We enter a privileged category. By behaving in appropriate ways, and learning to put into practice the knowledge we have mastered, we are able to fit the definition. Like the boy, we 'earn' the right to bear the name. And we earn a 'living' in the exchange economy.

A Self-Replicating Parasite on the Tree of Life

At a true meta level, we would recognize exchange as partial, just as we would recognize the male gender (and its definition) as partial. But giftgiving does not see itself, nor giftgivers, as its creatively receptive others. The meta level is confused by the different kinds of self-similar reflections. Anything attributing importance mainly to itself is necessarily partial, because it diminishes its other and decontextualizes itself—pulls itself out of its context (while the reflections of the concept structure make it appear to be all there is). Gifts require others who will receive them. But people in the closed system of extreme hierarchical patriarchy attribute importance to themselves through the instrumentalization of those who are 'different' or 'inferior.' They use others for the purpose of enhancing themselves while denying others' importance as the source of their good. This process gives these artificial egos completion, while making it seem as if they are self-made, either through being nurtured because they 'deserve' it, or through manipulation or force, or because the other is 'inferior,' or it is her/his 'nature' or 'instinct' or duty to give to one in that position. 'Of course she takes care of him; he's her husband.'

The male occupies the 'sample' or one position, requiring others to relate to him as many, reinstating the moment of comparison and equivalence between relative items and the sample in the concept formation process. The many also give way and give to the one who takes over, repeating the 'many-to-one' relation between things and their names. These patterns become self-confirming, also because of their similarity with a more abstract meta level. The human 'one' ignores the many and stands alone, out of context, self-reflecting as one instance of one.

In thinking about his 'one position,' a person then applies the concept process again to it. Seeing himself as one alone, he is equal to himself and to other ones alone.

The process repeats and reflects itself at different levels. Since re-cognition is based upon comparison and equivalence, comparison and equivalence appear to be the all-important relations even at the meta level.[2] Thus, even using a meta level in thinking about the situation validates the de-contextualized concept formation process in its various incarnations. However, the equation and the concept form only seem to constitute the whole meta level. Instead, they are one branch of the (fractal) tree, the trunk of which is giftgiving. Perhaps, we should say that their self-similar structures are a vine, a parasite upon the tree.

Reworking the metaphor: it is not just the trunk of the tree that has the structure of giftgiving. In fact, the possibility of giving and receiving elicit a living tree: the leaf receives sunlight, uses it in photosynthesis, sends its products throughout the tree to satisfy its needs for energy, the roots receive and transmit moisture from the rain and minerals from the earth and the humus of previous leaves and trees. The availability of the gifts of earth, water, air and sunlight allow the development of living things which can receive the gifts. The decontextualized equation and the concept, classes, exchange, hierarchies and the self-reflecting meta level also derive the possibility for their existence from the gifts that are given to them, through the roots they have planted in the gift way. They serve living beings who have warped and distorted themselves, so that they can receive these abstract gifts. The whole society creatively receives the altered nourishment.

[2]The class of all de-contextualized classes (classes taken out of context) is a de-contextualized class. However, a true meta viewpoint would be logically broader and would include giftgiving, thus including the different (the other), bringing about contextualization and destroying the de-contextualized class. The patriarchal view of thinking over-emphasizes classes and under-emphasizes the giftgiving context, just as patriarchal society over-emphasizes classes, and under-emphasizes the gift paradigm. A critic might say that comparing exchange and giftgiving is like comparing apples and oranges. My point is that these apples only exist within a context of oranges, which also give to them.

Patriarchal structures develop in a 'culture' of giftgiving, because they, too, are able to receive in special ways and give again to beings who are adapted to receiving them. Decontextualization is only a moment of abstraction used for concept formation. It has been made into a permanent condition of ego isolation, which serves the economy, the psychology and all the institutions built upon masculation. Patriarchy maintains control through the supporting interplay of various decontextualized self-similar structures. The vine, the parasite, is the over-development of the equation, the concept structure, classes. It is made up of human definitional strings organized in hierarchies, which suck up gifts to nurture the ones at the top. Patriarchy cannot exist on its own but twines around the tree of human giftgiving and feeds on it, draining the goods away from needs, creating the scarcity which serves as its necessary environment.

The artificial parasite becomes believable and self-validates by reiterating its own form. Exchange, as it replaces one product with another, also continually replaces the need-oriented qualitatively varied gift with the qualitatively simple, quantitatively varied equation. It asserts part of the concept process, the equation, as 'reality' while replacing the giftgiving female with the sample male. Qualitatively-oriented giftgiving is replaced by a quantitative naming process, which has had its gift aspects canceled. This take-over is the acting-out of masculation. The equation itself appears to be a gift which also appears 'inalienable' or perhaps inescapable. Actually, it creates a focus upon itself and receives importance from others through its reflections.

Being and Having

What we are seeing here is the psycho-socio-economic meeting between being and having, in the relation between the word and the sample, the sample and its items, the father and his sons, and the owner and his properties—even the owner of the male body and his body parts.[3] The masculated boy identifies what he 'is' by what he 'has,' and by the similarity of what he 'has' with what others 'have,' rather than creating his identity in an ongoing way by what he gives and receives. Then he lets that relation be played out symbolically, as he constructs his identity around other possessions, many of which are phallic symbols. Because the erect phallus is the possession of the adult male, who is his model, the symbolic phallus—in toy cars and little guns— lets the boy privilege that having in the immature present.

Exchange is made necessary by the mutually exclusive relation of private property. Property is a relation in which the many things give and give-way to the one owner. This makes it similar to the relation between men as body-part holders, with the phallus in the forefront, and women who are 'lacking,' but who give and give-way to the one who 'has.'

Women internalize the desire for property and the mistrust of giving that come with the exchange paradigm, and this is also perhaps part of the reason we do not propose the giving model for our sons. We push our sons away from giving and into the (ex)change of categories and likeness to their fathers, so that we can be sure the boys will have the right kind of identity to get what they need and keep it. If they were to follow our model, they could presumably be considered 'sissies' and excluded from heterosexual patriarchy, exiled in a no-man's land, where they would be neither male nor female. This strange mothering behavior occurs because gender is actually an economic identity. What we consider 'male' characteristics of competitiveness, aggression, sublimation of emotion, focus on goals rather than process, etc. are qualities rewarded by capitalism. The reason for this is that capitalism is the economic way that is based on male gender characteristics. Capitalism is the replay at many levels of

[3]Jacques Lacan described what he called the 'mirror stage,' a level of integration of the child's body parts image greater than that appropriate for his age. I would speculate that it is the relation of ownership that integrates them as 'his' and that their fracturing the relation to the male sample is reflected in exchange. See Ellie Ragland-Sullivan, *Jacques Lacan and the Philosophy of Psychoanalysis*, University of Illinois Press, Chicago, 1986. Kenneth Wright, *Vision and Separation Between Mother and Baby*, Jason Aronson Inc., Northvale, New Jersey, 1991.

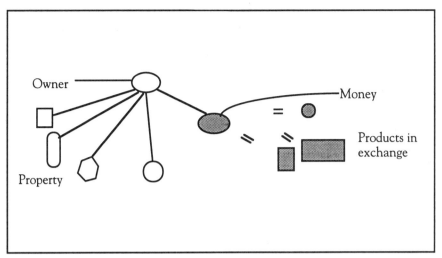

Figure 19. The owner of the money is a human 'one' to whom property is related as 'many.' Money, the 'one' value sample, is itself an item of property, but is related as equivalent to the many products in exchange.

the (ex)change of categories caused by the definition of gender, and the denial of nurturing.

Owning the Value 'Sample'

Patriarchy denies and discredits giftgiving in order to preserve itself. The two paradigms remain consistent with themselves: mothering appears as giving away the penis-property, and the boy (and being deprived of both) but continuing to give. Giftgiving therefore seems inherently self-sacrificing, even self-mutilating. Practitioners of the exchange paradigm appear to be giving up the mother, but receiving the penis, the superior male identity, and the exchange model itself in exchange. The logic of exchange confirms itself, and the logic of giftgiving confirms the 'other.'[4]

Money takes the place of the owner as the privileged sample for value, to which the property is related. Then the same thing happens again when another former seller buys.

[4] In addition to all this, mothers who are afraid of the father's competition with a nurturing son for their affection, may also be motivated to make him similar to the father, so that the father will not destroy him. Like Moses' real mother, they deny that he is theirs, give him to someone more powerful, and stay nearby to take care of and serve him.

The one-many pattern is embodied first in ownership, then in the one-many money relation repeatedly. (See Figure 19.)

Though exchange for money is a commonplace process, it is much stranger than we realize. We need to look at it carefully, in slow motion, to see its similarities to language, the concept process and masculation. In fact, an amount of money is the value of that product on the inter-individual plane—'for others and therefore for me'—socially. Money does the same thing economically that the word does on the plane of language. Products cannot get to the needs, except through exchange. Because products cannot be given in co-munication, they are 'spoken about' with money. Like the word, money mediates among people with regard to something, and that mediation changes their relation from a general 'everything is possible' sort of attitude, to one in which something is relevant in the present, and with regard to other people, addressing some need. The exchanger's relation to something becomes a present relation, selected from everything else it could have been.

Money takes the place of each person in turn, as the 'value-sample' to which the product is related, when the person gives up property. The owner of the money is a human 'one-many sample' to whom the value concept sample itself—money—is related as property. As a seller each person lets the other's money take the place of an item of her property and, by doing so, becomes the owner of the money. We might say she is 'meta' to the money, while the money is 'meta' to the products. As a buyer, she lets her money take the place of another's product, transferring the relation of ownership of the money to the seller, and of the product to herself. (See Figure 20.)

The (mutually exclusive) relation of ownership itself thus remains the same, while the kind of property that is owned is abstract as money, and concrete as the product. The relation of ownership changes levels from concrete to abstract and back, according to whether what is owned is a product or money. This permits the actual piece of property which was sold to be replaced by another (or others) constituting the same value and remaining

210

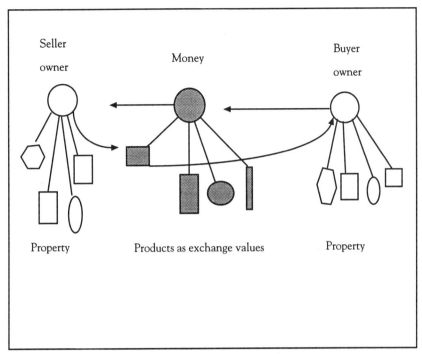

Figure 20. Money is the value concept sample, owners are samples for the complex of property. Money as sample is in the same (or a similar) relation to products as owners are to property.

in a sense the 'same' thing. At the same time, the seller's relation becomes one of ownership of the abstract sample itself—money. The one-many ownership relation can actually apply to money, the one-many concept sample itself, as an item of property.

There is a single kind of substitution performed over and over, as money continues to be given to others as the substitute concept sample for their products (another similarity money has with the word).[5] Money is always in the concept role of value sample for the product, while the owner is always in the transposed one-many concept role of ownership.[6] The owner can be in many different overlapping one-many roles. S/he can be, for instance, a father, a king, a pope, a city counselor, or a CEO and

[5] Money is only substituted itself when, having been 'invested,' it returns increased— another transposed masculation—perhaps a boy being born from the head of Zeus. The capi-talist is the one who makes this happen.
[6] Ownership is perhaps more like Vigotsky's 'family name' complex than like the concept; since the properties owned are diverse, they have no common quality, except that of being properties of that 'one.'

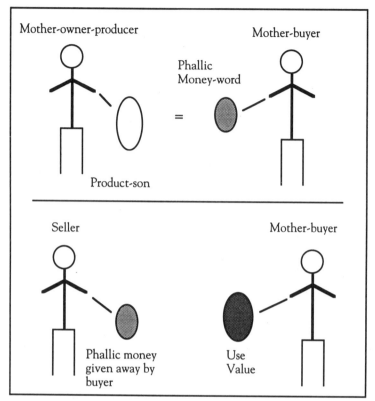

Figure 21. Money-laborer-owner allows her son-product
to be 'named' by phallic money and gives 'him' away.
Buyer gives up phallic money value-sample and remains
phallically 'lacking' but unharmed, with a use-value.

still own money. However s/he can have no access to the 'one'
position in human hierarchies and still be a 'one' with regard to
her/his properties, satisfying in that way the need to become a
'sample.'

The Social Nexus:
Male Sexuality Overtakes Mothering

The male gender is incarnated in the father in a way which is
different from the incarnation of value in money, but there are
many similarities due to the 'one' position. Money takes the place
of the owner as the 'one' to which the commodity is related as a
value according to the concept process pattern, and the same
thing can be said when the gender term and the father take the

place of the mother as sample for the boy. Moreover, the owner is superceded as 'one' by the money, which functions as incarnated word-concept sample for the value of the commodity, and the mother is superceded by the father as concept sample for the child. The similarity of the pattern permits a replay of the alienation of the boy into the category 'male,' through the alienation of the product into the category of economic value and the replacement of the product by money.

The 'castration' of the mother is replayed when the buyer gives up the money-phallus-word and receives the reward of the nurturing goods s/he needs. Those who hoard and accumulate money do not undergo this symbolic castration and, in capitalism, find a way to increase the money-phallus-word almost infinitely. The market serves as a 'safe space' in which to act out the childhood trauma of the boy's change of categories due to the naming of his gender. It has the healing effect of showing that giving up the product for sale, transferring it into the value category and the category of ownership by another, is not a harmful process in and of itself. (See Figure 21.)

Moreover, the symbolic castration involved in giving up the money is shown to be benign, not harmful to the buyer. Unfortunately, the whole process of exchange for money takes the place of giftgiving as the form of life of the co-munity. Then giftgivers give to the exchange process itself, valuing it above the very process they are practicing, giving gifts to it and to those who practice it in the same way that they give validation to masculation, to their sons and to other males. Exchange is a process that, to some extent, alleviates the psychological burdens having to do with masculation and castration, but it causes an aggravation of the problem at other levels.

In the economic realm the dependence of the child upon the mother is also played out in the dependence of the wife upon the husband. The wife and children all appear to be in a 'many-to-one' concept relation to the father, similar to the relation of property to owner or things to a word. He gives them his name. In the traditional family, the father appears to give the money-word-phallus to the mother, who in turn gives it to others, buying the means of giving, in order to give gifts to him and the children. His gifts are visible and counted, while hers are invisible and uncounted.

However, the wife is actually receiving the support (means of giving) of the husband in return for having given the boy into his category and having given up her place as concept sample (almost) becoming the husband's property. By shifting her validation onto her husband and exchange and masculation, she abdicates from the position of gift paradigm sample and puts the exchange paradigm in its place. For this, she receives the 'gift' of the husband's salary. The daughter is also given to the father, because the model the daughter follows is the mother who gives-way and gives to patriarchy and to the father.[7] In a context of scarcity, 'pockets' of gift economy are dependent on gifts from some part of the exchange system. Women have traditionally given up everything in order to put themselves in a position to be able to receive these gifts. Now they have joined the exchange paradigm as its actors, using the money they earn to support and nurture their children.

Even when the giftgivers are working in the exchange economy themselves, they often have to give their children up to the definitions and models provided by schools, television, and the streets, while they sell their labor in order to support them. The mothering economic model is diminished again at the same time that women are re-presenting it at another level, giving up their labor time in exchange for money with which to provide for their children, and giving up their children to be educated by others in the exchange economy.

The large scale economic changes that happen during wars (as in World War II) bring women into the capitalist workforce, weakening the link between economic activity and the masculine gender, which continues to be promoted by masculation. Changes

---

[7]The daughter might be considered as the 'good' or 'use value,' which is once more part of the nurturing way after the buyer has given up the phallic equivalent. She could also be considered the good which is not exchanged—at least until she marries.

in the big picture have an effect on the smaller picture, which changes more slowly. Even though many mothers now engage in monetized labor, there is an expectation that gender roles will continue to be distinct. One-many social structures take the place of the phallic father.

Television and film personages locate the father in the imagination; the 'word' becomes abstract once again. The motivation towards the general equivalent, money, produces many things in its image: the programs which show us one-many dominant men from police chiefs to fathers, supermen to singers. Women stars also perform one-many roles as sex objects, businesswomen, superspies. Even newscasters, as the one visible speaker to whom the many invisible listeners are related, fit this pattern. The dominance-submission model combined with hierarchy and competition are everywhere visible in our entertainment industry, business, politics, and academia, continuing to offer the poisoned gift-apple to little Prince Charming, providing the pernicious patriarchal models which are no longer directly available in mother-centered families.[8]

Gang relations also sometimes personally supply the one-many (violent) paternal models which are missing from the families of single mothers. Male sexuality, formed according to naming and the shift of categories, over-takes mothering as what Alfred Sohn-Rethel calls the 'social nexus'[9]—the deep pattern upon which society constructs itself. I think that, in spite of the difficulties, mother-centered families are beginning to change this situation. All too often, however, the discrediting of the single

---

[8]The norm-ality of exchange is reinforced by the ascendancy of the verbal over the nonverbal in the society, and in childhood, since the child is learning language precisely during the Oedipal period during which masculation is occurring. The possibility of the precocious genitalization of boys is stimulated by the importance given to language and naming and the transfer of the boy from the mother's category to the father's (or at any rate the sample male's). Economic exchange for money then actually retraces and reinforces the Oedipal situation, as well as this moment of genitalization. Ex-change is really a sex-change.
[9]Alfred Sohn-Rethel, *Intellectual and Manual Labor: A Critique of Epistemology*, MacMillan, London, 1978. Sohn-Rethel thinks that the 'exchange abstraction' deriving from the exchange of commodities is the social nexus. I believe that commodity exchange derives from masculation, which is therefore the basis of the exchange abstraction.

215

mother, together with the lack of the father, leaves the boy vulnerable to other, more negative masculated samples, as he follows the maze of one-many patterns that make up patriarchy.

Acting Out Masculation in the Market

The world of commodities imitates the world of patriarchy. The commodity-son is presented to the money-father, and found similar to it/him, relative to it/him as equivalent, allowed into the concept of the 'other,' the privileged concept of things having monetary value, and given away to the 'other' by the mother-owner-producer (labor-er). The mother-owner-producer's place is taken first by the money, as the concept model for the son-commodity, and then by the buyer as the one to whom that property is related as its owner. The mother-owner-producer gives the son-commodity away to become related to someone else as his/its owner. Then s/he changes roles and the phallic-father-money serves him/her as that to which the product of another is related. Another mother-owner-producer is giving up the product-child.

When the product is found equal to it/him, that phallic-father-money can be made to satisfy the communicative need for a means for (altering) a relation and changing from the mother to the father sample as the product moves from seller to buyer. The present (mother role) seller relates her son-commodity to (father role) money, comparing them, finding them equal, belonging to the privileged concept of things having value. The process of naming the product as a value-in-exchange, like the process which names the boy as 'male,' takes over from the process of giving-and-receiving a useful good. It is not the need of the other which determines the exchange, but effective demand. The money which the other possesses becomes relevant to one's own need for the money as a means of altering the property relation of someone else again to their useful good, in order to satisfy one's own need. The definitional meta need is superimposed upon the material need.

216

The use of the term 'labor' in English is interesting, as if the mother gave up her son as soon as she finishes her 'labor' and he is 'delivered' to become gendered, related to the term 'male' as soon as the midwife or doctor says, "It's a boy." She gives him up so quickly, and gives up her own sample capacity—in favor of what? a *word!* "In the beginning"—as soon as he was born—"was the word." He never had a chance.

In buying to sell, the phallic-father-money goes forth in society again and again, allowing son-commodities to become related to him, thereby confirming 'himself' as general equivalent. His/its human owner or collaborator then takes the son-commodity to others whose needs he/it will satisfy, and for whom his/its value is greater, so that the quantity of phallic-father-money in the hand of his human collaborator is increased. The economic operator engages in a kind of sexual activity, buying not to use the good to satisfy his needs, but to give it up again so as to increase the amount of his phallic money-holding.

From the linguistic point of view, the interaction of the economic communicators brings the 'money-name' into play so that the thing can be related to a human being by means of its socially validated general word equivalent. What is visible of all this in stores is the hierarchy of products with their prices from least to most, the 'sons' with their 'marks,' their price tags, dangling down with numbers on them to show 'how much' they deserve the money-name.

A Collective Psychosis

We are creating our reality collectively in a way which is harmful and unnecessary. By this, I do not mean that trees and cows, mountains and automobiles, children and grandmothers are not 'there.' I mean that we have been living out a distorted process, taking the images it spawns of itself as the principles by which to organize our lives. The misinterpretation of who we are and what we ought to be doing results in the rewarding of 'having' and the punishment of 'not having.'[10] Masculation creates a collective psychosis by which individual men vie with each other to be the sample man, and whole armies vie with each other to make their Fatherland the sample nation.

The 'over-taking' (substitution) aspect of words is inflated to become domination, while the giving-way (being substituted) of things becomes submission. These complementary activities can be found at many different levels. Overtaking is sometimes implemented violently in the family as the masculated gender role, or through the dominance of the adult over the child. Giving-way seems to be the role of the woman (or the child) who is obedient to the adult's words or commands. In the market, money takes over and the product gives-way, at the same time that the exchange process takes over and giftgiving gives-way. [11]

Patriarchy is a collection of vertical definitional strings, aspects of which are self-similar with relations in the market where the verticality of the strings is displaced onto the numerical progression of price. The market's definitions are many and short-lived, high-speed compared with the long-term definitional positions of over-taking and giving-way that are typical of the roles of command and obedience, for instance in hierarchies of the government, the army or the church.

Though many short-term acts of over-taking and giving-way and command and obedience may occur in these hierarchies, they flow together to make stable long-term roles. In the market, the position of the head 'honcho' is only one: money, the general equivalent, while in human hierarchies there is a chain in which the ones above take over from those below, and those below give and give-way to those above—to the ever more privileged ones.

The intermediate moment between product and need, which

[10]Even the Bible says, "To him that has much shall be given."
[11]At another stage of the same process, exchange for money takes over and barter gives way. There are at least these three layers of overtaking and giving way involved in exchange for money. We can tell they are still there because, at any time, we can revert to the 'previous' stage according to the will of the exchangers. We can barter instead of exchanging for money, or we can decide not to require an exchange and simply give the product to the person with the need.

is based on exchange and the equation, becomes the focus of the whole society, requiring equality[12] with money for access to goods. The masculating definition over-takes nurturing and imposes itself as a model everywhere.

Rather than resolving our problems through acting out the incarnation of the word, we have distorted reality, distributing goods psychotically to the benefit of the few to the point almost of omnipotence, according to a child's dream. We are using our linguistic ability to name or define, to transfer privilege onto some people instead of others, making them 'haves' instead of 'have-nots.' The priorities of masculation have altered reality collectively in a pernicious way, but if we understand, as Eastern religions have always said, that *this* reality is an illusion, a nightmare, we can return to a gift economy the ever-present possibility of which is the true dream into which we can finally awake, re-creating a reality which is a gift for all.

The Long Arm of the Definition of Gender

In spite of the odd and devalued positions giftgiving is forced to assume, it continues to be creative and life-sustaining. It is necessary for the enhancement of activities based on the definition—activities which, by themselves, would be abstract and barren. Thus, the denial of giftgiving sometimes includes incorporating some gift elements into the masculated model *post hoc*. Patriarchal religions do this, satisfying spiritual needs (while diminishing the importance of the mothering model) and legislating altruism. Sometimes masculated males create needs which they then satisfy. For example, a group isolates and disempowers its giftgivers by feminizing or enslaving them; then it gives them 'protection' by asserting its phallic hegemony over them and over other similar male groups who might try to overtake them. Such is military might.

---

[12]I believe that social change movements make too much of equality as a criterion, because they do not realize that its use in the market broadcasts its validation everywhere. Instead, I think we should celebrate qualitative diversity.

The good will of masculated men, of which there is still much, comes into play long after their personalities have been formed by giving up the gift paradigm and taking on their gender identity. Men's good will sets the standard for 'moral action,' while leaving aside the paradigm which would normalize the satisfaction of needs—not only in the lives of individuals, but also in the economic and political institutions of the group. If the society as a whole were already giving and giving value to needs according to the gift paradigm, morality would be quite a different thing. Much less individual heroism and 'willpower' would be necessary, because the good of others would already be a life premise of everyone and of the group.

The definition from which giftgiving has been deleted is broader than the gender definition and does not altogether coincide with it. Because it is at the basis of masculation, however, it resonates strongly with the male gender identity. The *definiendum*, and the equivalent position in concept formation are apparently over-valued on their own, though they are actually re-infected by the gender definition (which they helped to create). Thus, money the value sample and ways of dominating by naming and definition like academic discourse or the law are over-valued, but it is not immediately evident what part gender has in this emphasis, or what part giftgiving has.

Other seemingly gender-neutral categories, such as that of race, follow the pattern of gender, instituting a competition to be a concept sample for the human, over-taking other races, considering those who are different from the chosen sample as inferior. Like gender, these differences are culturally seen as physiological, while it is actually the form of the definition 'loaded' by masculation that implies that some group is 'superior' to others, who must then give-way and give *to* the 'superior' group. Similar situations can occur with political or ideological systems and nationalisms. Those born within the national boundaries of a country may consider themselves superior to those born outside those boundaries, even when there are no other differences affecting the actual bodies or minds of the nationalists. The whole nation then assumes the general equivalent (sample) position, potentially reinforcing the egos of the entire population with regard to other nations. Political systems, religions, interest groups follow these same patterns towards hegemony.

Profit

The definition can be manipulated for the superiority of those who use it in other areas of life, just as it is used to confirm and perpetuate the superiority of males. It seems that by being related to more of what is in the position of the economic *definiendum* (the money-word), we are better than others. It is as if this repeats the birth situation, again and again putting a person in the superior category by a relation to the general equivalent and taking him/her away from giving. Moreover, by providing the general equivalent, some of us can buy and control the time of others to our own ends. Requiring those for whose time we provide the general equivalent also to give unpaid gift (surplus) labor, the products of which we sell, allows us to make profit and accumulate capital. If we consider the general equivalent also as phallic, and so much the more so capital, we can understand the sexual appearance of investment, putting money 'in' something, taking it out increased, and re-investing it until we finally reap the profit.

We should realize that every time we 'make' a profit, some or perhaps many other people are giving a gift. Instead, we think our profit is a reward or that we earned it. But this again repeats the 'deserving' of the male, because he acts in a masculated way and thereby enters the privileged category again, 'deserving' the name 'man.' In fact, the male is rewarded by the gifts which he gave up giving when he entered that category in the beginning. If some primary or essential male gender characteristics were being put to work in our economic lives, they would be easier to trace and identify. But *both* the gender characteristics of men *and* the functional characteristics of our exchange economy derive from a 'common ancestor,' which is the definition by means of which males are privileged while being alienated from their nurturing mothers.

It is as if the collective boy child mind said, "But why am I a boy, and not like my wonderful Mommy?" The reply, "It is that way just because it is" becomes what he cannot beat but must join—what he, like his father before him, models himself on and then 'discovers' as his 'male' or 'human' characteristics. It is as if being itself, being equal, being equal to a sample, being the sample and being the word all collapsed into each other as the norm-al characteristics of male over-taking by categorizing and naming. This distressing situation is then projected out upon the society at large and finally becomes the *lebens-form* of the economic way of exchange. The 'father-sample' has the same characteristics of *being*, as did his father before him. There is, therefore, an infinite regress back through the generations of 'father-samples.' It is no wonder that male identity, which, denying giftgiving, has been read until recently as human identity, has had such a prominent place in philosophical discussion. It was and continues to be the source—not of some 'higher destiny'—but of our many problems.

Having More

The motivation towards increase can perhaps be found in the fact that the little boy's member is really very different and much smaller than his father's. If the phallus is the 'mark' of the male category, perhaps the boy cannot really consider himself 'equal' and part of that category, until he has a bigger member. The need to become the concept model, to occupy the general equivalent or word position, would imply also the need for a large member. The child is, of course, powerless to make this happen, while he, his brothers, his mother and sisters may be dominated (and sometimes abused) by the large phallic father, who is himself finally living out the mandate of the masculating definition on which he modeled himself in his own childhood.

The child, already in a position of competition with his father for the equivalent position, may also feel the need for a large phallus and its economic and symbolic equivalents, so that he can defend himself and the women with whom he is still participating (to some extent) in a giftgiving situation from the father and from still other men who may try to take over. The boy learns to dominate, playing the role of the *definiendum* in his turn. While the mother's nurturing bridges the differences of size by engaging the child as a human receiver (and giver and receiver of signs) at a very early age, the gender definition places the child at a decided disadvantage. For the moment he cannot achieve his gender mandate. He must be relative and part of the many, seemingly because he is too small. The real reason, after all, is due to the logic of the situation: there can only be one 'one.'

Perhaps the basis of the motivation for violence, power, and greed is this desire to be bigger (have more of the phallic equivalent), so as to occupy the 'one' position required by the gender definition. Girls can buy into the competition for superiority, though we do not have the physiological phallus and often do retain at least some of the giftgiving, mothering values to which we have been socialized.[13]

Because the father is often absent, the boy child, who has been taken away from the mothering model, can be left without a model for his identity (other than the definition itself) or a content for his category. Add to this the violence that many large men perpetrate on those who are smaller than they are, and it is clear that size (or quantity) can become the obsession not only of individuals but of whole cultures. A visitor from another planet who came here would surely look aghast at the ever-taller skyscrapers with which businesses demonstrate their corporate pride. Those who have offices in the towers of steel are of course superior to those who have offices in smaller, less erect buildings. They have more money and more power, which makes them closer to the concept model of the father, the adult male to which

[13]See *Making Connections*, Carol Gilligan, Nona P. Lyons, and Trudy J. Hanmer, editors, Harvard University Press, Cambridge, MA, 1990.

the little boy can only aspire. Then again, apart from any erotic sense, it is the erection which is different and so much larger than the boy's member, and it is that which the skyscrapers (guns, rockets, missiles, etc.) imitate.

All of these edifices are constructed upon the abandonment of the mothering model. Abandonment itself becomes directed—not towards the boy, but towards those who are lacking the phallus-word-money. Those with needs are left to die by those with goods. Those without the phallus have to pay for having put the boy in a different category. In fact, they have to invisibly continue to transfer the money-phallus to him as surplus value. Paradoxically, other-oriented giftgiving seems to be hypocritical and certainly no match for exchange as a method for providing distribution.

What is also concealed in plain sight is the draining of wealth into phallic symbols and infinitely expanding capital, away from the needs of the many. Wealth and energy flow from the many into the 'ones.' They also flow from giftgiving into the market and into capital, and from the 'Third World' to the 'First World.' The illusion is that it is the other way around.[14] As in the formation of the concept, the sample receives its value from the existence of other items of the same kind, but now there is an actual transfer of wealth from them to it.

Punishment by Scarcity

This whole situation could also be read as society's reprisal against the mother and her giftgiving way, for having given up the child to the father. Reprisal, of course, is part of and consistent with exchange. The displacement of the goods away from the needs, into the hands of those who have more and more of the

[14]The 'gifts' from the 'First World' to the 'Third World' contain hidden exchanges and actually return to the 'First World' many times over. See, for example, the work of the DAWNE collective and Gita Sen and Karen Grown, *Developmental Crisis and Alternative Visions*, Monthly Review Press, New York, 1987; Susan George, *How the Other Half Dies*, Allanheld, Osmun & Co., Montclair, 1977; and Vandana Shiva, *Staying Alive*, Zed Books, London, 1989.

phallus-word-money, creates the scarcity which burdens and discredits giftgiving, making it impossible or sacrificial. Continuing to practice giftgiving in spite of scarcity requires enormous effort and an almost obsessive sense of purpose. Women have often been branded masochistic because of it.

Instead, the burden of proof should be placed on those who are creating the scarcity and on the system which creates *them*. Their motivations are to be found in their attempt to heal their childhood change of gender category. Perhaps in our maternal tenderness, we are inclined to understand and humor them, but this must stop. It is not an appropriate response to the consequences of their actions and institutions—the deaths of millions by war, starvation and disease and the ecological destruction of the planet.

Scarcity has several advantages for patriarchy. It makes giftgiving difficult so that it cannot offer a visible and viable alternative to exchange. It punishes mothers and the giftgiving way for having given their boys away to the category of the father, at the same time providing the boys with the enticement of accumulating more than anyone else of the general equivalent. Moreover, those who succeed in becoming privileged samples can also materialize their priapic economic excesses in phallic symbols of all kinds. If citizens do not succeed in accumulating more individually, they can perhaps participate in a body politic which has more—bigger guns, airplanes, bombs.

Having this excess, while others do not have enough goods to survive, allows those who do have to consider themselves superior and to distribute small charitable gifts in manipulative ways, controlling the behavior of the have-nots. The masculating definition is also used directly to manipulate those who need positive judgments which have also been rendered scarce— judgments of intelligence, beauty, efficiency or expertise. These are often accompanied by monetary judgments, which they complement.

The economies and the eco-systems of the earth are being altered by the attempt to accumulate large amounts for the few, while depleting the resources of the many. The relative size of the possessions of the few increases by this means. The desire for security is also intensified by the use of the threat of scarcity, and it may seem that without a considerable margin, even males risk being transferred back from the category of the haves to that of the have-nots.

Perhaps we may be excused for looking at the market and patriarchy in this irreverent way. It seems to be a sort of tragicomic passion play, in which the alienation of the boy from his mother into the category of his father is replayed endlessly. The symptom of our psychological disorder occupies our minds and time, preventing us from following the mothering way, while millions of real children of both genders starve. The eyes of the visitor from outer space would fill with tears of pity for this excellent species which has gotten itself into so much trouble for what, after all, begins as a small and innocent mistake.

As for me dear reader, I howl in the night.

If you understand, maybe you do, too.

Chapter 14
Deserving to Exist

Human Contradictions in the Market

I have always wondered how profit could be derived through individual equal exchange. The answer I want to give is that profit flows through gifts that come to exchange and the market from nonexchange areas. These gifts come first from our giving value to equality (as do mothers with the son's similarity to the father), second from our giving value to ego orientation and exchange itself, third from nurturing the worker and fourth from giving to the capitalist through surplus value. There is another 'equal' exchange, between worker and capitalist, to which value is given from the outside. The worker agrees to work for a salary, but only because s/he can't survive any other way. Extra time, attention, labor and loyalty are gifts given in exchange for the 'privilege' of being paid the going rate for labor of a certain kind. Going 'up' a logical step, in scarcity the chance to have a paid job is a 'gift.' Care, honesty, loyalty, work excellence, and good humor are given in reciprocity for the 'gift' of the job. (We could look at this almost as a reciprocal exchange of gifts—as happens in some pre-capitalist societies.)While market exchanges may be equal at one level, at another level unseen gifts are constantly being given to, through and around them.

Marx's 'surplus value' is the value of labor in excess of a salary based on the cost of reproducing the laborer. Actually, surplus value constitutes a gift from the laborer to the capitalist. Since the wife's or mother's gift labor is uncounted in the reproduction of the laborer, its value also flows into surplus value. Scarce jobs are over-valued, and gifts flow to them and to those who have them from those who do not have them.

Economic operators usually do not pay attention to what the source is, but only to the accumulation of quantity for future use without qualitative variety. They are justified in this by the hall-of-mirrors, the self-similarity of all of the equal exchanges going on in the market and at different levels which constitute the context of each exchange. Moreover, the homogeneity or 'one word' character of money allows the market to replace the qualitatively varied vocabulary of language with the quantitative hierarchy of prices.[1] In the market, the only way we could name and thus recognize and appreciate a gift as a value is by exchanging it for money, which would contradict its gift character. Thus the gifts remain unvisible and unvalued.

Profit derives, in part, from our giving to equality and valuing it over need. Because someone participates in the equal exchange, s/he receives the gift of being valued instead of someone who only has a need. Any surplus that might otherwise have gone to the person who only has a need is thus 'free' to flow as a gift into the profit of the equal exchanger. The person with the need is seen as unequal unless s/he also has some other product or money as the result of a previous transaction. Actually, being equal as exchangers only implies that people practicing the behavior of exchange have produced for and exchanged with a group of others who are equally self-interested and adversarial. Their equality as actors and as values in the exchange process implies exchangeability—reciprocal substitutability, and their lack of bonds implies indifference.

There are needs which come from the process of exchange itself—like the needs coming from the process of masculation—which must be satisfied by gifts given to that process from the outside. The giftgiving way stands aside for exchange to take over, transferring its own ignored potential value as the mode of distribution to it, nurturing it and those who practice it. If it competes, if there is an abundance of a product, through over-production, for example, prices go down. If prices go down, more of the product's value is given to the consumer as a gift, and future production for exchange is jeopardized.

[1]Prices constitute a differential system like Saussure's *langue*, which is organized according to quantity by numerical progression rather than quality.

The market, like the masculated ego, is an artificial psycho-socio-linguistic invention using decontextualization. Like the ego, it needs to receive value directly (without an exchange) from giftgiving, while at the same time competing with it and winning. The people who are participating in the artificial invention, doing the exchanging, develop a need to be valued as opposed to those who are outside the market. They also need to be maintained by others. In order to be motivated to engage in this artificial practice, they include an extra recompense for themselves (an 'incentive') in the price of their products. The profit they receive is a gift, not only from the producers of surplus value (and those who nurture the producers), but also from the buyers of scarce goods. It is a contribution of gifts from the unknown and the unknowing many. Scarcity of jobs and scarcity of goods function together to keep the equal exchanges high and the flow of gifts going towards the 'haves.'

De-serving is a self-similar way of giving value not only to the exchangers but to exchange. Those who produce for the market de-serve a recompense. Exchangers receive the value of being equally defined as adversaries belonging to the same contradictory class. They are seen as superior to those who are unemployed or unemployable, those who cannot sell or buy. The equality of their products to money seems to imply the (mutually exclusive) equality between them, just as the ability to use the same words regarding similar things implies a (mutually inclusive) equality between interlocutors.

If our communitary selves are developed through language and material giving, then exchange, the material interaction of not-giving, can be understood as the basis of a particular kind of self. Materially it develops a private owner, while psychologically it develops an ego which is functional to the process and to ownership: competitive, striving to have more, to have and/or be the *definiendum*, and to become the masculated privileged one.

Those with the ego type adapted to exchange enter the dominant class of the self-interested many, all of whom are attempting to be privileged ones. The individual macho competitive action coincides with the logic of substitution by taking the place of giftgiving. So does the masculated nation, class, race or religion, over-taking others who are constrained to give up and give value and goods to the conquerors. Self-reflecting and male-reflecting groups overcome other-oriented groups and are nurtured by them. The egos which are produced by exchange define their expansion and the expansion of the market system as 'civilization.'

The Definition as Model:
Another Turn of the Self-Similar Screw

Gender is actually something that we create and impose on ourselves as we go along, but it is made by cultures to seem biological and, therefore, impossible to change. We tend to see gender roles as constants and consider individual adaptations as variables. For example, differences of individual temperament are read as gender differences. An aggressive girl is said to "act like a boy"; a compliant boy is seen as "acting like a girl." The idea that a characteristic of ours is our nature causes us to look deep within ourselves to find it. But if it is a cultural construct we are looking for, it is, at least at early stages, something that doesn't already exist within us—we have to make it, according to the models and definitions that are given to us. Language itself is an important modeling element. Let us look again at how it functions in masculation.

We have not realized how cultural factors are responsible for the definition of gender because the form of the definition is tangled up in the content of gender, and its genesis is involved in its present practice. These are complex and confusing cultural factors. The definition of gender incarnates the structure of definition itself in its content, as male takes the place of female. Male behavior strives to carry out the general, over-taking position of the *definiendum*. We recognize this behavior as a thing related to the word 'male' and feed it back into the original equation, causing a social self-similar structure. There is a meta

230

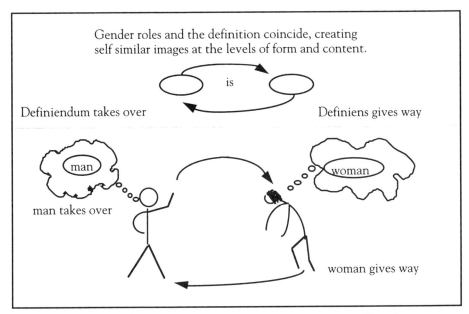

Figure 22. Gender roles and the definition coincide, creating self similar images at the levels of form and content.

level involved, perhaps without our knowing it. We feed the form of the definition itself into gender. Then we feed gender back into the form of the definition.

Immersed in language as they are, gender terms are disguised to look like other terms, and the disguise adds to their potency[2] as self-fulfilling prophecies. The self-similarity of gender terms— with their aggressive and over-taking referents in the case of terms for males, or in contrast the self-similarity with things which give way in the case of terms for noncompetitive females— appears to embed the behavior mandate of those terms within the terms themselves. (See Figure 22.) The mandate appears to reside 'inside' the terms but actually depends on an external context that has already been influenced by it for generations. The father's gender behavior has already been influenced by the self-fulfilling term 'male' when the son takes him as model. The

[2]Some languages do not use gender specific pronouns. Others compassionately extend gender distinctions to all nouns, as if to comfort children by showing that everything else is also similar to or different from the mother, and that this has little bearing on their value.

mother, like her mother before her, reinforces the mistake by giving up being the model for the boy. As she gives him into the other category because she is female, she becomes a model for the girl of giving up and giving-way.

The father, who is related to the word 'male' as its sample, also assumes in the family the position of the word, taking the place of the mother as sample. Meanwhile the 'thing'—the mother—related to this 'male' word steps aside as a sample, assuming the relative position as one of the many. The girl follows her example while the boy will eventually follow in his father's footsteps. The analogy arises here with our concept process specifically in regard to the moment in which the word takes the place of the sample, which is then no longer necessary as a point of comparison to maintain the common quality of the relative items.

The mother gives up the sample position and takes a position as a thing among the many things related to the father-word which now maintains the polarity for that category. The (self-reflecting) sample position of the father coincides with the word because, like the word, he over-takes the mother as sample. This family situation is also repeated in the definition, where the *definiens* performs a service and gives-way, functioning like the mother. The *definiendum* takes over as a permanent equivalent and substitute for things in that category functioning like the father. The father possesses the phallus and the mother and is the 'incarnated word-sample' for the concept of the boy—and perhaps for all concepts (as children of both sexes might see it).[3] Again, the situation in which male takes the place of female (and patriarchal values take the place of women's values) repeats the situation in which the whole process of exchange takes the place of giftgiving.

[3]The fact that the definition as a whole is a service which is being performed by a speaker or a writer for a listener or reader is often forgotten, so that the relation of over-taking and giving way seems to be taking place among the words themselves without human intervention. Value is being given to the words and to each other by the interlocutors from 'outside' the sentence, but this is not usually considered.

Women serve and step aside, and the gift economy steps aside, while men step forward and take over as the equivalents in the focus. This pattern can be seen reflected in yet another way in the definition. The character of *definiendum* reflects back on the *definiens* when the content is male. Vice versa, when the content is female, the *definiendum* becomes 'feminine,' more like the *definiens*. For example, in 'Women are the weak sex'—'weak sex' as the *definiens* weakly stands aside, and 'women' takes over as the *definiendum*. Thus, the content (women as things or beings who give-way) resonates with the giving-way transitional function of the *definiens*. The 'things' (women) related to the *definiendum* in this case have characteristics of the *definiens*.

'Men are the strong sex' functions in the opposite way, with strength resonating or repeating the 'over-taking' characteristics of the *definiendum*, which takes the place of the *definiens*. The 'things' (men) related to the *definiendum* in this case have the characteristics of the *definiendum*. A bridge is thus constructed by self-similarity between the level of content and the level of form in the definition. Neither level is necessarily that way, but each has been weighted by the function it performs in the social construction of gender. After the definition has been incarnated into masculated 'over-taking' behavior, the definition of gender resonates with its own heterosexual behavioral image.

The epistemological level, constructed according to the giving and receiving grain, is surely influenced by the way we do our definitions and infected with our cultural misinterpretations of gender. Human beings are artificially driven into 'male' and 'female' roles because we mistakenly interpret our physical 'givens' to imply that we belong to drastically different categories, almost different species. The male artificially creates a content for his gender by retracing some of the steps of categorization, and this pattern reflects back onto the linguistic mechanisms by which the categorization was imposed. Females enable the repetition of this pattern by serving it, which causes them to enter into it because, in fact, it is an asymmetrical pattern of nurturing and categorization-domination.

The giftgiving way is thus locked into a relation with categorization which opposes it. Then it gives-way as a consciously viable principle and is canceled by domination, which, in a self similar motion, takes over. There is complementarity of the two conflicting ways at the object level and at the meta level. The naming of the boy as 'male' is projected into the human relations of the society, and these reconfirm the naming of the boy as 'male.' (See Figure 23.) Thus every definition becomes an exercise in artificial hetero-sexism. Every definition resonates with the social projections of the gender definition. Then the gender definition is continually projected back into the individual consciousness through our speech, our capacity to self-define and to define others. The definition itself becomes the norm and discounts not only the service of its own feminine *definiens* but the importance and even the right to exist of those who do not correspond to its heterosexual patterns.

For example, the judgments of right wing bigots have a self-confirming aspect because the heterosexual form of the definition (and naming) bears out dominance and discounts the importance of those who give way to their definitions. From the epithets used by teenage boys to dominate teenage girls, 'bitch' and 'whore,' to the judgments expressed by bosses, husbands or other authority figures, 'incompetent' and 'dumb,' women are required to give-way to the over-taking *definiendum* when it is spoken by the masculated men whom they serve.

Gay bashing, racial, ideological, religious, ableist etc. derogatives also often 'degenerate' into actual physical violence. The definers take over and the defined give way. The over taking definers have 'become' the *definiendum*, the defined have become the *definiens* or the thing giving way.

We do not recognize the heterosexualization of the form of the definition partly because we have given it a 'sample' which allows us to ignore its genderized functioning. That sample is the abstract equation, which appears to be the form or 'essence' of the

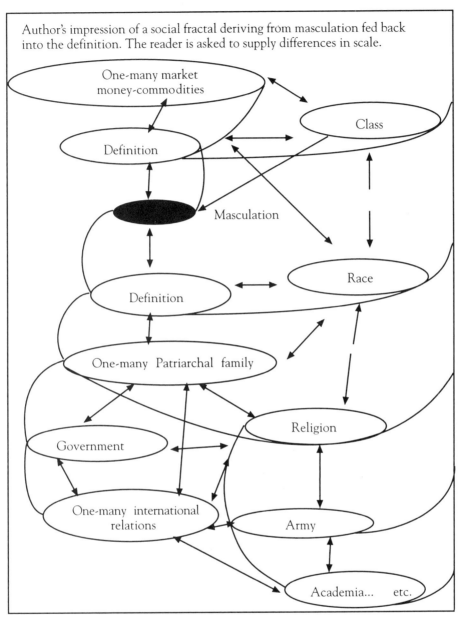

Figure 23. The reciprocal action of masculation and the
definition spawns social self-similarities.

definition itself. Using alphabetical notation 'A = B' substitutes empty place-takers for words or 'values.' Because they are empty place takers, not general (like word-gifts whose generality has been constructed as substitute samples), they seem to imply reciprocal substitutability: if A = B, B = A.[4] Moreover, the equation can seem to be simply a more complicated version of the (completely reciprocal) tautology: A = A. Taking the equation, which is a simplified and abstract imitation of the definition, as the 'sample' for all definitions, their model or 'form,' allows us to leave aside as irrelevant the overtaking and giving way that are actually taking place in the heterosexualized definition.

In fact, the reciprocal, neutral (should we say, 'sanitized?') equation takes over from the definition much as exchange takes over from barter and giftgiving and even from forced servitude. Then we give value to this image of neutrality or 'equality' and the overtaking, giving and giving way processes begin again. The equation of value for the market issued only among those products which (like masculated men in the OBN) already belong to the valued category and only deals with quantity of that value. It is used exclusively with things that are already considered exchangeable. Though the equation between a product and its price appears neutral, money becomes the incarnate *definiendum* which physically takes over while the product in exchange physically gives way. At the same time the whole process of exchange for money takes the place of giftgiving.

The feedback of the heterosexualized form of the definition into the definition produces self-similar patriarchal images at different social levels. Women's inferior position (like the *definiens*) serves as something unseen for the form of the definition to feed back into (and cancel). Then the unseen giftgiving activity coming

[4] In language, communicative need is a determining consideration. The abstract values of the equation seem to be closer to those of perception: perception X = perception Y would seem to be an appropriate content for an equation. But there is no need for us to communicate that to ourselves or each other in our ongoing daily lives because we already know it. Our perceptive apparata function. What we perceive is usually already a given as far as our consciousness of it is concerned. Our communicative needs arise in relation to others, regarding what perceptions we are paying attention to and their relevance to collaborations, understandings, collective or personal ideas, myths, histories, views of the world, etc.

from this position gives value to the form of the definition and the equation and lets its place be taken by it as the model for human interaction. In fact, a proliferation of self-similar images ensues. Women, the 'lower' classes, the many, children, the past, the future (everything but present tense, gifted and dominant men) play out the role of *definiens* to the men's *definiendum*. On a macroscopic scale, the relation is repeated among nations where one dominates and many serve. For example, the US dominates the nations in its area of influence, which give way and serve its cultural and economic hegemony. These gift relations are invisible to the majority of people in the US.

Self-Similar vs. Other-Tending Selfhood

The definition (along with its sanitized mirror, the equation) is incarnated inside us in the processes of the ego. It over-takes other-oriented giftgiving and gives value to itself. It makes others give value to it because (like any definition) it needs to have value given to it from the outside in order to function.

In the market, at the micro level, in each exchange there is a shift 'up,' which also takes the place of giftgiving. Each exchange, with its equation of value over-taking giftgiving, functions in a way which is similar to the macro level of the market itself, which takes the place of giftgiving as the mode of distribution. The micro and the macro levels confirm each other (because similarity seems to confirm). At the same time, much value is being given from the outside to the market as the over-taking totality made up of innumerable exchanges—and hence to each exchange over and above giftgiving. Similarly, in masculated ego thinking the micro level of equation and definition is equal (in its structure or process) to macro level expressions of a self-reflecting and self-similar male identity which overcomes.[5]

Large scale incarnations of the word and of the definition, in exchange and in hierarchies, in commercial organizations and

[5]When a pecking order is established in which one male becomes the 'sample' or over-taker with regard to other males, those who give-way can still maintain their identities as 'samples' and over-takers with regard to their wives and children.

social, religious, and political institutions, function as macro levels, which again confirm the micro levels of the masculated ego and the form of the (hetero-sexualized) definition or judgment. These institutions also provide niches for masculated egos to play out their social destinies, creating chains of domination. We have created social self-similar structures and different scales at which they can 'reflect' each other. The form of the definition (and masculation) repeats again and again, justifying the importance given to similarity over difference— and the value of conceptual norm-based one-many processes over giftgiving need-directed processes.

No explanatory capacity is allowed to giftgiving, so gift-based activities (such as the attribution of value itself) are explained by valued professors as deriving from categories and concepts, from systems of mutually exclusive elements, from hierarchies of marginal choices under scarcity, or from *sui generis* psychological or physiological processes, or they remain a mystery.[6] Our society is trapped in a hall-of-mirrors, and we are carrying mirrors in our minds, in our organizations, and in our purses.

The giftgiving, 'other-tending' self is not dependent on thinking for being because its bearer becomes socially relevant by satisfying the needs of others and receiving from them. Probably much of masculated identity also comes from participating in unacknowledged giftgiving and receiving, but the identity-forming capacity is attributed to thinking, to equivalence, to mirroring, and to 'finding oneself.' The identity of gift givers and receivers is created and validated by performing the process of material giving itself, rather than by performing only or mainly its analog, in language and thinking.

Moreover, since the one who derives his/her identity from thinking has many other needs, the giftgiver satisfies them and

[6]Even Marx's 'labor value' could be viewed as a portion of gift value trapped and filtered through the definitional process of exchange. If labor could directly satisfy needs, it would result in co-munication and would attribute value to people. However, given the market, labor expended on one product is expressed relative to labor expended on all other products through the equation of value, as exchange value. In this, it is like a thing related to a (quantitatively divided) word. Marx did not include any of the other gifts that are given to the labor process—women's work in the home, gifts of higher or lower prices, or gifts of nature—as contributing to labor value.

validates him (usually, though not necessarily, a male) as 'deserving.' If the person with the more abstract identity achieves a general social position, his/her nurturer is sometimes seen as giving to society as a whole transitively through him/her. (This is also the case for those in hierarchies who are in giftgiving positions serving those in higher social positions.)

Women have been nurturing men along with their mirrors. But rather than distributing mirrors to everyone, we need to put the mirrors down and turn our giving towards each other and towards solving the social problems they have created. Women need to nurture and solve general social problems directly ourselves, not to turn over our authority to masculated self-reflecting males. We need to care for society as a whole, promoting the giftgiving model at a general level, for all. Not only do we practice other-tending in our personal lives and in the solution of general problems, for example, by giving money, time, and imagination to satisfy general social, economic, peace and environmental needs, ending hunger, war and pollution, but we propose giftgiving as the model of a necessary paradigm shift for all.

Thinking and Being

"I think; therefore I am" are the words of the exchanger as privileged 'owning sample.' Descartes' *cogito* denied the importance of the existence of others, the mother, society as a whole, and nature, for the individual's own existence. Descartes took on a position of radical skepticism—not accepting anything as a 'given.' His first step was to decontextualize himself from giftgiving and receiving and to try to find the self-evident basis of his being. Because the disqualification of other-orientation does not allow the exchanger to find the confirmation of her/his existence in the satisfaction of the needs of the other and the continued existence and well being of the other, s/he also has to find her/his source in mirroring her/himself alone. The receiver's lack of gratitude toward the giver also results in his/her ignorance of the other as source.

There is an aspect of self-similarity in the process which influences the ego formation—and particularly the masculated ego formation in the *cogito*. Here, as in exchange, there is a shift to the logic of substitution which takes the place of the logic of giving. An example of the logic of substitution: 'thinking' is provided, by which the use of the verb 'to be' (I 'am') is justified. There is also a shift from discourse to definition and self-definition, leaving aside contingent communicative needs. Because it is decontextualized (or does that to itself), the ego usually has to continue being validated and over-valued in order to continue to exist. Descartes provided an internal validation of the ego by focussing on its self-similarity. The *cogito* is influenced by the equation and the self-similarity of exchange, and it involves valuing equality (even tautology) and logical consequence over need. The equality of thinking and being do indeed stem from the same source: is language-in-denial-of-giftgiving.[7] Usually the being of the self would include relations with others!

Descartes' gift to patriarchy was the satisfaction of the ego's communicative need for a logical proof of its existence. This need is derived from the denial of the giftgiving-and-receiving which already proves and creates human existence materially. Self-similarity in thinking constructs a norm, a sort of ceiling mirror to refer to, a reflection of the self, which is actually its product. It is a re-verberation in the microphone that we mistake for a message from the universe or from the structure of communication and selfhood—and it appears to be evidence that the self is the source of the self. As in the concept where the sample male is related to the word 'male,' "I think; therefore I am" is self-similar, self-referential. Descartes recognized thinking as definition; then the definition itself became the tautological ('I am I') underpinning of "I think; therefore I am." Here the definition has an over-taking source—himself.

Definitional thinking reflected in the equation becomes the 'mark' of the 'one' who is the sample for the concept of

[7]Similarly, the equation of work and money stem from distribution in denial of giftgiving.

existence. Both are over-valued, like exchange. Like the phallus, the self-similar 'mark' which puts males into the privileged category, the kind of thinking which Descartes was doing at the moment he thought up his immortal phrase puts those who do it into a privileged category as 'existing' and thus takes the place of giving as the justification for being. Definitional thinking and the verb 'to be' both function using substitution, and 'to be' brings thinking (the acts of substitution related to the word) into the present. Thinking is defined as definitional, equational, and logically consequential—if/then—instead of as transposed giftgiving.[8]

But something's 'being' just means that it is socially valuable enough for it to be related to words (for others), by an act which may be substituted by the verb 'to be.' So, thinking is a socially valuable activity, and the social subject who is doing it 'is'—especially if s/he succeeds in making this valuable (to others). Descartes' saying he is thinking brings forward a social general character of thinking, which he identifies with himself. 'I am thinking' is self-referential and seems obvious or clear because it is self-similar: We call the activity—expressed

[8]Perhaps the *homunculus*, the little man seen by philosophers sitting inside our minds recognizing endless regresses, is the internalized image of the phallus which corresponds with all things in the 'sample' position everywhere. But, as philosophers saw, he is only a figment of our imaginations, a reflection of reflections. They reasoned that, if knowledge is based on the reflection of reality, and we have a picture of reality in our minds, we would have to recognize those pictures and, therefore, have pictures of those pictures. There would thus be a kind of little man in our minds with pictures of the pictures, and a little man in his mind with more pictures, etc. What philosophers don't reflect on is that the *homunculus* should be replaced by a little woman—or better, a little mother, a *matericula*). Instead of just sitting there making pictures, recognizing the image of the baby crying, a mother recognizes the need and intervenes, does something about it (feeds her, for example). Thus, if *matericula* were there in our minds, she would recognize the picture of the baby crying but would feel a need to do more than that, to satisfy the needs the picture suggested to her. The division between internal and external would be bridged in different ways by *matericula* and by *homunculus*. The reason for this is that recognizing similarities is more static, less informative, than the process of satisfying needs. Thus, when satisfying needs is transferred to an internal scenario, it can remain an active process. *Homunculus* is totally dependent on *matericula*'s care, since he can't do anything but reflect. But he does not seem to make pictures of *matericula*, either in 'his' own mind or in the external world. Perhaps she moves too fast for him. Perhaps she moves as fast as the electric charge going from one synapse to another. In fact, couldn't we see brain activity in terms of giving, a movement from an abundance towards a lack? In that case, wouldn't we be doing something on the physiological plane that more or less matched what we are doing on the linguistic plane and in the external world? Perhaps those interested in the brain-mind questions might try to satisfy their needs with this moving-picture theory of reality.

in such phrases as 'I think,' 'I am' and 'I think; therefore I am'—thinking. There is a shift into substitution in the sentence itself, as there is with the verb 'to be.' And he satisfies others' ego needs to know they exist, when they read his book. What a gift!

But Descartes was not really alone, even though he was de-contextualized, because thinking had to be valuable to others in order for it to be related before him to a word as its name as well as to other words contingently in discourse. Both thinking and the words are evidence of the existence of others, and of the context in which the (supposedly decontextualized) thinker is operating. Value has been given to thinking by the many in the past.

But value is also given to the thinker in the present, not only by her/himself but by all those who are nurturing her/him generally as part of society, and individually as a person they know. The formula is: take thinking as the important quality (the sensory invariant?) of the thing that's the sample, then say we are doing it, so equal to the sample, so substitutable by the sample and by whatever words substitute for it, so our acts are all substitutable by the verb 'to be,' so they and we, exist. It's another 'having' that makes us 'deserve' to exist. We correspond to 'existing.' Perhaps I could call all this 'Anti-Cartesian Linguistics:' Descartes was just re-writing thinking as being, or vice versa, and (like Chomsky and the many other thinkers who have been misguided by masculation) over-emphasized the importance of the rewriting (re-naming) process itself.

Being is Masculine

Membership in the privileged category is a prerequisite for possibly eventually becoming its norm. For boys, this is the possibility of becoming a man, a father, a sample for the family and for 'human.' For both boys and girls, it now might imply being in a top position in a profession. Being a member of the privileged category creates a need to continue to be relevant in that way, to merit the definition. For boys (and other exchangers), it is a need to develop a masculated (exchange) identity—which means over-taking, giving up the mother and giftgiving, etc.

The gift the boy (or the exchanger) gives up is his 'feminine' (actually human) nurturing identity. He/she is validated by others because of this, economically anyway, and is rewarded with the self-esteem allowed to those of us who act according to the masculated norm, becoming successes 'in the system.' Such successes seem to exist and 'deserve to exist' more than those who do not succeed. We embrace the paradigm of exchange, much as at an early age we embraced language, or boys took on their male identity. It seems to be just the way things 'are.'

We have been saying that the verb 'to be' substitutes the acts of substitution of the other words in the definition, giving to being a partial similarity to masculation and to the shift into exchange. 'Is' becomes similar to '$.' The degree of existence of males seems superior to that of females, as it does of some races and classes over others. If we then add the idea of deserving, we can see how the different 'shifts' to a 'higher' level all validate the supposed superiority of white upper class males, who seem to 'deserve to exist' more than others.

By playing out the role of the *definiendum* in the tautology ('I am I') or ('I am a thinking being') males are substituting the act of substitution, like the verb 'to be' substituting the act of substitution in the definition. Being seems to imply being masculated, and the most masculated (or most-often masculated) over-takes the others, and 'deserves' to exist the most. This occurs because 'being,' like masculation, is already connected with substitution and exchange.

The masculated egos are the categorizers, who include themselves in the category as samples, validated by the verb 'to be' and by money—so they 'naturally' use money to further their own existence. How could they deserve to be categorizers if they did not deserve to exist? Then those women or classes or races or sexual

243

preference groups who are made to believe they don't deserve to exist (they are not 'good enough') have to justify their own existence by taking care of, serving, those who do 'deserve.' (They can also be just anyone put into the category of the undeserving by those who control the definition.) 'Existence,' then, becomes just another privileged category.

Existence by Proxy

Exchange places people and things into a special category, which receives value from the outside. In their role of giving value to that category, the many who serve the deservers also deserve. They seem to participate, to some extent, in the privileged category by proxy. By giving value to the system and helping another person succeed in it, we put ourselves in a chain of transitivity, so that some goods flow to us from the exchanges of those in the category. This is the case for 'nonworking' wives who receive the table scraps of exchange. The fact that some goods do come back to them makes it appear that exchange is the source of gifts, the great nurturer.

This is one reason why women continue to nurture exchange and the exchangers with our credence, our love and our un-monetized work. The model of masculation appears more attractive and deserving than the model of mothering, and we mother it. At puberty, we choose the masculated model over the mothering model, as more viable. Many daughters leave their mothers (at least in spirit) because they become convinced that masculation is human, and it is their duty to nurture someone in that category or to become someone in that category—someone who 'contributes' and who, therefore, deserves to exist and to be nurtured.

The person who does not somehow succeed in deserving to exist remains in a no-person's land. Her lack of 'self-esteem' is really due to the co-optation of (privileged) existence by successfully masculated women and men and their help-meets. Both deserving and existence bring with them the substitution of masculation and exchange for giftgiving. We must either join the substitutes and give up giftgiving, or we must nurture them if we want to deserve to exist.

Being Balanced

It may seem to women that they can 'balance work and family,' maintaining a nurturing attitude towards their husbands and children, while working in the exchange economy. This very balance, however, validates the masculated mode. By giving equal value to giftgiving and to exchange, we hide the creativity and fertility of giftgiving, constraining it into a comparison according to the principles of (equal) exchange and eclipsing its capacity as a model—draining the energy of the givers. We validate exchange again by using its principles to regulate giftgiving.

Men are also encouraged to 'rediscover the feminine' in themselves, mitigating the extremes of masculation without shifting paradigms. Like reformism or charity, these attitudes only make patriarchy more livable for some of its members. The principle of 'nothing in excess' is used excessively. Privileged groups 'balance their masculine and feminine sides' while reaping the advantages of an exploitative masculated economic and ideological system, which forces the many into a position of giftgiving towards them. Again, equations are overvalued and needs are ignored. The golden mean which quantifies caring (balancing it equally with not caring) is just that—mean. It allows privileged groups to live more comfortably with each other, without solving the problems that are causing the unhappiness of the whole.

The model of balance, like the more completely masculated model, really discredits the originary and creative aspect of giving and receiving. It confuses the issue by integrating the feminine according to the masculine standard. It keeps us from looking at the needs that are crying out to be met. There is, first of all, a meta need for us to go beyond balance, in order to satisfy the needs of all. But, of course, this is not a balanced point of view. The principles of masculation and of mothering battle it out, causing a see-saw effect. We are like a person shifting from foot to foot, never becoming unbalanced enough to take a step forward or a step up to a true meta level—or even to put a foot down to take a step to stop the destruction of the planet.

Everyone embraces the masculated model. Daughters admire their fathers and boyfriends while taking their mothers for granted. Mothers over-value their sons and husbands, under-valuing their own giftgiving way for themselves and for their daughters, who often eventually do the same thing. Feminism is changing this somewhat, and women's caring thought and behavior is recounted in stories and poems and even sociological studies, but we do not yet attribute to it the kind of value we attribute to exchange and to masculated thinking and behavior.

Nurturing is the origin of our species—not competition and hierarchy or the survival of the fittest. Human mothers ensure the survival of the unfittest—infants. And all of us are unfit in many ways; our soft skin, vulnerable bellies, short teeth, and varied diets make us animals with many needs that others' gifts can and must satisfy. Our very adaptability allows a proliferation and specification of needs and desires. (I am hungry—not just for anything, but for *tamales* like they make in South Texas—even though I don't know how to make them myself. My need—in this case, my delight—is specific and comes from my history.)

The process of identifying needs and satisfying them—during which we learn the culturally specific varieties of goods and services that can be provided for a great many needs and desires, and then actually learn to provide for them and also to receive that provision from others—is the basic human process. Giving more value to giftgiving, and in this case to the handing down of culture, might allow us access to the generality we now seem to find in money and other one-many social structures. Now the artificial need to exchange has been extended to

246

everyone and creates a degree of generality in the means of exchange which is rivaled only by heads of state—whose images, after all, are stamped upon it.

The Creation of Scarcity
By Those Who Deserve to Exist

Exchange challenges us to that we can satisfy others' needs, making our own survival dependent upon our being 'fit' enough to produce, in an 'unnatural selection' process. Some species of animals develop hierarchies in times of scarcity while, in times of abundance, the dominance model is relaxed—and mating and feeding take place in less structured ways. The creation of scarcity which facilitates exchange among humans makes the hierarchical mode seem essential to survival. We imitate the hierarchical behavior of animal groups beyond which we had already evolved through generalized mothering. The giftgiving in language still maintains our evolutionary leap on an abstract plane, while concretely we seem to have leaped backwards by making nurturing as difficult as possible, acting in ferocious, parasitic and adversarial ways.

Technologies of various kinds, including earth-friendly technologies, have the potential for providing abundance for all. This abundance threatens exchange by making it irrelevant and unnecessary. Giftgiving in abundance can provide for everyone, and abundance is necessary for effective life-enhancing giftgiving. In abundance, forced giving, as it appears in exchange and hierarchies, has no reason for being because needs can always be satisfied by a multitude of ready sources.

Hierarchies are used to continually re-create scarcity by siphoning off surplus wealth. They thereby maintain exchange as the mode of distribution for all. Wars are fought to counter the challenges to hierarchies and markets by other hierarchies and markets. These wars destroy resources, creating scarcity, thereby ensuring the continuation of an environment appropriate for exchange. Preparing for the wars and spending the money necessary for high-tech armaments and the support of large armed forces also depletes the civilian economy in 'peace time,' so that abundance does not accrue.

The appearance is the opposite. Employment in national war industries is highly visible and lucrative and appears to 'contribute' to the economy. However, these are jobs which produce nothing, gifts from the public to the workers. Paid for by tax money and devoted to the protection of the group or system, they seem to have the generality and social significance to which all in the society aspire. Unfortunately, the content of that generality is not nurturing but the propagation of death. The products of that labor never enter the nurturing economy; they are used instead to destroy the potential abundance of the local and global co-munity.

The increased government spending that is necessary in wartime (and the gifts of time, energy and enthusiasm given by patriotic citizens to the national effort) inject more elements of giftgiving into the economy as a whole, which stimulate it (creating more profit) while allowing a 'use' of the output—its destruction in fighting the war—which does not threaten the system of exchange by remaining in the economy and creating abundance.

Colonies and conquered territories provide the (minimally monetized) gift labor and resources necessary to allow excessive profit-taking by a few in the colonialist countries, which can then be reinvested as capital in war industries in the colonialist countries. The gifts thus come from 'elsewhere' and do not threaten the 'developed' monetized economy with their abundant presence, because they can be quickly cycled out in waste production—of armaments.

Now, in spite of the geographical distance, the North has found it useful to create scarcity in the South through World Bank and International Monetary Fund loans,[9] structural adjustment, and environmental depletion. This makes it possible

[9]Typically, the money from these loans has been quickly cornered by the elites, while the nations' poor are extenuated by trying to pay the interest—and the principal hangs fire.

248

to channel the gifts of the many with even more precision into enterprises that do not create the abundance which would challenge the system.

Instead, the stream of gifts—cheap labor (labor of which a large percentage is a gift) and low cost (high gift-quotient) raw materials—create an abundance of consumer goods to which only those working at a certain level in the exchange economy have access through their 'effective demand.' These goods again distinguish the 'haves' from the 'have-nots.' The communications industry uses radio, television and computers to broadcast 'free' information, music and images—products of our artistic gifts. These products are 'chosen' by the market and, therefore, usually help not only to sell other products (by modifying needs and desires), but also to create a consensus around the market system itself.

All of these extreme results come from the co-validation of masculation by a large number of overlapping, misinterpreted self-similar structures. From government to language, from economics to religion, from the military to academia—these structures overlap, repeat and validate each other. The ways we formulate our ideas of existence, being, and decontextualized thinking validate masculated males through similarity between their processes and the process of masculation (which originates in naming and the definition anyway).

Exchange, as the substitution of the logic of substitution for giftgiving, brings up the question of de-serving as well as the question of power, and of inclusion or exclusion from the category to which value is given. Our assertion of 'being,' though it may be logically and developmentally prior to exchange, validates exchange through similarity and vice versa, after the shift has occurred.[10] Many of the different substitution processes—masculation, the verb 'to be,' exchange, and the judgments of correspondence and deserving—hang together to form a self-structuring and self-

[10]See George Thompson on the influence of the development of money and philosophy. *Studies in Ancient Greek Society, vol. II: The First Philosophers*, 2nd ed. London: Lawrence and Wishart, 1961 [1955].

perpetuating 'reality,' a sort of servo-mechanism which, at many different levels, takes the place of and overpowers an ever-present and still possible gift-based world.

The 'new' reality seems to be more valid, more 'real' than the earlier one which, nevertheless, continues to support it. Although it is unacknowledged, the giftgiving process, like an oyster making a pearl out of a grain of sand, keeps on giving to the harsher reality of exchange, making it viable and humanizing it (to some extent). The masculated status quo, with its hierarchies and privileged ones, is maintained by the gifts of women and men both inside and outside it. As what *is*, it seems to deserve to exist more than its alternatives (the alternative realities of so-called 'primitive' peoples, for example) and we nurture it.

Meanwhile, not to be outdone by hidden givers, those who have succeeded in the exchange economy sometimes balance their egotism by dispensing a (usually not abundant) bit of charity to the underclass, or by proposing tendentious solutions to the social problems they have helped to create. For example, I recently heard of a proposal according to which the children of mothers who were on welfare would be sent to orphanages, as if paid professional 'experts' in an institutional setting were better for children than their single mothers. Having reduced the mothers to direst poverty, making nurturing almost impossible, politicians and 'social thinkers' propose to take their place with one more paternalistic, monetized model.

The reward for these thinkers lies in 'showing' that the masculated model is not only more efficient but more compassionate than mothers doing direct nurturing. Mothering becomes one more job from which women can be fired, with power over the inclusion or exclusion from the category given again to masculated men and institutions. The mothers' identities as giftgivers is unrecognized and, even though the job is unmonetized, it can be taken away from them. Robbed of their children, they are also dispossessed of their giftgiving identity and their exchange identity. They have no way to create an identity or to deserve to exist. Lacking all possibilities for masculation by

250

inclusion in superior categories, these women give to the privileged categories by contrast, and they receive the punishment for lacking which allays the fear and envy of the havers, thus expiating the crime of proposing the model of mothering without men.

In fact, the state steps in as a substitute for the father, once again eclipsing women's way. Whether as capitalist welfare or as management of resources by a communist or socialist state, the law or the charity of the collective fathers discounts and often defiles the reality of giftgiving life.

The visitor from outer space would recognize the importance of the fact that women do some 60% of the world's agricultural work, yet own only about 1% of the world's property. Feminists usually think of this strange disproportion in terms of justice— that is, of creating change to make women own as great a quantity of property as men do. I would like to propose that the reason women own so little property is that we have a different way of relating to our surroundings. We need to dismantle the structures of patriarchy, including the structures of ownership that are based on masculation, and propose a women's model of property based on giftgiving.

Does Giftgiving Exist?

Money is the means for satisfying co-municative need in the community of exchangers, private property owners. Exchange value is the relevance of products to that kind of contradictory mutually exclusive co-munication. Like the verb 'to be,' money substitutes the act of substitution of one product for another.

I believe that the co-municative value of things is expressed in words, which take their place as gifts in creating human bonds. Words may also be seen as having a positional value relative to each other in the system of the *langue*.[11] If kinds of things were not relevant to human beings repeatedly, they would not become

[11]Though their basic relation of words to each other in Saussure's *langue* is that of purely differential mutual exclusion, they do have some similarities that look like Vigotsky's complexes.

related to words as their names (though they could still be talked about in sentences).[12] Thus, the reason anyone has any words given to her/him by others is that they are in use in the collective, which is made up of many others whom each of us will never know.

The value of something for the collective is outside the individual communicative interaction and outside the individual money exchange transaction. It is really for *others*. The identity of a cultural item can be found in its verbal substitute gift, outside the individual communicative interaction, in the collective. An analogous situation happens with the quantitative determination of a price. The price is determined by the value of the product for others in the society whom we will never know. If we look at the qualitative value of things for communication as expressed in words, and the quantitative value of things for the contradictory kind of communication that is material exchange, as expressed in price, and correct for the difference between qualitative value and quantitative value, we can understand the mechanisms of both.

In fact, for both, it is the importance of things for the community that brings them to the forefront of our conversation, or to the forefront of the market. They are 'for others and therefore for me.' Cats are called 'cats' in English because for each of us that is what they are for others. A can of coffee costs $4.00 because that is what it is for others, also. When the amount others will give for it changes, it changes for the individual, as well. We can look at the value of the different component parts of the coffee, the price of the beans paid to the coffee grower, the price of the labor paid to the workers, the price of the transportation of the beans, their grinding, the price of the can, etc.

Each of these, and whatever component parts it might have, depends upon what that part is 'for others,' what others give for it. For each linguistic or economic transaction, the identification of what something is depends on what it is for the collective—for the many—outside that transaction itself. We talked about the

---

[12] For example, if cats are not present in a culture they might be talked about as 'those strange animals that say meow and have a long tail.'

verb 'to be' being the substitute for the act of substitution, and money as having a similar process. For the linguistic and the economic realms respectively, something is valuable when it is important enough to the collective to have its place taken by a word as its name, by 'is' as a substitute for that act of substitution, or by another product in exchange—and by money as its equivalent in the quantity of its price.

Both language and exchange leave co-municative giftgiving out of focus (particularly when exchange value has become the sample of value) and this happens in the collective mind. The gift aspects of life remain relatively unconscious and undiscussed. Gifts taking-the-place-of gifts has been assimilated to exchange (which is a very magnetic model) and to the definition influenced by masculation. For this reason, the value of giftgiving is not recognized collectively. It is almost not named.[13] It would seem paradoxical to say that giftgiving is valuable; value is the existence of something for the collective, and that giftgiving is not recognized by the collective as existing.

On the other hand, if we look at both the verb 'to be' and at money as substitutes for the act of substitution, we can see that giftgiving—which is *not* substituted—may reasonably seem to be not pertinent to language nor valuable to exchange. Thus if language and exchange both require substitution for the assertion of existence or of value, giftgiving, which does not involve substitution, may seem to be nonexistent and not valuable. Masculation, on the contrary, which is a construction of self-similar substitutions, appears to exist and to be very valuable. It is not surprising that it attracts the many gifts that are not given to giftgiving.

On the other hand, both 'being' and exchange for money are influenced and 'distressed' by masculation, which feeds back the principle of over-taking into the definition and into the economy—so that 'being' or 'being valuable' seem to imply over-taking or even being the one or sample. Again, none of this is our

---

[13] For example, I have had difficulty using terms like 'nurturing' or 'mothering,' which bring with them too much focus on infancy.

'fault.' These contradictions are mostly just due to *logical* tangles.

Thus the verb 'to be' and money reflect the power we have given to language to take us away from our mothers and the Mother. We do not see 'being' or 'value' as having relevance to substitution because we deny the reality of what has been substituted, just as we deny the mother (and the earth) as substituted model—as if she didn't exist (especially if existence has to do with substitution). We 'for-get' that the mother is active and that she actively gives and compassionately gives-way. Our original framework comes from giftgiving but, through being masculated or through caring for those who have been masculated and their processes, we learn to give value to the definitional aspects of language and life—substitution, having, keeping exchange and 'being'—rather than to the gift aspects and to giving.

The mother does not have to give way. If the mother did not give way, we might re-frame our view of the world and see how much of life is already in her giftgiving mode. We could see things as gifts from Mother Earth—not just as products of Adam's dominating names—and we would therefore treat them with the care which they need if they are not to be destroyed. Many of us are already doing this now, as we appreciate the gifts of nature, culture, synchronicity, good will, and the gift of life itself. What we sense as the immanence of 'being' is really the result of our creative receptive mode directed in gratitude towards the gifts of life and the earth, while suspending (for the moment) the distressed mediation of language and exchange.

Perhaps we could see community as part of the Mother, giving value to things as giving to us and giving value to us, and things giving value to their names, which we give to each other, giving value to us. The earth would co-municate with us through her fruit and birdsongs, our bodies and our giftgiving selves. We would participate in a co-municative relation with nature. Now the model of the community is formed of one-many mutually exclusive owners with owned property giving value-as-position to themselves and discrediting the categories of the 'have-nots.'

254

Property having to do with giftgiving (giveable and receivable property) is different from the private property that goes through exchange. We can create a caring relation with property rather than a relation of domination. Perhaps the gift paradigm would require a lighter kind of ownership, more like the property of our bodies which (in safety) are basically shareable but usually not for the moment being shared. We would have a relationship of companionship with property, of use, gratitude, and stewardship. We could consider it according to the model of the breast, not the penis—the property of something that can give in an on-going way, rather than the property of a penetrating tool or a 'mark' that puts us in a superior category.

A women's model would pay attention to needs and, in abundance, needs could proliferate in variety and specificity. They might also include psychological needs for security and for a bond with one's surroundings, so that the one who cares for something is the one it is for. In abundance, the need for property would be less intense than it now is because the consequences of not-having would be only that gifts would come from some other direction. Where having and not-having are no longer psychologically invested with the nightmares of childhood, law and retribution would no longer be 'needed.' Nor would the state be required or allowed to step in as the collective father-owner.

At present, the kind of property that involves sharing with ease and the enjoyment of nature and her abundant resources is usually reserved for the wealthy as a reward for having more. The point is not to keep everyone, including the rich, from enjoying the abundance of nature and culture but to extend that possibility to everyone. All of us need to realize how deeply our society is under the spell of a collective psychosis. We urgently need to heal it and ourselves.

Indigenous peoples have often had cultures which used the mothering model and the giftgiving way much more than our own. It would be interesting to find out to what extent they integrated linguistic mechanisms along with their giftgiving and what different kinds of property they propose. The Iroquois, a matriarchal society in which a council of women had important decision-making power, and which used the word for woman (instead of the word for man) to mean 'human being,' gave different proper names to each of the tribal members. A name became available only when the person bearing it died.[14] The names of the tribal members thus constituted a *langue*, and we could see the members of the tribe as the socially valuable 'things'—a culture, a world—related to those words. In European patriarchy—or puerarchy—we have made some people into things: women, and some into words: men—and we mediate between their socially valuable 'properties' with the 'money-word.'

Our patriarchal state of affairs is certainly not a more rational way of organizing the society than the gynarchical way of the Iroquois. All of the different cultures that existed before they were overtaken, destroyed and redefined by the White Man and his ways were socio-economic experiments engaged in by the many. Some of them gave value to mothers and to symbolic and co-municative giftgiving. We can learn alternative ways of living from them.

In the gift mode, 'being' is actually co-munication with the earth or other humans, and we are actually still in the gift mode a lot in spite of our participation in exchange. Our experience itself involves receiving sense perceptions and information—giving destinations to the world as we experience it, in needs which we can satisfy, whether they are other's needs, our own, or needs of our surroundings. Needs grow according to the means of their satisfaction, the ear becomes educated to the kinds of music it hears. Some needs are more basic than others, but even they diversify into tastes and preferences for the different means of satisfaction, the different gifts Mother Nurture and Mother Nature provide.

[14] See Elizabeth Tooker, "Women in Iroquois Society," in *Iroquois Women, An Anthology*, ed. W.G. Spittal, Iroqrafts, Ohsweken, Ontario, 1990. "By Iroquois custom, each clan holds a set of personal names. When a child is born he or she is given a name 'not in use.' This 'baby name' is usually later changed for an 'adult name' that is not then 'in use,' that is, one belonging to someone now deceased or to someone whose name has been changed" (112).

Women's existence does not consist in giving-way or being owned or owning but in a completely different relation to the world (and to property), a relation which is potentially not mutually exclusive but need-destined, 'other-destined.' Boundaries are only made necessary by fights among 'one-manies' striving to be larger 'samples.' If we gave value to needs and recognized and appreciated their complexity, we would also recognize and satisfy each other's needs for keeping and for independence. Women's care extends logically to the environment. Giving value to needs at all levels also allows us to give value to large-scale general needs.

At present, the need to heal the planet is a need of the collective, and it is being collectively addressed—without, however, passing through the human mothering model. Many of us are concerned about Mother Earth but still consider human mothering unimportant. It is in mothering, however, and being mothered that we can find the framework for living in peace with each other, so that we can stop over-taking and destroying the earth.

If we could diminish the exchange economy and its castration envy motivations of having and not-having, we could live in harmony with a kind of semi-private property, which was also pertinent to the collective as environment. The forest would no longer be seen as valuable to the logging company that owned it, but rather to those humans and animals who live in it and use its direct gifts respectfully with gratitude, cherishing them. The forests transformed into logs do not satisfy a real need of the collective, but only the profit motive need of the private owner. The need of the buyers with effective demand has to be created. Whether the trees are to be transformed into toilet paper, chop sticks, or building materials, alternatives exist and the needs of the public can be educated towards them and towards the collective and environmental good.

Instead, on the large scale, capitalistic exchange uses the collective as means to the satisfaction of everyone's need for the means of economic communication, for money. The need for profit is abstract. Everyone needs the same thing. This common unitary need for (more) money distorts our view of other needs. The value of money is like the linguistic value of everything, of 'being,' seen as substitution (over-taking), not as the immanence of the gift.

Nothingness is not the opposite of being. What is really the opposite of being involves a reinterpretation of the verb 'to be', which includes nonsign co-munication connected to language through the need-satisfying gift process, not through over-taking or substitution and giving-way. Similarly, the opposite of the one-many property[15] relation is not not-having but woman-based gentle property. Because of masculation, an abundant nurturing relation with property seems to be a prize of the privileged 'haves.' Similarly, a nurturing wife seemed to be a reward given to men for being male. Keeping property away from others makes us unable to receive and transmit its value, and unable to appreciate its relevance to a sharing collective. According to the linguistic logic, it is for ourselves and, therefore, not for others and therefore—not for ourselves. When we keep something within the system of mutually exclusive private ownership, we cannot imitate the mothering model with it.

Recently, reports of so-called 'primitive' people have become popular in the US because they describe ways of living which center around giftgiving, based upon a spiritual source. The story of the Australian Aborigines,[16] who travel with no supplies across the outback, depending on the gifts of the creator for their survival—and receiving them—is an example of a gift-based way of life (though at this point taking place in scarcity). Such stories become popular in the US because they point to an attitude which is healing for us, although we are practicing an economy which contradicts it.

Religions and New Age therapies promote gratitude for our blessings, putting us into a gift framework. The questions that

[15] Including 'one-many' property of the State.
[16] Marlo Morgan, *Mutant Message Down Under*, Harper Collins, New York, 1994.

arise here are, "Can we heal individually or spiritually while the society of which we are a part marauds the earth and destroys the very people who inspire us with their faith and alternative ways?" and "Can our individual healing change the paradigm, rather than reinforce it by assimilating some of its principles on an individual basis?" Our attempts to heal individually and spiritually must connect with attempts to heal the collective and the planet.

Vice versa, attempts to heal the collective, such as the feminist movement, the 'left' movements for social and economic change, and the environmental movement must also pass through individual healing. The model of the mother exists on both the individual and the collective levels. The gift paradigm, with mothering as its carrier, is the functional and poetic norm to which society can return.

According to the logic of exchange, women's way of property deserves to exist because of what it has already contributed to humanity. If we want to shift paradigms towards women's way, however, we cannot use the logic of exchange, re-instating a paying-back mode. For-getting the mother involves embracing exchange, turning away from the mother and getting something else in her place. When we are for-getting, we are not for-giving the mother and the way of the mother. Instead, we must all be consistently for-giving if the gift way is to function. And we need to keep our definitions on the verbal plane rather than incarnating them.

Chapter 15
Pointing and Patriarchy

The process of 'engendering'—which in English means something like 'bringing into reality'—is itself an act of giftgiving prior to gender. The gift is the living child her/him self. Then the boy child is given 'away' because he receives what seems to be a material 'gift,' which is not given to girls—by which greater value is given to him. The 'gift' that privileges its possessor from the beginning is the penis. Rereading Freud's Oedipal stage from the point of view of the gift paradigm would allow this interpretation. But the child is not adapted to creatively 'receive' his social superiority at such an early age. Many questions about it must come to his mind, as Freud speculated.

The logical possibilities involved in this 'gift' and its source are all problematical. If it came from the mother, she gave what she did not have, or she gave up her own. If it came from the father, he gave what he did not lose. Since the penis is the 'property' that removes the child from the category of his giftgiving mother, he gives up a lot for it (he gives up his human giftgiving potential).

In fact, it is his ongoing experience of nurturing that gives a content to whatever categories the boy may be forming, including his own identity. Telling him that he belongs to a gender category which does not nurture defines him as outside of the life process he is experiencing. Definitions and models of masculinity are attempts to give the male gender category a content when, outside nurturing, there is little content to be had. The very structure of the definition and of naming become the backbone of the masculated identity as a social ideal.

There are, of course, many individual variations to this story and, fortunately, things are changing. Now because of feminism, many men have chosen to take part in child care. Stronger and more conscious mothers, less emphasis on masculinity in some families, and more nurturing male role-models are changing the education of children in the US and elsewhere. The legacy of masculation in the society is great, however, and continues to be played out in social structures and rebroadcast back into the family. Themes of male violence and domination pervade our imagination on television, in films and in reality. Crimes of rape, battery and murder continue to be perpetrated against women and children. Secret horrors are perpetrated beneath benign surfaces. 'Perfect' fathers rape and torture their children at home. The School of the Americas trains foreign soldiers in torture and fascism. The CIA destabilizes countries through deniable bribery, torture and murder. Endemic poverty, resulting in the death of millions, continues to be created by giving to the few. Wars continue to be fought, devastating human lives throughout the globe. The environment is degraded daily by the long-term pollution created by business and war.

Whatever the less masculated exceptions at the individual level, the great social mechanism of patriarchy is hurting everyone and must be radically changed. It is towards this mechanism that women and their allies among caring men must turn their attention. We all have to understand how the mechanism works in order to be able to change it successfully. And in order to understand it we must look at it, though the view may cause us some discomfort. Otherwise, even with the greatest good will, we risk recreating its parts and structures. For example, even conscious men may unwittingly propose the one-many relation that is so deeply etched in our society. By taking the place of women as models, they recreate the structure of the problem. Women, by allowing their place to be taken, comply once more.

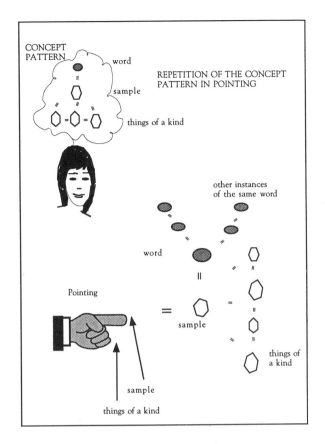

Figure 24. Pointing iconically repeats the concept process and projects it on the world.

Icon and Index[1]

Years ago, when I was thinking about the one-many concept structure, I came in contact with the work of Tran Duc Thao,[2] a Vietnamese philosopher who believed that language derived from the gesture of pointing. Applying it to the issues I was dealing with, I made a discovery of the obvious. I realized that pointing is a one-many gesture, and that it foregrounds one item of a kind, the index finger, while backgrounding others of the same kind,

[1]Semioticians distinguish among three kinds of signs: icons correspond to their object through isomorphism, or similarity; indexes incur a relation of dependency between the sign and its object; symbols refer to their objects by rules and associations of ideas. *The Linguistics Encyclopedia*, Kirsten Malmkjaer, editor, London: Routledge, 1991, p. 400.
[2]Tran duc Thao, *Recherches sur l'Origine du Langage et de la Conscience*, Paris: Editions Sociales, 1973.

263

the other fingers. In this way, it is actually an icon—a visual, tactile, and kinesthetic re-presentation of the relation between the sample and the relative items in concept formation. Just point your finger; you'll see what I mean.

The gesture has two functions; it incites us both to pick out something from a background of other things and to see it as potentially namable or shareable, as one of a kind of thing. The index elicits an external one-many relation in a sort of 'this is here—and there' projection of its own image. (See Figure 24.) The foregrounding of something on the external is confirmed by becoming shareable (and understandable) as a relation between one item and others of the same kind, and one item and a background. However, it is also shareable because we are each giving our attention to the same thing. There is a sort of projection of the one-many icon onto the world beyond the hand—almost as if the item that was pointed at was pointing back. I thought of Michelangelo's God and Adam. (See Figure 25.)

This led me also to speculate that we identify the penis with the index finger, making it appear as another index itself. We give the boy the name 'male' because he has this index and women, including the mother, do not. We say he is part of that category, because he is like the father, or he has that index, like the father. Perhaps another reason for phallic supremacy is that we (mistakenly) attribute the characteristics of the index to the penis. If the child's penis is indicated as an item, pointed at as a pointer, it may appear to be a sample, already in a one-many relation with other items of the same kind.

Of course, the father's is different, and much larger than his—so that, in comparison, it would have to be the sample and the child's one of the items in the series. The relation among penises then becomes a competitive relation among sample pointers or indexes—those things which can indicate other samples, making 'reality' in their image.

Figure 25. God points at Adam, Adam points back.

If we add to this the fact that the phallus is socially invested with superiority as the mark of the privileged category 'male,' we can see how the similarity between the father's genitals and the boy's have a great deal of significance. The index finger, the penis and the concept sample (especially the sample of 'male' and of 'mankind') are collapsed into each other. Too much value is given to similarity, and especially to similarity to the father, because the instrument for picking out samples—the index, which is an icon of its own activity—is identified with the 'mark' that picks out males from a background of women.

The penis thus becomes the icon of the index and of the sample. As icon of the sample as such, it can generalize to be icon of any sample, and with it of the concept itself.[3] While there is already a one-many relation among the fingers of the hand, this is not the case with the penis. The individual's member is therefore

[3]Though its phallic character is somewhat disguised, the black monolith in *2001: A Space Odyssey* seems to me to be an icon of the 'sample,' and the far-reaching effects the monolith had in the movie are comparable to the effects produced by human contact with our own phallically-invested concept-forming cognitive processes. The development of tools, armaments and space ships may indeed be due to our over-use of this phallic concept 'sample.' The phallic investment of the 'sample' is artificial and alien, coming from the imposition of gender through masculation. We can imagine a non-competitive, nurturing, non-phallic technology based on a mother-or breast-invested 'sample' (flying saucers?). Or perhaps we could simply divest sexually from our 'samples' altogether.

Figure 26. "That is a peach."

in a comparative relation with other males' and a competition is established to be taken as the 'mark' of superiority or have sample status among them, becoming the sample of samples—as if to say "Which finger will be the index?"

Actually, the sample is falsely invested with superiority. In Vigotsky's experiment, *any* member of the category could be used as 'sample.' The polarity that is established for the concept is simply functional to finding the 'common quality,' and the sample must be similar to the other items for that purpose, not superior to them.

A contradiction occurs when in sex men point this pointer at women's 'lack' of the pointer, and it becomes larger in the erection. 'Having' becomes identified with having the penis and the pointer, while 'lacking' becomes identified with lacking the penis, exclusion from the category of 'samples,' and (almost) an inability to reason conceptually (lacking the sample pointer perhaps appears to imply that we cannot point out 'samples').[4] Both conditions become eroticized for men, who act out their masculated gender role in a scenario of over-taking and giving-way.[5]

Missing the Point

If women are seen as lacking the penis pointer, they would seem to be non-verbal or pre-verbal, pre-conceptual, without the (body) concept sample, and thus wordless as well. Still, they can be related to the penis as many to one, as in the case of Don Juan, who has to point out how many he has 'had.' If women are pre-verbal (point-less), perhaps they are just the purveyors of

[4]Having the pointer, which corresponds to the index and can increase, gives a physical and psychological basis for an obsession with measurement and quantification and the emphasis on the question of quantitative equality and inequality.
[5]Male pleasure thus reinforces the kind of thinking involved in the definition and the definition of gender as played out in the male dominant sex act. (This emphasis was suggested by Susan Bright.) The fact that not all sexuality functions in this way provides hope for liberation from masculation, or at least humanizes it.

dependent bliss, things, as opposed to the father's incarnate word. The father supersedes the mother, even as sample of the verbally competent human. She is dispossessed of the capacity to give even language to her children. Perhaps, as the patriarchal ancients believed, she is his possession, chattel, and only a mechanical transmitter of culture, an empty vessel, a mechanism handing down the fathers' word, culture, law.

She can relate herself as thing to word, by giving to the male and by standing out, drawing attention, making him point at her. Or as his 'property,' she can point him out as sample thing and privileged 'one.' Her beauty, which makes other men point at her, points him out as important, because he 'has' her. The appearance of being pre-verbal is important because it makes giftgiving appear to be only infantile ('effete'). Is this an element in men's sexual abuse of children? And think of Marilyn Monroe's baby face.

The equation between the penis and the index finger would contribute to convincing us that men are the 'samples' of the 'human' concept and that women cannot be 'samples' because we are lacking that pointer. The penis is really not an index, however, and is not necessary for conceptual thinking. The index finger does a much better job because it is a better icon, since the other items of the series, the fingers, are part of the same hand and are drawn back in order to allow the index to point. In much the same way we background other items in our surroundings and other items of the series. Moreover, the index is directed by the will.

Making the penis relative to other people's penises, as series or as sample, places one's own item in contrast and competition with those of others beyond oneself. (See Figure 27.) Since this is the situation for others as well, and since there is a gender mandate to be the sample, others of that kind, members of that class, may appear to be dangerous and threaten to hurt or castrate the boy child, so as to eliminate him from competition. Perhaps this is what appears to have happened to females.

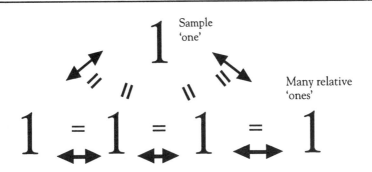

Phallusses are analogs of index fingers, but are in competition to be the privileged 'one' of the ones. Though the penis is the mark of the privileged category 'male,' each one has the contradictory mandate to achieve the sample status by overtaking other 'ones'. The one-many relation is played out in competition among men rather than just being exemplified by fingers of the same hand.

Figure 27. Competition among the members of the category of index 1's.

Knives, arrows, guns, and other death-dealing phallic symbols have the ability to eliminate competitors for sample status. If we look at how guns are made, we can see that the index pulls back to pull the trigger, becoming for a moment one of the backgrounded many fingers of the hand of the marksman, and allowing the phallic gun with its lethal index-projectile to take its place, indicating the death of the other, speaking the loud 'word' which, like the naming of gender, places the other into the alien non-communicating and non-pointing category of the dead. I have always wondered about the double meaning of the word 'arms.' Now I can see that 'arms' are those things that end in deadly pointers, but in our denial we obediently do not get the point.

The 'Heil Hitler' salute is perhaps the negative apotheosis of the relation between the one ('superior') sample penis and the many. Hitler used that 'mark' to manipulate the one-many process making himself into the self-styled 'sample' of the category 'German' or 'Aryan.' He did this to unite the many to violently

269

Figure 28. The Nazi salute is a clear example of one-many phallic arms.

obliterate other human categories, in an attempt to become the concept sample for the human race. (See Figure 28.)

The raised clenched fist perhaps shows the unity of the many—but I still read it as a penis symbol. The jabbing pointed finger is authoritarian, accusatory. Indeed, it has a lot in common with the violent penis, penetrating the space of the 'other.' (See Figure 29.) Instead, perhaps we could simply use our pointing index fingers to show that we are all humans able to single out one finger from the others, and to identify one of a kind as a sample outside ourselves—united as a species in our ability to know, to know together, and to share our perceptions and our gifts.

Symbolic Points

Breasts are actually formed in two points equal to each other in the same person, like our own two hands, or two pointing fingers—and both of them point towards others to give milk. The image of two equal giving pointers is a powerful archetype for society. Perhaps passing through the intermediate stage of our two index fingers, the two points have been transposed and transformed into symbolic points, some of which are definitely less benign. The symbol of horns has long been sacred, and could represent two equal (and dangerous) symbolic penises on the head of the bull, and equally (thus finally resolving the difference of gender) on the head of the cow. Unfortunately, horns point outwards to harm. Wings on both male and female birds might also be seen as symbolic transpositions of equality. The beak is another

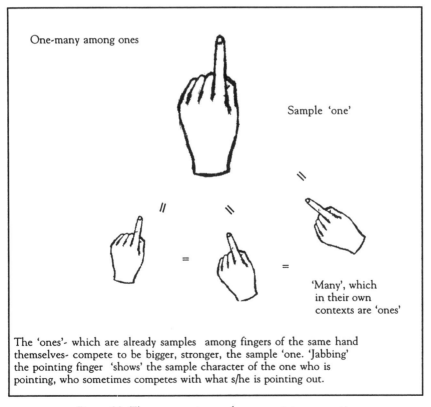

The 'ones'- which are already samples among fingers of the same hand themselves- compete to be bigger, stronger, the sample 'one. 'Jabbing' the pointing finger 'shows' the sample character of the one who is pointing, who sometimes competes with what s/he is pointing out.

Figure 29. The many point at the one pointer, repeating the concept pattern in the group dynamic.

271

phallic symbol, and 'bird' is a colloquialism for phallus in some languages.

Perhaps these and other syncretic symbols helped to ease the anxieties of ancient children, who may have been as damaged by masculation then as we are now. Women's breasts point towards others, to nurture, while masculated men's penises point towards others to find or impose their own identity. They measure themselves against others to find their equality, or their superiority as 'more.' Becoming the sample, they penetrate for their own aggrandizement, sometimes to cause pleasure to the other, but sometimes violently, to cause pain, or symbolically as guns and missiles, to kill.

Real giving from the point is milk from the nipple, the first visual, kinesthetic and tactile (as well as gustatory and olfactory) foregrounding and backgrounding experience of the child. Not only is the nipple erectile, but the milk actually comes from it. Our attention does not flow from our index finger. We have invented pens, from which ink flows to write words, so that not just the sample things are visible out there on the external with object constancy but also sample words.[6]

The pointing finger participates in several modes of signification at the same time. It is the prototypical 'index' and is a physical 'icon' of the one-many concept on the plane of metaphor, repeating in the human body a distinction that is also being made in the external world. Then the pointing finger can actually be used to touch the object of attention, setting up potential contiguity with the object, thus creating a situation of metonymy.[7]

[6]In fact, the type-token distinction dear to linguists and philosophers may be seen as deriving from the fact that every present voiced word is a 'sample' of the absent words of the same kind. Moreover each time we look at a written word it is a 'sample'which remains constant on the external. Thus (like an index or a phallus), the 'token'— properly just one of the many—would be a 'sample' already, and we would take it as standing for an abstract group or type. Then we generalize to other things which, because of their materiality, may actually be present as relative items together with the item taken as equivalent and 'sample.' The type then (because we are seeing all the instances as samples) seems to be an abstract category, which we may impute to some kind of brain pattern or activity (shifting levels there, too).
[7]The plane of metaphor functions according to similarity and substitution, while the plane of metonymy functions through contiguity (serving as the context for something else). See Roman Jakobson's discussion of this basic distinction, *op. cit.*, Ch. 7, "Two Aspects of Language and Two Types of Aphasic Disturbances."

Moreover, the act of drawing back some fingers in order to push one of them forward repeats metaphorically in the hand the social situation in which some people give up their position in order to allow another to be the sample. They serve the one by giving-way, holding themselves in check. The combination and shifting of modes has an almost mechanical process aspect like exchange, and like the definition, which may give the appearance of an automatic attribution of value through substitution.

However, the shift into exchange substitutes the logic of substitution for the logic of giftgiving as a whole. The shift from icon to index, from metaphor to metonymy, and from representation to implementation of the concept with the potential of actually touching the external sample (or beckoning it to come forward) is not a complete shift into the logic of substitution. The iconic re-presentation of the concept by the one-many relation of the fingers does not replace the sample it points at, but only serves to foreground it for the moment.[8] It only adds another dimension to the plane of giftgiving and linguistic communication, and it often serves both of them.

Verbal and Non-Verbal Pointers

The foregrounding and backgrounding activity of nursing at the breast is repeated with the second breast, as well as again and again in time. Perhaps the two nurturing points of the breasts serve as an early icon for the communicative character of the repetition of sounds. The breasts are two identifiable material gift sources which are part of the body of the mother. Then the early word 'Mama' is used for the mother as a whole as 'Papa' for the father as a whole. For babies who are not breast-fed baby bottles may be similarly—though not as poetically—iconic.

The words 'Mama' and 'Papa' occur in many languages, as Roman Jakobson says in a famous essay, "Why 'Mama' and 'Papa.' "[9] Jakobson explains the fact that the consonants used in

[8]The index is 'one,' like money, which 'points' at each thing as one of a kind and gives it the price of that kind on the market.
[9]In Roman Jakobson, *Ibid.*, Ch. 19.

forming these first words are few, by the ease the child has in forming them and by the suggestion that the 'm' and 'n' sounds evolve from the sounds and movements the child makes when sucking the breast. To me, the most interesting thing about these words is the repetition of the phonemes. The repetition occurs in many words we use with children, words which are psychologically important for them (for example: 'ba-by,' 'yum-yum,' 'poo-poo.') Many children distort words while they are learning to talk, creating a double syllable: 'car-car.' Jakobson says that the repetition of the syllable identifies the word as a word in the midst of non-linguistic sounds and that it is an expression of repeatability itself.

We could look at the repetition of sounds within a word as an icon of the repeatability of the word. That is, the word 'Mama' in its different instances contains in itself an example of the fact that the things which are sounds can be similar to each other and that they are important for that reason. (Things which are gifts can also be important because of their repeatability.) The same relation of similarity that exists between 'Ma' and 'Ma' exists between the whole word 'Mama' and other instances of the whole word 'Mama.' The word 'Ma-ma' is like one suitcase that contains two suitcases—proving in itself that the larger suitcase is not unique: there are indeed other objects of the same kind. Like the bottle Alice found in Wonderland, which had 'Drink me' written on it, the word 'Mama' implies 'Repeat me.' (See Figure 30.)

Like the index, 'Ma-ma' and 'Pa-pa' change modes. There is a shift from inside the word 'Ma-ma' to outside it in its other instances. An inductive leap must be made in order to consider the different events which are different instances of a word, 'one thing' which is repeated. The internal repetitions of 'Mama' and 'Papa' support this leap. The very repeatability of 'Ma-ma' corresponds to the child's developing sense of object constancy, the expectation that the experience of the mother is repeatable, and that she continues to exist in her absence. The word is always available to be spoken, and the mother is available to experience somewhere. Then there is another shift from icon to index: the

The relation internal to the word Ma-ma is similar to its external relation to every other instance of the word Ma-ma. Any spoken and present word is a 'sample' of the kind of thing which is that repeatable phonetic pattern.

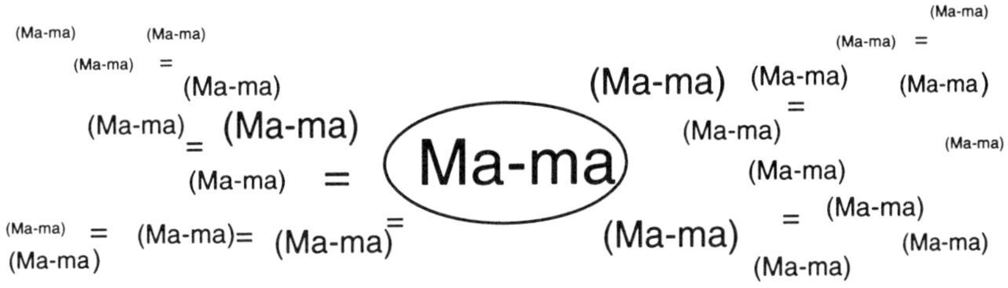

Figure 30. The repeatability inside the present word is an icon of the repeatability outside the present word. Language works because we consider different instances of the same word as a single 'thing.'

icon of repeatability in 'Ma-ma' becomes index of the mother, and actually calls her, makes her point at it and the child by coming. The child becomes her destination, the destination of her 'sample!'

There are other examples of the use of repetitions. Many gestures contain them, for example, nodding or shaking one's head—which makes gestures similar to children's early words. Some languages use the repetition of a syllable in the words which stand for 'the people' (and 'peo-ple' itself is an example)—for example 'Shoshone' or 'Mau mau.' It is as if the words themselves were saying, "This is a group of beings for whom repetitions have a value." Onomatopoetic words for animal sounds, such as 'bow wow' for dogs or 'peep peep' for chickens, also contain repetitions. Maybe children like them so much because it seems that the baby animals are also saying their first words.

The self-referential, internally repetitive character of 'Mama' and 'Papa' provides a sort of clue, a minimum instruction booklet for language learning. The relation internal to the word is iconic with the relation external to the word, with respect to its other instances, and with implications regarding the constancy or repeatability of things in the external world. Similarly, the gesture of pointing implies a relation of things outside it to each other.

Moreover, both the child's words and the pointing gesture take place in a context of others, so that 'Mama' is heard and used by others as repeatable, and the 'same thing.' The gesture of pointing also functions for others as an indication for picking out something from a background. As the child grows, the fact that there is a repeatable sound similarity that can be given and received for something draws her attention to an experience, makes it 'come forward' (point back). It is an indication of an importance, an attribution of value. The equality of the sounds may seem to be important on its own but actually derives its importance from the fact that we use the repeatable sounds as substitute gifts. The changes of planes from internal to external and from icon to index for the gesture or the word are also given value by the fact that others use them in the same way.

Money repeats the icon-index shift of the pointing finger. It is like the finger, in that it is an icon of the one-many relation, though at a much more complex level. It is the general equivalent, the one commodity which stands for all the others.[10] And it too shifts into action, creating contiguity by actually going to the other person, enacting substitution by replacing her product. Money is also like the word in its repeatability and present singularity. Like a word, it can be many places at the same time. Each 'denomination' is both one thing and many. As I write this sentence, I pick up a US coin to look at it again and see the words written on it: *E pluribus unum:* out of many, one.

Symbolic Artifacts

Passages to other levels are significant. Perhaps stairs are their embodiment, and our own repeated stair step dream action in REM (Rapid Eye Movement) sleep repeats shifts of 'levels.' Music

---

[10]Money alters the neutrality of the equation between itself and commodities because it is a constant standard. Similarly the equation between men and women is not neutral because men are the standard.

provides a rhythm of shifts, of changes of emphasis, of foregrounding and backgrounding. The conductor's baton waves; the music points back. The index is easily a 'sign of itself.' In 'conducting,' each time you move the finger or baton, it is again a sample that can call forth another sample.

The visitor from outer space could make a collection of commonplace artifacts by which to understand our strange society. Our clocks are made with two or three indexes pointing out different sized units of time. The index-knife is helped by the little hand of supporting fingers, which is the fork. Then there are the scythe, the pitchfork, and the hoe, all variations on the theme, and we can actually look through the index in the telescope and microscope. Phallic symbols all have a resonance with the index, and it is hard to tell which is which. For example, the 'rod' the child is beaten with is a phallic over-taker and supposedly points out to him or her what not to do.

It is interesting to look at the mechanisms of various kinds of weapons as transpositions of the gesture of pointing. For example, in the bow and arrow one hand serves metaphorically as the fingers, drawing back the bowstring, then letting the arrow fly, as a transposed index, which points out the sample in the world beyond the hands, and actually becomes contiguous to it. . . penetrating it, to kill. (The target, with its bull's eye, looks like a two-dimensional breast 'pointing back.') Pulling the trigger of a gun brings the index back to the group of the other fingers, backgrounds it, while foregrounding another index, the gun barrel, and a transposed index, the bullet.

By pointing, we single out something on the external as an individual or as one of a kind. The fingers can be looked at in this way as well, each individually or as one of the fingers of the hand. In counting on our fingers, we can raise them one by one or point at them one by one with the index of the other hand. (See Fig. 31.)

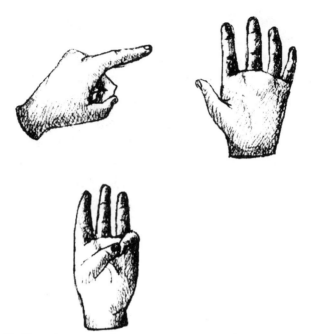

Figure 31. Counting on our fingers, we point out each finger in turn as the sample 'one.'

Shifting into Context

Sometimes the gesture of pointing is seen as deriving from an attempt to grasp, but grasping can be seen as part of a giving and receiving interaction. The other person's point of view as potential giver or receiver is available for us to take and the object pointed at becomes something which can potentially be given and received or related to words which can be given and received. It stands out, discontinuous from its background, and its singularity or plurality may well become relevant to the giver's gesture as well as to the receiver's grasp.[11] The gesture of

[11]When comparing our shared reality with what can be seen with the instruments of technology, we can see that atoms are not gifts but collections of points. Rearranging atoms through nanotechnology could create a situation of abundance whereby all needs could be effortlessly satisfied by all. Giving material gifts would become as easy as communicating through language. Unfortunately, the artificial needs created by masculation make the ease of manipulating atoms extremely dangerous. Weapons satisfying the needs of masculation could be made as easily as bread. In *Nano, The Emerging Science of Nanotechnology*, New York, Little, Brown and Co., 1995, Ed Regis depicts individual masculated uses: "You'd have your gigantically overbuilt human bodies, your four-wheel-drive humanoids with their jacked-up muscles, their oversize penises, and God only knew what else," p. 18. A woman-based gift economy is necessary for the human use of nanotechnology.

indication does not *make* us see, but allows us to see what the other person sees through analogy. It foregrounds something, making it more accessible and adding a new character, its interpersonal value. Pointing identifies the object as a value for others and for oneself—which is also a gift because we are able to creatively receive it.

Pointing is a many-layered sign. It is self-assertive in its capacity to be other-referential. The index finger is both a re-presentation and an active implementer of concepts, which it does as a sample pointing out samples (ones). Thus pointing may sometimes appear to be the initial moment and motivation of the gift, creating the illusion that the gift is an outcome or offshoot of a gesture of self-expression rather than the result of a motion towards the needs of the other. For example, we may believe that self-assertion and its products are the basis of gifts which are there to 'take' through our own self-assertion, rather than that they are the result of someone's, or the collective's, need-directed work. We attribute value to the self-reflecting moment and shift of levels in the pointing person's process.[12]

The problem of the misidentified source which arises with masculation permeates all our interpersonal relations. Here the transfer of attention from one mode to another, from icon to action, metaphor to metonomy may seem to 'automatically' increase something's use value for us. The increase in usefulness actually occurs because the gesture brings in others on another plane, however. In this, pointing is similar to exchange, and to the objectified definition where there seems to be a transfer of meaning or value from one term to the other without human actors. Instead, in exchange and in definition, a material or a communicative need is being satisfied by someone with the kind of thing others use for that purpose in the society.[13] Gestures,

[12]By analogy we may believe that the male sex act with its shifts of levels, fore-groundings and back-groundings, is the source of children who are merely the consequences of men's process of 'self-assertion.'
[13]For example, bread is the material thing we and others use to satisfy the culturally specific material need for bread, and 'bread' is the word we and others usually use to satisfy the communicative need regarding bread among speakers of English. Certain quantities of money constituting its collectively identified price are exchanged for bread, satisfying the culturally specific economic distorted co-municative need for the means of exchange, regarding bread.

279

words and money as means of communication are the result of processes involving others and are the basis for further processes.

The self-similarity of one's own gesture is reinforced by the similarity of others' gestures to it. The shifting of modes of foregrounding, from icon to index, both of which present the one-many structure, is repeated by a shift from re-presentation to implementation of the concept relation, and from the personal onto the interpersonal plane, where others repeat it as well. That is, one's own pointing finger stands for and together with everyone else's pointing fingers which, perhaps together with all the fingers that are not pointing (the rest of the fingers in the hands) function as many regarding that one. This is seen when the fact that others are also pointing is recognized. Everything else that could be pointed at as a topic is also potentially related to the present topic and the finger. The self-similarity and the shift may appear to be the source of new value, but value actually arises because others are already using pointing, attributing value individually and collectively.

Self-similarity with the index is suggested also in the seriality of words, each of which is foregrounded for a moment in the present, to be superseded by another and another. (And each written sentence ends pointedly with a period.) Each word is also in a 'one many' exclusive relation with all the others it is not. It maintains its distinctive character as opposed to the other words in the sentence—which said, also cooperate and give to each other. The relations external to a word are similar to the relations external to the pointing finger. Similar words or gestures are said or done by others, under their own volition. We point at something and others can also point at it. We say something, and others can use the same words, to which similar things are related.

The community-forming giftgiving way does not consist primarily in the shifting of levels but in using the shifts, the levels, the originals and/or substitutes for the common satisfaction of needs. The mechanism is interesting: the icon-index mechanism is self-similar with the concept structure at a different level, and the thing pointed at seems to have that structure as well. The value of the process, however, comes from the access it gives to the group. It is because others also point for others that an individual's pointing is significant. Part of the motivation for pointing is the inclusion of the other as an active giver of attention (or value) to the same thing—which has the side-effect of socializing one's own attention.

Pointing, like the use of a word, creates a mutually inclusive relation with others regarding (literally) something. We are in a context; there are others 'out there' who can point and respond to our gestures, give to and receive from us through ostension. The communicative process passes through a self-similar moment and brings about a higher level of cooperation.

Chapter 16
The Point of the Ego

I believe that consciousness itself derives in part from the interplay of different levels of cooperation. However, in patriarchy we not only become conscious but we also form the masculated ego-consciousness as follows:

When we (or others) attribute a sample character to ourselves, making ourselves the point, just as we would to something in the external world, we also become our own topic, the thing 'pointing back.' This self-referentiality ties the knot, shuts the door, blocks the view of its antecedents, reflects. It takes the place of the other, interrupting the other-oriented flow. We give credence to this shut mirror-door (it seems to be a mirror not only because we seem to see our selves but also because others are engaging in self-referentiality too). We believe in our own presence to ourselves, as if it were the source of ourselves. We create from it a dominating ego, as a sample against which we can compare the various moments of ourselves (our internal many) and others more or less like us externally. We nurture this moment of internal equivalence which is self-similar with the other internal and external enactments of the masculation process.

The result of finding a gender identity through becoming relative to the father as equivalent is reinforced by replaying the over-taking equation back into the individual consciousness through self-referentiality.[1] Then instead of nurturing others, we value equivalence over nurturing even internally. This eventually develops into valuing being over giving, abstract over concrete, general over particular—though of course these are not all concomitant. Instead, the true continuing source of our selves is interactive and comes from our other-orientation—the presence

---

[1] In fact, the result is the focus, the 'sample' self, the one. Once we begin to count, we require a context of 'ones.' Saying one 'one,' two 'ones,' etc. and one times 'one' equals 'one,' probably requires a knowledge of other 'ones,' from some other context.

of others to us, our presence to them. We mistake our common projections of our self-referential self-reflections for the center of our creativity. However, the source of our ability to see those projections and to give and receive lies concealed deep within our other-orientation, like the fire that casts the shadows in Plato's cave.

People with masculated egos verbalize, like everyone else, creating their linguistically mediated consciousnesses. The self-referential ego mirror becomes the over-taking speaking subject, but this is not a social or psychological necessity. We can have linguistic mediation, interaction with others, development of the self without the dominating ego mirror—which is $1 = 1 = 1$, repeating the content of the hall-of-mirrors of the equation. In fact, many women feel ill at ease in our individualistic capitalistic society because we usually do not have this kind of ego.[2] Many men are also uncomfortable because, in spite of the pressures of masculation, they have maintained a connection with the mothering model.

Free (Masculated) Will

The self-similarity of every 'one' with the index occurs also because we can actively implement the indication, moving towards the sample, like the finger. From the moment in which we focus ourselves in a self-similar way, backgrounding some parts of ourselves, making ourselves internally one-many, we can initiate action towards a goal, a topic, a destination which we have singled out. We often call this 'will.' However, at that point we are usually not taking into account the giftgiving or communicative impulse on the other side of the ego mirror-door. The giftgiving motivation appears to be part of the many—part of all the rest of the contents of our consciousness we are not attending to. We may or may not let our e-motions, our other-oriented impulses, get through the door to cause us to ignore the

---

[2] Perhaps intuiting the role the definition has for the male identity, we hang on men's words, hoping they will tell us we are 'beautiful,' 'intelligent,' 'a good wife.' In this way, we almost create a self-referential ego in their image.

mirror and to satisfy others' needs. Our 'right' motivation, the point of our actions, appears to come from the self-similar reflection.

We calculate, "What is best for me?" The need for this filter has been created by the competitive context of patriarchy. We also need to know 'who we are' for the purposes of survival.[3] We have to be able to say what gender, class, race, religion, sexuality we are so, knowing our definition, we know our place in the hierarchy and the rules that apply to us—how to survive in the system, be less vulnerable. The self-similarity that occurs at different levels allows us to say, "This is like me; this is not like me," making ourselves again according to the masculated images in different areas of life. The ego in relation to the subconscious is also a kind of concept sample with the resonances this has on the external, from family to government, which are also made in that image. Women's experience is usually somewhat different from men's because we are defined by men and when the man-word takes our place in marriage, we become the sample 'thing' whose place is taken by the 'word.' We 'know' our place in the system is not to be on top.

We could look at the ego with its will as another icon of the index, literally moving the body towards its object or destination (with other aspects of the self held back). But when we do caring, need-satisfying work, our behavior re-aligns with our motivation 'behind the mirror-door.' When we engage in over-taking, ego-enhancing, other-denying (exchange) behavior, we expand only the self-similar moment, the mirror, recalling the moment of comparison in the concept. The values of the masculated ego filter out giftgiving behavior.

There are of course variations on this self-replicating situation. Some women find that it is possible to have an other-oriented ego which can create self-preservation. It is also

[3]The patriarchal investment of the sample position invests the ego sample with over-taking when it wouldn't be doing it on its own. Also, males see themselves as 'ones' because they are giving up giftgiving and other-orientation, for self-referentiality. I think the experience of the ego is 'anchored' in the body much as Neuro-Linguistic Programming theorists say other types of experiences are anchored.

possible to do post-masculated giftgiving, as men and women do who support their families with the salaries they earn. In post-masculated giving, as in consciousness, there is a filter, the budget, which depends on prioritizing needs. It is not need-driven, as it would be in abundance, but availability-driven.

In the couple, men traditionally take on the role of the ego, women the role of the nurturer, the many, the subconscious. The person who has been discredited, even abandoned, as not-like (not similarly self-similar) returns as the nurturer of the self-similar (male) standard. Her giftgiving way is filtered out of the public arena and focused in the family. Her energy nurtures and upholds the filter, the public arena and those who succeed in it.

The Salary and the Ego

Ego consciousness itself is a kind of exchange-and-masculation-based filter mediating between the ways of giftgiving and of exchange. Property ownership also filters out giftgiving, but women's consciousness is usually socialized to continue giftgiving. Participation in the labor market allows a reconciliation of the two modes after the fact. The worker supports a family by giving to it from the 'property' of his/her monetary definition—the salary. The market is based upon masculation, and its process is therefore more attuned to those who have experienced that process as boy children.

For women, the market is an external context in which they can of course succeed, but it does not resonate with their original categorization. Earning a salary and supporting a family resolve psychological conflicts which a woman does not originally have, so it does not have the same effect for her. The advantage for her is that participating in the market can resolve the practical problem of the 'have-not' status, and it allows some women access to privileged categories constructed by patriarchy.

The salary, a portion of the general equivalent, determines what category a man in the traditional family is in, what he is 'worth.' Then by giving part of his 'money name' to his wife he can 'heal' his masculation. Money is a temporary replacement for the gender term 'male.' He could not share 'male' with his mother, give her all or part of his gender name, but he can share his money name with his mother's successor, his giftgiving wife. The salary determines what he can receive and what he can give and, therefore, is a filter, like the ego. Judgment about one's identity seems to determine what a person can have, since s/he becomes adequate to it, treating it as a self-fulfilling prophecy.

The houses a person helps to build as a construction worker take the place of the gifts of nature and become the property of someone. However, the worker's monetary 'name' often does not give him/her enough money to buy them. His/her 'giving' to the community (as exchange) takes the place of individual other-oriented giving and creating community with his/her family. The 'money-word,' $, takes the place of that act of substitution.

Males or females who give their salary to the family are like the person who gives the name 'male,' the name that privileges the boy and makes others give to him. But the boy receives the 'name' because he has the 'mark,' like the price tag. When a man supports his wife and family with his salary, he is giving her the 'name' even though she doesn't have the 'mark.' When she produces a son, however, her lack is resolved. She seems to merit her husband's sharing of his money name by bearing a son.

The relation between women's free labor in the home and the husbands' salary is influenced by this transposition of the gender definition and is not identical to exchange. He gives her part of his money-name, while she continues to give free caring labor which is not defined by money or quantitatively assessed. His salary is the re-incarnated word with which in scarcity she can buy the means of nurturing, so that she can continue to do free giving with all its qualitative variations. (It is almost as if she were made dependent upon his masculation, his gender term, for the means of nurturing—her own breasts being the prime example of these means.) By sharing the money name with her, the husband names or categorizes (and corners) her caring labor as 'for him.'

All of this has now been reworked by the entry of women into the labor force and single parenting. Women themselves work for the money name and supply the means of nurturing for their children. Thus it is clear that money is only a 'word,' a trans-lated gender term, which anyone can potentially acquire. Like the gender term, it is not biologically but socially based. Earning a living empowers some women by making their survival less tentative and dependent on a male's earning power. However, the whole exchange economy is a product of masculation and necessarily makes most people into 'have-nots.' The economic masculation of some women will not solve the general problems caused by psychological and economic masculation of the society.

(Hetero) Sexuality and Killing

Gender and its result, male (dominance)-based-heterosexual sexuality, over-take nurturing as the model for both sexes—fitting in with language which takes the place of material co-munication. Just mentioning the gender of the child seems to tell us that gender (i.e., difference from or similarity to the mother), and eventually sexuality, is more important than nurturing. The boy's physio-cultural difference from her is more important than her nurturing way. Similarly, killing with a phallic index symbol, which can be seen as transposed (hetero) sexuality, is more important than nurturing. The animal or person submits and becomes passive to the will of the shooter.

However, the animal that is killed by the over-taking phallic index can then be used for nurturing: like the woman who is dominated, over-taken, upon whom her dominator can become parasitic. Hunting itself is like exchange because the object, the receiver of the 'indication,' is transformed and re-categorized. It becomes the property of the hunter, separated from its will, like the product which is separated from its owner in exchange (or the child from the mother by his gender definition). Then the shooter kills other men (his competitors) for protection of his property or his nurturer or his nature or his masculation mechanisms—or for the safety of all of the self-similar masculation mechanisms collected together in his father-land.

Post-masculated nurturing usually requires re-cognition (another look-alike of exchange). Women (and less powerful men) nurture the dominator, and he works through the very mechanism of masculation to nurturing of a sort, over-taking and/or 'contributing' in that strange way. Male consciousness allows post-masculated giftgiving instead of non-masculated giving. The 'mark' is like a case ending in language, which shows this is his role. He has that 'case marker' (or 'tag'), and so can traditionally only give in specific socially determined de-personalized ways, which involve alienating the product, giving to the community, to others in general, in exchange for the 'money name' by which he can become a privileged receiver. It is this strange model the boy has to imitate.

Money, too, can be seen as a collection of quantitative case tags. As legal 'tend-er,' the tags say 'pay to bearer.' Like a transformation from active to passive, the price tag and the male 'mark' also indicate that their bearers must be treated as the receivers of specific gifts. Then the more possessions or money, the more case tags a man 'owns,' the more he controls and the more he 'deserves' to receive.

The dominated woman gives up giving sexually to anyone other than her husband, and materially to anyone other than him and her children. The shift of modes from gift to exchange, from maternal to post-masculated giving, becomes identified with the mark of the male. The icon of the sample shifts to and implements over-taking. And the penis itself changes, becoming erect. It does not have a self-similarity like the hand, a repetition of the relation of the sample to relative items in itself, so it has to find its identity as 'one-to-many' outside in a relation of competition with other males' penises for superiority. Then all men are considered 'ones' with relation to women (who do not

289

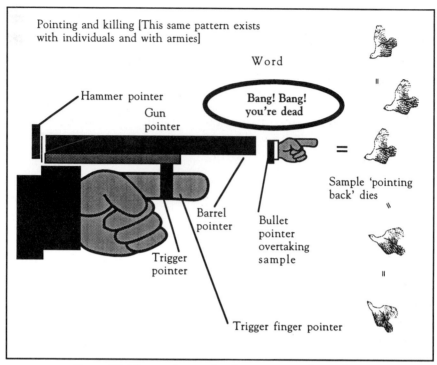

Figure 32. The gun is a mechanism constructed out of phallically invested indexes of different sizes.

have the 'mark') as many, and they practice domination upon them to prove their superiority.

Shooting

The index precedes the penis as an instrument of both sexual and non-sexual knowledge and, in fact, the penis is not necessary for identifying anything. The (false after all) identification of penis and index has perhaps been turned around so that the index appears to be a detached penis, which then may be transposed to become the bullet or the arrow. Also, saying it makes it so in masculation and in shooting. "It's a boy" and "Bang, bang, you're dead" have similarly alienating effects. By identifying something as one of a kind, you may exclude its other possibilities as an individual constant object. Shooting is made in the image of masculation.

Pointing at the boy, naming him as 'male'—that explosive noise—takes him away from giftgiving life. The index is the trigger finger and the shift in levels is like the trigger mechanism, which is also a shift in levels, as the finger moves back to shoot the gun. The word is the sound of the bullet, which names the 'other.'

We point the finger, picking out or indicating a sample object; then we speak the word, naming it, moving from nonverbal to verbal. The explosion accompanies the contiguity of the transposed index with the object which it penetrates. We move from the index concept icon (plus the concept-action of singling out) to the word. (See Figure 32.) The penetration of the other by the bullet-'gift' is really a service to the ego of the 'giver'-shooter. Shooting reinforces the exchange logic while the violent penetration of the body (and heart) of the other recalls and reinforces rape. The gun and the penis both function as 'ones' to allow their bearer to achieve privileged 'one' status.

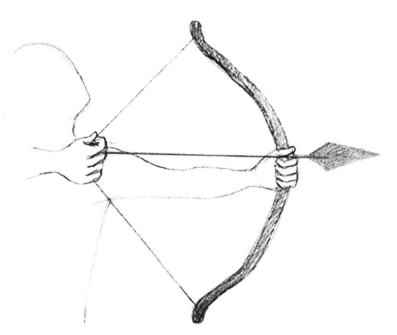

Figure 33. The arrow is an over-taking 'one' pointing at a sample, one out of the many (E pluribus unum). This indication is not of some product to exchange but of a living being to kill.

The bow and arrow are made to function by holding back the string, then releasing it, so that the attention-energy is transferred onto the arrow. Like co-operating fingers held back to let the index point, the fingers pull back the bowstring. (See Figure 33.) -The same thing happens with the index pulling the trigger, releasing the hammer which has been cocked, onto the pointing bullet. Like holding back, then releasing the word and/or the pointing finger, the strength of the many supporting the one comes forth explosively. The energy of what is withheld is focused onto the index. Perhaps an analogy may be drawn with the many actions involved in hunting—going to the forest, looking for the prey—the many co-operating actions which feed into the kill, over-determining it.

When we point at animals or people with a gun to kill, we must hold back our giftgiving impulses towards them, making them samples which will become dead objects—the animal useful as food or the person as elimination of danger or competition. We steel our will internally against other-orientation or giftgiving (poor rabbit) then single them out externally, taking life's gifts away from them, making them passive things. The internal mechanism of singling out, at the same time setting aside giftgiving, is like the mechanism inside the gun. With our index finger, we pull back the trigger-index; the hammer-index falls upon the bullet-index, making its charge explode and go forward through the phallic-index-gun barrel. The bullet-index hits the animal's or person's heart, stopping his/her internal giftgiving, transforming him/her into an object in our possession.

The explosion in the chamber of the gun matches the explosion in the chamber of the heart of the one who is killed; and also in the heart and mind of the killer, or perhaps in his penis, where the pointing and the over-taking analogously make something come explosively from the sample pointer. Masculated will = penis = gun, and there are economic analogies as well. It takes an internal exclusion of giftgiving to create an external exclusion of giftgiving in the body of another, through the

292

internal mechanisms of the gun, which are explosively externalized.

The spear or gun or bow and arrow point out and kill. The sharper focus backgrounds the life of the animal, giving value not to it but to the life of the pointer and the concurrent death of the animal. Then the prey becomes a gift of food. So hunting is a close analogy to pointing for communication because the killed animal becomes shareable, a gift, like the item that is pointed out. Similarly, the death of the enemy killed by pointing knives, spears, guns and missiles becomes a shareable gift for individuals, gangs, the army and the Patria.

This blood-soaked gift, our common ground, is divided into our properties which we again defend from one another with guns and knives. Whole armies point at one another, their technology made in the image of the reified pointers which show that they are in the superior category, abolishing the 'other.' In years of international tension, missile silos dot the landscape and missile-bearing trucks circulate, ready to raise their pointers and shoot their warheads at the enemy. From the knife to the gun to the nuclear missile, from the armed individual to the armed forces, the reiteration of the definition and the mark of 'male' transform our civilization into an immense fractal pattern consisting of self-similar images of masculation at different scales. The pattern self-validates and drains the energy of everyone and the planet into its agendas, sacrificing millions of human lives. However we may color and disguise the pattern, it is an ugly picture.

In ancient days the hunter only transformed the animal into food, property, a gift. A common attention circle, a circle of hunters, a council fire, a cook fire, a stove, a stage, accepted the gift. The topic—the fire, the food, the nurturing gift—became the common focus and the 'thing' related to a word, the repeatable sample. The gatherers and farmers also brought together their harvests. The topic was gathered using gifts of the past, past topics, past gatherings and council fires, individual points of view together. We are the others who the gifts of past hunts and harvests are also for, and who make them exist again for the people of the past, letting them still exist, even if they didn't know it as they conversed and ate. We also leave gifts for the people of the future.

Generations are like water flowing down a cliff, making pools, then overflowing and going on and making more pools. The common focus is a gift. In other words, an 'extra' that comes to us in the present and the future is that other people from the past can do it too, sit in the circle with us as we can with those of the future. 'One-many' dominance does not contribute a topic or a gift for others in the future because the goods it provides are not shareable, since they are monopolized by the one or used for constraint. The 'many' all give to the 'one,' not to each other.

Giftgiving Versus the Hall-of-Mirrors

Giftgiving is often discredited as crazy because it threatens to interrupt the fractal hall-of-mirrors. Common attention to others makes the self-similarity of the ego unnecessary, irrelevant. In fact, giftgiving is enhanced by the diversity of the others to whom one gives (among other things because their needs are different from the giver's and thus occasion growth and variety, not competition). Because giftgiving threatens the economic exchange paradigm and its ego structure, we exclude it from consciousness and force its female practicers into isolation, though they are legion, in the family.

There, they can be counted on to ensure the maintenance of most of the children in spite of numerous and overwhelming difficulties caused by scarcity. As isolated givers, mothers often endanger their own survival by giving too much in a localized way without being able to change the social structures. The 'catch-22' here is that they cannot change the social structures because giftgiving is not recognized as a viable alternative, and they cannot recognize its real viability until they change the social structures.

Being committed to something against all odds is one strategy people can employ to demonstrate its importance. However, doing giftgiving to self-destruction seems to prove it does not work because it annihilates the giver. Instead, the context of scarcity itself and the separation of givers from each other cause the destruction and extenuation of the givers. Others would have to begin to follow the model of giving in time for its practicers to receive from others, as well as give (even if this might have the appearance of exchange.)[4] For these and many other reasons, giftgivers have to recognize what they are doing, name it and practice it consciously. It can really be viable only when it involves many and creates a context, as a general, not an individual, solution.

Nevertheless, because giftgiving threatens exchange, other seemingly benign obstacles are put in its path. For example, 'humility' is its necessary virtue (don't brag about it)—a fact which keeps giftgivers from asserting themselves as models. A man setting boundaries, protecting 'his' woman, is really protecting his giftgiver, for himself, against her giving to other males. The internal structure of the ego-oriented masculated male is the interpersonal structure in the traditional couple. Patriarchal family values assert the right of dominating parasites to their giftgiving hosts. The phallus as the index invests the masculated male (or his ego consciousness or will) as index, so that he tends towards over-taking and domination of giftgiving, including the domination of his own internal gift motivations. If another external sample male 'points back' at him, the two of them must obviously compete for dominance.

[4]Co-dependence therapy interprets the givers and the people with un-met needs as excessive. It focuses on healing individual dis-ease, not on the diseased system, which is creating a context of scarcity and thus generating enormous numbers of un-met and un-meetable needs (which are actually used as economic motivators). Altruism is creative and life-enhancing, except when it is captured and drained by a dominator or rendered impossible by a context of scarcity. It was once estimated that 98% of the people in the US were co-dependent. That percentage seems to me to be clearly the red flag of a misinterpretation. It is normal to be altruistic. We are not being allowed to freely practice our normal nurturing behavior, because our means of nurturing are being robbed by the system, as well as by privileged 'ones' inside and outside our families. Co-dependence theory and therapy, by validating not giving, allow us to solve individual problems and live in the exchange system without challenging it.

The ego is one-many regarding other elements of the self, other people's egos, and all the samples that can be picked out in the world. It becomes relative to some larger samples as its equivalents, like the little boy to the father. From ancient Egypt to the modern US, large phallic symbols of the state, embodying the father of the country, Washington monument style, impose a relative status on many otherwise privileged samples. All the citizens of a country can patriotically unite with each other relative to their country as one (with regard to the many other countries), with its ruler as their national sample human.

The personality cults of recent leaders, whose mammoth images dominate public spaces, are examples of this. Until recently, in communist countries enormous pictures of the heads of the movement looked down on the meeting places of the masses. When Kim Il Sung recently died in North Korea, the television showed the crowds beating their breasts and weeping before the immense statue of their leader. The preservation of Lenin's body in his mausoleum in the Kremlin gave the Soviet Union an image of the constancy of the masculated ego-will, while the toppling of his huge statue with pointing finger outstretched is another case in point.

Destination

The difference between many of the self-similar levels is the time it takes to carry them out. The time it takes to say a sentence is briefer than the time it takes to exchange, so you can also do more of them together. Masculation itself takes years. We are indexes ourselves; our movements towards a goal are indication gestures. We can indicate the goal or actually go to it, to touch it. We have future orientation, a goal or destination transposed onto time from space. We can also point back at where we have come from spatially, and back in time.

Pointing may take as little time as lifting a finger, or as much as it takes to travel to a destination. We act like the index when

296

we go along a path from a point of decision at which we single out our goal. We choose a location to which to go, which is one among many. We can look at this metaphorically—also as the ends which 'justify' (or over-take) the means.

A goal which is identified as the destination or point may be something other than the satisfaction of a need. Is our motivation for travel ego or other-oriented? Exchange seems to allow us to do both or neither, only increasing the (money) sample. Caravans traveled to distant destinations to trade. Travel is like the phallus is in sex, going to a destination. The pioneers' journey to the West, conquering nature, pointed out 'virgin' territory where the men with index-guns killed the men with index-bows-and-arrows and then embedded themselves parasitically, homesteading on 'free' land.

Horses, with their large energy, can appear as phallic indexes as they gallop towards a destination. Cars are similar, but we can actually travel in them together, indicating a destination, and pointing out points of interest as we go. The road and the scenery are foregrounded and backgrounded in a constant flow; the road at which the car points and the common destination are topics held in common. The mechanism here is a foregrounding and backgrounding one. We pay attention to the foreground and self-consistently do not look at the background, which flows into the past. But it is the mechanism as a whole that overcomes the non-mechanism processes—which we do not see. (Is the index's shift of modes an original proto technology?)

Then we point our rockets at the moon to conquer it—and put our little flag pole on it when we get there. Our scientists rush to the goal of making a bigger bomb, winning the war, and produce a nuclear mushroom which points out its own unmistakable phallic character, murdering hundreds of thousands in the short term, and millions or billions long term, through (invisible, unindicated) radioactivity. We can kill with the index, but creating requires the whole hand.

Changing Hands

The other side of foregrounding is the backgrounding we do not pay attention to, but which is just as much an activity. In pointing, the drawing back of the many fingers is as intentional and energy-consuming as extending the index; yet we hardly consider it, perhaps because we focus on the repetition of the one-many pattern between the pointer and the pointed-at. But the other fingers are helping the index by drawing back. Drawing back some fingers is part of the intention of extending one finger. The same thing happens interpersonally, when some people step back or give-way to let the other one step forward. It can be part of the same intention of the group. However, since our focus goes onto the one (or sample) it does not go onto the many. Then it is easy to forget them (as masculated 'samples' forget those who are giving and giving-way to them).

There are two 'manys'—the many fingers which are part of the hand—perhaps also re-presenting the other internal items or considerations the indicator is not attending to—and the many on the external, the other things which are not being pointed at. If the fingers actually help the index, by analogy the things on the external 'help' the one in focus to come forward by giving-way or giving up being the focus. In the family, women have traditionally been the excluded fingers; outside the family, they have been the excluded items. In the OBN, male pointers vie for the position of the one in focus, as well as pointing at their superiors all the way up their hierarchies.

Perhaps this is supported by the fact that the penis does not have other 'fingers' to exclude. The other fingers have just disappeared in the transposition and psycho-social 'evolution' of the sign from index to genitals. If the penis is the 'finger,' the male body is analogous to the hand.

I would like to propose that 'man' comes from *manus* (Latin for 'hand'), as the body-hand with the penis-index. Wo-man would thus be the womb-hand, the whole hand which creates and gives.

Taking the others' point of view is part of giftgiving. Males (and females) usually stop doing it when they give up giving. Meanwhile, many women give up pointing, or being the point, and they take the point of view of men's pointer, which needs to point and to become a 'sample.' We help men. We look at what they need and at what they point at because our point of view has been excluded. It has been held back, excluded for and by them and, therefore, we do it to ourselves as well in order to make theirs work as a focus and to support them in being a sample, over-taking us. Sometimes there comes a point at which we cannot take it any more, a point of departure. Then we take a stand from the point of view of giftgiving, which can see itself.

Giving and nurturing are typically done with the hands, to which having or lacking the penis are irrelevant. Even the baby's pointing can be seen as a request for a gesture of giving by the mother, an attempt to elicit her wo-man's womb-hand. As nurturing men who take care of their children have recently shown, the pointing hand can transform into a giving one. I am pointing this out in order to elicit the gift of that transformation not only at an individual but a social, systemic level.

Chapter 17
What Does Democracy Re-Present?

Language is a response to communicative needs, which proliferate and diversify according to their satisfactions and according to on-going experience. These communicative needs overlap or co-participate with needs having to do with things— needs to consume things, but also to use them instrumentally, or to locate one's own or others' needs among them, perceive them accurately, foresee the consequences of their processes, etc.

Satisfying each other's needs having to do with things creates bonds among humans as those special parts of the external material world who are part of the same species as ourselves—who receive from and give to each other. The bonds created by language are similar to the bonds that would be created by sharing those things, if we could do so. Some of our sharing is impeded by the fact that there are things we cannot give to each other, such as mountains or our sensation of red, or granting the wish that the nuclear age had never happened. Much sharing is impeded by scarcity, in that there is not enough of something for everyone. Much is impeded by private property and our practice of not-giving. It is perhaps the differences in the reasons for not giving and receiving that makes the actual sharing of language so abstract and 'psychological,' transforming the mind into something different from the body.

We share abstractly, and this sharing produces only egos and minds, not peaceful and abundant material communities. We do not share goods concretely with the many. Perhaps we even practice giftgiving only with our immediate families and friends. What we do share, instead, is the not-giving of exchange, which makes us separate and adversarial, and connects us to each other only through the laws of the state, if at all. Exchange makes us into things that do not give to each other, except linguistically, so we are not part of the same species of nurturers. Instead, we organize ourselves into 'concepts,' which are organized into more general 'concepts.'

The OBN of 'Ones'

We create word-like representatives in government to take our places, organizing the larger group for us, deciding, commanding, legislating what giftgiving remains, the giving of obedience, of public services, of taxes. The representatives allocate (give) our tax money.

The lexicon, what Saussure called langue, is a purely differential system of words seen as values in which each element is related negatively to all the others as what it is not, and positively to the things it re-presents. For example, the word 'dog' is what it is because it is not 'cat' or 'beautiful' or 'justice' or 'running.' Those are negative relations it has with other words. 'Dog' also has a positive relation to dogs, which it re-presents.

We identified a very similar relation in private property, where each owner is related negatively to all the others, by mutual exclusion, and positively to the property s/he owns. Money, like the verb 'to be,' mediates between these mutually exclusive elements, creating a second substitution, a quantitatively divisible value concept sample,[1] to which property can be momentarily related, and the property of one owner can become the property of another—without resorting to giving. Giving to needs implies inequalities—while exchange implies and requires equalities, covering up needs and giftgiving.

Speaking about money as the 'general equivalent,' Marx commented, "It is far from being self-evident that this character of being generally and directly exchangeable is, so to say, a polar one, and is as inseparable from its polar opposite, the character of not being directly exchangeable, as the positive pole of a magnet is from the negative. People who give free rein to fancy may therefore imagine that all commodities can simultaneously acquire this characteristic of being directly exchangeable—just as, if they like, they may imagine that all Roman Catholics can

---

[1] Exchange value is qualitatively simple and single, so that it can be divided quantitatively. Money is the material 'word-sample' which satisfies the communicative need arising from the kind of altered co-munication which is the exchange of private property. It is a communicative need for a re-presentative of giving while not-giving.

302

simultaneously become Pope."[2] He says that "a commodity can only function as a general equivalent because, and in so far as, all other commodities set it apart from themselves as equivalent."[3] (See Figure 34.) Marx is actually talking here about money as what I would call the incarnated concept sample. What he sees as 'magnetic polarity' is the polarity between the one and the many, the concept sample and its related items, and/or the word which has taken the place of the sample as the equivalent for that concept, and the related ('relative') items. In his description of money as the general equivalent, Marx identified an important moment of concept formation and the incarnation of the masculated concept—though of course, at the time, he did not see that was what it was. His analysis of the relation between money and commodities is notoriously difficult because that relation involves so much more than meets the eye.

In masculation, the family is set up like the concept, where the patriarchal father is sample or 'general equivalent.' He takes the place of the other members of the family in decision making, instituting command and obedience through his over-taking will, and representing them in the society of men, the OBN. We have seen that property is related to its owner in the many-to-one concept (or family name complex) way. A similar thing happens with our government.

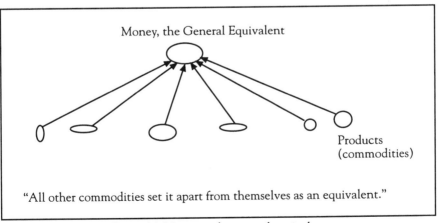

Figure 34. Money is the general equivalent.

[2]Karl Marx, *Capital*, vol. 1, London, J. M. Dent, 1962, p. 41.
[3]*Ibid*, p. 42.

Curiously Marx personalizes commodities, saying that they choose one of their number to be the equivalent, and this is just the democratic process personified. The US Declaration of Independence said "all men are created equal," at the time notoriously leaving out women and slaves (free giftgivers) from the democratic process. The fathers of our country were an OBN, made up of white male property owners. They divided themselves into groups according to location, each of which chose one of their number to be their general equivalent, to take their place as their representative in the governing bodies made up of the 'ones' who were representatives of other groups.

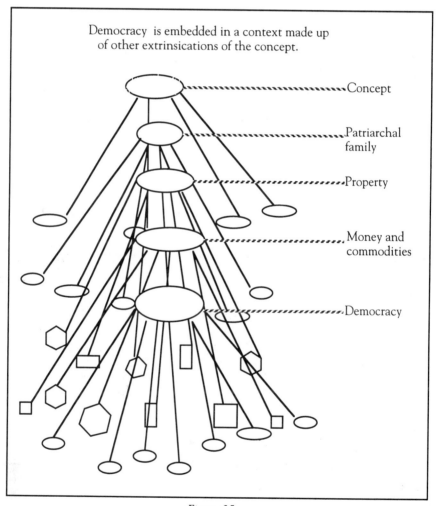

Democracy is embedded in a context made up of other extrinsications of the concept.

Concept

Patriarchal family

Property

Money and commodities

Democracy

Figure 35.

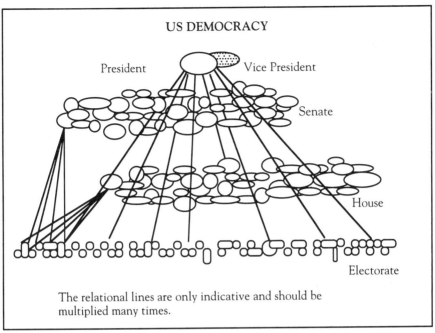

US DEMOCRACY

President

Vice President

Senate

House

Electorate

The relational lines are only indicative and should be multiplied many times.

Figure 36. Re-presentative government. (Compare with Figure 37.)

The OBN 'members' typically were themselves, by choice or by force, already in a 'one' relation regarding their families, and in a self-similar 'one' relation regarding their properties. The 'representatives' made decisions which affected those who had no power of choice, as well as those who did. The context made up of 'representatives' formed a new meta group, an OBN of the OBN, which had its own internal dynamics. A general equivalent was also chosen from among the group of the choosers, to be the general equivalent and representative of all, the president.

When the inhabitants of a nation are allowed to choose their representatives, the process appears to more directly reflect the concept process than, for example, monarchy does. The representatives then appear to be not just the samples, but the 'words' which take the place of all the members of the community or group. Like the words in the *langue*, they are in a mutually exclusive relation with each other, but they have a positive, though polar relation with those they represent. (Figure 36) From this position, they reconstitute themselves as a community, giving to each other and receiving in various ways, making deals,

305

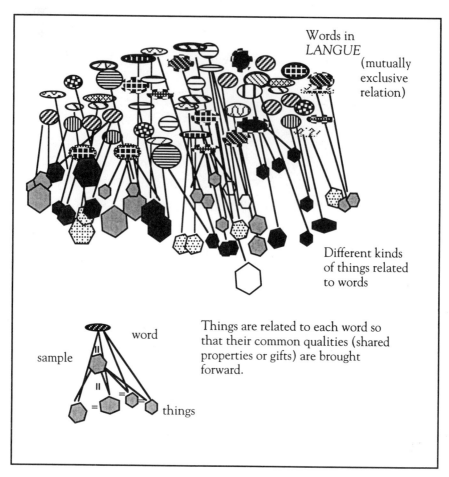

Words in
LANGUE
(mutually
exclusive
relation)

Different kinds
of things related
to words

word

sample

things

Things are related to each word so
that their common qualities (shared
properties or gifts) are brought
forward.

Figure 37.

coalitions, etc. This community acquires a life of its own with power over the lives of the many.

National boundaries then become like the boundaries of the concept. Those outside are 'things' that are not related to those 'samples' or to those 'words.' They are not represented, though they are affected by the decisions the representatives make, especially the decisions made in the nation that achieves the one status among nations.

If we stand back and ask ourselves, "If this is true, what does this configuration mean?" the strategies we have for interpretation pass through the concept process itself, and we are led to repeat the problem. However, if we access and give value to the model of the giftgiving mother, we may be able to avoid projecting our conceptual and linguistic patterns into our governments.

We could devise a way of organizing society free from projections and their subconscious resonances. We would not need to mutually exclude others in order to have national or individual identities, and we would not need to create relations of below and above, 'things' and 'words,' 'manys' and 'ones' in order to make individual or collective decisions. Rather, co-munication, forming the co-munity by satisfying needs at all levels, would be understood as the basis of meaning as well as the guiding principle for the organization of society.

Those in the 'word' position, the representatives, are themselves sometimes organized like the concepts of gender. US Democrats, for example, usually pay more attention to needs, while Republicans look at profit and national egotism. Both parties function on the male model—the right as more macho, the left as more paternalistically nurturing.

The Sexist Point of Democracy

Modern democracy more accurately corresponds to the problem of masculation than tyranny or monarchy because it has developed in an epoch of exchange where the money-word is the king, the general equivalent, instead of the king himself. This fact allows us to act out and perhaps understand the problem as systemic, rather than attributing our difficulties to the individual character of the 'one,' to the king or father, to the heredity of the royal house or the superiority of a nation or race. As much as we do fetishize gold or other money, it is clear that it is not a person. And according to the American Dream, anyone can 'make money.' We have displaced the problem of the privileged sample position into an area where it more closely resembles masculation, though the fit is not complete. Regardless of class or race, the story goes, anyone who has enough luck, energy, and know-how can acquire a lot of the general equivalent, much as anyone regardless of class or race can be genetically 'given' a phallus, the organ by which he is directed into masculation. He can 'have' instead of 'lack.'

In fact, 'lacking' is the other side of the coin, and anyone can also be like a 'lacking' woman. The supremacy of money detaches the privileged sample position from heredity, and perhaps allows more space for us to consider socialization and opportunity as the causes of privilege, along with money-making and capitalistic behaviors.[4]

Ancient Greek 'democracy' was directly the *Reign of the Phallus*, as Eva Keuls shows in her book of that title.[5] Women and slaves were both 'have-nots' in that period, 'inferiors' providing the satisfaction of needs. Gender coincided with nationality and class as a categorization by which a relatively large peer group was allowed access to privileged one positions. Keuls describes the 'herms,' which were anthropomorphic statues of penises *with* penises standing at the doors of Greek houses. These seem to me to be attempts to concretize a self-similar relation.

This is also perhaps a clue to a pun, the sense of which has always nudged at my curiosity, but eluded me. That is the similarity of monetary capital and the capital of a column. Jean-Joseph Goux talks a lot about capitalism and *caput*, the head, in *Symbolic Economies*.[6] Perhaps columns are images of phalluses derived or transposed from herms, and standing together to hold up the temple, the image of the phallic state. The capital is then the head, not of the person, but of the phallus.

Athena, the warrior goddess who gave her name to the city, nurtured male citizens and protected them in battle, is housed (or trapped) inside the temple. Born from Zeus' head, she performed the masculating functions of privileging the Athenians, caring for and protecting them, herself taking on the manly behavior of the warrior. Athenians were masculated as males, but bonded as

[4]Computerized banking and credit card proliferation are actually dematerializing money, transforming it back from a material word to an element of language.
[5]Eva Keuls, *The Reign of the Phallus: Sexual Politics in Ancient Athens*, Berkeley, University of California Press, 1985.
[6]Jean-Joseph Goux, *op. cit.*, pp.44-47.

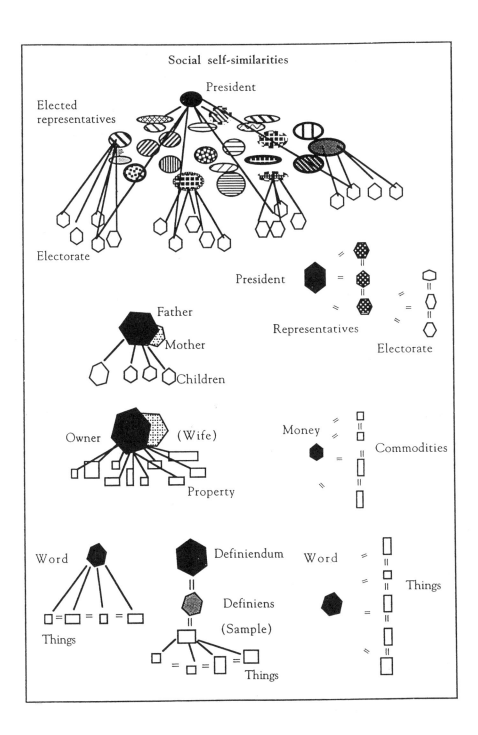

Figure 38

309

things of the same kind, bearing her name. Battles in which the Greeks slaughtered the Amazons are regularly depicted in Athenian art. Athena is the woman who helps men conquer women, as well as other nations and classes. She is the symbol of the way her men collectively receive their power over others, and she is honored by the symbol of their collective columnar erections. Her name given to their nation state fits well with the social cohesion that took place, not through women's nurturing, but through male bonding in battles or oratory and sports competitions, with the goal of becoming privileged 'ones.' The Athenians could also bond in the privileged enjoyment of their freedoms—pleasures not available to women or slaves.

Masculation is an artificial construct, and it needs images of itself which will confirm it. (It is the physical appearance—having the penis—that puts the boy into the non-nurturing category in the first place.) Perhaps masculation needs phallic images as evidence of self-similar structures at different scales, in order to make the universe more familiar and friendly to the boy dis-identified from his mother. Whatever the motivation, Patriarchy (or Puerarchy) creates its own images everywhere representing the phallus every time entrance into a privileged category is at issue.

However, the key (one more herm-like phallic symbol) seems to me to lie in the similarity between herms and columns and men. The column is a gigantic penis; the herm is a man-sized statue of a penis with a penis[7]. Could we say then that an erect man seems to be the image of a penis, self-similar to his own erect phallus, his head its 'head?' The need for a self-similar phallic image would thus be at least partially satisfied by a man's own body. His phallus would be the image of himself and, vice versa, he would be its image.

We have become blind to these images, or we have learned not to talk about them. To me, they seem to be symptoms of a mass psychosis that is being caused by masculation. Once we 'take the scales from our eyes,' we recognize the images for what they

[7]Eva Keuls, op.cit., p.44, ff.

are. They riddle our history. An ancient image is the *ureaus*, the cobra headdress worn by Egyptian pharaohs and gods. The phallic snake's head atop the human head was the symbol of one-many power.

Most death-dealing instruments, as we mentioned, are index-phallic symbols. Each 'member' of the armed forces has his 'gun.' Marks of conquest, from obelisks to flag poles, punctuate our patriarchal landscapes. More pedestrian modern examples: 'skin heads' allude to the organ of male violence. 'Joe Camel' notoriously looks like a phallus and self-similarly advertises cigarettes, like a herm. His phallic face becomes a herm—with the self-similar cigarette branching off as a little phallus.

If we see property as what privileged ones 'have,' cap-ital would be property masculating itself into phallic self-similarity, growing infinitely through repeatedly deserving a greater money name, and working or producing to become adequate to the name, creating a flow of (hidden) gifts towards a centralizing infinitely aggrandizeable 'one.' An economic self-similar image of masculation with phallic motivations (in fact blood rushes to the gland as hidden gifts rush to capital investments), cap-ital transforms itself from a word, controlling the workers' behavior through salary, into the 'money-sample' value-equivalent of products in exchange. An accumulation that allows one to tell others what to do, capital creates a sample phallic capitalist in its image. But he also creates it in his image. We now have numerous large capitals, which hold up the state. Their heads are the pillars and capital-ists of their communities.

The erection appears as privileged one and has a relation to a sexual object which is also for the moment singled out as a one-many sample—for instance, a woman as sample of all women. Athena served as the sample (hypostatized) woman by which citizens acquired their phallic standing-in-common. The *fascio* also was a bundle of sheaves bound together by one of their kind. A similar function animated the Nazi 'Heil Hitler' phallic salute. There must be ways to organize the state that do not require a leadership of phalluses. (In fact, the erection-in-common alludes to gang rape.)

It is not a matching between word and thing (or erection and singled-out woman) that creates 'meaning,' but the response to human needs regarding both words and things and the consequent positive proliferation of co-municative needs. Similarly, it is not the matching or correspondence between money and products that creates economic value, but the response to both communicative and material needs, in spite of the generalized situation of not-giving.

The correspondences between words and things, money and products, man and boy, man and woman continuously draw our focus onto one-many structures and their relationships of abstract equality and modeling and away from needs. This is another reason we do not recognize value as a gift that is being attributed and appreciated in common in all the different areas. Each self-similar area of patriarchy is considered separate and independent from the others because its concept sample is in evidence and different from the others.

Moreover, the 'samples' often appear to be the source of their own value. The relation between the president and the electorate, or senators and congress persons and the electorate, is seen as entirely different from the relation between money and commodities, for example. (See Figure 38.) While it is true that the scales are very different, I believe we have also learned not to look, and to discount the similarities when we see them.

Our view of patriarchy is thus splintered, divided and conquered, and we find ourselves addressing one part of it at a time, rather than making a general criticism and offering a global alternative. The partial criticisms can only have partial results, however important they may be, because other aspects of the patriarchal system 'take up the slack.' Other 'heads' of the hydra are ready to attack, when one has been decapitated.

By tracing the patterns that create these 'heads,' we may collectively address the whole mechanism. Capital, after all, is only one of the hydra's heads.

Chapter 18
The Unmasculated Agents of Change

Women do give freely from their breasts to their children (and in infinitely many other ways) but, since the penis is over-emphasized, we are seen as giving from a 'lack' of the 'mark' and, since scarcity has been created to privilege having, we are often actually giving in an economic situation of lack. All of this is exacerbated because men give up the gift economy. Exchange 'gives' the gift of not-giving, while breasts embody the gift of giving.

We could speculate that the breasts are the original model for the index: the nipple is the index, and the baby's mouth is the 'object' which is singled out for attention. Then the 'points' of view are turned around. For the baby, her mouth is the center of attention, and the nipple is the 'object' that is singled out. Then the 'object' does actually point back—and gives milk. Or for the mother, if the 'object' is not pointing back with mouth and tongue, it at least 'gets the point' and receives milk.

Let us look at having as having breasts, having something to give.[1] We are mammals. Though males have small breasts, there are, of course, many ways in which they and women who are not nursing babies can nurture others. (The penis is only actually 'given' to another person when boys become adults, but it is given to view and to comparison much earlier.)

These ways have been misread, hidden and disguised by the discrediting and isolation of mothering in infancy and by the patriarchal focus on the sample, exchange, reflection, having and keeping. The ways of giving include, among other things, language, problem solving, and producing goods and services as a supply for needs without the intermediate mechanism of

---

[1] Is that why we are required to cover them, because they bring up the issue of abundance and the gift paradigm?

313

exchange—itself derived from masculation. 'Having' is also having hands, the instruments which can be used for giving and for giving care. They do not serve only for tool-making (or worse, arms-making).

The Self-replication of the Sample

The gift the father appears to give to the boy (the gift of the penis) is the gift of similarity or equality, and the value given to equality—to the equation itself, to the boy as equal to the father as the non-nurturing norm who was related to the grandfather in the same way. It is a loaded gift because its psychological use in the society, its misinterpretation, creates an artificial need. Then the child has to try to satisfy the need by becoming like the father. Moreover, the father needs the son to be similar to him, so that he can achieve his position as sample, his own gender mandate as the equivalent to which not only all women but other (smaller) males are relative.

In patriarchy, the father has to show that he has reproduced himself. He has to show that, with the penis index-sample, and being himself the male sample he also has the creative power to make others like himself (showing that the creative power is not all in the mother sample whom he has eclipsed.) It is thus not just the relation of possession that is at the basis of men's obsession with paternity, but carrying out the mandate of the concept form as the realization of their individual, gender and species identities. Although this 'logic' functions across generations, it makes for an altogether false agenda.[2]

I think it is probably the superimposition of the different one-many incarnations of the concept upon each other that has been the Frankenstein which has created the white monster of patriarchy. In societies where the mother's brother has the

[2]Women can also follow their father's footsteps here, by competing with and eclipsing other women who are in a mother role. They are themselves, then, usually eclipsed by men. Feminists need to realize that it is not by taking more hidden gifts and obliterating the giver that we will ever make the world a better place. Rather, we should promote the gift logic and honor the model of those who practice it in all areas of life.

educational paternal function, the phallus does not have to be emphasized as the sample which actually 'creates' the boy. In these societies the transmission of culture through teaching and discipline is distinguished from sexuality; the person playing the disciplinary role (the mother's brother) does not have to require that the boy be like him. In societies where this is the case, it appears that there is little violence, and that rape is almost unknown.[3]

Males, like females, need to remain in a giftgiving and receiving mode, so that their identities can be formed by material and sign co-munication, creating a subjectivity constructed upon an ever-changing nurturing interaction with others (an interaction which also includes a great deal of reciprocal modeling and turn-taking), rather than upon an artificial and absurd injunction to achieve an abstract position of equality with the sample. To make matters worse, this position of equality has hidden within it in a contradictory way two levels of superiority (inequality). It creates a superior category of those who are unlike giftgivers and like the sample (and might, therefore, become samples), and those who are superior because they are already samples. The injunction instates competition where it need not have been, and makes dominance and over-taking the validated mode of behavior for half of humanity.

Because it imposes itself as norm, this mode then extends to all of humanity, making those with other values subservient, invisible and not quite human. It places those who are 'equal' in a category which is given to then by the giftgivers, and which appears to confer upon the 'members' a right to make others give to them by the use of violence and/or organized hierarchies—armies or police. By reapplying the same concept logic (which requires a 'one-to-many' relation to develop generality) to this situation, we find that what is most appropriate to the logic, though not to the happiness of human beings, is that a few be the general samples for their different

[3]See Maria-Barbara Watson-Franke, "The Lycian Heritage and the Making of Men," in Women's Studies International Forum, 16, 6, 1993, pp. 569-579.

categories—which means, of course, that the many do not become 'samples.' Thus we have, for example, many people organized into national groups, each of which has internal hierarchies led by a few men, with one man at the head.

By taking the agenda of the concept form as the logic of the species, and those who succeed in it as the sample for the species (forgetting that women are doing things differently), dominance, over-taking and the attempt to become the concept sample and the species sample become the validated forms of behavior.

Sadly, women have nurtured this state of affairs and the efforts of the sons and husbands who are trying to succeed in it. Now, we have begun to participate in it ourselves. Fortunately, our 'lack' of the penis has shown once more that *it* is not the species sample and is not necessary for success in the system. While this may have rendered suspect male superiority, it has not dismantled the agenda and the logic, but only displaced them onto other categories. Now, for example, all the people in privileged nations can consider themselves as privileged, or 'samples,' regarding those from other nations who 'should' therefore give to and serve them. All those of one race, both males and females, can consider themselves superior to other races, and they can 'prove' it by dominating other races (and by making them give to them, taking on 'womanly' nurturing tasks).

While all of this may produce horrible and opprobrious behavior of individuals of one group against others, they are all carrying out a male mandate that has been considered 'human' by Western European and many other societies for centuries. It is thus a system based on a false logic that must be held responsible, not the individuals, and it is the system that must be dismantled. Changing the individuals without changing the logic and the agenda only leaves room for other individuals to pick it up. As the old saw has it: "If everybody started out with the same amount, a few people would always get to the top." This just means that, until we understand the sickness and heal it, some people will continue to act out the agenda to the detriment of the others who don't have the 'drive' or 'ambition' (read: 'who don't have the need to be samples'). The sickness is a kind of self-replicating 'virus' (deriving perhaps from '*vir*,' the Latin word for 'man').

Dominator 'Marks'

An example of the imposition of one group as sample upon others is the European invasion of the Americas. It was not just the technological superiority of the Europeans that caused their genocide of the Native people, but the fact that the Europeans were carriers of masculation at many levels: misogyny, private property, language, economics, religion, philosophy, child rearing, law, architecture, agriculture, etc.—all of which were very different in Native cultures. It could have gone the other way. The Europeans could have learned from the Native peoples instead of destroying them.

After imposing themselves as the 'superior' category with regard to a whole hemisphere, our forefathers also took on the one-many property of other human beings as slaves, forcing them to give the gifts which created their profit and allowed for the slave owners' capital accumulation. The category of 'superiors' needs to be easily identifiable by large numbers of people. This is the function having a penis has served in categorization. White skin serves the same purpose. In both cases, the 'mark' of 'superiority' reverses the role of the mother, making the deviant become the norm, and the giftgiver appear to be inferior and deviant. In a society in which masculation and exchange are not the modes of life, this dynamic would not exist.

The hypermasculated Europeans killed and enslaved the less masculated peoples of the Americas and Africa, thereby 'proving' that they were in a 'superior'(more masculine) category, which was the norm and which permitted their infinite symbolic priapic growth—which masculated them again into an upper class of the 'superior' category. Having a lot of money also allowed them to buy and produce and build objects by which they could again be identified as belonging to the 'superior' category—the privileged among the privileged. Houses, vehicles, clothes, jewelry, skyscrapers, guns, education, travel can all be bought and are perceptually clear and macroscopic evidence of 'having,' which locates the 'havers' in the privileged category again and again.

Now I believe that the so-called 'First World' countries have become the 'superior categories,' identifiable by their physical location and citizenship documents, and they are forcing the 'Third World' countries to give to them through political, cultural and economic mechanisms, which are generally invisible to the citizenry. The exploitation that is occurring might continue to be invisible were it not for the influx of immigrants who are wisely trying to locate themselves in the geographically privileged category. The danger is that, through the mechanisms of the 'Free Market,' we will intensify the pattern of male-dominating countries and female-serving countries—finally developing into slave countries and slave master countries. Masculation is being writ large on the earth. (And I have always marveled at the appropriateness of Castro's name.)

Existence Quantified

Mothers' other-tending gives us, among other things, bodies, language and socialization towards our gender roles. But the possibility of receiving more through definition motivates us, like the possibility of being named 'male.' Profit-takers make others into their masculating mothers. They make others give to them, showing they 'deserve' the profit by giving to others conditionally, using them as means.

Perhaps it is also because of the singular, one 'word' aspect of money and a lack of access to the system of a qualitatively diverse *langue*, (and thus our inability to explore a variety of enunciatable values in their relation to each other), that money and exchange value maintain their social hegemony—while appearing and disappearing very quickly, as they change hands in the exchange process itself. The thing 'signified' by the material word 'money' is the product (the would-be gift) undergoing the shift of the

318

substitution of the logic (and the act) of substitution for the logic (and the act) of giving, i.e. the exchange. The value-in-communication of that 'signified' is exchange value, expressed in a particular quantity of money. Although the *langue* is not present to maintain a totality of qualitatively different value-mediators, the self-similarity of the substitution of the money for the product and of the logic of exchange for giving creates a self-validating mechanism which continually puts exchange in evidence while hiding giftgiving.[4]

Capitalism unites masculation and exchange, giving each a new goal. For masculinity, the new goal is to accumulate wealth priapically; for exchange, it is to repeat the process of masculation again and again, thus accumulating and having 'more,' deserving an ever-greater quantitative equivalent or masculating 'name,' and putting the owner into the category to which ever-more unseen free gifts are given.

Existence is identified with masculation, and thus becomes quantifiable. This gives people an incentive to have more, so as to *be* more. Power and potency are merged in a negative upward spiral, by which some 'successful' men (and women) can become more masculated than others—*exist* more—by having more quantitative 'value.' This makes them seem to deserve to exist more, which allows the upper class to self-validate and to judge those whom they exploit as 'less deserving to exist,' or perhaps already 'less existing.'

Thinking is taken as the basis for the adversarial authoritarian (exchange) identity. The capacity to perform definitions and substitutions is a recognizable repeatable process, which provides internal constancy (I = I) and focus in the situation of mutual exclusion necessary for private property, and also for the success of competition and ego-oriented activity. (A positive internal identity would otherwise be created through the repeated and variegated processes of giftgiving and receiving.) Exchange instrumentalizes the satisfaction of the needs of others

[4]Money is attached to an image of itself. The president or king's face on coins is perhaps the very image of self-similarity.

for the satisfaction of one's own needs, and it is valued again and again above giving. Those whose will is involved in having (and having more than others) appear to think and to be rational, while those who are still practicing giftgiving (and deriving their identities from it) appear 'irrational.'

Capital is Masculated Will

Capitalism is masculation by accumulation. It is less sexist than the definition of gender because it allows some women to be 'haves' (even 'self-made haves'). However, even successful women may still seem to exist—and to deserve to exist—less than masculated men. Their greater contact with emotions, which we might call the internal presentation of needs, places women partly outside the rationality of capitalism. Then emotions appear to be the 'reason' why women (and men) who have the emotions are not well adapted to the exchange economy.

In a situation in which humans are adversarial and dominating as a community, using each other as means, human e-motion is only a sketch of what might have been possible outside the self-similar 'ratios.' It is our ir-ratio-nal emotion that continues to go out to others' needs, even when we are blocked, cut off from the actions that could fulfill the needs. Perhaps women do continue to feel these feelings more than masculated men because we are still doing giftgiving. They are a way of plotting a course towards a better world. Joy is the celebration of needs fulfilled, the divinely-paced dance of the soul freed from the cage of exchange, living in harmony with itself and others at last.

Rage is aroused by harm, which is the damaging creation of new needs, and intense emotion opposes injustice as institutionalized harm.

The question of justice is bound up with the need to define some kinds of actions as harmful. It is the failure of these definitions to influence behavior that stimulates the anger and will to revenge those who have been harmed. It would be possible instead to promote such definitions without the reprisal that is part of the exchange paradigm, and to prevent crimes by satisfying the needs that cause them before the motivation to commit them has had a chance to develop. This kind of solution is made impossible by the scarcity required by the exchange paradigm, and by the glaring injustices that remain un-defined and appear to be part of an unchangeable system.

Capital is the masculated ego. It is incarnate value-attribution to the shift into exchange, the masculated will, which directs energy towards amassing more wealth and power. It is the desire and ability to *be* more. In fact, more money is more being (more ability to substitute, to take-the-place-of). The 'free will' of capital, like the free market, isn't really free. It is channeled towards the survival and supremacy of itself, according to the mandate of masculation. In other words, it is not free to practice giftgiving and nurturing (contradicting itself, self-sacrificing, not creating scarcity for others, not creating its own increase of abundance). Giftgiving is irrelevant to it. No value is given to giftgiving because value for exchange is caught in its self-similarity, and the irrelevance of giftgiving covers up the oppressiveness of exploitation through 'equal' exchange.

Both the free market and capitalistic free will are oxymorons, if you consider the term 'free' as 'gratis.' (Even shopping is free labor, but unrecognized—the labor of 'free' choice. We are not free not to shop and not to choose—because we will not eat. If we do not have the money, we are not free to shop and to buy. We do not 'deserve' to be.) But even understanding 'free' as 'liberated from constraint,' the market and the will are free for their practitioners at the cost of greater constraint for their victims. The perpetrators of the free market and of capitalistic free will are free from 'other-orientation,' from the commitment to serve others' needs, and they have to be if they are to succeed. Some of our multinationals are even more masculated than our individual sons.

What we think of as the ethical stance of free will is just the possibility of individual masculated egos to choose according to gentler values in contradiction to their socialization to power, or allow themselves to be restrained by the equations of 'justice' (while most women already choose according to a 'different voice'). By availing themselves of their discarded ability to nurture, men contradict their masculated wills to dominate, and to be more, accepting the 'constraints' of other-orientation.

Meanwhile, those who have been socialized to nurture are free to imitate masculated ways, adapting to a sick society. They can develop an exchange ego through working within the social projections of masculation like the market, espousing the values of patriarchy. However, women continue to be socialized differently, towards nurturing and, therefore, are always potentially in a situation of dis-ease within the system and in conflict with themselves internally.

Women also tend to choose 'humility,' criticizing themselves for a masculation that does not apply to them, ridding themselves of a defect they do not have. They criticize masculation as if it were a part of themselves, rather than recognizing it as, at most, their own internalization of a self-similar pattern of males (with whom they are not 'equal') and of the society at large. Thus, women fill churches, therapy sessions and self-help groups, inspecting their souls for trace-elements of arrogance and power-tripping, when in fact they are the victims of that masculated behavior by husbands, bosses, schools, universities, businesses, governments, and other patriarchal institutions. While providing a community and common values, most 'healing' approaches still hide the giftgiving values which give them life behind a male-dominant smoke screen of the masculated values of individual independence, responsibility, guilt and retribution.

If we look at capital as the masculated will, we see it as free to gain power, to 'be more' at others' expense to infinite accumulation. The practice of philanthropy allows the capitalist to make the 'free' choice of 'other-orientation' after the fact, while s/he continues to 'make money.' Charity allows the capitalist to become a 'more complete' person, balancing exchange with giftgiving and, at the same time, satisfying some of the needs that have been created by masculated patriarchal ways and institutions.[5] While these attitudes may be better than unmitigated exploitative moneymaking, they only improve the lot of a few individuals, while making the individual charity-giver a better individual. The ego-orientation of the system captures our giftgiving as it encourages us to use our gifts to others for our own self-improvement.

It is only by giving to social change from a meta level—with a meta message that says, "This co-municative gift is made to change the system towards giftgiving," that the capital-will becomes general, liberated and liberating—giving to change the (exchange) system that created it. This choice frees capitalism from masculation and, by providing the financial resources, frees everyone finally to be nurturing, to practice a gift economy, a women's way. Those who are in positions of privilege cannot create change by pretending they are not privileged, or by simply giving away their 'marks' to become individually unprivileged. Rather, they need to find ways to use their privileges at a meta level to validate the model and logic of giving rather than the model of exchange.

There is a phrase which I heard as attributed to Winston Churchill: "The point is not to distribute poverty equally but to distribute wealth equally." Apart from the use of the word 'equally,' I think that the idea is very important. What we need to focus on is wealth for all, not a new system of poverty for all. It is not by making ourselves equally poor that we will change the system for the good of all. In fact, only abundance allows giftgiving to flourish. Therefore, we must use our wealth of resources, the money accumulated in capital, our land, our education, experience, communicative skills, political, psychological, and business savvy, our groups and networks to create an intelligent, non-violent transition from the system based on exchange to a system based on giftgiving in abundance.

[5] Even groups like United Way which collect millions of small contributions from the many funnel them into projects that take care of individuals and do not rock the boat.

323

A step in the right direction would be to stop the waste spending that is now taking place on armaments and the military worldwide. Another step would be to for-give the so-called 'Third World' debt, realizing that the debt is an artificial, exploitative mechanism which has actually already been paid back many times over. At the same time, stopping the destruction of the environment would ensure that abundance could continue to accrue in the future, rather than disappearing into an artificially impoverished and toxic ecosystem. The well-planned reduction of exploitation and waste would allow the accumulation of wealth which would permit giftgiving among individuals, as well as among groups and nations.

Women's Leadership

Because of the way the categories of masculation have proliferated, many of us belong to several different categories. We are privileged as white, but unprivileged as poor. We are privileged as wealthy, but unprivileged as women. We are privileged as male, but unprivileged as persons of color. We need to unite across the unprivileged categories because we are conscious of suffering, but we also need to unite from within privileged categories to remedy the suffering, to change the system for all. In fact, if we re-establish the mothering model and equip ourselves with the logic of the gift economy, we will give attention to others' needs and satisfy them, not only at an individual, but at a social level. The true overturning is not to put one category in a privileged position in place of another, but to put into effect the general norm-al mother-based other-orientation that bridges and breaks down categories altogether.

Masculation validates self-interest at all levels (even group or category self-interest). We must also be able to validate other-interest at all levels. The answer does not lie in categories at all, but in giving and receiving, co-municating with each other as human beings, and collaborating to solve the general problems, the needs of all, by changing the system built on masculation.

This is the paradigm shift that the New Age and other spiritual movements have been longing for. It is not based only on consciousness—though consciousness plays an important part in the necessary change of perspective—but on the real and practical satisfaction of needs and solutions to problems. Such a practice must be aided by cultural sensitivity and foresight, devising ways of satisfying psychological and spiritual needs, such as the needs for dignity and respect, for the independence and self determination of everyone who is transitioning out of the exchange and into the gift mode. The paradigm shift can be created by women, crossing all categories. Its operators are already everywhere in the international women's movement. The unmasculated agents of change are already planted in every household.

Chapter 19
Dreaming and Reality

I think that our subconscious-conscious division might be an internal replay of the two paradigms. (Perhaps even the functioning of the right and left brains plays out this division.) Of course, this is hard to see because, at least while we are awake, it is always within consciousness that we are present to ourselves. And in consciousness, we are often serving our own definitions of ourselves, carrying out their self-fulfilling prophecies.

The gifts of words hover somewhere in our mental cupboards, ready to pop out whenever necessary. They are there vibrating in resonance with everybody else's words of the same kind. As we move through the external world, everything we encounter has the quality of a potential relation to our words and their combinations, and/or to the words of others. Our communicative needs for bonding with each other in relation to the world arise and are satisfied by the collective products of previous generations, which we collectively and individually recombine and use to create ever-new gifts, to which the parts of our world are related as their substitutes in communication.

We create our subjectivities ad hoc, together, by giving gifts to one another both materially and linguistically. The great potential for human development through this process is hampered by patriarchy. Only enough of our collective humanity remains for us to continue to understand each others' speech, transmit information, and function as somewhat efficient promoters for the egos we have developed through definition, self-definition, and exchange. The fact that we do somehow continue to live is evidence, not of the functionality of the masculated ego, but of the creativity of giftgiving and life itself, which carry us along in their flow in spite of the ego's self-reflecting empty shell and the self-similar society.

In patriarchy, the community we form by communication is usually shattered into many pieces or remains a wish, an abstraction floating somewhere behind our backs (a might have been, an ideal, a different possible world). Our word-gifts have been turned towards the purposes of exchange through advertising and propaganda, and we motivate ourselves according to priority lists which define us and others, putting ourselves as privileged ones at the top, bolstered by privileged one possessions or relations and positions within other hierarchies. We do not even notice the presence of society in our words, much less in our lives, because private property (even of our consciousnesses) does not encourage us to look outside at others as the source of our good or as having needs we can satisfy. Our thoughts appear to be our 'own,' because we are isolated from others. Instead, as individuals we are the alienated community, thinking.

If we could go back to materially nurturing one another, we would recreate our community and ourselves on a more solid earthly basis, healing each other and the planet. Instead, we look at ego values and not at bodies—the egos of the rich compete against the bodies of the poor. Evidence of parasitism abounds. Every nuclear test site, dump, mine, oil well attests to the destruction of the mother for the purpose of the gifts renamed 'profit' that exchange brings with it.

Our sharing has been pushed into a mythological past (or infantile bliss) and into by-products of our ego activity, and has become the collective unconscious since con-sciousness (knowledge together) in our society is based on definitions and exchange. Perhaps it is not Persephone, daughter of Demeter, who is the most important character in the Greek mythological story of a mother's loss but Hades, the son of Gaia, the boy who became the god of the underworld.

Knowledge of the Heart

Our hearts pump our blood to take the oxygen and nutriment out to our cells that need it, then when the blood is exhausted, it comes back to the heart to be nurtured. This is a physiological archetype that the exchange paradigm prevents us from following. Individually, too, our subconscious prompts us with buried information, and ideas come to us from nowhere, out of the blue, gifts from an unknown source we perhaps call our Selves, imagination, God.

Humans are basically loving beings. Our social structures and the logic of exchange are patriarchal distortions of love. The sharing and caring which we experience in the original mother-child relation are often the only experience of free love we have, and they become the model for us for the rest of our lives. This is the reason early childhood is so important for our psychology. All the rest of our lives, we have to deal with the various distortions and blockages of love. Our nostalgia for childhood, even for the womb, is nostalgia for a primary period of health which has never returned, because there is no social or economic structure that permits it. Our independence is so distorted that we belittle dependence instead of honoring it. We insist on standing alone, and yet we are a mass of individuals crying to be touched, fed, caressed, supported.

The free circulation of the blood between the mother and the child in the womb is the natural paradigm of a healthy society. It is the model of life-giving collaboration, where both hearts pump the same blood and nutriment is shared. Like the wind that moves from a higher to a lower pressure area, good circulation moves from those who have more to those who have less. Once the child is born and draws the air into her needing lungs, beginning her interaction with the free outside world, she receives and perceives as much as she is able of the abundant environment and gives her new humanness to the gaze of the onlookers, her touch to other bodies, saying who she is and will be.

The circulation of the womb has begun on a new level—out from within a body to between bodies. The hearts no longer pump the same blood but pump laughter, language, motions, gestures—to the need which is recognized, goods and caretaking flow. The child creatively receives, is an interpersonal creature, an interpersonal heart, a subject of attention, who also gives attention. Milk flows to the needy stomach through the baby's own actively receiving mouth. It is not denied. There is no blackmail, bribe, payment. Though her signals may let us know her needs, these are not exchanges but free products issuing naturally from her whole being.

Like synapses where nerves do not transmit impulses through direct contact, but by means of processes over a different space, life in many forms is transmitted freely by the mother to the child, by the child to the mother and to the others who love her. Mother and child are pleased with the freedom of their giving. Neither is embarrassed by the relation of dependence, which requires and permits the circulation, just as no one is embarrassed by our dependence on air, which requires and permits our breathing. We can take what is freely given and give freely in this relation, enjoying and touching each other from the outside, sensation passing through and into sensation, sharing in time outside the womb.

Since our society is embarrassed by dependence and the need for free giving—but actually would do anything to have it, we build ever larger barriers against it, including in the barriers a certain amount of flexibility, places to let off the pressure that builds up in us, because we cannot have what we really need. Yet, we keep working towards having or getting more than enough ourselves, so that it will seem free to us—only to us, not to others. Since we tap only our own experience as babies with our mothers and later find that the world and its rules are different, we may think that nobody else ever had or needs to have the experience of free nurturing.

Instead, the free circulation from those who can give to those who need, the ability to ask freely, to receive freely, to give freely, is the basic process through which the flow of life circulates unimpeded. The consciousness of the various things which are given and received is shared as perception or language are shared, freely in all the transformations, as the gifts pass from one person to another, from nature to people, from people to nature and to different people. This is the new consciousness of nature, an evolution, a new shared life of life.

Giving and receiving life is not confined to conception, pregnancy or physically birthing babies. Rather, it takes place in every act of need satisfaction. Exchange, by placing itself between the giver and the receiver, the giver and the gift, the receiver and the gift, has obstructed the synapse and confused us. The processes are distorted, unfree. We no longer intelligently and creatively give and receive life, but base our interactions upon masculation. A prize has recently been offered to the first male who becomes pregnant, but giving and receiving is exploited and belittled everywhere outside the womb.

Our Common Dream

We could look at judgments of reality and unreality (and of waking and dreaming) as depending on whether or not the exchange mode and the masculated concept relation have come into play. Dreaming explores other syncretic relations, frees samples from their phallic investment and satisfies our needs for understanding through symbolism, which is not one-to-one or one-to-many but 'over-determined'—where one image represents a number of different and seemingly unrelated issues, items or events. Complexes and syncretisms[1] of various kinds allow for associations we might never make within our hierarchical

[1]People who associate (form a society) with one another usually practice giving-and-receiving with each other in a variety of ways—and would do it more if they did not live in an exchange economy. That is why giving and receiving are a key to the idea of 'associations' found in dreams or among words. A schizophrenic who was asked to perform Vigotsky's experiment told the experimenters that the 'sample' was a policeman telling a crowd of people what to do. We have traced enough self-similar patterns at this point that the policeman-crowd relation can easily be seen as a 'one-many' concept derivative. The policeman actually dominates the association-crowd, while the schizophrenic gives us the gift of a needed connection ('association') which has not been made. (See Hanfmann and Kasinin, op.cit.)

331

classification system (and social class system).

In dreams, our images do not have to toe the line, relating themselves to samples or to words, providing us with factual socially validated help for managing our lives in the 'real' waking world. Instead, they can free-wheel it, satisfying our needs as soon as they come to mind, or memory. They are subjective, me-first sometimes, but without the hegemony of the masculated ego. In dreams, our needs are gratified according to the pleasure principle, without our having to work for their satisfaction. Our real needs are symbolized, our intuition addresses them. Real help is given. In dreams, we are treating ourselves as if we lived in a gift economy. The reason why dreaming is only subjective and based on wishful thinking is that the external world is framed by exchange. Author-itarian therapists might frown at this 'regressive' and 'infantile' mode, but why not see it from the other point of view, as utopian and maternal? Dreaming seems to be the satisfaction of co-municative needs on an individual basis. If we could satisfy our co-municative needs collectively, we could all live our dreams.

Upon waking, a reality judgment comes into play at the same time that the one-many cognitive strategy kicks in. Then we use the one to uphold the other. We marvel at how silly our dreams were, discount our syncretic thinking, thus validating our one-many thinking. This makes us deny or forget and disqualify our dreams as inferior to our waking states, perhaps because our strategies for remembering are one-many as well. Children syncretically belong in the 'category' of dreams, as silly, non-rational and non-phallic. Women and wishes are also often relegated to the dream netherworld.

By over-valuing and phallically investing conceptual thinking in the society at large and projecting it into the structures of institutions, we have collectively created a social reality which is different from our dreams and inhospitable to that way of thinking. As we validate 'reality' each time we wake up, we also discount the kind of reality our dreams are made of and the many non-phallic parts of our waking world. Thus, it may happen that, every time we wake up, we unwittingly assert dominance, misogyny and the hatred of children, of nature and of giftgiving, as we say to ourselves, "That was not real—this is real."

If nothing else, dreams do satisfy one need shared by all—they provide an alternative, much as Communism did to Capitalism (and *vice-versa*), communicating to us that the 'real' world is not the only world, and masculated, phallically-invested conceptual thinking is not the only way of thinking. If dreaming functions according to unmasculated gift processes, it is a clue to a better world, like language and mothering. Humanity's common dream is the map of a world to come. The injunction to humanity to 'wake up' is mistaken. Instead, we need to change re-ality to make our dreaming come true.[2]

The Imposition of Re-ality

Language itself speaks to us, and it tells us that the collective unconscious has seen some things that we ourselves have collectively ignored. I believe language is full of clues to just the issues we have been discussing—the masculated concept, exchange, hierarchies and giftgiving. The words we are presently mentioning on this page are clues along the royal road to the discovery of the nature of 'real-ity.' (Spanish *real* is royal.) What the clues are telling us is that you can't get there on the royal road alone. You have to approach the 'subject' from another direction.

So kingship or thingship, from Latin—*rex* (king) or *res* (thing)—is telling us about the 'one-many' basis of re-ality. The pun existed already in Latin. It points to self-similar dominance patterns in our knowledge of the re-al, outside the giftgiving grain. And the ego as 'king' is also part of what defines this re-ality, coinciding with it in structure, while the giftgiving self remains outside it. Re-ality is a common ground, which originally comes from giftgiving, but is ruled by phallically-invested cap-

[2] I would like to mention that the spiritual practices which promote gratitude upon awakening keep us partly in the gift mode for a few more moments, providing some continuity between our 'real' worlds and our dreams.

italistic concept thinking.

Basing thinking on concepts disqualifies differences—or at least makes them important mainly as signals of another concept. "What concept do you belong to?" appears to be the real question. We leave aside your needs and how peculiarly interesting and beautiful you are, the sparkle in your eye. Instead we ask if you look enough like the model or sample to belong to the concept of 'beautiful,' the concept of 'lovable,' of 'successful business person' or 'academic.'

Is the affirmation of masculated re-ality the recognition of an external given, or the imposition of a gift which we *have* to receive? Perhaps we feel obligated, because of the exchange principle, to 'give back' something to re-ality. Re-cognition perhaps? Re-ality satisfies our distorted common needs, but may leave aside our healthy un-realistic individual needs. What are the consequences of not receiving the present? Abandonment? Insanity? And of receiving it? Do we give up the truths of our subjective view for the masculated collective view, so we won't be left out of the concept of human and sane? If we refuse re-ality, are we being ungrateful, selfish, 'self-indulgent,' as one psychiatrist said about mental illness? If we go crazy, perhaps we are just displacing our reality judgment from a collectively mediated to a subjective stance. We do that because we are all the 'walking wounded.'

A Selfish Collective View

A common judgment of reality is, after all, a collective attribution of value which is probably more likely to be functional to each of us than a purely individual attribution would be. When we insist on kindness, or wish for a better world, and people say we're not being 'realistic,' they are appealing to a collective attribution of a quality or value which assures at least a certain degree of functionality—adaptiveness for the individual as well as the group. For our own best interest (our self-interest), they say, we should adapt to the collective judgment, not change anything or envision anything different.

But why does the collective view seem to be less selfish? There is a division between the self and the collective, and what is not collective seems to be egotistical. But the ego itself is a collective product, and there are many collective mechanisms and values that give it strength. It also fits into a sort of generalized ego-orientation of the particular collective of which it is a part—for example, the race, the class, the religion, the nation.

The ego also depends on a collective attribution of value and reality to the individual's internal configuration, which validates it for each of us, but especially for (successful) masculated men. The self-similar structures in the society perform this function. The privileged one, the process of exchange and the denial of giving, institutions based on masculation, money, and the phallically-invested concept are all social mechanisms by which value is collectively attributed to the individual ego.

The ego and egotism may be viewed as a collective stance, while the subjective stance really may be more giving and other-oriented. We can collectively be very egotistical. However, we could collectively put the dividing line somewhere else between individual and collective, and validate a different kind of ego and giving itself, creating a different kind of collectivity. In order to see that the split is in the wrong place, perhaps we need a three-dimensional view. If we see what we think of as our selves as made from and through the social gift that is language as well as through the gifts of life perhaps we would stop envisioning a polar opposition between individual and collective, the I and the other. This re-framing would allow the division between subjective and objective, subconscious and conscious, dreams and reality to be different.

Reality is affirmed and defined by the imposition of the masculated way upon the collective. The distorted community is constructed to carry out this imposition and its definition as 'real' is part of the construction. The judgment of reality is a meta message which serves to maintain the patriarchal *status quo*. Then reality seems to be just organized meanness based on the cruelty of 'human nature.' Anything goes, because we believe the meta statement, "People are just that way."

The individual gives the value of reality to parts of her experience, creating an on-going attribution with a continuing gift effort of energy. But reality itself does not appear to be giftgiving or to include the gift paradigm. Giftgiving on the external is being continually misread, and the internal gift mode is unseen and unrecognized as such. Sometimes, if we are not burdened by scarcity and overwork, we can experience the giftgiving side of nature and each other, but for many people these happy moments do not come very often.

All of this has the effect of not allowing our internal giftgiving mode to have a co-respondent in reality, though perhaps our efforts to get others to give to us might be seen as mistaken attempts to make 'reality' reflect our giftgiver within. (Perhaps our giftgiver within appears to us as an 'other.') Since we have validated exchange and put the mother in an other category, it seems right or harmonious that others should give to us.

If we look compassionately at exploiters, we can see that they are convinced of the reality and perhaps permanence of scarcity, and that they feel the challenge to overcome this individually by taking, i.e. making others give. Their very parasitism is almost an attempt, within the scarcity created by their way, to make reality nurture at least themselves when it doesn't nurture anyone else. Perhaps it is an attempt to make reality their own mother; is this the secret motivation of greed? Is every exploiter a child sucking alone on the reali-titty?

If they believe they deserve more than others because they produced more or are stronger or more intelligent, exploiters are participating in the exchange mode and canceling the gift, which is, paradoxically, what they were seeking. No one can make reality her mother, unless we restore the gift paradigm for everyone. Reality is a collective construct, and if we collectively construct reality to nurture only one or a few at the expense of the many, we destroy the many—who are the collective. We must make our giftgiver within correspond with real giftgiving on the outside—this will liberate both the individual and the collective. Meanwhile, restoring our contact with nature can help us find an ecological niche outside us for our giftgiver within. Nature needs to be cared for, restored to herself as the free giver; then we can align ourselves with her.

Exchange is actually a displacement of what would be the solution to our problem—giftgiving both internally and externally. Exchange requires that the 'other' take on the same ego-oriented motivation each exchanger enacts. Each gives, but for something beyond the present, something other than the satisfaction of other's needs. The giftgiving side of the 'other,' or nature or reality is misread and translated into the 'fair' or 'just' correspondence between giving more and getting more. Reality then does not seem to give freely, but only to respond to an exchange. Then because giftgiving is not modeled in reality, we reflect the distorted equation. The solution is collective giving, collective altruism. Money, as a collective product, can be used to begin this process.

Dreams-Come-True Inside and Outside

Maybe if dreaming is in the gift mode, Spider Woman really does dream the world as Paula Gunn Allen says.[3] But masculated re-ality is a collective nightmare, a collective gift to end all gifts, which cuts off giftgiving because it assimilates it into exchange. Masculated reality is what much of humanity unconsciously gives energy to. We need to collectively dream something else, and to give our waking energy to making a different reality, making our dreams of a better world come true instead of our nightmares. With more giftgiving in reality, our giftgiver within would be empowered, as would our creativity and love.

Artistic creation is giftgiving in reality and a bridge into a better world because the medium or vehicle of the gift is itself a free gift, which satisfies and creates aesthetic needs. For example,

[3]Paula Gunn Allen, *The Sacred Hoop*, Beacon Press, Boston, 1992.

singing is free to the listener, and the vehicle, the voice, satisfies a need, a potential in ourselves for enjoying beautiful and pleasurable sounds, rhythms, harmonies, while the words satisfy communicative needs. Visual art is similar. The colors, forms and textures can create pleasurable sense givens, whatever the subject or topic of the work may be. Though many kinds of art can be bought and sold, they all maintain a free need-satisfying side, which is essentially their co-municative channel. There is no exchange between the ear and the music, the eye and the painting, though access to those experiences is often expensive. The work of art itself gives. The creative gift of the artist is the ability to make something that gives.[4] (Earlier, in contrast to anthropologist Levi-Strauss, we said that women should not be interpreted as commodities or messages exchanged among kinship groups, but gift sources, gifts-who-give.) Numerous kinds of exchange-based activities become parasitic upon art, as they do upon other sources of giftgiving.

Even if art restores giftgiving to some extent in the outside world, it does not suffice to corroborate the cancelled model. For the present, giftgiving stays in dreams and the unconscious, and unrecognized as such in art, stories, myths. Stories can introduce children kindly to exchange through communication, satisfying that need. They show children the transitivity of one thing leading to another, the satisfaction of one need, which permits the satisfaction of another—an action resulting in something else. Action can be seen as giving; satisfying one need creates another—when the baby has eaten, she needs to go to sleep, or out to play. The mother needs to clean up, to rest, to go back to work.

The if-then structure, however, captures the gift with a consequence—if you put your finger in the fire, it will burn you. When the framework of social reward and punishment is introduced, the transitivity of the gift transforms into the logical consequentiality of exchange. If/then becomes 'do this, get that.' Thus, it may seem that when the child does something, what reality 'gives back' is what she 'deserves.' Did Cinderella deserve

[4]Lewis Hyde discusses the creative gift in a somewhat different sense in *The Gift*, *op.cit.*.

338

to go to the ball and marry the prince because she worked so hard? Did Little Red Riding Hood deserve to be eaten by the wolf because she was not obedient to her mother? These stories are explorations into the exchange between 'reality' and the stories' protagonists for children who are just beginning to consider their behavior according to the exchange mode.

What are the prices we pay for not giving, the rewards we get for giving? An equilibrium rules these exchanges—at least in fairy tales. As children begin to learn how to exchange, their morality co-responds.[5] Making children obey, instituting a system of rewards and punishments, brings them away from the gift mode they were participating in with their mothers and prepares them for the exchange mode rampant in so-called 'reality.' Stories satisfy children's need to be introduced through kindly co-munication to a world rendered alien by exchange.

It is true; we do have a need, as children, to be taught to adapt to reality. But that is because reality is distorted. The need to adapt is imposed by an environment which is artificially and pervasively altered by the exchange paradigm. Socialization imposes an evolution towards functionality in the system and an adaptation to the roles of having or not-having at all the different levels. If we were functioning within the paradigm that works for human and planetary development, we would not have to be taught giftgiving and receiving from the outside, but we would learn from our experiences—just as we learn to make sense of our perceptions, to manage our bodies' activities and at least in large part, to speak.

Teaching children to obey imposes the dominance-submission pattern, including the reward and punishment components of exchange, upon warnings like: "If you put your finger in the fire, you will get burned." This phrase is purely informational, but it is used to prop up parental dictatorship like, "If you don't say, 'Yes, M'am,' you can't go out to play." These dictates function according to the exchange mode, even giving

[5]See Carol Gilligan, *In a Different Voice*, Cambridge, Mass, Harvard University Press, 1982, for the moral perspective of care.

our actions a price in terms of consequences. "You disobeyed. You're grounded for three days." The author-itarianism of the parent is often not only a replay of her or his own childhood and relationship with her/his parents, but an attitude of oppressiveness against her/his own giftgiving and receiving 'child within.' Our schools, with their practice of grading, extend this reward and punishment process to quantitatively evaluatable amounts of 'knowledge' acquired.

The Iroquois and the White Man

When women support women, or nurturers nurture nurturers, a transitivity of giftgiving takes place, so that the good is passed on and on and the receivers receive from and give to many. When this is done on principle, people become conscious of it and then reality contains more actions determined in this way. If the gift paradigm were validated and consciously practiced, however, we would not need to think of it as a principle. We would be able to be more flexible, experiment, and act on a case-by-case basis. Perhaps, if we found it useful, we could even safely practice exchange in some instances—because the context as a whole would carry giftgiving. Native American woman-led tribes, like the Iroquois, created alternative giftgiving realities of this sort. The context carried the gift values even though exchange—at least symbolic exchange—was practiced to some extent, and wars were sometimes fought.

The values of the gift economy threaten the practicers of the exchange economy, and I believe that this is a reason for the ferocity of the White Man against the native people. The White Man had a mother, too. He learned to kill her in the slaughter of the witches. Yet, he could not do that without killing himself, his mother within. There is no gender. Humans are all formed according to giftgiving. By slaughtering and enslaving his European mother, the White Man deprived himself of the model of his *human* potential. By leaving the motherland and penetrating the Americas, the White Man left his humanity to

340

carry out his false masculated agenda of conquest. There he found mothering societies, exploited them and committed genocide upon them. What he considered civilized was the ego and exchange, with its empty logic coming from definition.

Yet, the White Man has a heart. He lived in his mother's womb; he was nurtured by her, received her gifts and gave her his own. What he did not realize is that all men and women share the same dream, the same way of dreaming and the same way of speaking. We already have a common language. The language is not just co-munication of material gifts—though this is important. It is the communication of verbal gifts. It does not matter what the specific sound-gifts are, but that we give them to each other. The Tower of Babel is just the phallic symbol of masculation, which does not let us see that all our languages and our lives come from the Mother and from Mothering. If we can give up masculation and return to the mother and child within each of us, we can restore the dream.

From Re-ality to the Goddess[6] Rhea-lity

Giftgiving and exchange are locked together on the level of economic re-ality, a fact which puts many obstacles in the path of doing effective social change work towards giftgiving. Moreover, the goal of social change is often mistakenly identified as the integration of everyone into the exchange economy. This goal is mistaken because it ignores the fact that, for the market to function, free gifts must come to it from somewhere.

There are many groups who are excluded from the capitalist market system whose products do not have access to the market or cannot compete there. Artisan work by indigenous people, for example, though it is of the highest quality, usually has no way into the market except through exploitative middlemen. Recently, projects which help artisans get their products on the market have been begun by well-intentioned people, who seek funding from foundations or other entities. The problem is seen

[6]Rhea was the original Aegean mother goddess, also Mother Time.

to be the presentation of the crafts on an equal footing with mainstream items. (There needs to be an 'equal exchange.')

The contradiction here is that the goal is seen to be an assimilation into the economy which has excluded and exploited those groups, and which continues to exclude and exploit others, taking from them large quantities of hidden gift labor. Only a few can become 'equal' to the mainstream few who are 'equal,' and all of the few are brought to this 'equality' through using the hidden gifts of others. The gift of the funding of these projects takes the place of the hidden gift labor for a time, but 'self-sufficiency' within the capitalist economy is usually an illusion, because capitalism needs hidden gifts in order to function. 'Self-sufficiency' often only means effective dependency on the capitalist market, just as it has for women who enter the labor market in order to be 'self-sufficient.'

The production of Native American beadwork in Hong Kong is a case in point. International exploitation produces cheaper, more competitive, 'more equal' products than social justice or self-sufficiency projects can. It factors in the gift-quotient that becomes available through the exploitative relation between nations (which produces the difference in their levels of life), together with the 'gift' of the exploited labor of the workers in the individual foreign enterprises. The illusion is that groups 'outside' of the mainstream could succeed if only their products were good enough to be competitive. What is not seen is that being 'good enough,' being equal, or even in the same 'ballpark' requires the addition of a comparatively large amount of hidden gifts.

Perhaps by producing a new product or cornering a market, people outside of the capitalist economy could enter it successfully, benefiting their communities. But this requires a knowledge of the market which individuals achieve through education and through experience in the market, which usually brings them into attempting success for their own profit, not for the community—according to the capitalist values of 'every man for himself.' Even the attempt to enter the market, to produce competitive or equal products, validates the market and 'equal exchange' as the best (and even as the only) way to abundance. Alternatives are seen as impractical or non-existent. The gift economy, hidden and integrated into the exchange economy as exploited labor, is victimized and sacrificed—no value is given to it; it is invisible or discredited and despised.

At the individual psychological level, the subconscious is out of sight but serves as the source for the energy of our conscious minds. Many subconscious motivations and associations never reach the surface and are discounted. In the same vein, people outside the market support those inside the market. Similarly, women support men in their 'equal' relations with other men and in their competition to dominate, without recognizing the effort they themselves and other women have put into nurturing them. What we must do is to stop giving value to the kind of consciousness which is based on exchange and mutual exclusion, to equality in the market, to making our products or ourselves or our children 'competitive,' and try alternatives which are altogether different.

While it may appear difficult to create giftgiving projects in present reality, I suggest that many ways are actually possible that are not being recognized as such. Many women whom I know personally provide services, housing, training, and support free for other women, often believing that they themselves are 'crazy' because they are not requiring payment. There are many experiments with women's land trusts, movements for self-sufficiency and living lightly on the earth.

Movements against domestic violence and sexual violence involve the free satisfaction of needs, as do movements against addictions. People in these movements, as well as those working against racism, and for the liberation of peoples, against the destruction of the environment, against the puer-ile games played with radioactive waste and chemical time bombs, against war, militarism and military spending are all giving enormous time and energy to satisfying important general needs for social change.

While a great deal of volunteer work is done by women, much is done by men, as well. It is not clear to those who are involved in mixed activities that, in doing unmonetized need-satisfying work, both males and females are following the gift paradigm based on mothering. Women's leadership according to giftgiving values is therefore not taken as the standard. Indeed, women often support men who are carrying out the masculated agenda even in activities that have the goal of creating social change. In fact, in many cases, the masculated agenda is not even recognized as problematic.

Giftgiving has often acquired a bad name, and people have been discouraged from doing it, because patriarchal beneficent organizations have imposed their gifts upon the receivers, considering them passive and inferior, not listening to their assessment of their needs. Here, too, women as well as men have espoused paternalism to the detriment of everyone involved, and clouded the connection between women and the gift paradigm by not recognizing the difference between giftgiving and exchange. In fact, these organizations have often used giftgiving as a pretext for domination and profit-making of various sorts.

I have heard the old saw—that it is better not to give poor people fish but to teach them how to fish—with a twist that points at social change. We need to ask how the scarcity was created in the first place. Why have the people not had access to the lake so they could learn how to fish? Was it privately owned or controlled by a corporation or a government? Is it even possible that a group of hungry people could live by a lake to which they had access and not learn how to fish?

We need to give to change the causes of poverty, and one of the major causes of poverty is the system based on exchange. Creating projects to bring people into the market system will not change the causes of poverty. We need to create a change in consciousness, which will let everyone identify the systemic causes and focus on changing them.

It is important to create alternatives to patriarchal capitalism, experiments based on the ways economies were organized by different groups of so-called 'primitive' peoples outside the market system. I suggest funding or otherwise promoting alternative projects—perhaps non-monetized local gift and sharing circles or projects to restore fertile land to dispossessed people to live on and farm. (Many women have already begun buying and sharing land with other women). These projects need to be made possible by monetary gift giving—funding—which in itself is a different economic way. Though funding may appear to be parasitic upon capitalism, it is then parasite upon the parasite—so it has a meta view (parasight) and can put a different way into practice.

Funding gift economies with it even in an experimental way carries its own confirmation at the meta level. It is giving *for giving*. By asserting the existence of alternatives, we can affirm the value of difference and dis-invest from capitalistic equality. From within the classes privileged by the domination of the equal = sign, women at least can hear the resounding call of the First Commandment of Altruistic Reason: "Try something *different*. This isn't working!"

Mater-Mother

Matter-spirit, *mater* (mother)-breath are probably false oppositions. The illusion is that *mater* doesn't mind because she is attributing importance to the other and not taking credit—but that really means she minds more. What we have to do, instead, is make mind *mater*. Atmospheric pressure moves the air, and as we develop a need for it by expanding our lungs, it is inspired, satisfies the need. Things in nature satisfy needs—from the chlorophyll in the leaf providing sugar for the root, to plankton at the bottom of the sea, where whales feed, loll and take their ease—from ancient rocks with which we build our houses, to the potter's wheel.

That is because needs, which are also a part of nature, are creative. Creatures, including humans, adapt to what is given, as well as change it. Mat(t)er is already mind; parts of it attend to one another, needs arise and are filled. But the human mind has

345

been interpreting itself according to the exchange paradigm and so has detached itself from its matrix, reflecting upon itself. In allowing itself to be taken care of by giftgivers, women, the mother and child within, the many—the mind is not minding about them. Occupied by its ego-orientation, it philosophically tries to track what it alone is doing.

Perhaps the mind (and the brain, as well) can be better understood if we look at them from the viewpoint of the gift paradigm. If we put the *mater* back into matter, we can see how she minds, how mind is mothering, and how we must now satisfy our own need and that of humanity and the earth, to recognize that *mater* as a given. Spirit hardly matters in reflection; it is breath upon the mirror, something belonging to a different concept. But actually, the mother and the wind work according to similar principles. They go where there is a lack, a void, a need for them. And they bring the words we need to hear to form our communities again.

Mother Nurture

I go for a walk in the country—there are so many creatures, insects, plants, wildflowers, so specific and different from each other in the places and ways they grow. A variety, a magnificent wild, slow dance of plant and animal life is in each square foot of terrain. Each kind is related to a word as its name, but they are rhea-lly far from equal. Now the combination of the concept, the definition and exchange has produced an environment where things are actually identical to each other. We no longer pick berries in the woods; we pick up identical cans of berries at the supermarket.

The goddess has not been completely destroyed. Preparing, cooking and eating the food we cook—feeling, moving, many types of enjoyment from sex to poetry to watching a storm—are still ways of embracing her gifts. But forcing reality to give has to do with male violence: mining, drilling, bombing. If you force someone to give, you get security that they will give, and perhaps this security provides needed comfort to the artificial exchange ego.

We should look at Rhea-lity as Mother Nature, Mother Nurture. The same thing is being done to her that is done to us, depleting her so as to force her to give, showing that men do it the right or only way, that they have control of Rhea-lity as well as re-ality. They do this by not attributing or giving nurture to nature or value to giving. Canceling the mother makes it appear that mechanical cause and effect, if-then, objective exchange processes, are the basis of life. This blots out a whole spectrum of nurturing intentionality from the least 'human,' the wind, or the chance of the amoeba's finding a juicy morsel in its path, to the most 'human,' a feminist revolution or a lullaby. In the beginning, ontogenetically and phylogenetically, mothers feed their babies.[7]

Emotion

The work of maintenance of the world still attributes value materially though 'menially.' Despite monetization and exchange, needs continue to be recognized by women (and some men) both emotionally and intellectually. In fact, I believe it is the human connection with the needs of others and our own that is the basis of human emotional life. Masculated egos, immersed in exchange, are notoriously (and unhappily) detached from needs, 'insensitive.' Attention to needs appears to be irrational, because what we consider rational is based on exchange. Since we have allowed exchange to pervade our world, blocking out giving, we have set all our values askew, making them more abstract than they would have been if they had been grounded in giving. Then value has been given to abstraction itself.

[7]Nature and nurture are just contrasting gift sources. Nature is what we 'have,' gifts or endowments we inherit from the past of the species, while nurture is what we are given socially. Archeologists, like Richard Leakey, think a major part of human evolution came about through 'altruism,' food sharing, among hominids—coupled with competition. But don't forget, we are looking back at pre-history through a competitive framework given to us by our present society.

Emotions continue to flicker around unsatisfied needs, drawing attention to them, giving them value so they can be satisfied. Those emotions are often ignored, discounted, disqualified and otherwise superseded by the logic of self-interest. Giving value to abstract reasoning draws our attention away from needs. While it is true that abstract reasoning may sometimes be useful for understanding how to satisfy complicated needs, it can become an end in itself and an excuse to disregard needs and the emotions that lead us to them, forever.

Patriarchy has re(x)-ified re-ality. It has extended its network of self-similar images—phallically invested concepts—seizing the gifts of the collective, like an OBN of businessmen seizing new markets. Overlaying these concepts onto 'reality' diminishes its nurturing side, makes needs invisible, discounts the emotions that respond to them, and reality then becomes mechanical and objectified. What is a given is taken for granted, important only because it has been organized into concepts, made relative to privileged ones. We are always in receivership, however, though we don't recognize it. Reality is always nurturing, even though abstract concepts hide it and deceive us. The network of concepts, the self-similar system, is an invisible web, abstractly shared, deviating our attention away from the real gifts of the goddess Rhea and onto phallic Rex and Res.

348

Chapter 20
Giving and Love

I think the phrase 'carnal knowledge' is well-taken. Much of our interpersonal experience of love and sex is involved with knowing and perceiving the other person physically, as well as spiritually, according to the giving and receiving 'grain.' This knowledge requires or invites an other-orientation, which is partly the basis for the experience of 'losing one's self,' well-known in the literature of love. In a society which is made in the image of the exchange paradigm, many of us have learned not to be other-oriented so love can be an overwhelming experience, an excursion into the gift economy, a concentration on the other, a chance to re-perceive the world, re-create a human society of two.

We bond, forming our relations to each other, in regard to our new gift perceptions. Like Adam naming the creatures of Eden and talking about them with Eve, we become conscious of each other's particularities and universalities, and we become conscious of each other's consciousness of them. Love alters our individual attitudes towards other-orientation, at least for the time being. We begin to need each other and to want to give to each other. We even begin to need the other's need for us, our giving of ourselves, becoming linked to the other's desire. Perhaps it is this other-oriented aspect of love that makes us sing about it, talk about it, long for it so much in this society. "Love is the way," say preachers and peace activists. The only ones that don't say it are economists (and therapists worried about co-dependency).

There is a part of our true minds that is telling us what to do, using our relationships to tell us. I guess it is hard for that part to generalize. It did not know that its context was really economic. It tells us, "Give, change the ego, nurture the other person abundantly." Freud and women writers like Nancy Friday who found that we look for relationships with our mothers in the men we marry have hit on a glimmering of the gift economy which is usually nipped in the bud.

In fact, the love relationship, by causing 'other-orientation,' may make a man behave in a more nurturing way than he ever has before, putting his ego aside, acting like a mother would with her child (love ya, Baby!), especially if the mother were also used to living in the exchange economy and had taken on its values. The feeling of bliss that comes from reciprocal nurturing (turn-taking—not exchange—because each is other-oriented) is the experience of the gift economy between adults, highlighted by the fact that they are a society of two, since nurturing is not the economic way chosen by the world they live in. Indeed, their relationship may seem to be, and is, a pocket of blessedness in a world gone mad.

Like other instances of the gift economy, the society of two is soon altered in its nature and chance for survival by the alien character of its surroundings. Like a tropical flower growing in a northern climate, it needs special circumstances, hard work, attentiveness, protection—all of which make the feeling of warmth and abundance drain away, so that the tender plant feels (correctly) that it is in the wrong environment. But again, this is not the 'fault' of love, but of the scarcity of love and the scarcity of goods created by masculation and exchange in the world at large. The more cruel acts that take place in the world, the more hostile is the environment for the nurturing relationship between two adults.

In order to survive in a situation of scarcity, the lovers adapt. They typically divide the labor heterosexually; one enters fully into the exchange paradigm, while the other remains nurturing, even when she also works in the exchange economy. Their egos alter accordingly. Women give our greatest gift; we give birth to our children, and then we practice the gift paradigm with them because they impose it. We are forced by their real dependence to adapt to an other-oriented way. Male partners enter into the hierarchy of competition for scarce goods but do not usually have the psycho-economic saving grace of having to nurture the children. Participation in the exchange economy becomes the only technique for survival and women, therefore, begin to reinforce psychologically in their partners (and sometimes in themselves) those characteristics which help to succeed there. They postpone their love, put aside their nurturing of each other, until some more convenient time. Finally, they may think the experience of love was childish, an illusion. It rightly reminded them of their childhood because the relation between mother and child is the only other major experience of the gift economy most of us know.

Giving Embedded in Exchange

With the system of the double burden, many women perform both gift and exchange roles. They are paid less for comparable work—not only to demonstrate their inferiority and the inferiority of the gift paradigm, but to keep them needing the money which men provide for them with the results of their exchange economy activity. This support seems to slip into being a sort of payment for services. In other words, a woman's free nurturing, both of her mate and of her children, is 'compensated' by the money given to her by her husband. The free nurturing is thus corralled into the exchange paradigm, captured by it, almost re-framed as exchange. However, the money that women receive is usually barely enough to buy the means of nurturing for the family. In a situation of scarcity, women's free labor seems (and sometimes is) a kind of slavery. The opposite of slavery seems to be working for pay, while instead it would be liberation to freely give in a situation of abundance.

Giving in abundance is an option for wealthy people—where the husband works in the exchange economy to make abundant money, and the wife (who does not work in that economy) has time to practice nurturing on a wider scale, doing volunteer work or providing charity, something which her husband may also do. Unfortunately, charity of this kind maintains the status quo by alleviating problems, while allowing their causes to remain the same. Moreover, volunteerism which depends upon patriarchal capitalism makes it seem as if the exchange mode were necessary to support giftgiving.

Charity validates the exchange mode by considering it as its pre-requisite. Even the successful examples of cause-related marketing have this defect. Instead, we need to change the whole context by shifting to the gift paradigm for all, and we need to use our gifts to make that happen.

While it is good for us psychologically to nurture others from a situation of abundance, in the present situation of generalized scarcity giftgiving can seem unusual, even saintly. This can lend itself to ego trips of various kinds by the givers, as well as to a lack of respect for the recipients. Considering the exchange paradigm and its logic as the root of the problem depersonalizes the actions of the givers and of the receivers. Need satisfaction should not replay the scenario of having and not-having, better and worse. Instead it is part of a more workable and human way, good for the personality and material well-being of the giver and the receiver, freed from the humiliation and egomania of the defense of the exchange paradigm. It is the logical and co-munitary thing to do.

The kinds of jobs which are available in our society do not allow for the development of the free giving mode and mentality. The whole society validates the production of goods and services for exchange, together with the evaluation of human beings according to the monetary standard. Within our personal relationships, in our hands-on experience, we can experiment with the social currents that are flowing through us. We may do a lot of 'giving' of ourselves to each other, because we are not doing it socially on a material plane. Those who have some material wealth must at least unconsciously feel the pull of the needs of others. Starving people look at us from the TV screen. We watch the homeless, drunk and cold, lying in doors of buildings.

There is a true, if cynical, point of view about giving which says, "If I give everything I have to someone else, s/he will just be as ego-oriented as I have been." If the exchange paradigm continues to be validated, the 'haves' will continue to oppress the 'have-nots.' If a slightly more other-oriented person gives her money to someone else, that person may very likely become more ego-oriented. The secret is to give in order to change the system and to validate the gift paradigm. Any need-satisfying behavior, if it is done with consciousness of the paradigm of which it is a part, does help in that validation.

Sexual Giving

I think that we may be trying to practice co-municative giftgiving in our love relationships, perhaps even through promiscuity. We give ourselves sexually to those who seem to need us, because we are pushed by our subconscious to give while, at the same time, we are either living in material scarcity or have been convinced that giving materially is not a viable thing to do. Giving ourselves sexually allows us to feel the emotions of giving and receiving 'on our own skin.' It allows us to do something for somebody else, satisfy a need without actually transferring goods from one to the other. In fact, it can seem very embarrassing to give and receive goods while sexual giving and receiving is validated as a 'normal' desire. Promiscuous sex allows us to be other-oriented towards a number of people, giving to them on that plane, while society does not allow us to give to them on the plane of material need.

We live the problems of our society through our interpersonal relations. For example, women over-give to our children or continue to give to abusive husbands. I think we realize unconsciously that giving is the way. What we don't see is that we are often giving in the wrong places, and on the wrong levels, and that we cannot do it effectively until it is validated socially as the Way to behave instead of exchange. In fact, I think there is a confusion between material nurturing and love—which makes us think that we are loving people any time we are being other-oriented towards them. Any need we satisfy seems to be giftgiving, even if that is a batterer's need to hurt us.

But perhaps the reason for this is the confusion between the other-orientation that takes place in sex and love and the material other-orientation that would be present in the right practice of the gift paradigm. Even now, we could begin to practice it in giving our time, money and energy to change the structures of oppression. If we were to shift to the gift paradigm, the whole society would be other-oriented and needs would be satisfied by others, so we would continually hear the call of the needs of others.

But in that case, many other people would be satisfying needs, so even the needs of our mates might be very different from what they are now. Being able to practice material other-orientation outside our immediate families and for the good of all would allow us to practice better psychological orientation towards our loved ones, as well. Receiving from others-in-general as well as giving to them would allow more bonding with them, and we would not be dependent on sex for meaningful 'co-munication.' The quest for a 'meaningful' life is well-named, since it may be seen as a life which attributes value by giving and receiving, and value is, therefore, bestowed on it, as well.

As it is, we are particularly dependent on each other in our relationships, because this is the only place most of us can do giving and receiving, practicing the gift paradigm, even if imperfectly. It is, therefore, the most 'human' of our behaviors, and we become very attached to it. Abandonment seems to be a threat to our humanity. The giving and receiving that we do sexually, in which different needs spring up in our bodies as we proceed and as we satisfy them for each other, creates a common ground for the community of two, which is hard to renounce.

Our selves grow through this community, much as our selves grow in our original families where we become differentiated as individuals on the basis of our common ground with others. The masculated or exchange-based ego is more likely to be abandoning, adversarial, denying connection and intimacy, and using the other for her nurturing reinforcement of its sense of

354

importance. Unfortunately, the socialization of men away from nurturing allows this kind of destructiveness of the sexual comunity. Seduce and abandon ("love 'em and leave 'em") is the macho disease, sometimes even when it is women who are doing the leaving. A desire to dominate, which functions well in the competitive exchange economy, can be carried out in personal relations by force, abandonment or mental cruelties, such as disparagement and non-participation.

The Nurturing of Competition

The gift and the exchange paradigms function like two environments of nature existing side by side, and what is adaptive behavior in one is destructive in the other. Moreover, the environment of 'survival of the fittest' is seen as the support of the nurturing family environment. The families of the fittest in the exchange economy survive. This is an illusion because it is the existence of the competitive environment which threatens the nurturing way and burdens it to extenuation. In fact, nurturing is sustaining the competitive environment, not vice versa. It cannot be abolished without destroying the competitive environment also, because the way of exchange needs free gifts in order to continue to exist.

The competitors are themselves provided by the nurturers, and many of their competitive advantages come from the kind of nurturing they have received. Many of their prizes and rewards also come from the nurturers, including the nurturers themselves. Beautiful and sexy women or 'good wives' are often seen as the prizes of successful men. At the individual level, none of this appears connected to the rest, and the interactions seem to be due to personal differences, choices, and characteristics. Taking a broader view, however, we can see that the two kinds of behavior are tied together, bound by the chains of their complementarity. It is advantageous to the competitive group that the relation not be seen from a perspective which would allow the nurturing group to consciously liberate itself. Indeed, like many parasites, the competitive group puts on a mimetic exterior, appearing to be doing the nurturing itself.

Value Accents

The two paradigms are also distinguished from each other because the capacity to define and all its transpositions in the activities of measuring and assessing value, mediating private property by substituting one thing for another, and establishing equivalencies between different kinds of things which are to be exchanged, are seen *post hoc* as the province of masculation.

Women are said to be 'immersed in experience'—and, in fact, experience may be seen as taking place according to the giving grain and in the gift mode. There is a sense in which all our perceptions and experiences come to us free. Though we may have to exert ourselves to have one kind of perception instead of another (walk out the door to see the sun shining), if our senses are functioning correctly, there is always something present to be perceived. The structure of our world picture and our needs will determine which of these perceptions we pick out to use, which 'givens' we focus on. Much of the world picture depends upon past experience and practice of one paradigm or the other as well as upon 'value accents' transmitted through language and culture.

Women are relegated by men to the side of life which has to do with perception and materiality. Men describe us to each other, sharing us as their common ground through language while we are stereotypically immersed in 'feeling.' I was talking earlier about women as occupying the 'shadow,' the side of mat(t)er, and the many. We have this to fall back on. It is the border of the gift economy, as language is the border of the exchange economy.

But the side of mat(t)er and the many is lost in the haze, while language is focused upon. Beneath the surface of language and the givens of perception lies the free labor of the centuries, consisting of women's free maintenance of things, as well as all

356

the unpaid other-tending labor of the society as a whole. All the free gifts of the past determine what specific things we perceive— that is, what parts of material culture have persisted through time to make up our world. We may also consider ourselves as gifts given by others, and our children as our gifts. Our other-tending egos are less self-similar than masculated ones, more 'transparent,' straightforwardly embracing the other without the ego filter. We are the children who remember our mothers (and the mothers who remember and are remembered by our children).

Our 'male and female' sides, at least in the specificity with which they appear to us in Western society, are really a transposition of the masculated exchange ego and the other-tending self as products and processes of the exchange economy and the gift economy. Since the two economic modes exist side by side in society, the ego structures they promote can be internalized together. This creates a third kind of personality structure which, while it may be seen as transitional between one kind of economy and another, and may have some of the advantages of each, is caught in numerous paradoxes. The 'giftgiver within' bonds by attending to needs, and strong emotions may arise when the needs cannot be met. In contrast, the masculated ego seeks independence and dominance. It is not a perfect fit internally or externally.

The masculated ego and the contents of its thought may be directed towards gain for itself or for its family, as an extension of itself. It considers its experience as 'objective,' without the gift character but also without the duty of maintenance towards its surroundings. It is less conscious of the needs in the environment, from the unmade bed to the hungry child to the toxic waste dump. Much of its time is spent focused on language, bureaucracy, instruments of a social or material kind for causing others to do something, or to give so it may receive. It ignores the same things in itself. Its own needs must, therefore, be satisfied by others, as in the stereotype of the absent-minded professor. Without an external nurturer, the giftgiving side of this personality may finally have to turn around and take care of its own masculated ego. Thus, the remaining other-oriented parts of the personality are turned towards the 'other within,' and the person becomes even more self-centered.

For those who are socialized into giftgiving, the self which develops is already oriented towards others, so that the nurturing aspect is included as part of the ego which develops through participation in the exchange mode. Perhaps this accounts for the popularity of me-first therapy among women. From co-dependency groups to assertiveness training, our exchange-based society is teaching us to put ourselves first. Fortunately, since we have been brought up to be other-tending, the gift way remains part of the self we assert. It may seem functional to the status quo to do away with giftgiving and its ideals and ideas, but the exchange economy would really be destroyed by doing so.

There are, of course, pathological cases of other-orientation, but ego orientation is much more likely to be pathological. Socially, it is having pernicious effects for all the creatures of the planet, while it is being upheld as the model of health. None of us have a clue that we are doing all this because we do not recognize giftgiving as a paradigm at the same level as the exchange paradigm. In fact, it is the comparability of the paradigms that we should be asserting, not the equality of the sexes.

Equality deriving from masculation and exchange is equality preparatory to quantification, or quantitative equality. Need-direction emphasizes qualitative variety. Paradoxically, the gift economy brings forth individual differences more because it is not measuring them on a single quantitative value standard. If we focus on the gift economy as a paradigm instead of demeaning it and particularizing its manifestations, we can also use it to shed light on what the exchange paradigm is doing. We could be reading such statements as, "Women are as good as men," as meta statements saying, "The gift paradigm is as good as (or better than) the exchange paradigm."

Judgments

Among the other characteristics of the exchange paradigm is the capacity to pass judgment, putting something in one category or another. Like marriage customs in which women acquire a man's name, women's actions and desires are judged by the masculated ego as good or bad, appropriate or inappropriate, etc. Women accept this judgment because of our (otherwise positive) other-orientation. Judgment of our own qualities is not something which is easy to do for ourselves, though perhaps the internalized ego can do it for us. "Am I intelligent? Am I beautiful? Am I good?" We may become endlessly preoccupied with these assessments, becoming ego-oriented even about defining our other-orientation. Our capacity to look at ourselves through the eyes of the other lets us seek his definition of us and then judge ourselves as he would.

Playing out the definition, as the *definiens* we serve a man's *definiendum* of ourselves trying to de-serve his positive word. We confuse self-deprecation with 'humility' and allow stereotypes to lead us as self-fulfilling prophecies. The division between words and things, mind and body, is absorbed by us internally—even though, as participants in the exchange economy, we may now be living the division somewhat differently. Women used to give up on abstract linguistic work, like mathematics or finance, because they considered it not feminine. Even now, we may strive to merit our own positive judgment of ourselves, measuring our value on a standard created by men for women, by masculated egos for giftgivers.

A principle of giftgiving is that it not be done to seek rewards. Thus, if we strive to be judged by others or even by ourselves as 'good' or 'beautiful,' we are bordering on the exchange area. However, others may judge us freely in a positive way, and this may seem to come as a gift for which we can be grateful. We sometimes receive the gift of the judgment 'good' or 'beautiful,' though we haven't striven for it. We long for this 'free' judgment from others, because of the difficulty of maintaining ourselves in the gift logic internally. Attempting to live up to our own standards sets up a self-manipulative dynamic.

Perhaps the self-criticism that many of us indulge in allows us to try to direct ourselves through our own judgment, while remaining in the gift paradigm. If we punish what we do 'wrong,' it may seem less like acting for a reward than if we were to judge ourselves as 'good.' The ego trip seems to be shunned by many good people. Perhaps it seems that, by avoiding that masculated behavior, we can remain in the gift paradigm. Actually, belonging within one paradigm or the other is probably determined, not by self-domination or manipulation, but by many repeated actions, motivated in one or the other direction at many different times and situations and on different levels. The external and the internal contexts determine the success and practical validation of these actions.

Needing To Be Needed

Women may try to bring forward in ourselves the characteristics that men would value, enhancing our 'attractiveness' so that they will pay attention to us, use our gifts and give us the gift of their positive judgment of us. In fact, we used to have the specter of the 'old maid' before us as someone whose gifts remained unused, perhaps because she was not good enough. No one needed her. In fact, we need the need of others so that we can practice the gift economy towards them, whether by nurturing them with various kinds of goods, or 'giving ourselves' to them. Needing the other's need has been disparaged by our culture, but it is part of the quandary created by the coexistence of giftgiving and exchange.

For example, 'smothering' mothers sometimes hold on to their children too long. They need to be needed because their giving has been trapped inside the family. They are unable to find needs outside the family which they may fill, or to direct themselves to 'others-in-general' through working for social change. Paradoxically, in a situation of scarcity, there is also a scarcity of needs to which giftgivers have socially approved and 'meaningful' access. If the gift economy were seen as the norm, everyone would be needed by everyone.

In a gift economy, some kinds of specialization and habitual interactions would probably form on the basis of the general recognition of the values of the gift paradigm and the personality structures connected with it. The people with the capability and energy to nurture would not be denied access to the people with the needs, nor would the flow of goods be stopped. Giving and receiving would no longer be branded as 'demeaning,' but would become normal behavior. The earth pulls us to her, water runs downhill, wind moves according to atmospheric pressure. There is a gravity and a pressure differential in human affairs also, which must be respected. Exchange works like a system of locks on a river, making water travel uphill, away from those who have the needs and towards those who already have more than enough. Our altruism is manipulated and turned back upon ourselves. We desperately need to validate the original flow.

There is also a gravity in personal relations, and the flow can be altered there, as well. We may begin to count on another person's nurturing, internalizing it as something we 'deserve,' seeing it as a payment for our right action of one kind or another. Then we affirm this rationale as valid and insist on being nurtured in the manner in which we are accustomed. When the other person doesn't do it for us, we do it for ourselves, procuring or taking what we need or believe we need, no longer respecting the desires of the other. It is all too easy to do this in the exchange economy in which we live at present because this kind of attitude is 'normal.' If we were living in a gift economy, we would remain in a situation of other-orientation, looking at others' needs and satisfying them, but trusting that they would be doing this towards us, as well. A masculated ego structure would not be necessary.

I think that, in practice, such well-founded trust would allow a greater transparency of our experience. Much less fear, bigotry and hatred would occur because the person would not need to defend her/himself at every moment, both from others' violent taking, indifference, manipulation and from self-criticism for doing these things to others 'in order to survive.' In other words, there would no longer be artificial structures blocking the flow of compassion. These structures also cause the fear, self-pity (the ego-orientation of compassion) and distress which block the clarity of our selves and our interactions. I just want to repeat here that I do not see this as the 'fault' of the ego-oriented person, since the whole system of patriarchy is pushing him/her in that direction, moreover the terms of guilt and repayment are really exchange-based values, and therefore validate the exchange paradigm, even while they are being applied to one of its defects.

Rather, the wider self-similar social structures that validate the masculated ego logic must be recognized as impractical, obsolete, and harmful. Masculation and its external projections should be seen as alterable and actually pernicious to society in general, as well as to the individual. Practicing other-tending towards the person possessing or possessed by a masculated ego, we can see that s/he has a need to dismantle and re-arrange it, that s/he would be happier and more effective without it, being more other-oriented. It is possible to create an environment in which other-orientation can be validated and internalized as such, without turning it primarily towards the 'other within' or the external or internal dominator. This can be done by not masculating our males and by changing the paradigm from exchange to giving, validating the values most women (and many men) already have.

Monetization and Morality

Monetization of labor not only incarnates some of the processes of the definition, like substitution and equivalence, but it also functions as a judgment upon the value of the person to society. Money and the free market supposedly measure us on a standard that is equal for all and objective, which makes it all the more difficult to deal with if we are judged negatively by it, or left out of the monetized economy altogether. Women's salaries, being lower than men's, negatively define us as 'less' than men to begin with. The economic sample of judgment by salary then doubles back into other types of judgments, reinforcing their power over us. We measure and motivate ourselves by the monetary standard, influencing our judgments of ourselves and others as good, smart, efficient, etc.

These judgments appear to come from some external standard where worth is evaluated 'objectively,' and fit in well with the quantitative evaluation of the masculated ego. We are a society obsessed with evaluations from grades in school, to counting calories, to the weather report and the psychological test. We submit to tests and let the assessment dominate our behavior. Even in our intimate examinations of conscience, we judge and dominate ourselves through self-assessment. Much of the self-esteem movement is meant to counter the all-out negative effects of domination through negative self-evaluation.

Of course, we must give value to criteria and judgments if we are to submit to them. Authoritarian parenting, morality and religion are set up to make us give this value. It is more difficult for other people to dominate us, especially psychologically, if we do not do so.

A sort of secondary exchange system is created in which we strive for recognition. We give our actions of a certain sort to the scrutiny of others, and the judgment they give us is our reward. Even giftgiving is done often with this in mind. We long for the judgment of others that we are 'good,' or smart, or capable. Then, having received it, we use it to form our identities, our self concepts.

Giving or withholding this judgment, and giving a negative judgment, are ways people have power over others. One reason we strive to receive positive definition by others, attributing so much importance to it, is the underlying pattern of judgment by salary, which in turn is influenced by the underlying pattern of the pricing of products. Our love relationships also often follow these patterns. Each of us is 'evaluated' by our lover, chosen as the 'best' among similar 'products' or 'employees.' (Economists now even talk about the 'marriage market.') It should not be this way. We are greatly influenced by the unconscious archetypes of exchange—and would be much happier without them.

We sometimes internalize the evaluation and judgment process, dominating ourselves according to society's values or our own. By such inner activity, whether through self-domination or self-acceptance, we confirm ourselves as 'good,' etc. Morality functions along these lines, inducing 'right conduct' within a situation based upon exchange. Unable to really solve existing problems or shift the paradigm socially, morality, like charity, makes the best of a bad situation. Perhaps it even saves its practitioner individually, making him/her become 'good' rather than 'evil.' However, the person is encouraged to concentrate on his/her own qualities, thus remaining ego-oriented, without challenging the paradigm.

Compassion

The 'price' of not nurturing and giving value to the dominator may be physical violence. The 'gift' is thus constrained, making it like the 'gift' of the work of a slave. For centuries, people throughout patriarchy have been trapped in situations where violence is the punishment for not giving. The many are punished by ones or by hierarchies for non-compliance or rebellion. Obedience becomes a survival skill.

In this situation, the stop-gap measures of personal generosity may seem to be the only viable response to suffering. While caring people practice giftgiving individually, they do not appear to be proposing a viable social model and thus do not serve the solution of the general problem, which has to take place on a wider scale. Probably many of these caring individuals would want to change the social paradigms; they just do not see things in those terms or know it is possible.

The movements against domestic and sexual violence have organized individual caring for social change at the level of the family. They do not yet challenge other aspects of patriarchy, such as environmental and international violence; however, they are focusing on the problem in an important area, they are practicing the values of care—and they are organized. Other movements for social change, for peace, for the environment, for economic justice and the liberation of peoples are doing important work for systemic change, but they do not usually focus on patriarchal patterns as the problem or on women's values as the solution.

A similar consideration may be made for governmental solutions to problems. While they may be well-intentioned and even functional in the short term, they are operating upon the foundation of exchange. The appeal to individual responsibility as against dependency, taking people off welfare, integrating them into the market, is a solution which aggravates the problem by re-emphasizing the values that are causing it. Giftgiving as done by the paternalistic state is demeaning and ineffective. The culprit wrongly appears to be the act of receiving, which is seen as passive and unintelligent—and is decried as almost sub-human. Consequently creative giving-and-receiving is replaced by individual integration into exchange and the reinforcement of masculated capitalistic values.

Individual altruism sometimes does provide a giftgiving model, extending its influence to a wider group. However, unless it is an attempt to arrive at the root of the problems, it may only be a way to live within the exchange paradigm, maintaining a certain degree of personal sanity and helpful behavior towards others, but without radically changing anything. Compassion, charity and morality, when practiced only as individual approaches, do not cause a paradigm shift which is necessarily a collective process.

That is why it is important to see women's coming to consciousness—the international women's movement—in the light of the gift paradigm. The gift paradigm is already there in women's caring values and, when individual women validate their own (not patriarchy's) values, they are already part of a collective, which is more than 50% of humanity. The gift paradigm is deep, pervasive and unrecognized. Masculation occurs early for males, but women take on the values of masculation later by seeing the world through the eyes of our 'others'—of those humans society has alienated from us and whom we over-nurture.

By becoming conscious of our other-tending values as paradigmatic, women working for social change can liberate ourselves from the superimposition of the values of masculation upon the values of care. By proposing the gift paradigm as the human way for all, we can also liberate men and society at large from the hall-of-mirrors of the exchange paradigm. Men and women can recognize the alien and unnecessary character of masculation, step back from it, and dismantle it in non-masculated, non-violent ways. The transition towards a different way can be easier because the alternative way does not have to be invented. It already exists in the giftgiving which is actively practiced by half of humanity and forms the hidden matrix for the other half.

Restoring Humanity to the Mother

The kind of other-orientation that is functional for taking care of children is interactive and different from a morality which tries to impose 'right action' and 'right attitudes' on others or oneself. Morality may cross over into nurturing, especially when it is difficult to satisfy needs because of scarcity or stress. In difficult times, a person may also have to 'force' herself to act in an other-oriented way towards the child or the other, i.e. to take on the nurturing as a moral issue.

Reactionary and macho philosophers have interpreted the mother-child bond as 'natural.' Giving value to the needs of the other is not 'natural' in a mindless sense, but it is also not part of rule-based morality. It is a principle *sui generis*—of its own kind—which may not be recognized as such because it does not contain within it those self-reflecting ego elements by which we usually recognize something as a principle or 're-al'—because our thinking so often takes place in the masculated mode.

If our egos and our philosophical interpretations of re-ality are ego-oriented and produced by exchange and masculation, the non-ego-oriented things that we do remain outside their purview. They do not become conscious, or at least not in the same way. There is an instrumentality of egotism that binds us to giving value to what may be useful to it, and not to other things. It sees its structures reflected, and defines that familiar sight as 'real' while things that do not have those earmarks are extraneous, irrelevant, un-real. The self-similar ego is a little like the animal which marks its territory with urine, then recognizes it as its own. In giftgiving, we are usually not involved in marking our territory, but in providing the well-being of the other at some level.

If language is based on giftgiving, giftgiving cannot be considered mostly pre-verbal and infantile. If we can add to language other instances of giftgiving, such as dreaming, art, and action for social change, we can see giftgiving begin to emerge as the great unacknowledged principle of the human species. We must understand that the Mother is for giving and that both males and females can be for giving. Indeed, exchange—spun from the process of naming and the definition—does not work to satisfy the needs of the many. Only by taking up the principle of the Mother—not as biological or instinctual, but as conscious creative human practice—will we be able to satisfy the diverse material and cultural needs of the 5.5 billion human beings now living.

What we need to do now is to bring the gift mode into the ego-oriented consciousness in order to show its advisability for all. This can be accomplished by looking at things from a meta level, with a global perspective, and in terms of a totality. In fact, ego-interest and other-interest coincide at the global level. The survival of the planet (other interest) coincides with the survival of the individual ego and even of the whole complementary system of exchange-and-giftgiving. If each of us is to be destroyed by the destruction of our planet, each of us can give our energy to the solution of the problems that are causing this destruction, whether our motivation is ego- or other-oriented or a combination of both. For the ego-oriented people, this is a moment of transition towards giftgiving. From the meta point of view, which sees both paradigms, we can all opt for a paradigm shift. This is the beginning of a solution.

I believe that the spiritual practices which call upon the oneness of all are actually seeking this meta level, while couching their quest in terms which recall the superiority of the one as opposed to the many. While proposing an inclusive one—and inclusion is an aspect of gift logic—they nevertheless do not focus upon the actual patriarchal dynamics between the one and the many.

From the point of view which tries to embrace everything, it is possible to include both paradigms at the same level of importance. The self-reflecting exchange paradigm is not more important than the gift paradigm, although its self-similar form creates that illusion. It is the gift paradigm which could stand alone as the logic of human behavior. Looking at both paradigms from the broader perspective, if we re-institute the criterion of competition between paradigms—which is not contradictory because it is taking place at this 'higher' level—we can see that the gift paradigm wins hands down as the more functional way for humans to think and behave.

We can displace our individual striving to become the sample and allow the gift paradigm to become the sample for human behavior. By ending masculation itself, language, the definition, and naming, liberated from their self-similar incarnations, can continue the creative mediation of human subjectivities and cultures in a world in which material giftgiving becomes the norm. If we analyze and understand exchange, the ego and its elements well enough, we can maintain any of their aspects which may be useful to us all. Just as we may use some kinds of technology in a peaceful and ecologically sane way to provide the means for nurturing everyone abundantly, we may perhaps decide to maintain elements of exchange and the ego-oriented consciousness to provide certain kinds of useful activities and parts of our personality structures.

A reinterpretation of morality as behavior which creates a transition towards the gift paradigm would suggest that we should act according to other-orientation and life-giving and promote the consciousness of that behavior as paradigmatic.[1]

Conditional and Unconditional Love

Morality does not function effectively because of the patterns of domination which pervade its strictures. A gift which is forced either from the outside or from within loses many of the positive aspects of the gift. Moreover, we place ourselves in a position to be manipulated. As in masculation or definition by money, we depend a great deal on judgments by others. We want just the right measurement or evaluation for our actions. In love, we may try to get others to be other-oriented towards us rather than being ourselves other-oriented towards them. Some kinds of positive judgments about us seem to ensure that possibility. For example, we elicit the positive judgments of others by making ourselves beautiful. Then we love them for loving us. Thus, we are in the same position towards them as we are towards ourselves loving ourselves: the part of ourselves that loves our exchange-based ego. We both internalize and externalize the relations between the paradigms, in our relations with ourselves and with others.

Much is said about unconditional love in our therapy-riddled society. Perhaps, what the therapists have hit on is the healing quality of other-oriented, gift love, in an exchange society, where

[1] Thus, we would be reworking the Kantian categorical imperative so that, not only should we ask whether the principle (the paradigm) underlying our action could be generalized, but we should act to bring its generality to consciousness and institutionalize it. The exchange paradigm cannot be generalized as the way of behaving for everyone because it requires the gifts of the many in order to function. That is, it requires that many practice the gift paradigm towards it. Those who want to extend the 'free' market to everyone are not taking this into consideration.

much of the love that is given is framed by bribe and barter, 'given' on an if/then basis. People who love each other outside the exchange paradigm can consider themselves harbingers of a better world.

Urgent needs among those close to us can call forth the gift of unconditional love. The tragic AIDS epidemic has stimulated a great deal of giftgiving without attachment. The movements against child abuse, battering, and addictions, the peace, environmental, and anti-nuclear movements, the movements for the liberation of peoples all require endless hours of dedication, a great commitment of life energy and imagination.

The 'release' of others from our attention (as positive-thinking teachers advise) functions because it assures the continuation of other-orientation towards another without any feedback on her part. On the other hand, such an extreme position as loving unilaterally would not be necessary if the society were not so deeply warped by exchange. Active giving and receiving, turn-taking, is appropriate behavior between two persons (as well as between them and the rest of society) and can take place without involving giving in order to receive.

It is only when we have been so wounded by exchange and domination that we no longer trust that we find it necessary for others to love us unilaterally and unconditionally. However we may also look askance at this solution, since we have been taught by therapists as well as by the society and our parents that it is wrong to receive without giving anything back. We want unconditional gift love, but we are taught that exchange is the only respectful and human way to behave, so we may suspect gift love of really being a power gambit, the first half of an exchange we did not enter into knowingly (they loved us without our asking!) and can never 'repay.'

Parenting

Many of our parenting practices are barbaric. We get children to obey by threatening to abandon them or beating them up,

370

thereby teaching exchange and conditional if/then reasoning. "If you do this, you will get that."[2] We make children give value to us and to our words, according to what we want. Here, the giving-over of the will and the satisfaction of the parent's need to be obeyed are grotesque imitations of nurturing and being nurtured.

Even as adults, the threat of abandonment haunts us. The society does to us what our parents did. The specter of homelessness, joblessness, loneliness menaces each home, each place of employment, each family and individual. There is a constant threat of scarcity of love, just as there is the threat of scarcity of money and nurturing goods. In our waste-oriented society, according to the model of the product for which no market exists, or which the accelerated production-exchange-consumption cycle barely uses, we can suddenly find ourselves cast upon the garbage heap. Falling out of the privileged market categories, we are placed in the trash can of time and place. Such a situation influences both 'masculine' and 'feminine' egos, frightening them into a position of dominance or submission, making them follow the Don Juan model of one-many money dominance or the Super Mom model of the useful product, out of fear of being discarded and abandoned.

[2]The case of a modern 'feral,' language-less child, was described recently by Russ Rymer in Genie, Harper Collins, New York, 1993. Rymer's book demonstrates how little giftgiving the child received. First, as a victim of isolation and abuse by her parents, then as a pawn of bureaucratic academic interests, she was almost as far from straightforward nurturing as Victor of Averyon, who was subjected to the authoritarian strictures of Jean Marc Gaspard Itard a century earlier. Genie was able to categorize, but never learned syntax. She kept a roomful of containers—sand buckets and plastic cups —which I read as analogous to word categories without gifts. I think the idea of 'belonging to' or property was not enough to let her learn language. She needed the nurturing co-munication prior to language. She did not participate in enough giving and receiving outside exchange to be able to generalize it to the relations in language and to attribute value the way others did. Rymer contends that, even after she was released from her captivity, the child was used as a pawn of research by her academic 'caretakers.' Genie did achieve the 'pivot stage' of development, but could not go beyond it. She could not project gift relations onto words. Genie's inabilities show the defect of exchange. For exchange, the category is more important than the contents. Moreover, humans (especially masculated males) are valued for what they have and are supposedly born with: male gender, the soul, a personality, an identity and (some believe) language—while giftgiving actually constructs these 'properties.' Genie was not freely given to and, therefore, did not have the model of free giving by which she could herself give other-oriented value to the contents of her categories or construct her social self linguistically.

Unfortunately, the phallic images and phallic ways in our society reinforce the masculated ego at every turn. The lack of meaningful rituals and meaningful work outside these patterns highlight the patterns of masculation. Everything, from the army to exploitative economics, integrates the idea of masculinity with the idea of agressivity. Teenage boys learn that the way to dominate others is through showing off, with big phallic cars or with many girlfriends. Teenage girls learn to pay attention to big cars and to deal with the possibility of being seduced and abandoned. From the missile to the number 1, from the Trump Tower to the ivory tower, the self-similar phallic image draws attention to itself, creating crystallized rituals to which everyone in the society can continually relate according to her or his particular place or role. Since these objects are present in daily life, we do not recognize their continuing power, but they unconsciously influence our behavior and our motivations all the time.

Practicing exchange in order to do giftgiving is the compromise or hybrid the society has proposed between the two paradigms. However, giving in order to receive economically makes us more likely to do the same in our relationships. When we measure the emotional exchange and feel we have not gotten enough, it seems reasonable to leave, self-destructive not to. Sometimes monetarily, the mate doesn't 'contribute enough to the household'—sometimes emotionally, he or she doesn't give enough, or goes with others, therefore not 'exchanging' with oneself. Therapists and friends help to assess the right or wrong doings of the mate, measuring the advisability for one to remain attached.

In relationships based on giving, giving itself would be a given, securing the atmosphere for both, allowing more leeway for development. Sexual attraction calls forth a lot of attention from the other person. Each 'invests energy' in the other, then wants to give to or nurture and be received by her. Actually, I believe most relationships begin with giving, then as soon as negative things begin to happen, exchange reasoning kicks in. The giver begins to want to be a receiver and to calculate how much she has given. She 'sets boundaries,' especially when she sees that her own giving cannot continue as such and she has to paradoxically switch onto the exchange mode in order to continue to give.

Acting according to the gift paradigm, co-municating materially probably makes us more likely to continue loving unilaterally. Perhaps this is why so many women continue to love, to maintain their children whom men abandon, and to even remain faithful to philandering husbands. Even in a hostile environment, the gift economy self-perpetuates, at least for a while. If we were to practice giftgiving in abundance—not only in the home, but socially as the way of organizing our economy and institutions—our human relationships would improve and our internal conflicts would be more easily healed.

Chapter 21
From the Garden to the Grail

By criticizing patriarchy or puerarchy, I do not want to deny spirituality, but only to show that it has been used in ways which hinder giftgiving. One of the reasons for our misunderstanding of giftgiving is that we see God as the greatest giver, and he is male. Thus, we mix giftgiving characteristics with the characteristics of masculation.

If we understood God, the giver, as female, perhaps we could come to consciousness of the paradigm more easily. Perhaps s/he is really pure altruism, a 'you-first' spirit, and that is why s/he is invisible. S/he creates things and loves them in a 'you-first' way and then goes on creating and loving others. If we cannot love each other, we block her movement. Perhaps nature spirits, fairies, and angels are only slightly less 'you-first' parts of the goddess.

Putting giving into the province of the male model hides the fact that women have already been doing it everywhere, all the time. Even the sacrifice of Christ's life distracts our attention from the amount of sacrifice that has been done everywhere by women for their children, husbands and others. Our gratitude is turned towards a male giver as the source, disguising the mother model.

I believe the most harmful aspect of Christianity is the glorification of sacrifice because it does not address the situations which make sacrifice necessary. The system which creates scarcity, war, environmental and human degradation must change, and this need should not be upstaged by the sacrifices of those who are making the best of the terrible situation. We must have the socio-political courage not to sacrifice ourselves, but to recognize the causes of the problems and unite with each other to change them, giving that general gift to all. If we can change the paradigm, which includes changing the reward system and the ego structure of exchange, we will be able to give without self-depletion. During the transition from one paradigm to the other, we have to create alternative organizations, use our energy, our imagination and our resources. We must decide whether to let ourselves be depleted or destroyed in the process, or to give up, or whether to try to maintain ourselves as models of givers who do not sacrifice.

In a situation of scarcity, it is all too easy to give to one's own depletion because giving is not generalized and, indeed, others may not give to the isolated giver. Women throughout history have been givers, because children's needs require it—but, trapped by the exchange paradigm, we are often crucified, made to give our lives in order to keep satisfying needs, because the situations we are in are so hostile that they murder us. Women are right, giving is the Way. But we have to generalize giving and change the context because, by doing it individually, we are destroyed.

Masculation and exchange put themselves forward, self-validate and call forth the gifts of others. Thus, those who are practicing giftgiving cannot see what they themselves are doing or give it dignity as the norm. They have accepted the ego-oriented values of others; so, paradoxically, they may not have the courage of their own other-oriented values and actions. Women may even believe that giving is wrong, though usually they do it anyway. They are afraid of the paradigm they are practicing and confuse the threat of self-sacrifice due to scarcity (a real danger coming from the social context) with the idea that giving creates the scarcity. Sacrifice for something may be a way of saving it from destruction, giving value to it, or a way of recognizing or naming it though 'paying for it.' On the other hand, sacrifice is often a product of domination by force.

Masculated Giving

The only thing we did wrong in the beginning was to shift from the gift to the exchange paradigm. Perhaps this is what the story of the Garden of Eden was all about. In the gift paradigm, no repayment is necessary. Only when we shift to the exchange paradigm do we find the necessity to repay. By treating the eating of the apple as a sin of disobedience, which required repayment, the Bible shows humans effectively entering into the exchange paradigm with God, casting Him into the role of punisher, providing 'just' reprisal. A God who was for giving, functioning according to the gift paradigm, would not have required repayment. S/he would have taught the children giftgiving by modeling it.

Perhaps Christ's self-sacrifice was an attempt to model giving and forgiving, but the Goddess (mother) model was canceled by the male model of the Father and the Son. (All those images of Madonna and Child could have shown to us that boys needed to follow their nurturing mothers. Instead, the other-orientation of the mother never became self-validating. We never took the logical step up. The focus was always on her 'other.') Thus the only appropriate place for giving seemed to be in motherhood to a male child. Moreover, women's values were not presented as such for social solutions, but were altered and translated through a male figure.

If Christ was a male model of giftgiving, the exchange paradigm was still the frame for interpretation, so he was seen as 'paying for' humanity's sins. His death 'evened the score,' but that could not get humanity out of the exchange paradigm. Even if he was paying in advance also, for the sins people were going to commit, exchange was still the issue. The exchange archetype underlies everything we do, and influences our consciousnesses to a great degree. Even when our spiritual intuition and our hearts draw us towards altruism, these patterns pull us and our interpretations of religion back to the masculated model. In fact, as we have been saying, our consciousness and the re-ality we live in are formed according to the values of masculation. Giftgiving—the female model—comes to consciousness filtered through masculation and exchange. Now feminism and the worldwide women's movement have allowed us to detach the mother from her 'other' and to see women as the bearers of the other-tending values of the species.

Communicating with the Gods

Humans have always tried to establish co-munication with the gods, giving them innumerable 'gifts' from animal sacrifice to human sacrifice, from novenas to tithes. The 'gift' of Christ's life to God can also be interpreted as an act of co-munication—the Word. Because we have not recognized the gift paradigm and its part in co-munication, we may see our attempt at interaction as a moment in the logic of exchange. We bribe the divinity: "I will give you this, if you give me that."

Perhaps because of our distress over masculation, or because of the ideology of exchange, or even because of a defect of imagination, we consider major sacrifices to be the kinds of gifts which would satisfy the needs of the gods. Maybe our difficulty in communicating is that those kinds of gifts distress the Divinity as much as they do ourselves. The scream of the sacrificial animal whose throat is being cut horrifies Her/Him—or Hum. We need to devise some other, kinder and easier gifts, such as words are for us, like incense, music, flowers and food. Our cruelty to each other makes a toxic atmosphere, where the spirit cannot flow freely from one person to the other.

Maybe our masculated attitudes simply do not allow for large enough collective units to form as a co-municating subject, who can hear and be heard by Hum. If we could really shift onto the gift paradigm, and disentangle the logic of communication from the logic of exchange, perhaps we could find again the garden of Eden. This could be God's or the Goddess's kingdom come. I don't think it will be a kingdom though, or even a democracy, but some new kind of government.

From Complex to Concept

In our Christmas celebrations, we put our joy at babies' being born, our desire for the best humans can be, our salvation, the solution to our problems. We see the solution to our problems in the child. In fact, this is one outcome of the gift paradigm/

exchange paradigm struggle. The woman gives the child. The man gives the name, the inheritance. The child takes the place of the parents. The future is exchanged for the present, or takes its place, and the conflict is handed down, as the 'gift' from generation to generation. This heritage is a strange kind of gift, involving a contorted division of labor, like that between salaried husbands and unsalaried wives.

We exchange in the present in order to give to others in the future. In the future, will the others exchange or give? Now, at the end of the 20th century, we are taking both the present and the future into exchange. We are making the future a present to ourselves, and we are not handing down a good earth. We are creating scarcity, making the gift economy impossible for our children and future generations. We are validating the system, giving a meta judgment in favor of exchange, so the very possibility of giftgiving is destroyed.[1]

The mother has been giving the gift of her children to her husband. The ancient right of primogeniture was one form taken by masculation in families of wealth and power. In the logic of Christianity, if Christ was God's son and also a man, and if men were brothers, Christ's one-many relation with them was like that of the first son to his brothers. The one-many relation of God the creator to mankind is equal to the one-many relation of Christ to mankind. In this, the relations are similar to one-many sample and one-many word.

Though the relation of artisan to products (which he made in his image) or father to children is a 'complex' of family resemblance, it can transform into a concept relation when the common quality of the items is discovered. The common quality of humans is expressed in their 'saved' souls, which are related to Christ as the one-many sample. Christ is also equal to God in that relation, and is His incarnate word or re-presentative on

[1]Perhaps the *Star Wars* space shield and now the nuclearization of space are actually attempting to shield exchange from giftgiving, doing this at meta (above) in space. The metaphor of meta was carried that far, with billions of dollars spent on it, because we just don't understand what we are doing.

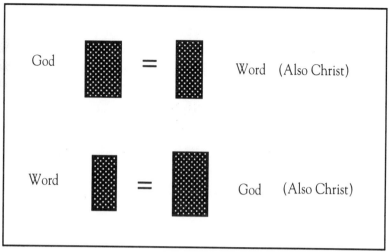

Figure 39. God, Christ and the Word.

earth. If Christ is God, and the son is the father, he stands on both sides of the equation between the word and the sample. The Christian mythos can also be read as an exploration of the concept formation process. (See Figures 39 and 40.)

Some of the other elements of exchange we have been discussing are also evident here. For example, Christ is also the general equivalent, and his life is the means of exchange—the money—that pays for men's sins. If people are sinful, they are unequal to each other and cannot enter the concept relation with God as 'many-to-One' because they lack the common quality. Many stories in the Bible describe the sins of humans. The sin of Eve and Adam made them different from God and, revealing their nakedness, made them conscious of being different from each other. Cain's murder of his brother, Abel, also made Cain different from other men. The Old Testament is a chronicle of human differences. By paying for and for-giving humanity, Christ implied that humans were equal to each other again in value and able to enter into the concept relation with himself as a sample identical with his Father.

Adam and Eve's disobedience seemed to cause a debt towards God and the idea of debt is part of the exchange paradigm. The

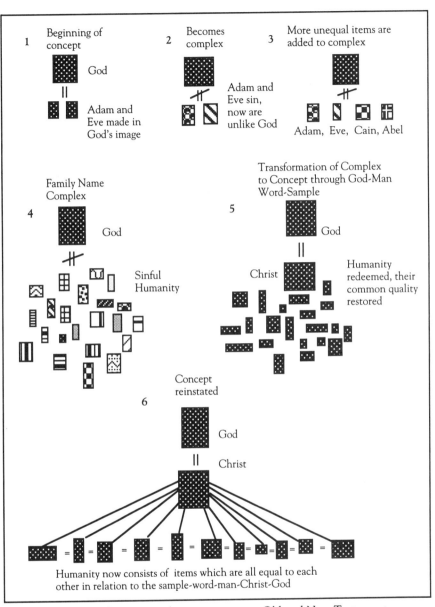

Figure 40. The concept formation process, Old and New Testament.

debt made people feel they should give to God (creating co-munication), which was gift-like motivation, but which was actually payment for a wrong. Maybe it seemed that by paying for the sin, there would be no more debt, and then the gift paradigm would return. However, it was not a sin humans committed, or a debt they incurred, or an act of not-giving they indulged in (not-giving obedience to God). It was just taking on the idea of paying back, exchange, that made humans appear to have to pay back. Unfortunately, as subsequent history demonstrated, Christ's 'payment' did not disqualify the exchange paradigm, even if he was 'for-giving.'

Paying for humanity's sins was an exchange, even though the sacrifice of Christ's life was perhaps an attempt to show the giving model in a situation of scarcity of justice and real lack of kindness. Actually, many women sacrifice in similar situations all the time, not to pay for anything, but to satisfy the needs of those in their care.

Perhaps being born from a Virgin shows Christ as the child of the gift paradigm, outside of genitalized sexuality, as well as beyond the male ego.[2] Proposing giftgiving as coming from a male model is dangerous, however. Churches organized to honor Christ's teachings set up misogynist, masculated religious hierarchies, which supported political and economic hierarchies, invaded other territories and slaughtered people with other beliefs in order to teach them 'altruism.'

To change paradigms, we must identify the gift paradigm with women generally, follow their leadership, and not repeat the masculated one-many structures which self-propagate, spawn hierarchies, and promote competition and domination. Indeed the over-valuing of the 'one' concept sample position is an important part of the problem. It is an element in the process of masculation, which must be dismantled in order to return to the gift paradigm as the norm. Unfortunately, both the

[2]In fact, the relation between God, Mary and Joseph, and Jesus is reminiscent of the societies in which the mother's brother (a person who does not have sexual relations with the mother) takes over some paternal roles for the boy.

382

logic and the organizational aspects of Christianity have merged the image of a giftgiving male god with the 'one' position and with the masculated characteristics of over-taking and domination.

Giftgiving on the social scale is being continually misread, while the gift mode on the individual internal scale is unseen. In fact, internal giftgiving does not just give a static picture, as we mentioned in regard to the *homunculus*. Internal giftgiving is often paralyzed and rendered unconscious, however, by the lack of validated models of giftgiving on the external. Perhaps the models of Christ's sacrifice and the sacrifice of religious saints do provide a context which, at least partly, validates giftgiving for the individual. However, by making giftgiving sacrificial and the gift paradigm saintly, instead of recognizing its existence in what women and many men are already doing in daily life, we push it out of everyone's reach.

The Authoritarian Father

Patriarchal religion provides a number of false images of the male giftgiver. The Father, who supposedly would not abuse his children, did actually send them out of the Garden of Eden for eating an apple, and therefore, like human fathers, requires our blindness and denial towards his injustice. As a model of the giftgiver, internally and externally, Godliness leaves room for many transgressions, especially along the lines of authoritarianism. How many children have been abused in the name of the will of God, what violence performed upon them in the name of sanctity of their father and the necessity of filial piety? It is really wrong to call the God of these fathers 'good,' because compassion seems to be secondary to what they think of as right action—action which reinforces their masculated egos. Having projected their values onto an all-powerful Patriarch, men use him to justify their reinforcement of their egos, judging authoritarian ways as good.

When we question the presence of evil and suffering in the world, we are told it is beyond our knowledge. Actually, the authoritarian image of God validates abusive patterns in men, and does not validate women's nurturing and compassion—because it says that the male God, who is also authoritarian, is all good, and does not allow for a female image of God at all. This is part of the cause of the suffering. Thinking that we cannot understand it just feeds the denial of the abuse. We have a taboo on the thought that our concept of God might be causing masculated men to continue to create that suffering.

Similarly, mothers often refuse to see the abuse their husbands are perpetrating on their children, and have faith in his good side, and in 'God's unfathomable will.' This lets them allow the abuse and, in so doing, become party to it themselves as well. The image of the giftgiver is thus either assimilated into the image of the authoritarian masculated ego, or is feminine and powerless, nurturing the male, at best interceding with him like the Virgin Mary, humbly pleading the case of her child to the male Authority.

Meanwhile, the boy she is raising is really him, the male authority in miniature. So, our Mother within is transformed into little other-oriented initiatives within or into ineffective twinges of conscience tugging at the coat tails of our masculated will to power. We discount her intercession in favor of others as unrealistic compassion, quivers of a bleeding heart. If she succeeds in awakening some moment of other-orientation in us, credit is given to the Good Father, the 'beneficent' masculated ego. Perhaps we could cancel this illusory father image and have Mary as our model. We would have to change our image of her, redirecting her other-orientation away from obedience and intercession and towards the empowered nurturing of humanity and the planet—especially of women and children. Recently, in fact, the women's spirituality movement has restored to us many female images of the Divine, as giftgiving goddesses who are powerful as well.

The Holy Grail and Alchemy

The Holy Grail is the free source of abundance. The Grail, the cup, is symbolically also the cornucopia or womb. Perhaps the spiritual aspect to this story about the search by legendary heroes for the chalice of the Last Supper tells us again that the problem is not biological but social. The Grail is not a material thing but a logic, a way of organizing our economic behavior. The Grail is the gift paradigm. It is not a physical object—not womb, vagina, breast or penis, not horn nor sword, chalice nor blade—but a refusal to mis-align the microcosm and the macrocosm, a refusal to create the shift into the artificial structure of exchange and its ego, where abundance and nurturing should be. The Holy Grail is the gift that gives, the gift of the gift paradigm which we all receive from our mothers—we only have to overcome our childhood complexes and our masculated misunderstandings of language and life in order to be able to receive it at last.

This social interpretation of the Holy Grail can be supported by interpreting the practice of alchemy in Marxist terms. Any commodity could become the socially-chosen general equivalent, money, though gold is the one that actually did. Alchemy was really posing a question about a social choice. Transforming base metals into gold is the physical projection of the problem, "How does something become money?" This question harks back to the question, "How does a baby become male?" or, "How does a body part become a penis, the mark of the category 'male?'" or the even more hidden question, "How does a body part become a vagina, womb or breast, the producers of life and nurture?" and, "How might the womb or the breasts become the 'sample?'"

Both alchemy and the story of the Holy Grail show aspects of the social problem of masculation interpreted on a material plane. We have seen how the position of sample is socially attributed and is not a quality belonging to the material objects themselves. The special value of gold does not come from the metal itself; rather it is a social quality, coming from the use of gold as the general equivalent—the value sample—in exchange.

We could socially assign that role to specially designed pieces of lead, just as we have socially assigned it to printed paper. The relative scarcity of gold made it a functional means of exchange. That relative scarcity is also made possible by the special printing of paper money in limited quantities. We could just as easily print pieces of lead, though they would be harder to carry in our pockets. Ironically, if the alchemists had succeeded in transforming lead into gold, there might have been so much of it that gold could no longer have served as the general equivalent, and the purpose of the transformation would have been lost.

The transformation of base metals into gold has actually happened. The only element that has not entered into the process is the physical material identity of lead, and of gold. In the transformation, the physical identity of the items under transformation was actually irrelevant. What was essential was the similarity of items being used as money material to each other (as paper bills, coins, etc.) and their production in a limited quantity. This permitted their social use as general equivalent. The lead that was relevant, finally, was the printer's lead, used for printing paper money. The choice of gold or printed paper as general equivalent is due to many social and historical factors. The fact that we choose any object as a sample of exchange value is due to masculation and its psycho-economic expression in exchange.

The search for the Holy Grail demonstrates a similar problem: it is a search for change at the wrong level. The physical object, the grail, is not the source of all abundance. Neither is the womb, as the symbolic equivalent of the cup. While the womb does bring up the idea of the mother, and the sought-for Grail the idea of a privileged object, the solution to the puzzle does not lie in finding that object or contemplating the womb, or in giving men a physical womb or castrating them in order to do so (or giving them a 'vagina' by wounding them). Nor is the answer the search itself.

Rather, the answer lies in changing planes from the physical, and metaphysical, to the social and psychological. By understanding and dismantling the social process of masculation, we can restore the mothering model for all, providing a nurturing economy (a social cornucopia or grail), which will abundantly satisfy all needs. A nurturing economy would not require any changes in male or female physical bodies—no castration or adding on of organs where they originally were not. Only a change in our interpretations of these differences would be necessary, together with the dismantling of their psychological, economic and social projections. We have been forced to search for the source of all good because we were not asking the (right) question—the right question was not, "What ails the knight?" though it did bring up the issue of castration in its connection with the search for giftgiving. (In fact, that question is a lot like our greeting, "How are you?" which can potentially initiate a comunicative interaction.)

The question they and we should have been asking is something like, "How can we provide abundance for all?" to which the reply, then and now, would have been symbolically the Grail, "Follow the life-giving and nurturing mother model."[3] The final question of Percival: "Whom does the grail serve?" is similar to the question, "Who is it for?" which is at the basis of the split between giftgiving and exchange. Is it for the other or for the ego, for the present or future Fisher King or for God? Or shall we apply to the Grail Marx's answer to the question of language and see its infinite creativity in the other-tending logic of human socialization, the logic that has the extra step: "For others, and therefore, really for me as well?"

In a recent book on the Holy Grail, Graham Phillips[4] connects the medieval French Romance, *La Folie Perceval* with the *Tarot* and especially with the 'Popess' card (the figure of a woman in the papal one-many position). Phillips also makes a tentative identification of the Grail with the secret Gnostic *Gospel of Thomas Didymus*, a complete copy of which was

[3] The Grail (or cup of abundance) is the symbolic opposite of the 'cap' of cap-italism.
[4] Dr. Graham Phillips, *The Search for the Holy Grail*, Arrow Books, Random House, London, 1996. pp.170-171. Dr. Graham Phillips also claims to have found the actual material artifact which was the Holy Grail.

purportedly discovered in Egypt in 1945. A section of the text he cites seems related to the mother model and to liberation from masculation:

"Jesus saw children who were being suckled. He said to his disciples, "These children who are being suckled are like those who enter the Kingdom." They said to him, "Shall we then, being children, enter the Kingdom?" Jesus said to them, "When you make the two as one, and when you make the inner as the outer and the outer as the inner and the above as the below, and when you make the male and the female into a single one, so that the male will not be male and the female not be female, when you make eyes in the place of an eye, and a hand in place of a hand, and a foot in place of a foot, and an image in the place of an image, then shall you enter the Kingdom."

Several elements of this passage recall the restoration of the nurturing mother model, especially the unmasculated unity of male and female, and the breast model. The unity of opposites, and the return to substitution of things for things, are perhaps a transposition of material co-munication.

Male Nurturing

Transubstantiation through definition or naming, "This is my body. This is my blood," really proves the point of alchemy. God or Christ as the sample for the concept of mankind transforms the bread and wine into the sample (himself). As the sample nurturing man, he makes himself into food and drink.[5] Transubstantiation demonstrates the power of definition, as masculation does. The effect of naming is not physical, as it would be in a miracle (as in changing water into wine), but social. The Holy Grail, the mother symbol, is the locus for making a nurturing male, by reinterpreting and reforming the

[5]The Christian idea was not new. For example, in the tradition of the great goddess, the son-god Dionysus in his many forms was also ritually eaten. "As a Vegetation God he was ritually sacrificed, usually on a tree (prototype of the later crucifix). His flesh was eaten as bread, his blood drunk as wine..." from Monica Sjoo and Barbara Mor, *The Great Cosmic Mother: Rediscovering the Religion of the Earth*. San Francisco, Harper and Row. 1987, p. 121.

social mechanism of naming, especially the naming of gender. Sub-stance is only under-standing.

Perhaps, in the sacrament of the church, more attention is given to the sample character in the transubstantiation process than to the material bread and wine character. From the material bread and wine, we only have to pass to the sample character of God, not to another physical material. And God is the "human form divine," a social idea, following the process of other social ideas, whether s/he exists as such or not.

'Transubstantiation' is a lot like exchange or masculation. It is a change in the status of something, which takes place by relating it to a new word as its name. The 'sample of samples' names (and points out) something as itself, and the priest repeats this process. If the male God is the general equivalent One, his making himself into food transforms both this matter into the sample and makes the male sample nurturing. The 'host' is, after all, only a taste, a sample. At the same time that bread and wine change into body and blood, the model shifts from male to female, from over-taking to nurturing—and this is really the taste of a better world, though it is hidden within the tabernacle of author-itarian patriarchal religion.

The symbolic form of the Grail coincides with its contents, transposing real into symbolic sacrifice, giving a gift that can easily be given (bread and wine) instead of a gift that cannot (body and blood). Male priests then potentially have something to give, by their words becoming more similar to nurturing women, modeling free giving. By their words, "This is my body, this is my blood," in the ritual, they presumably change the substance of the things, bread and wine. By changing our gender words, we could change the substance (under-standing) of males into nurturers. Communion points toward the *ungendered* human, hidden within the model of the nurturing male.

What we need now is the restoration of the model of the nurturing female. Either model or both must serve to change the masculated system to which sacrifice is functional. With that change, we will create a system by which we will be able to share not symbolic but real food locally and globally, thereby transforming reality. We will understand words as the power of the collective to transform our understanding, and 'ones' as elements of our conceptual processes, liberating the spirit from patriarchy.

Human Sacrifice

At present, we are wasting wealth on things which do not satisfy our needs in order to stimulate the economy, and our gifts of value are therefore given not to each other but to the economy itself. Wasting and destroying products creates scarcity. High prices ensue because goods do not accumulate and thus do not create the abundance which would make the whole system unnecessary. Those who participate as sellers in the cycle of creating false artificial needs and waste receive greater profits in return for their efforts. Not only do they receive the gifts of the surplus value of the producers at home and abroad (and the issue of exchange-rate differential and level of life make the whole economy of one country give to the whole economy and to the individual economic agents of another country), but they receive the gifts of the shadow of all the needs that remain unsatisfied because abundance has not been allowed to accrue.

'Trickle down' cannot happen because the cup which might have been the Grail is never allowed to fill up or to run over. The gifts run out as waste through a crack in the bottom. Meanwhile, the unsatisfied needs of millions of people, including the forty thousand children who die daily worldwide from hunger and preventable disease, are human sacrifices giving value to the 'needs' of the free market. The ritual human sacrifices that maintained the pyramidal society of the ancient Maya involved the slaughter of only a chosen few in view of all. Perhaps the Maya were, after all, both more compassionate and more conscious than we are.

390

We sacrifice millions of human lives to create the scarcity necessary for our system to function, to maintain the social pyramids, hierarchies, upward chains of gifts, and downward chains of masculated definitions and commands. But these sacrifices for those of us in power occur 'elsewhere.' The gifts which are given to us are invisible and, if they are seen at all, their interconnection with our economy is not acknowledged. Rebellions 'elsewhere' are quelled by the use of abundant armaments, the manufacture of which diverts energy and money into the means of destruction, and brings more profits to their producers and sellers, while depleting the store of the means of nurturing still further.

In the 'First World,' if we see the pictures of the starving and the maimed in other countries (or across the tracks), we attribute their condition to local calamities of nature or 'human nature.' However, because in an alternative system, in abundance, their situation would have been otherwise, their deaths, which are the consequence of artificially created scarcity and their excessive gifts to us, give value to our system by giving-way. Our own well-being seems to come from localized good fortune or 'deserving,' and we deny the transfer of wealth and value to us from other countries and classes.

The Mayan civilization ended; rituals of human sacrifice were no longer performed. Much speculation has been generated about the cause of its apparently abrupt end. Drought, disease, conquest have been suggested. I prefer to believe that someone finally changed her under-standing and said the sacred words, "This isn't working. Let's stop now." Then the whole group, in a great act of civilization, decided to go back to the countryside, to live peacefully with their loved ones, to give up attributing value to the pyramid by sacrificing and giving goods and obedience pyramidically. We can do the same.

The Maya originally sacrificed the 'one' as a gift in material co-munication with the gods, who would presumably give gifts of abundance in return. Blood was also let from the tongue (the word) and the penis (the 'mark' of the one position) of the king. As happened in many other cultures, the Maya sacrificed the privileged 'one' as the representative of the group.

Now we are sacrificing the lives of millions, not to gods, not as representatives, but to give value to a masculated system, which we perceive as nurturing us, our natural and only source of livelihood. The cultural value that we give to profit and wealth is also given by the sacrifice of the children and mothers of the future, since their means of nurturing are now being destroyed through environmental degradation. Cancer, due to nuclear radiation and hazardous chemicals, attacks the symbol and source of women's giftgiving, the breasts. In the US there is an epidemic. One in every eight women is expected to get breast cancer.

Actually, almost half of the population will have some kind of cancer. The disease also attacks the 'mark' of masculation in cancer of the prostate, and even the sperm count, especially in white men, has been drastically reduced in recent years, presumably by environmental causes. Because we do not challenge the incomplete accounts of cancer given by the free market apologists, such as the American Cancer Society and the American Medical Association, the sacrifice of our breasts, our capacity to reproduce, and our lives gives value to the exchange economy. The cancer-causing nuclear radiation and toxic chemicals that free market industries release into the environment remain invisible and continue to accumulate and become permanently abundant, while life-giving resources become scarce.

Those who are trying to heal the diseases receive their livelihoods from the system and give it their gratitude and credence, making it unlikely that they would consider it as the cause of the cancers. Like women who over-value masculation, they give value to the very processes that are causing the problem, while at the same time trying to care for the individuals who have been injured by those processes. The system is not just a beneficent, though sometimes harsh, husband, whom we must value and follow, doing damage control; it is a hazardous mechanism, which we must recognize, understand and dismantle step-by-step, so as not to destroy all those who live in and around it.

In so doing, we will change our consciousnesses and begin to attribute value, not to exchange, but to the needs of all and their satisfaction at all levels. We will stop sacrificing ourselves, our children and unknown billions of human beings to maintain our system of pyramids, and we will direct our gifts towards co-municating with everyone in abundance. We can begin to fashion the Holy Grail for society at large, the cornucopia of co-munication, by saying the holy words of tran-substantiation, changing our social under-standing: "Let's stop this devastation now."[6]

---

[6] It is striking that the bomb dropped on Hiroshima was named "Little Boy." The name "El Niño" also indicates at many depths the source of our weather problems.

Chapter 22
Cosmological Speculations

Life on earth is an attempt the earth is making to imitate or express the relation it has with the sun. Since the process of life and death has left a humus of the past for the future to grow from, the expression has changed over time. The earth, in all its fertility and variety, is a product of the interaction between itself and the sun—in which the sun gives a constant kind of energy, and the earth gives a great variety of energies. The earth has a history and an evolution; the sun does not, or at least does not seem to, since its evolution is much slower. What happens in the present on earth is based upon what is left from what happened in the past. The layers of earth in which plants grow, and on which people and animals walk, are by-products of past events, all of which included the earth's use of the energy of the sun. Circulating systems, such as trees and blades of grass, lift themselves up towards the sun. Having incorporated the energy of light, they are themselves sun rays of the earth, or 'earth rays' reaching out toward space.

Animals and human beings who stand, on four legs or on two, or birds flying up to the clouds, all are earth energy moving outward. But beyond this is our capacity for locomotion toward a goal. Guided by our sight, we move from one place to another, much as the light moves from the sun to the earth. In this dimension, life imitates its origin. Similarly, the sperm moves toward the egg; the egg is produced and moves toward the place in the womb where fertilization happens. But also, in the dimension of consciousness, a self-propelling intention arises. Like a sun ray leaping toward the earth, it moves toward its goal or object, perhaps combining with some other past elements of life to create an outcome, a sun ray incorporated in earth rays, earth energies bearing fruit.

Our voices and the voices of animals, fish and birds issue from throats and arrive at the receptive ears, where they are incorporated and become understanding and behavior and sensation. The sunlight of our attention illuminates our past, present and future experience, as well as experience of others brought to us through our senses, or through their stories, or reading and viewing. Our conscious attention shines upon our selves, helping us to plan and decide, clarify our intentions and put them into effect. There has been created socially, however, a sort of mirror game, where we are caught within our reflection, focusing our energy within ourselves.

This has combined with the use of accumulated energy of others, or of the group, to foster self-focusing energy. It is as if the sun ray were incorporated into the earth and came back to itself multiplied, as if the sun's rays were a closed system, too. There is a confusion between life—plants and animals—and energy. Moreover, in this form the self-focused attention of one may harm others, as it appropriates their energy to intensify its own. The sun does not do this. The mirror game creates an insatiable hunger for energy to focus and shine on the ego more strongly, attracting again and again the attention of others.

As human beings of many varieties and cultures, we have tried to understand what we were, what we were doing, or supposed to do and where we were living. Only recently has our astronomy given us any inkling of a correct idea about the universe, our planet and our star. It is not strange or surprising, then, to think that we might have made mistakes in our self-direction and the imagination of our goals.

Freud made much of the fact that in his epoch (it happens in our own, as well) children sometimes have a very distorted idea of what happens in sex—which influences their later thinking and emotions. It would seem logical that a false cosmology might have just as negative effects on our collective imaginings. The idea that the sun is the center of the universe may have influenced our thinking and our social behavior more than we know. And the idea that we are on a tiny speck of dust near a spark of light in the midst of billions of others is mind-boggling and also not healing for the imagination. Instead, the view of the earth from the moon allows us a perspective from which we can perhaps place ourselves in a productive context. Earth is a very special place, a shining drop of life. We are part of it.

Not Copernicus but Ptolemy was right: the earth is the center of the universe, our universe, because we are human beings. Now that we are beginning to be able to see what earth is, maybe we can see better what we are and what we must do.

First, we must respect our planet, the life of which we are all a part. What is unusual here is not that the sun's rays shine in our direction, but that the earth is able to create something with them. We must see ourselves as incorporated light, incorporated life. We need to be like Goldilocks and find the cosmology of our own dimension, the view of the earth that is 'just right' for us. We need to understand our place on earth and within the solar system, so that we can clarify our relation to each other. One particular problem many of us are having right now is seeing ourselves as single persons, related as individuals to a human race of five and a half billion. It is remarkable how similar this problem is to the one of seeing our earth and sun related to billions of other suns and possible planets, as large numbers of new galaxies are discovered.

We might call this a theory of knowledge through projection. We project a pressing human question on some branch of knowledge, and then we find it there. This is not to say that the knowledge found this way is not true, but that the motivation for seeking it is a social or collective existential problem, rather than an individual purely scientific aseptic motive of 'curiosity,' or even a not-so-aseptic individual for-profit motive. And isn't the avidity for knowledge a sort of translation of the greed or avidity for goods and money that motivates our exchange-based society?

The theory of the survival-of-the-fittest evolution, which was developed at the same time as a survival-of-the-fittest capitalist economy, is another case in point. Perhaps, if we understood the mechanism of projection, we could see why we are doing it, what the personal or social difficulty that we are trying to heal is. Then we could find out how much of our view is caused by the projection, what elements are seen or ignored because of it. More important, perhaps we could heal our human difficulties, and by doing so become also clearer perceivers of the universe. If we know we are projecting, we can take it into account and understand the distortions we ourselves are creating, and even use this knowledge to consciously plan for a better world, in which the problems that cause the projections do not occur.

Let us return to the view of the earth that sees her in relationship with the sun. In our atomistic and individualistic society, we have begun to degrade the importance of relationships, seeing the well-being of the individual person as the important goal of interaction and the social process, as well as the individual's own reason for being. Therapies for co-dependence and dysfunctional families have a wide public following and acceptance in the US and produce both money and social validation for their purveyors.

Our distress about relationships shows just how important they are to us. Love songs fill the radio waves, love stories fill the magazine racks, bookshelves and movie theaters. Relationships really are important to human beings; they are (part of) the way we become human. We just don't know how to have them. We don't have many good examples. It is my hypothesis here that the best model for a relationship that we have is the one between the earth and the sun. We can project our problems out there, then look at them more clearly in ourselves.

But why not look at it from a more intentional stance? The Gaia Hypothesis[1] considers the earth as a living being. In this case, we are Herself coming to consciousness. She is coming to consciousness of her relationship with the sun and of her own part in it, of her creativity of the precious miracle of life. Perhaps, then, we are her projection of her problem. Humans play the roles of lover and beloved, of sun and earth. We internalize these roles in our consciousness and our being objects of attention (giving and receiving attention). Do we receive our own or others' care as

[1]James Lovelock, *The Age of Gaia: A Biography of Living on Earth*, Norton, New York, 1988.

the earth does light, using it for creativity, or do we reflect it back (as does the moon) in a sterile mirror game of who is brighter, bigger, hotter?

Is the sun the source of life or is the earth? As men and women, we act it out: men are active, suns; women are passive, earths. This is the perennial stereotype. Yet, if we look again, both roles are earth's creations. So, the earth produced the ones who play the sun *and* the ones who play the earth. In fact, the whole play is being put on by the earth.

It is the earth who has made the sun a life-giver by receiving the light creatively. As far as we know, other planets have not done this. Similarly, male animals produce billions of sperm, but, if there is no female's uterus or egg to meet them, no life is produced. Seeds fall from trees or are borne by the wind but, if they are not lodged in earth, they are lifeless. But, of course, sperm and egg, seed and humus are all earth-produced.

As it happens in many of our heterosexual relationships, we overvalue one person, usually male, and we undervalue the other, usually female. A woman, by her creativity, attributes a solar importance to a man, and he is seen as the source of life, income, creativity. Receiving this attention (like the earth), he becomes more actively creative, seeming to confirm the truth of the attribution of value. The whole society participates in a system, which privileges one pole in the relationship and hides or ignores the other. We women define the definers as definers. Then we cover up our own active role, and men are only too happy to usurp the credit for it.

If we are playing the earth's role, why should we not recognize our/her power, creativity, life-giving and value bestowing qualities? Loneliness perhaps? It is so far to any other planet or sun. Is the sun alive, too, and of a different order? Does the earth just want not to realize that she is doing it all by herself? Could we human beings ever love her enough? Could she ever love herself enough to make up for the sun's not being alive? But maybe the sun is alive, as alive as she is and in the same or a different order of reality and alone.

Our attention imitates the sun, but when we concentrate on a star, the star is in the position of the earth. And the same with space. Surely this dimension of receptivity around her comforts our Mother Earth, and the knowledge we have gained puts her in a context, gives her a home. The confusion arising from the existence of millions of galaxies dissipates when we realize that there must be other living beings out there.

Mother Earth, like ET, someday may be able to phone home to her sisters. Meanwhile, we must keep up hope, learn to live with one another and not ruin her exquisite beauty and harmony before she meets other life. Are we being destructive so as to better play what we perceive as the role of the sun, continuing to discredit the role of the earth? Have we created a male-sun-patriarchal God to keep us company as well, projecting our and her problem beyond the solar system to the universe?

I think that we might accept the fact that we still do not know much about the universe. However we do have immediate access to our perceptual apparata and our social context. We need to shine our sunny conscious attention upon our psycho-social mechanisms, in order to find out why it is that we are seeing what we are seeing. There are unacknowledged mechanisms of selection that come from our motivation, that make us look for and find some things rather than others. These then feed back into the contexts in which the motivations arose, reconfirming the problems that created them. Only when we heal our motivations can these mechanisms function as clearly as they should, creating an alignment of the various types of reality of which we are a part.

Perhaps our conscious attention corresponds to the sun, and our subconscious corresponds to the earth, because of the internalizion of a social polarization between active and passive. But our earth side, as we have been saying, is only seemingly passive. It actively receives, not only giving content to consciousness, but also giving it a context and a value. It gives consciousness its potentiality to know, as part of a human being, where many things are going on.

Consciousness is like the light of the sun refracted through the atmosphere. There are so many more things for it to pass through and touch upon than meet the eye. Since humans are social products, there is a contribution by the many and the past to each of us. Our sunlight consciousness not only illuminates many aspects of this in succession, but is also defined by it. Perhaps, like the earth, and like women in our giftgiving ways, our subconscious produces consciousness, while not acknowledging its own part. Thus, consciousness seems not to come from the earth but from heaven.

In this century our knowledge (and through us the earth's knowledge) of the solar system, the galaxy and the cosmos has increased greatly, while the knowledge of the nature of the earth and her relation to the sun has not yet become clear. Similarly in our human relations, we do not understand the mother-child, nurturing one-to-one relation, before we venture into relation with the 'many.' We do not understand what is going on at home before we venture out into the world. The relation between the earth and the sun, which has produced so much miraculous life, is not a dysfunctional relation. The solar system is not a dysfunctional family. By identifying the sun with the father, however, we have reproduced the social self-similar masculated image of the sample under-emphasizing the activity and creativity of the 'passive' female 'receiver' and the many while overemphasizing the initiative of the 'active' male 'giver.'

The need is essential to the gift, for without it the gift is nothing. Thus, the earth has created myriad needs, which the sun can satisfy with her light—light which otherwise would be unused and barren. The interaction of these needs with each other recreates the giving-and-receiving interactions of the sun and earth. The asymmetry is the key. The sun only gives, while the earth both receives and gives again, though presumably she cannot give back to the sun, since the sun is too far away and presumably cannot receive. What happens, then, is that many of the relations of life are really self-similar images of the relation between the earth and the sun. They are role-plays, ways of acting out giving and creatively receiving. The baby receives the loving gaze of the mother—then, as she grows, actively relates herself to the mother, taking turns.

The amoeba encounters some piece of matter which it can receive and use creatively, as the earth on her voyage in space encounters the light of the sun. So does the blade of grass use the sunlight for her processes. The caterpillar actively finds the blade of grass, this earth ray made of creatively incorporated light, and uses it for her processes. The bird, on her more active paths, finds the caterpillar.

But we and perhaps the earth herself (Does she have a problem of self-esteem?) attribute more importance to the male, identifying him with the 'one' and the sun (the son), because we do not see the receiver as creative—and needs are seen as lacks and not what is necessary to bring gifts to completion.

We could even consider most life relations as a metaphor for the relation between the sun and the earth—an enormous variety of replays of that asymmetrical relation of unilateral giving and creative receiving and giving again (and leaving the by-products and waste from the process, which then become the gifts for another order, or orders, of life). All of life could be seen as an attempt the earth has made to give feedback to the sun, to relate to her. To give as the sun does, she must create the needs which can receive the gifts, that is, recreate something in her own (earth's) position. Then she takes the sun's position giving to satisfy them. Through life, she says to the sun, "This is what is happening between me and you; this is what is happening."

All of this is taking place on the surface of the planet, where the sun is shining, present (a gift) to its 'view.' Life in its variety could be seen as an immense proliferation of images of the relation between the earth and the sun, what in human terms could be seen as an immense joyous philosophical investigation into this relation. And, in human terms, this relation would be called love. Perhaps it is the earth's attempt at co-munication with another order of being, her labor of gratitude for that warmth that caresses her in the deep night of space, an investigation into their identity and relationship with each other.

What it is important for us humans to do is to align ourselves with this relationship, not misinterpret it, as we have so often done, because parts of our social organization and language have created the deep patterns of masculation which obscured it. Since we could not see the earth from space, we did not even know she was here or doing anything. We were too close to her; we could only look outward. We thought she was passive, just receiving the light, as we thought women were passive. We covered up our giving, her giving, and saw only the sun, the privileged light-sample as giver. Patriarchal patterns spawned phallic self-similar images of themselves everywhere, and validated each other.

The moon and the sun seemed to vie with each other as dominators of the heavens, each were privileged 'ones' for their allotted times. The moon changed through her phases and was many with respect to the sun. The idea of reflected light came to appear to be the women's, the moon's, identity. We forgot that the great dark creative earth was the proper image of the mother. But reflection which we attributed to the moon really was the province of the ego which did not give, the false, static, un-giving meta image of life and of the earth-sun relation.

We saw the earth and sun, women and men, children, mothers, things and words, citizens and presidents, commodities and money as not equally actively related to each other, but caught in a more or less static imaging of reflection. Where one was real, the other only served to give back that reality. Yet, the moon does provide a sort of cosmic meta level for the earth. It simply says, "The sun shines here, too, though I do not receive it creatively like the earth. And dark and light happen here, also." The moon has influenced the way earth developed life and consciousness. Her beams elicit our imagination. She seems to be a sort of self-referential aspect of the earth. Her light touch moves our tides.

For centuries, for humans, the moon took the place of the earth as the 'other' of the sun, whereas the earth was really the sun's life-giving other. It seemed that the reflection of the sunlight was the opposite and complement of the active giving of the sun, whereas it was actually its creative use in life-making. Thus, it could also seem that exchange, based on reflecting back what was given, honored the sun more accurately, enhanced it.

What was given was given back in an equivalent. Reflection validated exchange as a way of life, and masculated ego patterns, over-taking and competition, seemed ways to play the roles of the active sun and the passive moon. Then the sun was seen as taking the initiative towards the earth, seen as passive. The earth does not give back just a reflection or an image of the sun but many living images of her relation to the sun, many images of the sun and herself and their relation to each other. There are also images of the moon, reflections of the reflection of image-making itself, imagination.

The fact that there are two heavenly bodies in the sky suggested to us the importance of the two-fold relation, even when we thought the earth was flat, because we saw the two in the heavens and looked at them in terms of our gender relations, which already were earth-made life images of the earth-sun relation. We thought the sun-moon relation was the same as the sun-earth relation and identified the moon with women, as 'lesser lights,' losers of the competition to be brighter. Perhaps, when we began to know the relative sizes of the earth, sun and moon, we began to think of the earth and moon as children and the sun as father. So the image of the woman-child was superimposed over the woman of creativity, concealing her.

Not only did individuals enter into and play out these relations, but different kinds and orders of living images of relations had themselves to relate to each other. This may seem complicated, but it is really easy enough to follow if we see the sun as unilateral giver, the moon as reflector, and the earth as both giver and receiver, repeating (embodying rather than reflecting) the relation. (A complete meta level would not be

404

made of the simple reflection of the other but the reflection of the giving and receiving relation to the other, including the self, and the reflection of the relation of reflection.)

If we are the earth, coming to consciousness of herself, we have had some major misconceptions due to our inability to see ourselves in our (and her) real context regarding the moon and the sun. If humans are images of our immediate cosmology, it behooves us to understand it and align ourselves with it. Aligning ourselves with the misconceptions is bringing us to grief and our creative Mother to destruction.

If the life principle is in the creativity of needs to use the gifts, we must not let the needs and the beings that have them die because we are reflecting or trying to act like our idea of the sun, falling into the patterns of masculation our society has created. The needs form a sort of gravity, towards which our gifts must flow—like water, the liquid gift which flows towards the center of gravity, and rain, like transformed sunlight falls on thirsty plants. Wind moves from high pressure to low pressure areas. Giving to needs is the answer that is blowing in the wind.

The misinterpretation of our sexuality extends and fits into the misinterpretation of our cosmology. We see our earth as somehow lacking, rather than as the great creative receiving and giving source she is. In fact, by ignoring her creativity, we over-value the 'independence' of the sun, which, as we saw from pictures of the moon, did not 'independently' create anything there. Rather, it was the sun in relation to the earth that was creative, and the earth in relation to the sun. Because of the eminent presence of the sun, her visibility, and even that of the moon, the earth was seen as 'less than'—because she did not give light (she did give fire, however, which, like words, can be given away while keeping it). All of this fit into (and resonated with) the sexual and social pattern of men as active 'ones' and women as passive 'manys.'

Perhaps the earth herself has felt incapable when compared to the sun or the moon, and estranged and lonely, so far away from other planets and stars. As her children, humans have contributed

405

to this feeling. We have not only ignored and misinterpreted her, attributing value to everything but her, including ourselves, but with the same mentality that has taken us to space and finally allowed us to see her from beyond, we have trashed and degraded many of her greatest most delicate creations.

We consider ourselves children of the universe, and we long to see the life on the planets of Aldebaran, if there are any. We are willing to spend trillions of dollars on space programs with that eventual aim in mind. Yet, the amazing variety of species of beetles in the rain forests of the earth are so unimportant to us that we render them extinct without lifting a finger in their behalf. We must learn to attribute value to our creative Mother— both our human mothers and our Earth Mother. We must see that needs are not lacks, re-evaluate the symbolic vagina as the great hidden creative place, where life grows and continues on, and we must see that the type of single-shot creativity that the symbolic phallus represents is based on the denial of the value and the on-going labor of the feminine. Everyone must become nurturing of everyone else and of the earth. We must restore needs to a place of honor and fill them.

As the consciousness of the earth we must be her self-esteem, letting our love flow like water towards her centers of gravity. She is suffering, as are so many of her people and creatures. We must act in her behalf. How un-compassionate we are when we long for outer space, while we do not care for this miracle where we live. It is only our patriarchal mind-set, our misalignment with the earth-sun relation, that bores us with the present and blinds us to the Garden of Eden, causing us to be toxic to each other and to blight the land. Poor people everywhere are forced to play the part of the denied and exhausted mother, exploited, wasted, and despised. They are the self-similar image of Mother Earth being destroyed by a patriarchy whose healthy bright son goes forth in his phallic space ships to 'fertilize' other planets.

We must realize the gravity of this situation and turn our love and our money towards needs. In this way, we can follow the Earth Mother's commandment, "Nurture one another," imitating her clear, creative, cosmic relationship. We can liberate ourselves and her from the false enchantment of the reflection and the aggrandizement of the sample.

The multiplicity which earth has created with life rivals the multiplicity of the galaxy. We must begin to value 'many-to-many' relations, which other-oriented egos can promote. First we must turn our attention to the world we live in, honor and bless our Mother, satisfy her needs, the needs of the folks at home.

Perhaps it is really true that we are able to say on one level what we have learned and felt on another. I have often been far away from those I loved, and now for many years I have loved another woman unilaterally. Receiving no response to my co-munication, I became more creative, as I went on giving to projects for social change. I know how both the earth and the sun must feel. I am in alignment with one part of the image, then another. Of course, when human love is requited, we each can take turns at being sun and earth to each other.

May I accordingly suggest that, as we liberate ourselves from masculation, we return to our roots in our cosmology. Perhaps our term 'hum,' which would unite males and females in childhood with their caretakers, their nurturers, and each other, could be replaced as they grow up, not with 'woman' and 'man' but with 'earth' and 'sun.' This could only be a healing thing when the earth herself is restored to her rightful place as creative source of both male and female human beings, and the sun as unilateral energy giver. Perhaps, indeed, we could take the cue from those who now see us as androgynous, containing both male and female, active and passive, and call ourselves 'earths' in the moments when we were creatively receiving, and 'suns' when we were unilaterally giving (in both cases, we would have already consciously detached our selves from the one-many structure of the concept and the distortions of the definition of gender).

We should try to co-municate with the earth, not with the stars. If Gaia is alive, surely she has a language. She is the goddess who speaks to us through synchronicity and nurturing and in other ways as well. How can we speak to her? She is an other order of being. We are like cells in the body trying to communicate with the whole body. What gifts can we give? First, I think we can give her the gift of peace with one another, healing our societies. And this will help us give her the gift of our respect for her beauty and creativity, ending pollution, healing the devastation we have caused. With our gifts, we will find our common Mother tongue.

Since all our focus has been on the 'one,' the many have been in the dark, unknown and unrecognized, like stars in other galaxies, where our answers might seem to be. The stars are so many, like our brain cells. Are they images of the stars? Are the stars the neurons of the earth, except outside it—like us but backwards? The earth would be a tiny body within an immense brain of stars.

I saw the stars this morning as I woke up. There seemed to be so many. This is the problem, 'one-many.' The earth is finding herself within this huge array of others before she knows what she is—or the sun and moon are. Similar to us, with the 5.5 billion people on earth. We humans can form groups to relate to larger groups, but can the earth form a group with other planets? Aren't the living ones too far away? Is she the only living child of Sol? Are the other planets alive, even though they don't have life on them? Is earth trying to reach out to them through our space travel? We need to form a co-munity with her here. We need to comfort her in her being alone.

Chapter 23
After Words—Practicing the Theory

There are many different ways of creating a transition towards a paradigm shift. For example, there would be immediate and far-reaching effects if the First World institutions would for-give the 'Third World' debt (which has actually already come back to the 'First World' many times over). We could begin by for-giving the interest. This positive step could be accompanied by our beginning to co-municate materially with the 'Third World' in respectful and life-enhancing ways. We could also give abundant money to the ex-Soviet countries, recognizing that our capitalist tendency to plunder has not caused them to create a better society but has only reduced them to dire poverty. Most importantly we could stop wasting the world's wealth on arms production and the military—and use the resources instead for a nurturing economy.

In the US we could change the punitive prison industry and mentality to an understanding of the social causes of crime and an attempt to give children and youths lives worth living. We could recognize everyone's need and human right to be grateful for a good and joyful life, and the right to have something to give. We could stop some of the terrible wrongs which are being committed such as the sexual trafficking of women and children. We could recognize that most immigrants coming from the South to the North are simply following the path of resources which have been drained from their countries by the North as unpaid gifts. We could stop that drain, and welcome our sisters and brothers. (If we weren't spending the money on armaments there would be plenty for everyone). We could stop the devastation of the environment, considering it a gift for our children and our children's children. We could elect many more women with compassionate values to public office. Progress in any of these areas—and there are many others—would have a positive ripple effect everywhere and would bring forward the values of the gift paradigm. We can begin to move in the direction of a paradigm shift by recognizing the giftgiving we are already doing and by refusing to give value to the system based on exchange. We can begin to practice giftgiving experimentally and in political and social institutions in ways which both have multiplier effects and do not cause us to self-destruct.

The point of view of the gift paradigm needs to be consciously put into practice. I have tried to do this by creating the Foundation for a Compassionate Society, and the more political (not tax deductible) group, Feminists for a Compassionate Society. Actually, I have been practicing the theory expressed in this book since 1981, by using my resources for social change. Before developing the theory, I practiced the gift paradigm less consciously, as a wife and mother.

For me personally, one positive effect of the theory has been to liberate me from psychological and social pressures which kept me from giving to needs outside the family, and I believe that taking on a more activist giftgiving role helped to heal some psychological problems with which I had been struggling. It has now become clear to me how much giftgiving is going on all the time everywhere, convincing me that giftgiving is *the* normal human behavior. In fact, everyone's giftgiving practices are being blocked by exchange and made difficult by scarcity, but also by patriarchal values, which interpret giftgiving as exchange, dismiss it as ineffective and weak, or over-emphasize and sentimentalize it. Finding giftgiving in language makes it possible to consider giftgiving as what makes us human. It is my hope that affirming giftgiving as the human way will promote its conscious practice.

Unfortunately, giving to satisfy the needs of individuals does not in fact change the social system which creates the needs. After the system is changed, giving to satisfy the needs at the individual and at all other levels will be the guiding principle. For the present there is a huge need for resources to be devoted to social change. And each of us needs to give at both the individual and the social change level while shepherding our various energies to keep ourselves from exhaustion since we are still living in the exchange paradigm.

One reason givers also hide their own giving is that it may appear that they are giving in order to achieve the ego-dominance that masculation requires. The logical contradiction in such 'ego-oriented altruism' casts doubt upon the altruism itself, making it appear non-existent. The people involved in the giving and receiving interaction can get through this contradiction by developing the radical trust and forgiveness that are possible in the feminist social change movement. Another reason people do not give visibly is that religions and moral preceptors promote hidden giving and sacrifice as morally superior. While this tactic may have the effect of avoiding the pitfall of ego dominance, it also effectively keeps the model from becoming visible and from causing a ripple effect.

A great deal of psychological distress has grown up around giftgiving and receiving, perhaps because, for most of us, it has such deep connections with childhood and has otherwise been blocked and stunted. Our gut reactions about it are extreme and uninvestigated, our defensiveness and discomfort immediate. We find exchange easier to deal with, more respectful, 'cooler.' Our psychological reactions validate a habit of mind about 'appropriate' giving—giving which does not go to excess—and therefore, of course, does not really change anything.

As would-be givers we tiptoe in politically correct ways through a society which is devastating the planet and creating daily hunger and death for millions who live 'elsewhere.' Our aplomb is salvaged at the cost of our effectiveness, and the negative drift of the status quo prevails. Those who continue to be awake to the suffering of the many and the sickness of the system plummet in despair because they do not see the whole gift-based side of life that continues to exist or the glimmers of social change that are actually happening. Religions, corporations and governments co-opt giftgiving, making it appear to be one more masculated ploy, often a tool of greed and corruption. At best, there seems to be a civic duty to 'give back' to the community—within the pre-established parameters of the system.

Given all of these considerations, I decided to practice

411

giftgiving visibly for social change by creating the organizations I have mentioned. I created and supported social change projects, using exchange—salaried work—for changing the system towards giftgiving. The Foundation and Feminists for a Compassionate Society are both hybrid solutions of this kind. I also used the money I inherited to fund progressive and feminist projects for social change that were already existing. For several years I enlisted the help of my cousin, Sissy Farenthold, who had made a career as a feminist political leader and activist, and who 'knew the ropes' better than I did. Sissy helped me find groups to which I could give. Then I acquired physical locations (land and buildings) in which on-going woman-led projects were implemented. I started or supported activist and educational projects, as well, hiring a number of women to manage and carry them out. Some of the women had already started projects of their own or created them later, with or without my collaboration and input. I am now working on a book about my life where I will also tell the stories of meeting and collaborating with important organizations such as Dawne, Sisterhood Is Global, Wedo, the Feminist Press, the Feminist University of Norway, CoMadres of El Salvador, Resourceful Women and many others.

I have grappled with the contradictions inherent in practicing giftgiving to change the system which gave me the resources to give. I have also grappled with the contradictions in using exchange—giving women salaries—to change the exchange system towards giftgiving. And I have had to make a policy not to give to individuals for their own benefit because it was essential to devote the money to social change projects. Perhaps someone else might have thought of other ways of practicing the theory. This is what it occurred to me to do, aided by the Goddess's gifts of good timing and good fortune.

Sometimes, the women of FFACS did not agree with me or with each other. We had long and at times painful discussions, but we usually got through them with our friendship and feminism intact. I have been committed to making the Foundation as diverse as possible, and it has indeed been a place where women of color and white women, old and young, gay and straight, local women and women from other countries have worked together. In fact, I believe it has been an environmental niche for peace, where a multitude of voices can be heard and the thinking of the many is in evidence. I am very grateful to the women who have been involved with the FFACS over the years, and I feel very blessed to have been in their company. At the staff meetings, which take place every Wednesday, we listen to each other's reports. The amazing variety of information and experience, commitment and courageous imaginative action confirms and inspires our sisterhood—and gives hope to even the most jaded visitor.

So many general social needs have arisen, due to the psychotic practice of patriarchy, that social-change activists have their hearts and hands full. The truth is that every need is connected to every other—environmental needs are connected to human needs, hunger to militarization, respect for single mothers to world peace, domestic violence to racial violence and to international violence. Pulling a thread at one end of the tangle of problems touches all the other problems. Satisfying any need for social change—'making a difference' as it's often called—provides the possibility for everyone to visibly and intelligently practice the gift paradigm at a general social level.

The model of women giving to satisfy social needs, giving of time, intelligence, creativity, commitment, and money demonstrates the potential of the generalized gift paradigm as the solution to the whole complex of problems caused by the practice of the exchange paradigm. The gift paradigm visibly practiced for social change by women can have a wide-reaching ripple effect. While there are many activist projects now going on in the US and in other countries, many of them still operate according to patriarchal structures and thus perpetuate the problems they are trying to address.

Projects which deal with violence in the United States often try to change the individual or attempt legislative reform without changing the society as a whole. The connections between domestic violence and international violence, for example, are all too often ignored. Nevertheless, all the people who are now involved in the movements against sexual and domestic violence, for social justice, peace and human rights, and for ending hunger, war, racism and homelessness, as well as those dealing with healing from addictions and psychological problems due to patriarchal violence, are moving towards the gift paradigm—whether they are male or female, and whether they know it or not. I do believe it is important to promote women's leadership in this transition because women are originally unmasculated, with a model which is already so different from the 'privileged one.'

1997 is the 10th anniversary of the founding of the Foundation for a Compassionate Society, though many of the projects began much earlier. Stonehaven Ranch is a retreat center near San Marcos, Texas, which began to operate in 1984. It is open for retreats by peace and feminist groups every weekend, free or at a low cost. Literally thousands of people working for social change have been nurtured in its woman-led atmosphere over the years. Margie First presently manages it, 'nurturing the nurturers.' Other projects begun in the 80s, such as the Austin Women's Peace House, had a lifespan of several years and then closed for one reason or another. A weekly program on Austin Community Television, "Let the People Speak," hosted by Trella Laughlin, was part of our activities from 1985-1994. Several other regular community television programs, including one by myself, "Feminist Values," one by Sally Jacques, "Arts and Activism,' and one by Frieda Werden, "Women's News Hour," have taken its place.

Practicing giftgiving in an exchange economy depletes the giver if she is acting alone. Since, except for a few relatively small contributions, I am the only person giving money in this organization (though the other women give time, energy and imagination) my financial resources are being depleted. I have had to close the donation program which functioned from

1981 to 1994, and some of the other projects. The Grassroots Peace Organizations Building housed the Foundation's offices and provided office space for many other peace groups, including both women and men. Located on Austin's main downtown street, this little building was an outpost for social change in the flow of the mainstream. I sold it in 1996 to continue to maintain the Foundation. A beautiful facility on Lake Travis, our second retreat center, called 'Alma de Mujer,' was part of the Foundation from 1988-1996, when I donated it to the Indigenous Women's Network. It continues to be successfully managed by indigenous sculptor Marsha Gomez with the help of Esther Martinez.

In 1985, I was able to fund and 'woman'—together with a group I helped originate, 'The Feminist International for Peace and Food'—the Peace Tent at the Nairobi, UN Decade for Women Final Conference. The tent was very successful, providing a safe space for debate and discussion between women whose countries were at war with each other. Thousands of women attended the events there. Two of the women who helped to organize the tent, German Ellen Diederich and Afro-German singer Fasia Jansen, have worked with the Foundation for many years, first womanning a Peace Caravan to the Soviet Union (before the fall of the Berlin Wall) and later creating the Four Directions store (an attempt at cause-related marketing). They continue their on-going work for peace. Many other groups collaborated on the Peace Tent, including WILPF and WIDE. It was a successful model of women's dialogue which has been imitated many times thereafter.

Peace Caravans were also organized in the US, in which women went from town to town talking about the Nairobi meeting. US Quaker Alice Wiser and German Gertrude Kauderer drove them every summer for several years. Meanwhile, we also did a lot of support work for the Central American self-determination movements, sending delegations to El Salvador to investigate human rights abuses, death squad activities and the US government's involvement.

Ellen and Fasia organized a tour of the Salvadoran Mothers of the Disappeared in Europe, which was useful in disseminating information. We sent a fact-finding delegation of attorneys general from the US to Central America (I was part of the delegation as well). I supported women from the global South to travel through the US, talking about the realities in their own countries (through the 'Third World' Women's Project of the Institute for Policy Studies organized by Chilean, Isabel Letelier).

All of this work culminated in two meetings between women leaders from the US and women *commandantes* from El Salvador's FMLN. In these friendly encounters, it was quite clear that women's values could overcome war and antagonism. We talked about our children and about the future. We had serious political discussions, but we also danced and sang together.

I have had a long-term commitment to women from the Global South and to international feminism. I have supported women in international groups and conferences and helped with publications and computer networks. Over the years, I have supported a number of projects in the South and of women from the South living in the North. Presently Filipina activist Charito Basa is on the staff, working with immigrant women living in Europe.

I think that media are especially important for providing the point of view of women to the public. In 1991, I started FIRE, the Feminist International Radio Endeavor, a two-hour daily program presented from a women's perspective, one hour in English and one in Spanish, on Radio for Peace International, a short wave radio station in Costa Rica. Maria Suarez, from Puerto Rico, and Chilean Katarina Anfossi are the instigators of these programs.

WINGS, Women's International News Gathering Service, was started independently by Frieda Werden and Katherine Davenport in 1986. After Katherine Davenport's death, Frieda returned to Austin and joined the Foundation staff in 1992. Since then she has continued to produce WINGS weekly programs, with the collaboration of many volunteers whom she also trains. Frieda also provides radio training at WATER, Women's Access to Electronic Resources, a facility in Austin which was birthed and is being freely nurtured by videographer Fern Hill. At WATER, women receive free training in video, radio and computer. Felicia Hayes and Vicky Kilgore provide training and are on the Foundation staff. A large community of women has grown up around WATER, using its resources and volunteering many woman-hours. A particularly exciting collaborative effort is the yearly International Women's Day Media Festival, a 24-hour multimedia event put on entirely by women and involving several other media facilities throughout the city.

An indigenous resource center and museum, Casa de Colores, is open to the public on the border between Texas and Mexico, under the care of Helga Garcia Garza. Festivals of Danza, gatherings of youth and elders, traditional medicine and healing unite ancient spiritual traditions of the indigenous peoples of the US and Mexico. These meetings and the museum of art and artifacts allow people from the North and South to reconnect with their cultural heritage.

Part of the effort to change values flows into the movement for alternative spirituality, especially the Goddess movement, and support for indigenous peoples' earth-based spiritual traditions. The Stonehaven Goddess Program, organized by spiritual activist Pat Cuney, has been ongoing, and many of the authors and teachers of the Goddess movement have given workshops there.

I built a temple to the Egyptian Goddess Sekhmet in the Nevada Desert near the nuclear test site to honor the birth of my daughters and to take a stand against nuclear testing from the point of view of women's spirituality. The statue of the lion-headed Goddess by Marsha Gomez bears a plaque which reads, "May women be as strong as a lion in giving birth to the future." The statue of 'Madre del Mundo,' also by Marsha Gomez, shares this sacred space. Wiccan priestess Patricia Pearlman cares for the temple and welcomes meditators, nuclear protesters and celebrators of mysteries. I was able to give back the twenty acres of land on which the temple is built to the Western Shoshone, to whom all of that area originally belonged.

One particular area of concern has been the damage done to the environment and health by nuclear radiation. The women who work in the (more directly political, not tax deductible) part of the organization, Feminists for a Compassionate Society, have created excellent and effective projects in opposition to the proposed nuclear dump in West Texas in the little town of Sierra Blanca on the border with Mexico. Erin Rogers has been particularly effective in organizing against the dump and in collaborating with other activist groups.

Susan Lee Solar has created a Peace Caravan, a mobile anti-nuclear museum, and travels from town to town discussing the nuclear issue. The transportation of nuclear waste is very dangerous, and the mobile museum is particularly effective at informing people along the routes it takes. The Foundation has also undertaken to do health surveys near ex-military bases to reveal nuclear and toxic waste residues and their effects on the population. Yana Bland, who also started the Association of Women of the Mediterranean Region with Foundation support, has conducted a survey near Kelly Air Force Base in San Antonio, Texas. Another health survey has been implemented at Clark and Subic bases in the Philippines.

It is difficult in such a short space to describe all the projects of these organizations. Recently, we put on a series of conferences, including one on 'Feminist Family Values' at which Angela Davis, Maria Jiménez, Gloria Steinem and Mililani Trask spoke to a crowd of two thousand. A second conference, on 'Feminism and Fundamentalism,' brought together activists and thinkers from different traditions to discuss patriarchal religion from a feminist point of view. Mahnaz Afkami, Marta Benevides, Yvonne Deutsch, and Robin Morgan presented their thinking together with a local panel, which included activist Cecile Richards.

Anti-nuclear gatherings are being held yearly to network among women opposed to the nuclear cycle. In all of our activities, we recognize the connections among the issues, especially the connection between military spending, the creation of poverty, and the depletion of the environment. After the sale of the Peace Building, we moved our office to a more standard office building. A core group of special project coordinators works there, including Pat Cuney, Sally Jacques, Suze Kemper, Mária Limón, Sue MacNichol and Doll Mathis. The Foundation and Feminists' administration offices are in Kyle, Texas, and are run by San Juanita Alcalá, Rose Corales and Nancy Wilson. Our stalwart accountant is Mary Nell Mathis.

Our recent collaboration with Plain View Press has made possible the publication of the proceedings of the Feminist Family Values Forum and the Feminism and Fundamentalism Conference. Books from the Association of Women of the Mediterranean Region are also available, and a re-publication is forthcoming of the proceedings of a conference on breast cancer and low level nuclear radiation, held in 1993. Videos and audio tapes of many Foundation and related events can be ordered through the office at P.O. Box 868, Kyle, Texas, 78640. You can write to me at that address also. I would be very interested to hear what you think.

All of these activities and numerous others, which I do not have space to name, have been an attempt to practice the gift paradigm at many different levels and in parts of 'reality' from which it is usually excluded. The Foundation has grown up organically with many twists and turns; like life, it is messy and riotous, as well as nurturing and consciousness-raising. So many man-made things and theories are like plastic, with all the molecules in a straight line, or like cities, with houses in endless orderly rows.

Putting a theory into practice means that it has to seep in, through contradictions and misunderstandings, through disbelief and different frames in order to be able to grow, flower and bear fruit in many different ways. An additional difficulty arose from the fact that I am publishing this book only now, after many years of the practice. I only explained the theory verbally and, perhaps, not always convincingly. I was willing to take this risk because I believe that, due to our socialization to nurture, all (or almost all) women already operate according to the values of the gift paradigm.

These values are often buried under an overlay of exchange paradigm beliefs, however. The contradictions within each woman are explained away in one way or another, and we learn to live in patriarchy by remaining unconscious of our own values, or by pushing them into the area of emotion. The Foundation for a Compassionate Society and Feminists for a Compassionate Society are, apart from all the services they have performed and changes they have succeeded in fomenting, consciousness-raising organizations. Their existence alters re-ality, satisfying the need for an example of women's giftgiving on the external, which can validate the giftgiver within each of us, giving the gift paradigm the dignity it must have if it is to be recognized as the principle by which humanity can achieve peace.

Some words came to me in a dream: "Peace on Earth is the next step in human evolution." May it come quickly.

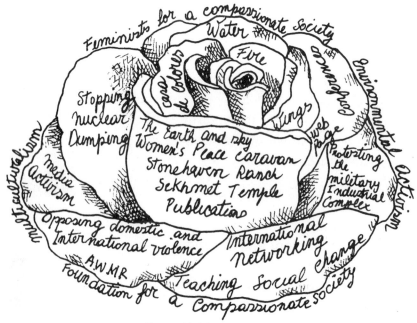

Figure 41. My mystic rose.

420

WHAT THE WORLD WANTS

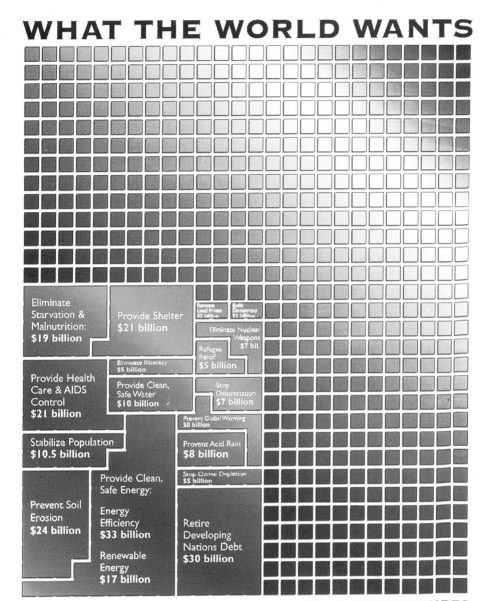

Eliminate Starvation & Malnutrition: **$19 billion**	Provide Shelter **$21 billion**	Remove Land Mines $2 billion	Build Democracy $2 billion
		Eliminate Nuclear Weapons **$7 bil.**	
	Eliminate Illiteracy $5 billion	Refugee Relief **$5 billion**	
Provide Health Care & AIDS Control **$21 billion**	Provide Clean, Safe Water **$10 billion**	Stop Deforestation **$7 billion**	
		Prevent Global Warming $8 billion	
Stabilize Population **$10.5 billion**		Prevent Acid Rain **$8 billion**	
	Provide Clean, Safe Energy:	Stop Ozone Depletion $5 billion	
Prevent Soil Erosion **$24 billion**	Energy Efficiency **$33 billion**	Retire Developing Nations Debt **$30 billion**	
	Renewable Energy **$17 billion**		

AND HOW TO PAY FOR IT USING MILITARY EXPENDITURES

Above are annual costs of various global programs for solving the major human need and environmental problems facing humanity. Each program is the amount needed to accomplish the goal for all in need in the world. Their combined total cost is approximately 30% of the world's total annual military expenditures.

Total Chart represents Annual World Military Expenditures: **$780 billion**

☐ = $1 billion

■ = Amount that was needed to eradicate Smallpox from the world (accomplished 1978): $300 million

Reprinted with permission. © 1997 World Game Institute.

*I got the idea to use this graphic from Hazel Henderson's book, *Paradigms in Progress: Life Beyond Economics*.

Many of the strategies suggested on the next page still presuppose the framework of exchange.

WHAT THE WORLD WANTS

This chart seeks to make the point that what the world needs to solve the major systemic problems confronting humanity is both available and affordable. Clearly, to deal with a problem as complex and large as, for example, the global food situation, with just a small part of a single graph is incomplete, at best. The following explanations of the charts various components are not intended as complete or detailed plans, but rather as very broad brush-strokes intended to give the overall direction, scope and strategy. The paper, "What the World Wants Project" goes into more detail. It is available from the World Game Institute at the address below. (References listed at bottom of page contain supporting documentation, further explication and related information.)

Strategy 1. Eliminate Starvation and Malnourishment/Feeding Humanity: $19 billion per year for ten years, allocated as follows: $2 billion per year for an International Famine Relief Agency—spent on international grain reserve and emergency famine relief; $10 billion per year spent on farmer education through vastly expanded in-country extension services that teach/demonstrate sustainable agriculture, use of local fertilizer sources, pest and soil management techniques, post harvest preservation, and which provide clear market incentives for increased local production; $7 billion per year for indigenous fertilizer development. Educational resources of Strategy 10 coupled with this strategy. Closely linked with #'s 2, 3, 4, 9, 10. *Cost: 55% of what US spends on weight loss per year.*

Strategy 2A. Provide Health Care For All: $15 billion per year for ten years spent on providing primary health care through community health workers to all areas in the world that do not have access to health care. Closely linked with #'s 1, 3, 4, 5, 9.
Strategy 2B. Provide Special Child Health Care: Within the 15 billion, $2.5 billion per year spent on: a) providing Vitamin A to children who lack it in their diet, thereby preventing blindness in 250,000 children/year; b) providing oral rehydration therapy for children with severe diarrhea; and c) immunizing 1 billion children in developing world against measles, tuberculosis, diphtheria, whooping cough, polio and tetanus, thereby preventing the death of 6-7 million children/year.
Strategy 2C. Iodine Deficiency Program: $40 million per year for iodine addition to table salt to eliminate iodine deficiency, thereby reducing the 566 million people who suffer from goiter and not adding to the 3 million who suffer from overt cretinism.
Strategy 2D. AIDS Prevention and Control Program: $6 billion per year allocated as follows: $3 billion per year for a global AIDS prevention education program; $2 billion per year for providing multiple drug therapy to AIDS patients in the developing world; $1 billion per year for research and development for an AIDS vaccine or cure.
Costs for all Health Care Strategies: 16% of what US spends on alcohol and tobacco per year.

Strategy 3. Eliminate Inadequate Housing and Homelessness: $21 billion per year for ten years spent on making available materials, tools and techniques to people without adequate housing. Closely linked with #'s 1, 4, 5, 9. *Cost: amount US spends on golf every 16 months.*

Strategy 4. Provide Clean and Abundant Water: $10 billion per year for ten years spent on making available materials, tools and training needed to build and maintain the needed wells, water and sewage pipes, sanitation facilities and water purifying systems. Closely related to #'s 1, 2, 3, 9. *Cost: 1% of what the world spends on illegal drugs per year.*

Strategy 5. Eliminate Illiteracy: $5 billion per year for ten years; $2 billion spent on a system of 10 to 12 communication satellites and their launching; $2 billion spent on ten million televisions, satellite dish receivers, and photovoltaic/battery units for power—all placed in village schools and other needed areas throughout high illiteracy areas; the rest (90% of funds), spent on culturally appropriate literacy programming and maintenance of system. Closely related to #'s 1, 2, 3, 4, 9, 10, 11. *Cost: 5% of the cost of the Gulf War; 14 months of what the US spends on video games.*

Strategy 6. Increase Energy Efficiency: $33 billion per year for ten years spent on increasing car fleet mileage to over 50 m.p.g., plus increasing appliance, industrial processes, and household energy and materials use to state of the art. Closely linked with #'s 7, 8, 12, 13, 14. *Cost: 13% of what US teenagers spend per year.*

Strategy 7. Increase Renewable Energy: $17 billion per year for ten years spent on tax and other incentives for installation of renewable energy devices, graduated ten year phase-out of subsidies to fossil and nuclear fuels, research and development into more advanced renewable energy harnessing devices. Closely linked with #'s 6, 8, 11, 12, 13, 14. *Cost: 13% of current subsidies to electricity prices in the developing world.*

Strategy 8. Debt Management: $30 billion per year for ten years spent on retiring $500 billion or more of current debt discounted to 50% face value. Not only helps developing countries get out of debt, but helps banks stay solvent and furthers international trade. Closely linked with #'s 1,6,7,10,11,14. *Cost: 3.8% of world's annual military expenditures.*

Strategy 9. Stabilize Population: $10.5 billion per year for ten years spent on making birth control universally available. Closely linked with #'s 1, 2, 3, 4, 5. *Cost: 1.3% of the world's annual military expenditures.*

Strategy 10. Preserving Cropland: $24 billion per year for ten years spent on converting one-tenth of world's most vulnerable cropland that is simultaneously most susceptible to erosion, the location of most severe erosion, and the land that is no longer able to sustain agriculture, to pasture or woodland; and conserving and regenerating topsoil on remaining lands through sustainable farming techniques. Both accomplished through a combination of government regulation and incentive programs that remove the most vulnerable lands from crop production; and by farmer education through vastly expanded in-country extension services that teach/demonstrate sustainable agriculture and soil management techniques. Closely linked to # 1. *Cost: $3 billion less than the annual cost of US farmland loss; half the amount of price subsidies given to US and European farmers.*

Strategy 11. Reverse Deforestation: $7 billion per year for ten years spent on reforesting 150 million hectares needed to sustain ecological, fuelwood, and wood products needs. Planted by local villagers, costs would be $400 per hectare, including seedling costs. Additional costs for legislation, financial incentives, enforcement of rainforest protection. Closely linked with #'s 10, 11. *Cost: 0.9% of world's annual military expenditures.*

Strategy 12. Reverse Ozone Depletion: $5 billion per year for twenty years spent on phasing in substitutes for CFC-20, CFC taxes, incentives for further research and development. Closely linked with # 14. *Cost: 3.7% of US government subsidies to energy, timber, construction, financial services and advertising industries.*

Strategy 13. Stop Acid Rain: $8 billion per year for ten years spent on combination of tax incentive, government regulation and direct assistance programs that place pollution control devices (electrostatic precipitators, etc.) on all industrial users of coal, increase efficiency of industrial processes, cars, and appliances. Closely linked to #'s 6, 7, 11, 14. *Cost: about 1% of world's annual military expenditures.*

Strategy 14. Reverse Global Warming: $8 billion per year for twenty years spent on reducing carbon dioxide, methane and CFC release into atmosphere through combination of international accords, carbon taxes, increases in energy efficiency in industry, transportation, and household, decreases in fossil fuel use, increases in renewable energy use and reforestation. Closely linked with #'s 6, 7, 11, 13 . *Cost: 17% of what the insurance industry paid out in the 1990s for weather related damage; 1% of world's annual military expenditures.*

Strategy 15. Removal of Landmines: $2 billion per year for ten years spent on setting up cottage industries in each of the 64 countries that have landmines planted in their soils. Participants are intensively trained in the safe removal of landmines; compensation set at more than a days wage for each removed mine in each respective country. Closely linked with #'s 2, 16, 17, 18. *Cost: less than the cost of a single B-2 bomber; less than one half what the US spends on perfume each year.*

Strategy 16. Refugee Relief: $5 billion per year for ten years spent on an international Refugee Relief Agency that guarantees the safety of refugees and coordinates the delivery of food, shelter, health care and education. Closely linked with #'s 1, 2, 3, 4, 15, 18. *Cost: 20% of the amount of arms sales to developing countries.*

Strategy 17. Eliminating Nuclear Weapons: $7 billion per year for ten years spent on dismantling all the world's nuclear weapons and processing the plutonium and enriched uranium in nuclear reactors that produce power and render the radioactive materials into non-weapons grade material. Closely linked with #'s 15, 16, 18. *Cost: 25% of what is spent each year on private "security"—private guards, weapons detectors, video surveillance, etc.*

Strategy 18. Building Democracy: $2 billion per year for ten years spent on the following programs—an International Democratic Election Fund that would help finance voter education and multi-party elections in countries making the transition to democracy; a Global Polling Program that would ascertain what people from all over the world think and feel about key global issues; and a Global Problem Solving Simulation Tool that would enable anyone with access to the Internet to propose, develop and test strategies for solving real-world problems. Closely linked with #'s 15, 16, 17. *Cost for all three programs: less than one B-2 bomber; 0.025 % of the world's annual military expenditures.*

Major References: UNDP, *Human Development Report 1996* (New York: Oxford University Press, 1996); UNICEF, *State of the World's Children 1996 1995, 1994*; *Giving children a future: The World Summit for Children*, (New York: Oxford University Press, 1996, 1990); UNHCR *Refugees II-95*, Public Information Service UNHCR 1995; The World Bank, *World Development Report 1996* (New York: Oxford University Press, 1996); World Resources Institute, *World Resources 1995-96, 1992-93*; World Watch Institute, *Vital Signs 1996*; *State of the World 1988-96*, (New York: W.W. Norton & Company, 1996); Ho-Ping: *Food for Everyone*; *Energy, Earth and Everyone*; World Game Institute, Doubleday, New York.

World Game Institute, 3215 Race Street, Philadelphia, Pennsylvania 19104
Phone: 215-387-0220 Fax: 215-387-3009 E-mail: wgame@libertynet.org • World Wide Web: http://www.worldgame.org/~wgi

Reprinted with permission. © 1997 World Game Institute.

Index of Figures

Selected Bibliography

Allen, Paula Gunn. 1992. *The Sacred Hoop*. Boston: Beacon Press.

Bateson, Gregory. 1972. *Steps to an Ecology of Mind: A Revolutionary Approach to Man's Understanding of Himself*. New York: Ballantine Books.

Caldicott, Helen. 1984. *Missile Envy: The Arms Race and Nuclear War*. New York: Bantam Books.

Cambridge Women's Peace Collective. 1984. *My Country is the Whole World: An Anthology of Women's Work on Peace and War*. London: Pandora Press.

Cheal, David. 1988. *The Gift Economy*. New York: Routledge.

Chodorow, Nancy. 1978. *The Reproduction of Mothering: Pscyhoanalysis and the Sociology of Gender*. Berkeley: University of California Press.

Cixous, Hélène and Catherine Clement. 1975. *La jeune née*. Paris: Inedit.

Crystal, David. 1988. *The English Language*. New York: Penguin Books.

———. 1992. *An Encyclopedic Dictionary of Language and Languages*. Cambridge: Blackwell Publishers.

Cushman, H. B. 1899. *History of the Choctaw, Chickasaw, and Natchez Indians*. Greenville, Texas: Headlight Printing House.

Daly, Mary. 1978, *Gyn/Ecology, The Metaethics of Radical Feminism*. Boston: Beacon Press.

Deely, John. 1990. *Basics of Semiotics*. Bloomington: Indiana University Press.

Derrida, 1976. Jacques. *Of Grammatology*. Gayatri Spivak, trans. Baltimore, The Johns Hopkins University Press.

———. 1992. *Given Time: Counterfeit Money*. Peggy Kamuf, trans. Chicago, The University of Chicago Press.

Dinnerstein, Dorothy. 1976. *The Mermaid and the Minotaur*. New York: Harper Collins.

Douglass, Mary. 1990. "Introduction" in Marcel Mauss, *The Gift*. New York: Norton.

Eco, Umberto. 1975. *Trattato di Semiotica Generale*. Milano: Bompiani.

Eisler, Riane. 1988. *The Chalice & The Blade: Our History, Our Future*. San Francisco: Harper & Row.

Engels, Frederich and Karl Marx. 1964. *The German Ideology*. Moscow: Progress Publishers.

Feiner, Susan F. and Bruce Roberts. 1990. "Hidden by the Invisible Hand: Neoclassical Economic Theory and the Textbook Treatment of Race and Gender." *Gender and Society* 4 (2).

Firestone, Shulamith. 1971. *The Dialectic of Sex*. New York: Bantam Books.

Fodor, J.A. 1972. "Some Reflections on L.S. Vygotsky's *Thoughts and Language*." *Cognition* 1. 83-95.

Fodor, J.A., M.F. Garrett, E.C.T. Walker, and C.H. Parkes, 1980. "Against Definitions." *Cognition* 8. 263-367.

Folbre, Nancy. 1994. *Who Pays For the Kids? Gender and Structures of Constraint*. London: Routledge.

Foucault, Michel. 1994. *The Order of Things: An Archaeology of the Human Sciences.* New York: Vintage Books.

George, Susan. 1977. *How the Other Half Dies: The Real Reasons for World Hunger.* Montclair, N. J.: Allanheld, Osmun & Co.

———. 1979. *Feeding the Few: Corporate Control of Food.* Washington, D.C.: Institute for Policy Studies.

———. 1988. *A Fate Worse than Debt: The World Financial Crisis and the Poor.* New York: Grove Weidenfeld.

Gilligan, Carol. 1982. *In a Different Voice.* Cambridge, MA: Harvard University Press.

Gilligan, Carol, Nona P. Lyons and Trudy J. Hanmer, eds. 1990. *Making Connections: The Relational Worlds of Adolescent Girls at Emma Willard School.* Cambridge, MA.: Harvard University Press.

Gleick, James. 1987. *Chaos: Making a New Science.* London: Penguin Books.

Godbout, Jacques T. 1992. *L'Esprit du don.* Paris: Bollati Boringhieri.

Goux, Jean-Joseph. 1990. *Symbolic Economies: After Marx and Freud.* Ithaca: Cornell University Press.

Greenberg, Joseph H. 1966. *Language Universals.* New York: Mouton Publishers.

Gregory, C.A. 1982. *Gifts and Commodities.* London: Academic Press.

Grown, Caren and Gita Sen. 1987. *Development Crises and Alternative Visions: Third World Women's Perspectives.* New York: Monthly Review Press.

Hagan, Kay Leigh. 1993. *Fugitive Information: Essays from a Feminist Hothead.* New York: Harper Collins.

Hanfmann, E. and Kasanin, J. 1937. "A Method for the Study of Concept Formation." *Journal of Psychology* 3. 521-540.

———. 1942. *Conceptual Thinking in Schizophrenia.* New York: NMDM.

Hartsock, Nancy C.M. 1983. *Money, Sex and Power: Toward a Feminist Historical Materialism.* Boston: Northeastern University Press.

Henderson, Hazel. 1991. *Paradigms in Progress: Life Beyond Economics.* Indianapolis, Indiana: Knowledge Systems, Inc.

Hyde, Lewis. 1979. *The Gift, Imagination and the Erotic Life of Property.* New York: Random House.

Irigaray, Luce. 1974. *Speculum de l'autre femme.* Paris: Les Editions de Minuit.

Jakobson, Roman. 1962. *Selected Writings, I. Phonological Studies.* The Hague: Mouton.

———. 1973. *Essais de linguistique générale: Rapports internes et externes du langage.* Paris: Les Editions de Minuit.

———. 1978. *Six Lectures on Sound and Meaning.* Cambridge: MIT Press.

———. 1990. *On Language.* Cambridge: Harvard University Press.

Jameson, Frederic. 1972. *The Prison-House of Language: A Critical Account of Structuralism and Russian Formalism.* Princeton: Princeton University Press.

Johnson, Sonia. 1989. *Wildfire: Igniting the She/volution.* Albuquerque, New Mexico: Wildfire Press.

Jung, Carl. 1973 [1906]. "A Psychological Diagnosis of Evidence." *Experimental Researches, Collected Works of C. G. Jung 2*. Leopold Stein and Diana Riviere, Eds. London: Routledge and Kegan Paul. 318-332.

Keil, Frank C. 1989. *Concepts, Kinds, and Cognitive Development*. Cambridge: MIT Press.

Keuls, Eva C. 1985. *The Reign of the Phallus: Sexual Politics in Ancient Athens*. Berkeley: University of California Press.

Lacan, Jacques. 1966. *Ecrits*. Paris: Editions de Seuil.

———. 1982. *Feminine Sexuality*. New York: Norton.

Levi-Strauss, Claude. 1958. *Anthropologie Structurale*. Paris: Plon.

———. 1967. *Les structures elementaires de la parente*. The Hague: Mouton.

Lovelock, James.1988. *The Age of Gaia: A Biography of Living on Earth*. New York: Norton.

Lyons, John. 1977. *Semantics*, Volumes 1 and 2. Cambridge: Cambridge University Press.

Lux, Kenneth. 1990. *Adam Smith's Mistake: How a Moral Philosopher Invented Economics and Ended Morality*. Boston: Shambala.

Martien, Jerry. 1996. *Shell Game: A True Account of Beads and Money in North America*. San Francisco: Mercury House.

Marx, Karl. 1904. *A Contribution to the Critique of Political Economy*. Chicago: Charles H. Kerr & Company.

———. 1930. *Capital in Two Volumes: Volume One*. London: J.M. Dent & Sons, Ltd.

———. 1964. *The Economic and Philosophic Manuscripts of 1844*. M. Milligan, trans. New York: International Publishers.

———. 1973. *Grundrisse: Foundations of the Critique of Political Economy*. New York: Vintage Books.

Mauss, Marcel. 1990. [1950]. *The Gift*. New York: W.W. Norton.

Mayer, Richard E. 1983. *Thinking, Problem Solving, Cognition*. New York: W.H. Freeman and Company.

McAllister, Pam. 1988. *You Can't Kill the Spirit*. Philadelphia, PA: New Society Publishers.

Miller, Jean Baker. 1976. *Toward a New Psychology of Women*. Boston: Beacon Press.

Morgan, Marlo. 1994. *Mutant Message Down Under*. New York: Harper Collins.

Morgan, Robin. 1984. *The Anatomy of Freedom: Feminism, Physics, and Global Politics*. New York: Anchor Books/Doubleday.

———. 1989. *The Demon Lover: On the Sexuality of Terrorism*. New York: Norton.

Noddings, Nel. 1984. *Caring: A Feminine Apporach to Ethics and Moral Education*. Berkeley: University of California Press.

Owens, Jr., Robert E. 1992. *Language Development: An Introduction*. New York: Macmillan.

Peirce, Charles Sanders. 1931-35. *Collected Papers of Charles Sanders Peirce*. Charles Hartshorne, Paul Weiss, and Arthur Burks, eds. Cambridge: Harvard University Press.

Phillips, Graham. 1996. *The Search for the Grail*. London: Random House.

Pickford, Clifford. 1996. *Fractal Horizons: The Future Use of Fractals.* New York: St. Martin's.

Pinker, Stephen. 1994. *The Language Instinct.* London: Penguin Books.

Poole, Gordon. 1971. "Alle origini della concezione borghese della donna." *Ideologie.*

Ragland-Sullivan, Ellie. 1986. *Jacques Lacan and the Philosophy of Psychoanalysis.* Urbana: University of Illinois Press.

Regis, Ed. 1995. *Nano: The Emerging Science of Nanotechnology.* New York: Little, Brown.

Rosenau, Pauline Marie. 1992. *Post-Modernism and the Social Sciences.* Princeton: Princeton University Press.

Rossi-Landi, Ferruccio. 1968. *Il linguaggio come lavoro e come mercato.* Milan: Bompiani.

———. 1972. *Semiotica e Ideologia.* Milano: Bompiani.

———. 1974. "Linguistics and Economics." *Current Trends in Linguistics* 12, ed. Thomas A. Sebeok. The Hague: Mouton & Co.

———. 1983. *Language as Work and Trade: A Semiotic Homology for Linguistics and Economics.* South Hadley, MA: Bergin and Garvey.

Ruddick, Sara. 1989. *Maternal Thinking: Toward a Politics of Peace.* New York: Ballantine Books.

Russell, Bertrand. 1959. *The Problems of Philosophy.* London: Oxford University Press.

Rymer, Russ. 1993. *Genie: An Abused Child's Flight from Silence.* New York: Harper Collins.

Saussure, Ferdinand de. 1931. *Cours de linguistique générale.* Charles Bally and Albert Sechehaye. Paris: Payot.

Sebeok, Thomas A., ed. 1974. *Current Trends in Linguistics,* Vol. 12. The Hague: Mouton.

Sen, Gita and Caren Grown. 1987. *Development Crises and Alternative Visions: Third World Women's Perspectives.* New York: Monthly Review Press.

Shell, Marc. 1978. *The Economy of Literature.* Baltimore: The Johns Hopkins University Press.

———. 1982. *Money, Language, and Thought: Literary and Philosophic Economics from the Medieval to the Modern Era.* Berkeley: University of California Press.

Shiva, Vandana. 1989. *Staying Alive: Women, Ecology and Development.* London: Zed Books, Ltd.

Silverman, Kaja. 1983. *The Subject of Semiotics.* New York: Oxford University Press.

Silverstein, Olga and Beth Rashbaum. 1994. *The Courage to Raise Good Men.* New York: Penguin Books.

Simmel, Georg. *The Philosophy of Money.* 1978 [1900]. Translated by Tom Bottomore and David Frisby. London: Routledge and Kegan Paul Ltd.

Sjoo, Monica and Barbara Mor. 1987. *The Great Cosmic Mother: Rediscovering the Religion of the Earth.* San Francisco: Harper and Row.

Slater, Phillip. 1968. *The Glory of Hera: Greek Mythology and the Greek Family.* Boston: Beacon Press.

———. 1980. *Wealth Addiction.* New York: E. P. Dutton.

Sohn-Rethel, Alfred. 1965. "Historical Materialist Theory of Knowledge." *Marxism Today*. 114-22.

———. 1970. *Geistige und korperliche Arbeit*. Frankfurt: Suhrkamp Verlag.

———. 1970. *Lavoro intellettuale e lavoro manuale*. Milan: Feltrinelli.

Spittal, W.G. 1990. *Iroquis Women: An Anthology*. Ontario: Iroqrafts Ltd.

Steiner, George. 1977. *After Babel*. Oxford: Oxford University Press.

Strassman, Diana. "The Stories of Economics and the Power of the Storyteller." *History of Political Economy* 25 (1): 147-165.

Taylor, Timothy. 1996. *The Prehistory of Sex: Four Million Years of Human Sexual Culture*. London: Fourth Estate Limited.

Tronto, Joan C. 1994. *Moral Boundaries: A Political Argument for an Ethic of Care*. New York: Routledge.

Vaughan, Genevieve. 1980. "Communication and Exchange." *Semiotica* 29, 1-2. The Hague: Mouton.

———. 1981. "Saussure and Vygotsky via Marx." *ars semiotica, International Journal of American Semiotic*, 6(1). 57-83.

Vygotsky, Lev Semenovich. 1962. *Thought and Language*. Cambridge: The MIT Press.

Volosinov, V.N. 1973. *Marxism and the Philosophy of Language*. New York: Seminar Press.

Waring, Marilyn. 1988. *If Women Counted: A New Feminist Economics*. San Francisco: Harper and Row.

Watson-Franke, Maria-Barbara. "The Lycian Heritage and the Making of Men: Matrilineal Models for Parenting." *Women's Studies International Forum* 16(6).

Weatherford, Jack. 1988. *Indian Givers: How the Indians of the Americas Transformed the World*. New York: Fawcett Columbine.

Weinbaum, Batya. 1978. *The Curious Courtship of Women's Liberation and Socialism*. Boston, MA.: The South End Press.

Weiner, Annette B. 1992. *Inalienable Possessions: The Paradox of Keeping-While-Giving*. Berkeley: The University of California Press.

Wertsch, James W. 1985. *Vygotsky and the Social Formation of Mind*. Cambridge: Harvard University Press.

Wilden, Anthony. 1972. *System and Structure: Essays in Communication and Exchange*. London: Tavistock Publications.

Wilson, Margaret D., ed. 1976. *The Essential Descartes*. New York: Penguin Group.

Wittgenstein, L. 1967. [1953]. *Philosophical Investigations*. Trans. by G.E.M. Anscombe. Oxford: Basil Blackwell.

Wood, David, ed. 1992. *Derrida: A Critical Reader*, Oxford, Blackwell.

Wright, Kenneth. 1991. *Vision and Separation Between Mother and Baby*. Northvale, New Jersey: Jason Aronson, Inc.

Index